GCSE Media Studies

Editors: Vivienne Clark and Richard Harvey

Colin Bulman
Vivienne Clark
Richard Harvey
Richard Horsman
Tim Leadbeater
Eileen Lewis
William Malyszko

Edinburgh Gate
Harlow, Essex

Pearson Education Limited
Edinburgh Gate
Harlow
Essex
CM20 2JE
England and Associated Companies throughout the World

ISBN 0582 32833 0

First published 2002

Printed in Singapore

The Publisher's policy is to use paper manufactured from sustainable forests.

Editor acknowledgements

The editors would like to thank, first and foremost, their families and friends for their support. They would also like to thank the many students they have taught over the years, for their enthusiasm and creativity.

Gratitude is also due to the team of co-authors: Colin Bulman, Richard Horsman, Tim Leadbeater, Eileen Lewis and William Malyszko for their considerable expertise and patience.

We should like to express thanks to Lorna Cocking at Pearson Education for her guidance and patience during the production of this textbook and to Alison Gilbert and Phoebe Clapham for their assistance. Jane Klima deserves a special mention for her excellent work for this project and thanks are due also to Rachel Viney.

Vivienne Clark and Richard Harvey

Contents

Introduction

VIVIENNE CLARK AND RICHARD HARVEY

WHAT IS MEDIA STUDIES?

Media Studies is the study of the methods and effects of mass communication.

A **medium** (singular) is a method of communication, a form used by humans to communicate with each other. An artist may use the medium of oil paint or charcoal to communicate her interpretation of a person or place, for example, to whomever looks at it. Someone may use a spiritual medium to try to communicate with the deceased. So, in a sense, a medium is something that is in the middle, between the creator (**producer**) and the person or people (**audience**) with whom they wish to communicate. Television, film, newspapers, radio and magazines are all **media** (plural) forms and we have come to call them, collectively, **the media**.

There are many different methods of communication that we study for Media Studies, but we can put them into *three* main areas:

- **Audio-visual media**
  Moving image media (film, television, video), radio and photography
- **Print-based media**
  Newspapers, magazines, comics / cartoons and posters, brochures etc
- **ICT-based media**
  Digital vision / sound editing and image manipulation technologies (software and hardware), including communications technologies such as the Internet, CD-ROM, DVD, MPEG and interactive / multi-media, e-mails and word-processing

NB News, advertising and music are described as **cross-media forms**, as they are produced across more than one media form.

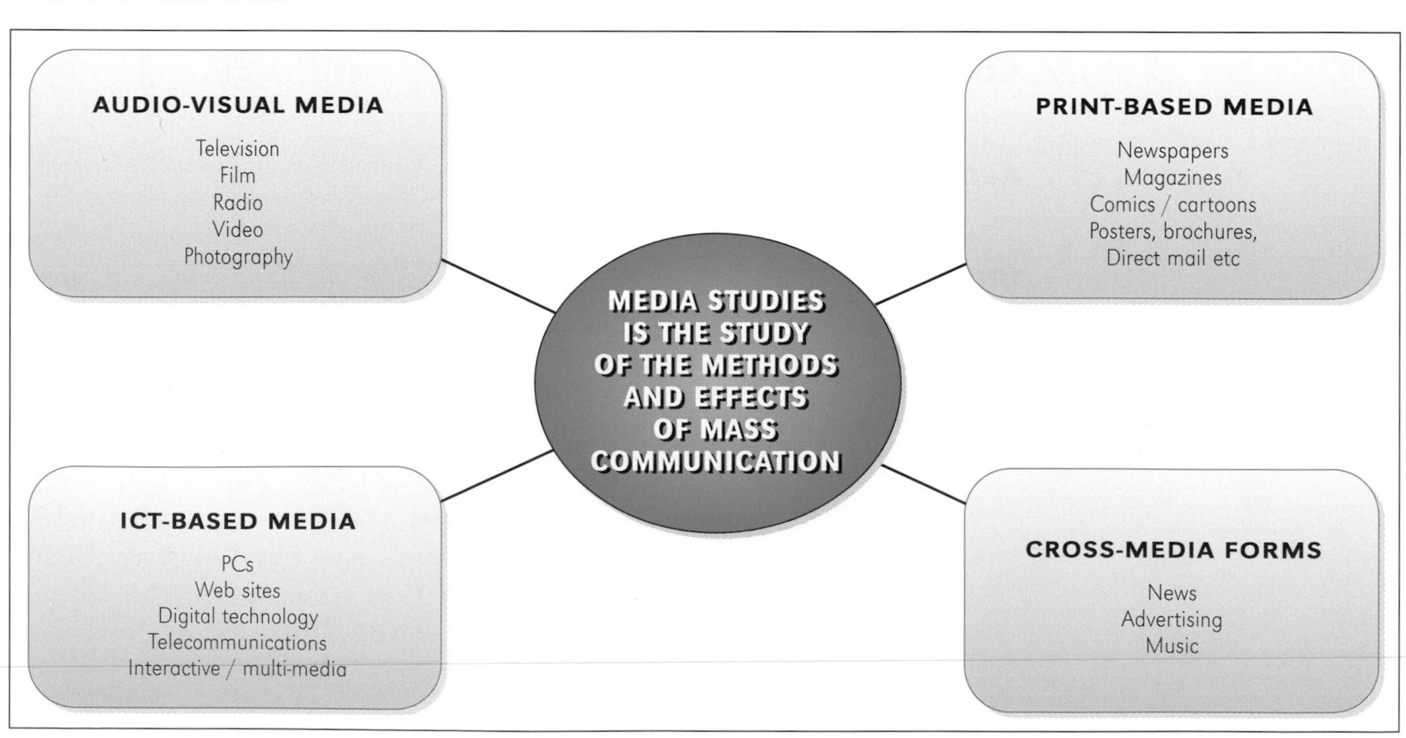

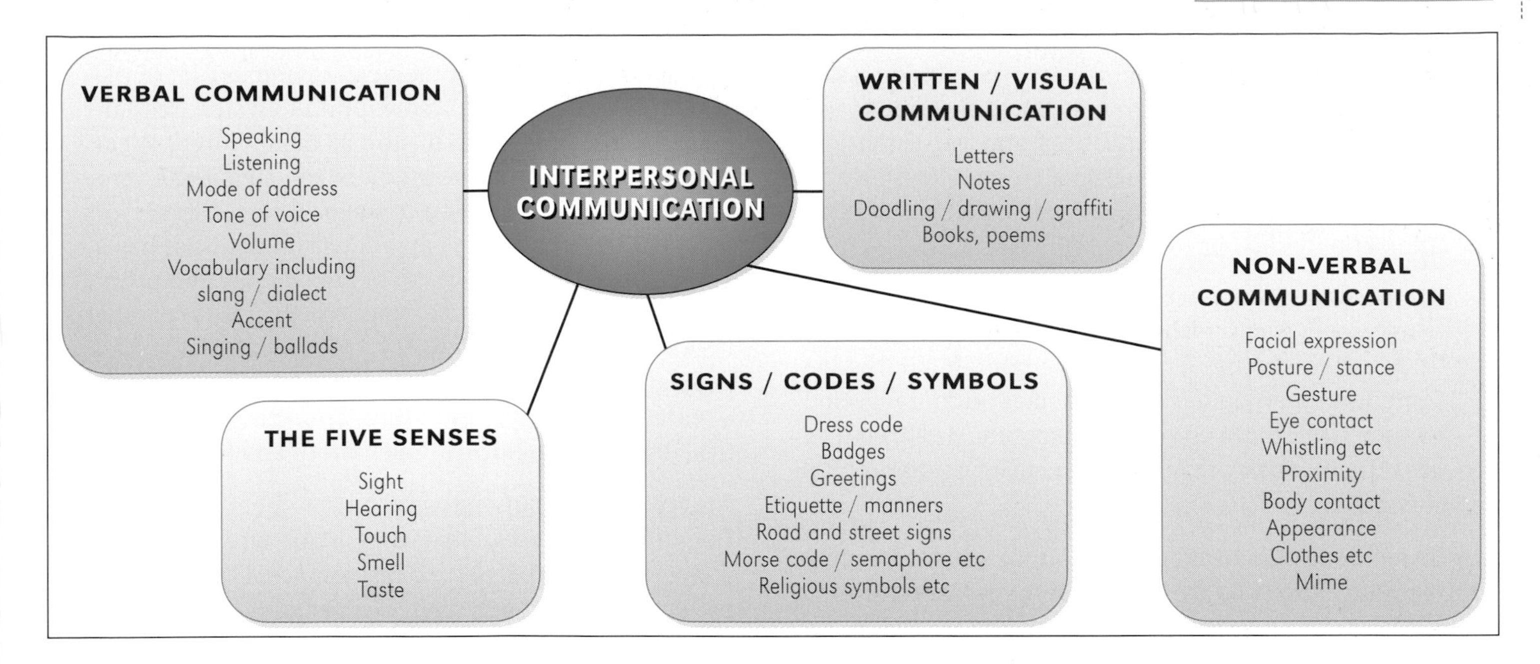

Before any of the above media forms were invented (and you will learn all about their invention in the chapters that follow), humans relied on various forms of **interpersonal communication** (communication between people) and we still do. It is worth considering first how we communicate with each other before we think about mass media communication, as many aspects of interpersonal communication are used to make meaning in newspapers, television, films etc.

We use our **five senses** to help us to send and receive communication, but they cannot make any sense of what they receive without the help of our **brain**. For example, the eye, one of our essential tools of communication, cannot make sense of, or interpret, anything that it sees. It is just a lens through which we see our world. **Seeing** is the optical process of looking. **Perception** requires us to use our brains to interpret and understand what our eyes see. The same is true of the other four senses.

Our brain is like a powerful computer that collects a vast store of information during our lives, even from before we are born. We use this store of information, mostly without even thinking about it, in order to make sense of what we see, often by making links, or associations, with what we have previously experienced.

Different colours, sounds, shapes, symbols, smells, typefaces, words, objects and images can trigger our memories and help us to make connections between our experience and understanding of our daily lives.

However, not everyone perceives the world around them in quite the same way or makes the same interpretations. The differences in perception between people will be one of the important aspects of communication that we look at in Media Studies, for example when studying the key concept of **Media Messages and Values**.

Human beings have always loved stories and our literature, art and history are full of stories, either true or made up, that show what mankind has felt, thought and experienced over the centuries. We have used all kinds of ways to tell stories, by drawing, painting, singing songs and nursery rhymes, telling jokes, fireside tales; even a large public sculpture, or cathedral or temple, tells a story about a person, a country or the relationship between people and their god. Music and fashion are also stories about what we value at different times and in different places.

As each century has dawned, we have found new ways of telling stories and recording our existence on the Earth. In English, we look at stories told in novels, plays and poems. In Media Studies, we look at stories told in television programmes, of breaking news or events in other countries, in the fantasy and escapism of films old and new, on the radio, in newspapers and photographs. The media have offered us other ways of recording human experience and creativity and in Media Studies we look at how these methods of communication work and why they have such a prominent place in our daily experience.

Communication of any kind is a **two-way process**. It is the process by which messages are **sent** and **received**. Someone speaks to us and we listen and think about what they have said; we may respond by speaking or doing something. We see a sign and we think about whether to follow it or not.

In the same way, we watch television and have responses ('That's really awful!', 'Did you see that?', 'It was so funny!'); when we watch films, we sometimes jump in our seats if something unexpected happens, we might cry when a character we liked dies on screen, or we may grip our seats at something shocking.

So we don't just sit there, soaking up what we watch, read and hear. We are not **passive**, but **active**. Also we cannot possibly watch, read or listen to everything! So we choose what to watch, read or listen to – we deliberately **select** and sift through information, sometimes even without thinking about it. While flicking through a magazine, we may stop to read a particular article or look at a particular photograph or advert. When 'zapping' through our TV channels, we may decide to pause and watch the rest of a music video or part of an old comedy programme.

In Media Studies you will learn about how we all make use of the media and how media companies find out what we enjoy and use that knowledge to sell us their latest products.

In addition, the companies that produce media texts do not do so just to pass the time, giving us, out of the goodness of their hearts, something to watch, read or listen to, just to be nice, to stop us being bored! What you will learn is that the study of the media has very little to do with watching a video in lesson times or studying trivial pastimes and entertainment but has a great deal to do with looking at how money and profit are created for these companies. By the way, the USA's No. 1 export industry is entertainment – so people who say 'It's only a film!' are missing the point – entertainment, as well as information, is BIG business and you'll learn much more about that later.

Also, we learn many important ideas from the media. Our attitudes about what is right or wrong, fair or unfair, in fashion or out of fashion are all influenced by the media as much as by our families and friends. Our ideas about how people live in other countries are also often shaped by what we read, watch or listen to – we cannot visit every country in the world or meet everyone in the world to decide for ourselves what we think. So we mostly have to depend on where we travel to, and whom or what we can see, from the comfort of our own sitting room.

Media Studies is the study of the methods and effects of mass communication, but you could also say that it is **the study of the power of money and the power of ideas**.

The media are such a part of our daily lives, always there, so *why* should we study the media and *how*?

WHY SHOULD WE STUDY THE MEDIA?

Media consumption – we are said to **consume** media texts when we see or hear them.

Just to take one example, the watching of films. Fifty years ago we would all have to go to the cinema to see a film. In 1955 there were 4,483 cinemas in the United Kingdom but by 1987 the number had dropped to an all-time low of 1,215. Many people would go to the cinema two or three times in one week. In 1950 over 1,400 million visits were made to cinemas: by the mid-1980s this figure had dropped to fewer than 100 million. Today it is possible to carry your cinema with you. Some of the newer, and more expensive, laptop computers have DVD capability so you can watch feature films wherever you may be.

ACTIVITY 1

- Ask your parents or grandparents how they listened to music when they were your age. Compare this with the ways in which you listen to music today.

ACTIVITY 2

- Keep a diary for one week of your consumption of the media. Make a note of all that you see or hear throughout the day and how long each activity takes. You should include listening to the radio, watching television, reading newspapers or magazines, playing computer games, listening to personal music systems, use of the Internet or any other activity that you consider to be consuming media products.
- Calculate the total amount of time that you spend on each different medium. You might also like to record time spent discussing any media that you have consumed during the previous day.

Extension activity

- Discuss in class how the details recorded in your diary might be used as reasons for studying the media.

We are often not fully aware of just how much of the media we consume. Think about how large a part the media play in your daily life.

Most of the information we receive about the world is through the media. We rely on the media to keep us informed and also to entertain us. We probably talk more about the media with our friends than about anything else. Does a day go by when you do not discuss with friends or family a film or television programme that you have seen or a piece of music that you have listened to?

The media, then, play a very important part in our lives. Something as important as this should be understood much better than it is. As a subject for study Media Studies offers the opportunity to think critically and imaginatively about the relationship between the media, the individual and society. Some students are concerned that in studying the media personal enjoyment will be spoiled, but this is certainly not the case. When we develop a deeper understanding of how and why media texts are created we are able to enjoy them even more.

This book is intended to help you, as a student of the media, to develop the knowledge and skills necessary to explore the media effectively. It is important to be able to think about the media from your own point of view based upon thorough knowledge and understanding: you need to be informed before you can offer a convincing point of view. Analysis and interpretation may need some guidance, which is what this book offers. It will not give you all the answers – you will be expected to do some of your own research and independent study.

HOW CAN WE STUDY THE MEDIA?

For the purposes of media study, we can call any product of a media production process a **media text**. A magazine advert, a film, a radio news bulletin – they are all defined as texts, because, by **reading** them (studying them closely), we may find out a number of things about them. This includes anything that you produce yourself during the course for your practical work. What we study about media texts are called the **key concepts** of Media Studies.

THE KEY CONCEPTS

A **concept** is an idea, a way of thinking about something. Over the years, *three* key concepts have been developed by academics and teachers about how to study the media. The concepts are 'key' because they unlock ways of understanding media texts that we may not have considered before. A key-stone in an arch is the most important one, as it supports the whole arch by locking the other stones together. So a key concept is one which supports the structure of the study of Media Studies.

Every subject that you study for GCSE has its own key concepts. For English GCSE, some main concepts might be Language, Structure and Form, for example, or Character and Setting, and you will be asked to demonstrate your skills in Reading, Writing, Speaking and Listening, with a range of different texts, from Shakespeare to advertising.

In 1948, an American, Harold Dwight Lasswell (a political scientist and Director of War Communications Research who looked at propaganda during war), published his model of five stages of communication:

WHO?
SAYS WHAT?
IN WHICH CHANNEL (MEDIUM)?
TO WHOM?
WITH WHAT EFFECT?

This model still provides us with a clear and simple starting point for the key concepts and questions we use to study media texts and processes of communication in Media Studies.

For the OCR GCSE Media Studies specification you have to study media texts using the **key concepts** below. If you are following the AQA or WJEC specification, we have put their terms for these concepts underneath to help you:

- **Media Languages and Categories**
  AQA: Media Language – Forms and Conventions
  WJEC: Media Texts
- **Media Producers and Audiences**
  AQA: Audience; Institutions
  WJEC: Media Organisations; Media Audiences
- **Media Messages and Values**
  AQA: Representation
  WJEC: Media Texts

As you will see from the list below, there are many questions to be asked when we study a media text, but to try and find out everything about every text would be impossible (for there will be some questions that you will not be able to find the answers to). Therefore, the GCSE specification you are studying will ask you to focus on one or two aspects of a text or topic at a time. Nevertheless, you might like to refer back to the following questions during the GCSE course to remind yourself of the way that we can use the key concepts to study media texts.

This way of thinking and studying is often described as **analytical** or **critical** and as you develop these skills you'll find them essential life skills beyond GCSE, important to you in your daily adult life, whether or not you go on to work in, or study, the media.

Media Languages and Categories

The languages used by audio-visual, print- and ICT-based media to produce meaning and the categories and conventions used to organise and structure them.

The Key Questions to ask here are...

- What is this text called and what associations do we have with this title/name?
- What is this text about? What does this text 'say'?
- How does it 'say' it? What are its languages (print, moving images, sounds)?

- How are these languages put together, or constructed, to make this text?
- What category, or genre, of text is it? How can you identify this?
- What can we learn about this text from its appearance, opening minutes or front cover?
- What codes and conventions does it follow?
- What languages and categories do I need to consider and use when making my own media text?

Media Producers and Audiences

For this concept we study the participants with roles in the media production process, the institutions they represent, how they are financed and generate profit, and the processes of media production themselves. We also look at the relationship between the media and audiences, who are made up of individuals and social / cultural groups, and are involved in the consumption of media texts, and at their responses to them.

The Key Questions to ask here are...

- How was the text produced (production processes)?
- By whom (company, individual, team) and why (entertainment / information) was it produced? What else have they made?
- Who is in it? What else have they made / appeared in? How does this affect our understanding of this text?
- When and where was it produced and how did this influence the production of the text?
- What is it similar to? Why might this be relevant?
- What was / is its competition / market?
- For whom (target audience) was it produced?
- Who actually watches / reads / listens to it? How do we know?
- How was it financed and by whom? How much profit did it make?
- How did it reach its audience? How / where / when was it advertised? Where is it shown, sold or available?
- How do audiences respond to or interpret / make use of the text?
- What expectations and pleasures do audiences have in response to the text? What effects does it have on them? How do we know this?
- What have other people (critics, academics etc) said about this text?
- How do I respond to this text and why?
- What do I need to consider when producing my own media text?

Media Messages and Values

For the study of this concept, we look at the relationships between people, places, events, ideas, values and beliefs and at their representations in the media; and at the issues and debates arising from these representations. This includes how you might choose to create representations of yourself, your family and surroundings. We also look at how we make sense of the meanings of media texts and how these meanings contribute to the ways in which our society and communities function.

The Key Questions to ask here are...

- Whose interests does the text serve?
- Who is present in this text? Who is absent from this text?
- Who or what can it be said to represent?
- What does the text tell us about who made it and when and where they made it?
- Has its meaning changed over the years and in what ways?
- What judgements do you make about the truth, accuracy or effect of this text?
- What judgements might other people or groups make about it?
- What values are offered, either directly or indirectly, by the text?
- What conclusions can we draw from it, what issues does it raise?
- What do I need to consider when making my own media text? What messages and values am I using in my decision-making?

GCSE MEDIA STUDIES SKILLS

There are two main **subject-specific skills** that you will need to develop for GCSE Media Studies:

- **Textual analysis skills**
- **Practical media production skills**

TEXTUAL ANALYSIS SKILLS

To **analyse** something means that you are studying it in detail. We sometimes use the term **deconstruct**, to take apart, which is similar. To some degree, Media Studies is about taking apart what has already been put together, or **constructed**, in order to see how it works or how to make sense of it.

There are some further important questions to ask when analysing any media text. You can use the questions above during the course, like a checklist, to help you to find out these details in order to analyse a media text, either in preparation for your exams or when undertaking your coursework projects.

You will be expected to learn and use **subject-specific vocabulary** related to the key concepts and media texts, for example:

- Vocabulary specific to **media production processes**, for all three media areas, audio-visual media, print-based media and ICT-based media (such as *close-up, edit, masthead, web browser* etc)
- Vocabulary associated with the **key conceptual areas** of the subject (such as *representation, mise-en-scène* etc)

This book is full of useful subject-specific vocabulary for you to learn and use – it is printed in bold type throughout the textbook with definitions and examples.

PRACTICAL MEDIA PRODUCTION SKILLS

The purpose of producing your own media texts is not really to teach you technical skills at a *vocational* level, as this may be beyond the capabilities and training of schools and teachers. Media production at GCSE (and AS / A and GNVQ levels, too) is seen as an effective way of engaging you in creative activities making and technical processes used in the media. So there's no point in thinking that your grade A* in GCSE Media Studies will get you a job at the BBC, Capital Radio or IPC Magazines!

In practical work, you are asked to reflect on and explain the decisions and processes you used when making your magazine, newspaper, radio programme or short film in order to show that you understand the links between theory (ideas and concepts) and practice (making and doing).

Media professionals don't need to study Media Studies to make a film or be an editor of a magazine, because they have learned from different kinds of training and experience they have had along the way.

Also, GCSE Media Studies has only been available at school since the mid-1980s and A level Media Studies from 1990, so it is a relatively young subject compared to others, such as History or Science. In the same way, most great writers have not studied English Literature at A level, let alone at university!

However, we hope that you will gain two things from your practical work:

- that the 'hands-on' approach afforded by practical media production will help you find new ways to express yourself and be creative;
- that the discovery and development of particular talents or skills will encourage you to go a stage further, either in higher academic study or in seeking appropriate work experience and vocational training, to pursue a media career.

An increasing number of successful media professionals once studied Media Studies at A level or for a degree – perhaps you will join them soon?

GCSE MEDIA STUDIES – TYPES OF ASSESSMENT

All three awarding bodies which offer a GCSE in Media Studies use similar methods to assess the standard of what you have learnt about Media Studies.

The *three* main **intellectual skills** that you will need to use are the same for many of the other subjects that you study:

- Knowledge and Understanding
- Analysis and Interpretation
- Production and Evaluation

There are *two* main **methods of assessment** used for GCSE Media Studies:

- **Coursework**: This is worth 50% of your final grade. Coursework is work that you produce in response to tasks set by your teacher during the course. This may be in the form of written essays (of varying lengths up to 1,500 words) on media topics or media **production** tasks (including preparation and planning for production work, called **pre-production** work). You may also have to keep a log of each stage of the work as you do it and you may have to make a presentation of your work to the teacher in an interview.
- **Examination**: This is worth 50% of your final grade. You may have one or two examinations, of varying lengths, depending on which awarding body you are entered for. For the AQA specification, it is called a controlled test.

  There are *two* types of examination:

- **Unseen extracts from media texts**: All three awarding bodies set this kind of assessment. It is similar to those set for your English or English Literature GCSE, where you have to answer questions on a passage from a novel or poem, or, in the case of an English Media paper, an advertisement or newspaper extract. You will be prepared during the course to study various types of media texts (film or television trailers or extracts, newspaper or magazine extracts or advertisements). You will then be presented with an extract in the exam, without knowing which one before the day itself, together with a set of questions to answer. Your teacher will give you several opportunities to practise for this during your course. You will see how learning to use and apply the **key concepts** and **key questions**, mentioned in this book, will help to prepare you for this examination with confidence. Each chapter is full of useful examples of textual analysis.
- **Set exam topics**: Each awarding body has set different topics for you to study in advance to answer questions on in the examination. You will find that this book contains essential background facts and historical information that will be of use to you in your preparation for these topics, as well as specific case studies.

Your teacher will provide you with the exact details of the specification you are following. Or you might like to visit the web site for your awarding body (OCR, AQA or WJEC), whose site addresses we give in the Appendix at the end of this book, to check the details for yourself.

Whether you are interested in pursuing a career in the media or not, we hope that this book is useful to you in your study and enjoyment of the media.

1 Film

WILLIAM MALYSZKO

Coming up

In this chapter we will be looking at:

- why and how we study films
- the history and development of cinema
- the major system of film-making in the world: the Hollywood studio system
- the people who make films
- the production, exhibition and distribution of film
- the process of film production
- textual analysis
- genre
- representation

INTRODUCTION

First of all, what is the difference between **film** and **cinema**?

Film is the **medium** itself (as opposed to any other, such as television, radio, magazines), the specific product and **media text**.

Cinema means the situation of **reception**, where we 'receive' / see the films, and involves related ideas such as **national cinema** and **institutions**.

Look at the diagram on page 13. Film and cinema may be some or all of the following:

A technology:

- an **industry**: a complex and diverse group of people and companies who are involved in the production and manufacture of a product
- a **business**: the products are made in order to make money; companies and individuals invest money in the hope of making a **profit** (a return on their investment)
- an **invention factory**: the product being made is one of imagination in order to entertain, even though it may also do a lot more than this
- **economic power**: the sums of money involved in some of the major companies give them immense power – they can affect related industries such as pop music and television

An art form:

- an **historical document**: film is a reflection of the time in which it is made; it can be a permanent historical document which shows future generations what it was like in its contemporary period, e.g. films made during the Second World War, such as *In Which We Serve* (Noel Coward, Rank, 1942), quite vividly capture the experience of the times

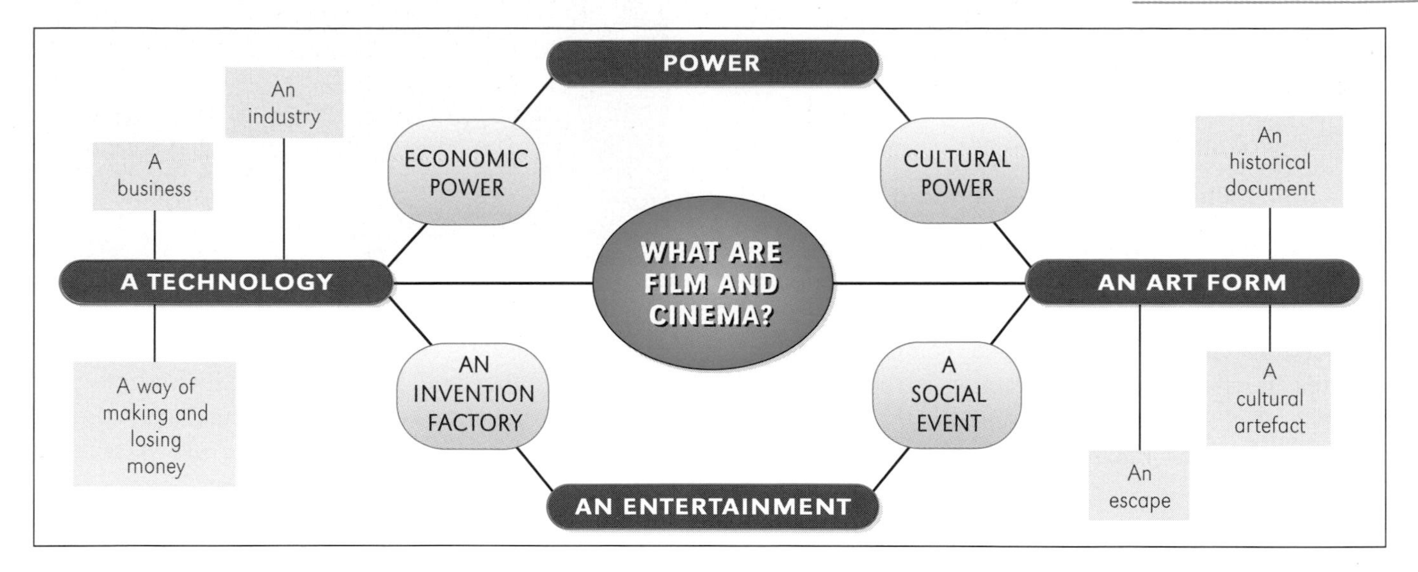

- a **social event**: we watch films with other people in a cinema; the act of going to these picture palaces is frequently a social one with friends
- a **cultural artefact**: films are reflections of a culture; they show us different aspects of our own society and that of other peoples, ethnic groups, nationalities, e.g. *Trainspotting* (Danny Boyle, Channel 4 Films et al, 1996), *East is East* (Damien O'Donnell, Assassin Films et al, 1999)
- an **escape**: as an entertainment it is an escape from the real world which we inhabit to others which can be dream worlds, imaginary worlds, exciting flights of fancy, e.g. *The Matrix* (Andy and Larry Wachowski, Grouch II Film Partnership et al, 1999)
- **cultural power**: as products which can quickly be sold around the world they are also instrumental in 'selling' a culture and giving a nation a more powerful position

WHY STUDY FILM?

This medium is important because:

- It is a powerful or **dominant art form**.
- It is a major **economic force** – i.e. a wealthy industry.
- It is **popular** – it usually has very large audiences.
- It tells **stories** – an attractive way of documenting and understanding ourselves and our world.

But what about the question, 'Why *study* films?' This change in emphasis leads us to other answers:

- It leads to a greater **understanding** of the medium.
- It helps the **imagination** of those who will create texts (e.g. Hollywood directors, independent film-makers, GCSE pupils).
- It is fun – **entertainment** is something that human beings need.

DO FILMS MATTER?

There are numerous reasons why films matter to many millions of people. To answer the question we may begin by looking at:

- our **history**
- our **society**
- our **economy**
- our **culture**
- **ourselves**

Remember that film is an art form and the answers to the question, 'Why study the arts?' usually apply to the study of film. Probably the most important answer is: 'Because we learn more about ourselves.'

- *Do films matter? Do they matter to you? Do they matter to society? What do you think?*
- *What reasons would you give for your answer?*

MAKING THE PICTURE

The basic process is in two parts:

Photography ⇨ **Editing**

The first part is **photographing**, or **filming**, the actors etc, to create the **footage** that is needed to make the finished film. The film made each day is referred to as the **dailies**, also commonly called **rushes**. Each time a piece of action is recorded it is given a number at the beginning so that it can be found easily later. Each of these attempts is called a **take**.

Once the **director** and **editor** have all the footage together they can pick the precise pieces of film that they wish to use by **cutting** them out and then **splicing** them together in the right order. This is called **editing**. It is one of the most important aspects of making a film – in fact, film-maker Alfred Hitchcock said that, after the **script**, it was *the* most important aspect.

Filming in progress for *Sense and Sensibility* (Ang Lee, Columbia, 1995)

Once the director and editor have put the whole picture together and are happy that it is in the right order and that they have used the best takes of each **shot**, they have their **print**. But the film is still not finished. They may need to add any or all of the following:

- **Music**
- **Sound effects**
- **Dubbing** (i.e. voices over the pictures)
- **Special effects**
- **Digital effects**

THE HISTORY OF FILM

Film, in its current form, has been around since 1895. Many originally considered the idea of moving images as toys or entertainments, but it did not take long before inventors saw the commercial promise and full potential of this powerful medium.

Two significant aspects are:

1. The history of film is very closely tied to the history of the twentieth century – and now the twenty-first century. As related inventions were introduced, they were integrated into the production of film. As events occurred in history they were introduced into the content of the stories in cinema, e.g. daring exploits of British soldiers during the Second World War, the spate of Vietnam War films from the late 1960s onwards.
2. The biggest influence, by far, was that of the United States of America, although other cinemas have had an important influence on the medium, such as the British, Russian, French, German, Australian, Chinese, Indian and Scandinavian cinemas, to name just a few. The USA invested immense amounts of money and talent in the industry.

The history of film can be examined in two major ways:

- **Technology** – *how* was film made?
- **Texts** – *what* was made for an audience to watch?

The three major stages in the evolution and development of film were:

- How can we record images?
- How can we make images move?
- How can we add sound?

In the beginning, film was thought to be best used as a way of recording the real world in a **documentary** format. Film was used to capture everyday events and some historic moments. But it was not long before the human imagination took over and **fiction** film became heavily sought after.

- *Before the invention of photography and film how do you think real life was documented or captured?*

KEY DATES

c.1000 First record of the use of the ***camera obscura*** principle by the Arabic scholar Ibn al-Haytham. The principle is that when light enters a dark chamber through a small hole (an **aperture**) it projects a picture of the outside, inverted and upside down, on to the surface opposite the hole

c.1100 Shadow play puppets become popular throughout Asia

c.1500 The *camera obscura* arrives in Europe

1671 The magic lantern is introduced as a form of entertainment

1822 The discovery of the use of the substance lime to create light promotes the widespread use of the magic lantern

1826 Niepce creates the first successful **photograph**

1839 Louis Daguerre launches his **daguerrotype** process to the public. Daguerre has developed the invention of Niepce to create a process whereby a silver surface on a copper plate is used to create a positive image

William Fox Talbot, an Englishman, exposes images on light-sensitive paper and discovers the process for producing **negatives** of photographs

(Whether Daguerre or Fox Talbot is the father of modern photography is debatable)

1851 Production of the first sewing machine by Singer – a similar process will be used for making pictures move

1875 Thomas A. Edison develops the **phonograph**, the **microphone** and the light bulb

1882 Marey manages to expose 12 images in one second on a plate with his invention, the **chron-photograph**

1887 **Celluloid film** is invented

1892 Edison presents his **kinetoscope**

1894 A shop selling kinetoscopes opens in New York

1895 **The official year of the birth of film**

In Berlin, on 1 November, the Skladanowsky Brothers win the race to be the first to exhibit the process of 'living photographs'

Eight weeks later in Paris on 28 December the Lumière brothers present their technically superior ***cinematographe***

HOLLYWOOD

1887 Harvey Henderson Wilcox registers his 120-acre ranch in an area just north-west of Los Angeles. His wife, Daeida, decides it should be called **Hollywood** due to the large number of holly trees growing there

1902 Thomas Talley, known for running exhibitions, opens the first cinema, the Electric Cinema, which seats 200

1903 The village of Hollywood has grown so quickly that it is incorporated as a suburb of Los Angeles

1907 Director Francis Boggs visits Hollywood with the first film crew to shoot coastal locations for the Selig Polyscope production of the costume drama adventure of *The Count of Monte Cristo*

1908 The company owner, Col Selig, likes the locations and the area so much that he decides to stay and he begins the construction of the first film studio in Edendale

1909 The New York Motion Picture Company also builds a studio in Edendale

1910 Several New York film companies begin to use Hollywood on a regular basis to make their films. By now the population of Hollywood is 5,000

1911 The Nestor studio is built as the first movie studio in Hollywood itself

The New York Motion Picture Company builds a studio near Santa Monica, outside Hollywood, for filming westerns under the producer-director, Thomas Ince

1914 D. W. Griffiths uses the Mutual Triangle Studio, later the Griffiths Fine Arts Studio, where he films his best-known early feature-length films, *Birth of a Nation* and *Intolerance*

1915 Carl Laemmle opens his new **Universal Studios** in the nearby San Fernando Valley

1917 The Fox Film Corporation, later **Twentieth Century Fox**, moves into a studio on Sunset Boulevard

1918 Louis B. Mayer arrives. He goes on to build the studio known as **Metro-Goldwyn-Mayer**

The four major Hollywood studios

1919 The population of Hollywood has grown to 35,000. By 1925 it will grow to 130,000

Douglas Fairbanks and his wife, Mary Pickford, the first two **stars** of Hollywood, buy a huge house in Beverly Hills and start the trend of the glamorous film star lifestyle

THE GROWTH AND IMPORTANCE OF HOLLYWOOD

Hollywood grew very quickly in the next few decades to become the most powerful and richest film industry in the world. It successfully sold its product abroad with aggressive **marketing** and a **populist** choice of product – it captured popular imagination and millions wished to see these products.

The key aspects of Hollywood's success were:

- Its **location**. This particular part of America had many advantages: large areas of cheap land; a sunny and dependable climate; cheap labour and a variety of ethnic types and locations.
- The **support of the government**. President Woodrow Wilson said in 1917 that the USA needed Hollywood to sell America abroad.
- The **exploitation of technological advances** such as:
    - the coming of **sound** and better quality delivery – from *The Jazz Singer* (Alan Crosland, Warner Bros) in 1927 to Dolby Stereo and beyond
    - the **size of the screen**: using anamorphic projection to squeeze a wider screen on to the standard 35mm film stock; using 70mm film to develop a very wide screen
    - the use of **colour**, especially expanding in the 1950s to compete with television
    - the use of better quality **film stock**
    - the use of **smaller and better cameras** such as **steadicam** so that films could be shot on location and with better results
    - the use of **tricks**, such as 3D films and *The Tingler* (William Castle, Columbia, 1959) in which the audience were given an electric shock
    - the invention of **new cinemas** from drive-ins to IMAX
    - the use of **digital technology** to produce, distribute and exhibit the film as with *Toy Story 2* (Ash Brennon/John Lasseter, Pixar/Walt Disney, 1999)

From sound to digital technology: *The Jazz Singer* and *Toy Story 2*

- The **talent**: actors, writers, directors, producers. In particular the **star system** was created, whereby individual popular actors were turned into stars – another commodity for the studio to own, exploit and sell. The stars were tied to a seven-year contract and therefore had to work for, or be hired out by, that studio.
- The **system**: everything under one roof. By creating huge **studios** which specialised in making films the companies could create an efficient production line, much the same as assembly lines today. These studios would have everything they needed on site so that the whole film could be made quickly and cheaply. It is referred to as the **Hollywood Studio System**.
- The hard-hitting **business approach** – such as buying into television, subsidiary links with magazines, product merchandising and a high media profile from the start.
- By distributing and exhibiting its own films – the studios bought up as many cinemas as they could so that they controlled which films were shown to the public. This is sometimes referred to as **vertical integration**.
- The use of popular **genres**, such as the love story, the musical, the gangster film, the horror film.
- It created a way of applauding itself and selling the products at the same time: the **Academy Awards** or **Oscars**.

In addition to these strengths, look at the diagram below to see why and how Hollywood grew.

ACTIVITY 1

- Take each of the categories in the diagram and find out why each factor was important in the growth of Hollywood.

HOLLYWOOD TODAY

By looking carefully at the history of Hollywood we can see how the Hollywood of today has evolved. Many aspects of the studio system had a long-term and profound effect. For example, look at how important to modern Hollywood the cult of the director and the star system are. These men and women are used to sell the product, in much the same way as they were necessary in the early decades.

ACTIVITY 2

- Find modern examples of the cult of the director and the use of the star.
- What other aspects of the history of Hollywood are still to be seen in modern Hollywood?
- What are the major differences?

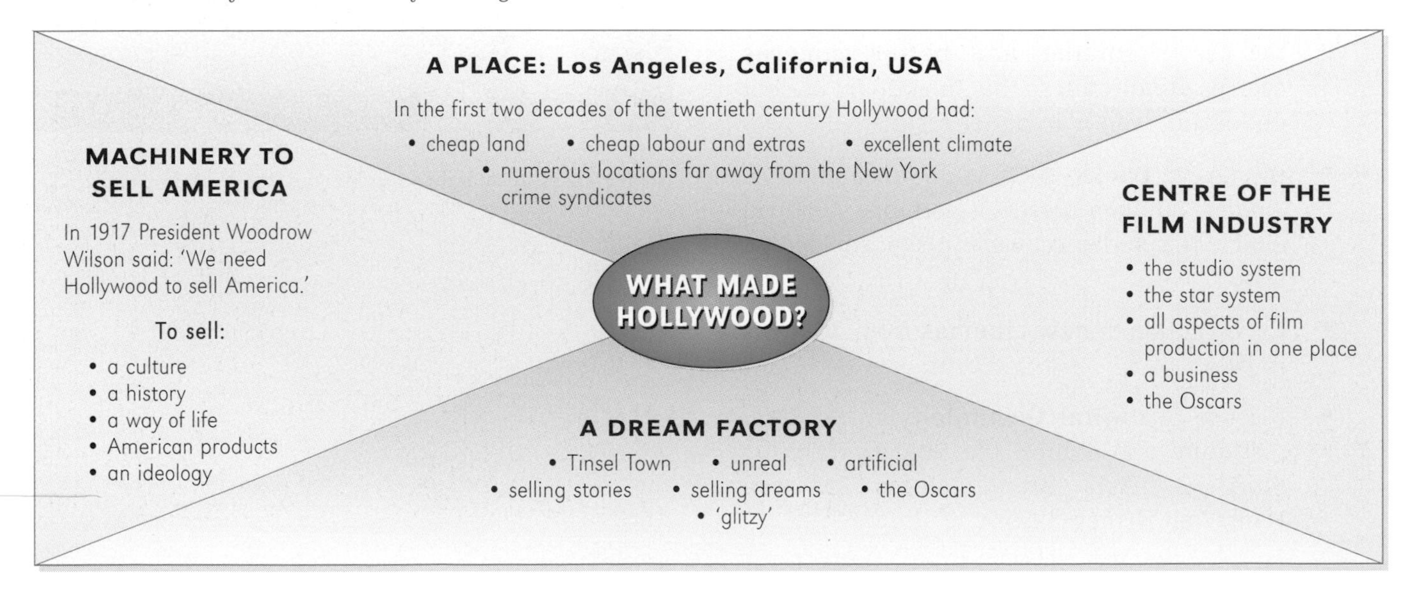

MEDIA PRODUCERS AND AUDIENCES

WHO MAKES FILM?

This question can be approached in a number of ways. Consider the following diagram:

	EAST IS EAST	*GLADIATOR*	*BILLY ELLIOT*	*YOUR FAVOURITE FILM*
INDIVIDUAL	Damien O'Donnell	Ridley Scott	Stephen Daldry	?
COMPANY	Assassin Films BBC Channel 4 Films	Dream Works SKG Scott Free Prod Universal Pictures	BBC Tiger Aspect Working Title	?
COUNTRY	UK	USA	UK	?
YEAR	1999	2000	2000	?

Who makes film?

The first thing we need to realise is that manufacturing a film, like all mass media texts, is a **collaborative** exercise. This means that these products are made by more than one person – they are made by groups of people, ranging from just a handful for a short five-minute film, to hundreds (and even thousands) for major studio films and epics.

If you make a short video for your practical work you will find it necessary to work in a group as there is so much to do.

Look at the table above. Can you complete the blanks for some of your favourite films? Use the Internet as a resource (www.imdb.com).

East is East

Billy Elliot

Gladiator

The Individuals

ROLE	EXPLANATION	EXAMPLE
WRITER	Writes the screenplay – the blueprint for the film. May also involve the original novelist if it is an adaption	Frank Darabont (screenplay), Stephen King (novel) – *The Green Mile*
DIRECTOR	In charge of the creative aspects of making the film, especially during the principal photography	Sam Mendes – *American Beauty*
PRODUCER	In charge of the whole production – deals with the money and major aspects of the business side	Andrew Macdonald – *Trainspotting*
EDITOR	Cuts and edits together the dailies into a complete and coherent whole	Masahiro Hirakubo – *The Beach*
CASTING DIRECTOR	Allocates the roles to actors	Dianne Crittenden – *Pretty Woman*
DIRECTOR OF PHOTOGRAPHY	In charge of the way in which the film is photographed – works particularly closely with the director. Lighting design is also involved	Adam Greenberg – *Terminator 2*
DESIGNER	Designs the set – will have a strong influence over the mise-en-scène and the style of the film. Lighting design is also involved	Anton Furst – *Batman*
COMPOSER	Creates the musical score for the film – may also conduct the orchestra	Maurice Jarre – *Ghost*
SPECIAL EFFECTS	In charge of all special effects which are very difficult to create in reality – such as scale models, stunts, explosions	Stan Winston – *Terminator 2*
MAKE-UP ARTIST	Design the make-up for the actors/characters	Stan Winston – *Batman Returns*
COSTUME DESIGNER	Designs the clothes that the characters will wear	Giorgio Armani (wardrobe) – *The Untouchables*
ACTORS	The people who act the roles and create the characters	Leonardo di Caprio – *Titanic*

In addition to this list there are many others such as camera operator, continuity person, title designer, musicians, key grip, extras, but the above list gives a clear line-up of the important players.

ACTIVITY 3

- Look out for names of famous people in the film industry and research them using books and a film database on the web. Create a dossier of their work.
- Can you spot any similarities in the work of particular stars, directors, writers, composers, directors of photography?

The Companies

The companies similarly can range from small **independents** to huge international **conglomerates** (i.e. a large company that incorporates many businesses, such as Time Warner). The important difference we need to look at first of all is between Hollywood and independents.

The Hollywoood studios, having established a power base, are unlikely to let go. They invest heavily not only in their own films but in others as well. The reason for spreading their investments is because of the heavy risk factor in making films. William Goldman, a well-known script-writer, once said about making Hollywood films:

> "Nobody knows anything."

What he meant by this is that it is frequently difficult to predict the public's response to a film – it is not just a question of, 'Is it any good?' When a big expensive picture loses $100 million it can jeopardise the very existence of that company or studio.

So if a major Hollywood studio knows from previous experience that some films are unexpected winners and some are not, it makes sense to invest wisely and widely. The diagram below gives an indication of the groups or companies behind most film-making.

ACTIVITY 4

- Choose a few of your favourite films and find out where the finance came from. Use movie mags, books and the Internet to help you. Is there a difference between American films and British films? In what aspects is it visible?

Remember, the film industry is not just one big industry – it is broken down into smaller companies / institutions / groups. Some people argue that we basically have two categories:

- Hollywood
- everything else – i.e. independents

Others take the view that there is rarely such a thing as an independent film nowadays as Hollywood always manages to get involved somewhere along the film-making process.

The Countries

You may have noticed that a film can be identified by:

a where the **film was made**

or b where the **money came from** to make the film

or c where the **director and / or the cast and crew came from**

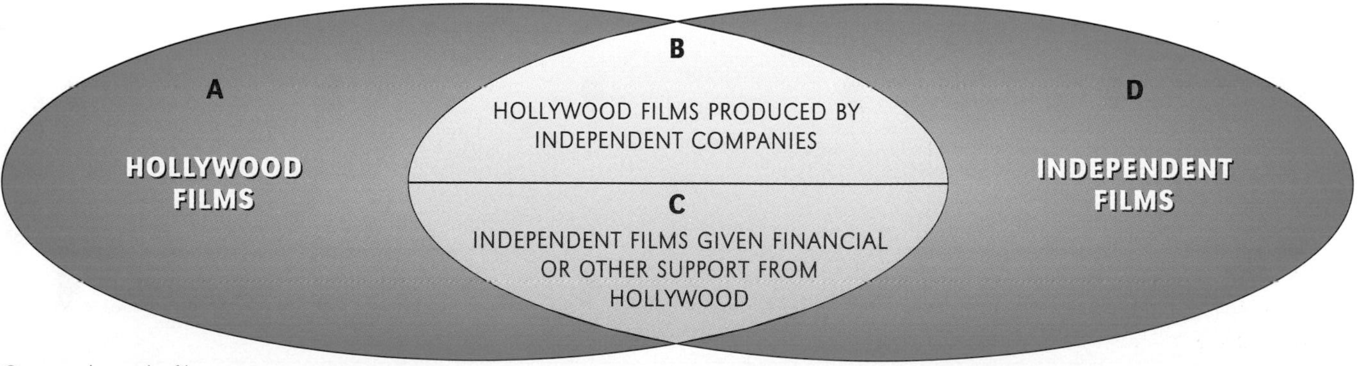

Groups who make films

ACTIVITY 5

- Why do you think it is important in each case? Does it matter that a film has a country of origin?
- Find out the answer to **a**, **b** and **c** above in relation to *Shakespeare in Love* (John Madden, Bedford Falls/Miramax/Universal, 1998). Is the answer surprising?

In the present age it is frequently difficult to state the national origin of a film. Many people believe, for example, that the Bond franchise must be British as it has a British cast on the whole, it was created by an Englishman, the hero is English and England is his home base. However, if we look at the producers and the financial aspects of the film we could arrive at a different conclusion.

The Producers

These are the people who are involved in the production and business side of film-making. They include:

- **Movie moguls** – the people who own and/or run a studio. They decide which films the studio will make and how much money to allocate to the initial budget
- **Producers** – the people in charge of the production side of a film. They are primarily businessmen, although some are heavily involved in all aspects of the making of the film and some have the power to fire the director or decide on the **casting** of the film. Notice how many men control the industry and how few women are involved. Why is this?
- **Investors** – these are people who give their money to a production company in order to receive a **return** on this investment when, or if, the film makes a profit
- **Distributors** – these people are interested in buying the **rights** to a film after it is made in order to distribute it around a country or the world
- **Exhibitors** – these people own cinemas or cinema chains and will show films in order to obtain a **revenue**

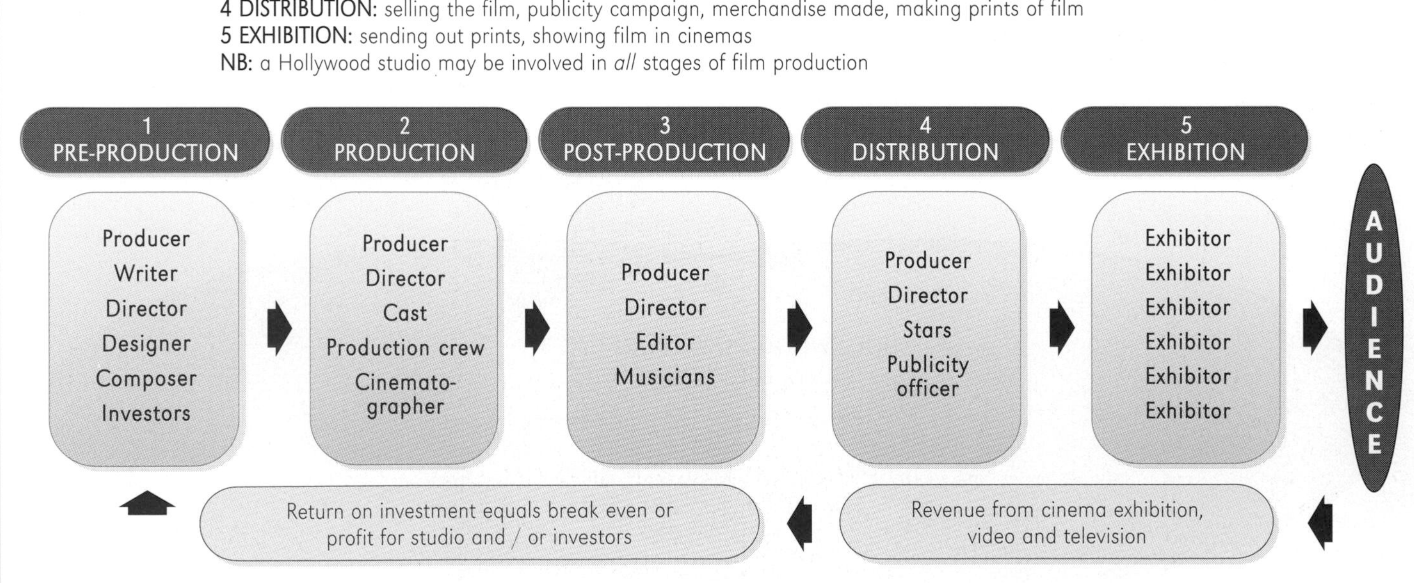

This list is not as simple as it seems. Some companies can make films, distribute them and exhibit them, e.g. Warner Bros. In other cases a production may find that its revenue is split by quite a number of people at each stage of the production.

When you watch a film look closely at the credit sequence at the very beginning. The names of the companies and personnel will give you an indication of its production origin. You will, for example, see the name of a Hollywood studio frequently in this sequence somewhere, or one of its subsidiaries. Disney may invest in a film using the name Buena Vista, for example.

Another interesting aspect of film production is where the actual money comes from:

- individuals, and / or
- companies

Independently wealthy individuals can invest in individual films, depending upon how the film is financed in the first place.

Then there are companies which specialise in making films and these can provide all, or a part, of the finance. The greater the percentage of their investment, the more say they will have in details of production.

Quite frequently major companies in other industries invest in film production because they have similar or vested interests, such as Sony or Coca-Cola. In some cases we can see **product placement** in action whereby certain products are showcased in the film, such as BMW in recent Bond movies.

ACTIVITY 6

- Look at *Back to the Future* (Robert Zemeckis, Universal, 1985) and see if you can spot any significant product placement. Do you think that product placement is an acceptable form of advertising? What might be the objections to it?
- Look at the end credits to see if famous company names are acknowledged for their 'assistance'.
- Which companies are involved in the soundtrack of some recent blockbusters? Can you find out if they have any investment in the production of the film itself? Use the film databases on the Web.
- Do you think it matters that men tend to control the film industry? What differences might one expect if more women had more say in film production?

Product placement: BMW and Bond

The Artists

These are the people who are primarily interested in the **artistic** and **creative** side of the production. They will include:

- **Directors** – these people are in charge of decision-making and production when the film is actually being shot. They are likely to have a lot of input into other areas, such as the script, the design and the editing

- **Writers** – these are the people who write the shooting script. They may be the ones who come up with the original idea, or **pitch**, or they may adapt other works such as novels or biographies
- **Editors** – these are the ones who finally **cut** the film from the **dailies** or **rushes**, and assemble it together in the **edited** version that we see
- **Designers** – these people will design the look of the film such as the costumes, sets, lighting
- **Composers** – these musicians will write and **orchestrate** the music for the **soundtrack**

There are of course numerous other people who are important on a film location, such as builders, stunt men, caterers, drivers and **gofers** (people who do odd jobs, run errands – from *go for*).

THE FILM PRODUCTION CYCLE

On page 22 we saw a diagram of the full cycle of a typical **big-budget film**. We will look at some of these key aspects.

The three major parts of making a film are:

Production ⇨ Distribution ⇨ Exhibition

1 Production

This splits into three parts:

Pre-production – where the **script**, **storyboard** and **designs** are prepared and the shooting schedules are drawn up. Some of the sets may be built in preparation for filming.

Production – the **principal photography** and **second unit** filming takes place. Sets may be built simultaneously during this period.

Post-production – the editing of the **final cut** and the preparations for **delivery** to an audience. At this stage some digital effects may be added if necessary.

2 Distribution

This vital part involves getting the film to the audience around the country and the world. This is a very expensive business as many of the following are likely to be involved in this process and many individual companies may be employed who specialise in each of these areas:

- making the most economical number of **prints** as they are expensive
- **booking** the right cinemas in the right places at the right time
- making a **trailer** for audiences prior to the opening
- designing **posters** for billboards, magazines, etc
- creating **tag-lines** for the ads
- creating a **web site**
- mounting the **teaser campaign**, used to create initial interest or to use on television
- publicising the USP – the **unique selling point** – to make the film seem different
- putting together the EPK – **electronic press kit** – for critics, reviewers and general publicity in magazines, newpapers and television
- setting up the **celebrity** interviews with stars, directors, writers, designers etc, as well as associated publicity in the 'gossip trade'
- deciding on the timing of **press releases**
- creating a CD **soundtrack**
- producing additional **merchandise**, if possible, to help sell the film and, more importantly for the investors, to make more money
- setting up **tie-ins** to complementary industries such as food chains to create an additional buzz
- timing the exhibition to fit in with other **competition** or particular **seasons**
- using **film festivals** to get additional publicity or **awards**

You can see from the above that **advertising** is a very important aspect at this stage. Huge amounts of money are spent on advertising films so that the public is informed. After this stage **word-of-mouth** becomes important – that is when an audience has seen the film and spreads the word on whether it is worth seeing or not. This includes you as a **consumer** of film.

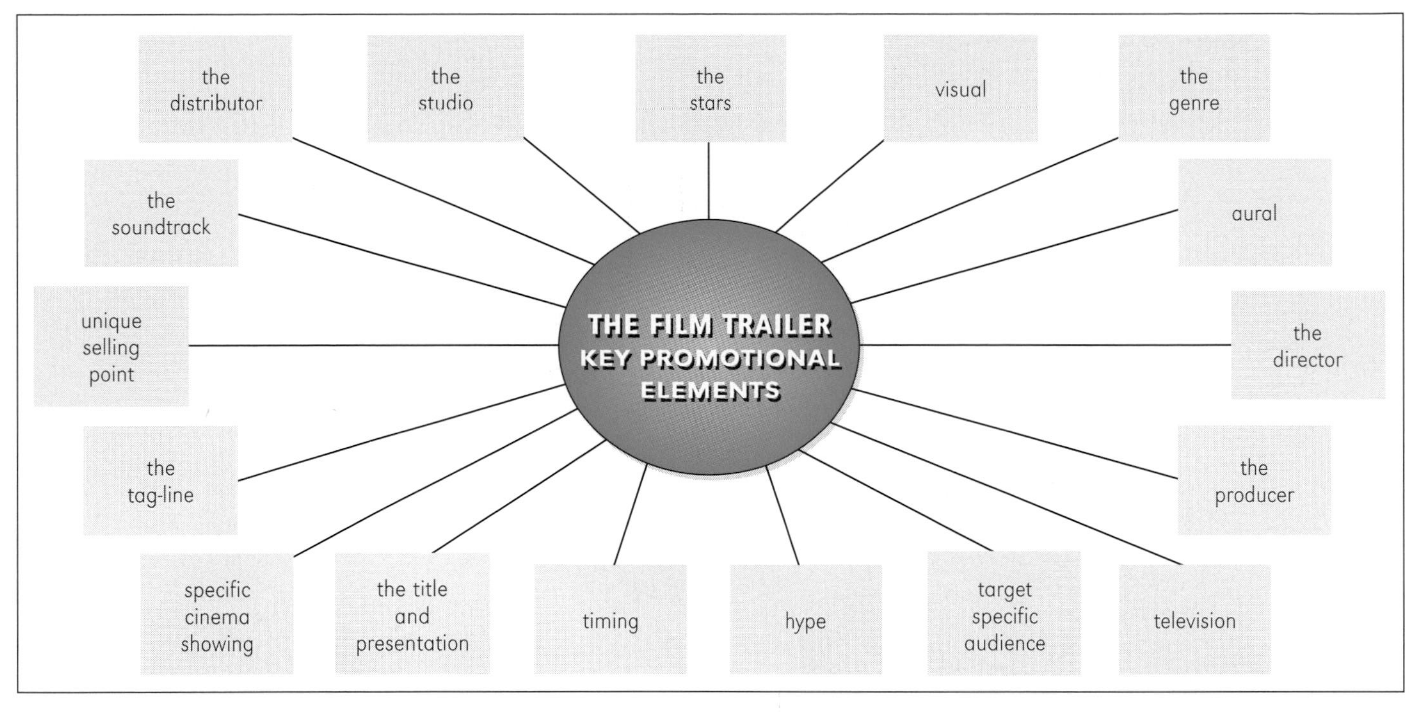
THE FILM TRAILER
KEY PROMOTIONAL ELEMENTS
the distributor
the studio
the stars
visual
the genre
the soundtrack
aural
unique selling point
the director
the tag-line
the producer
specific cinema showing
the title and presentation
timing
hype
target specific audience
television

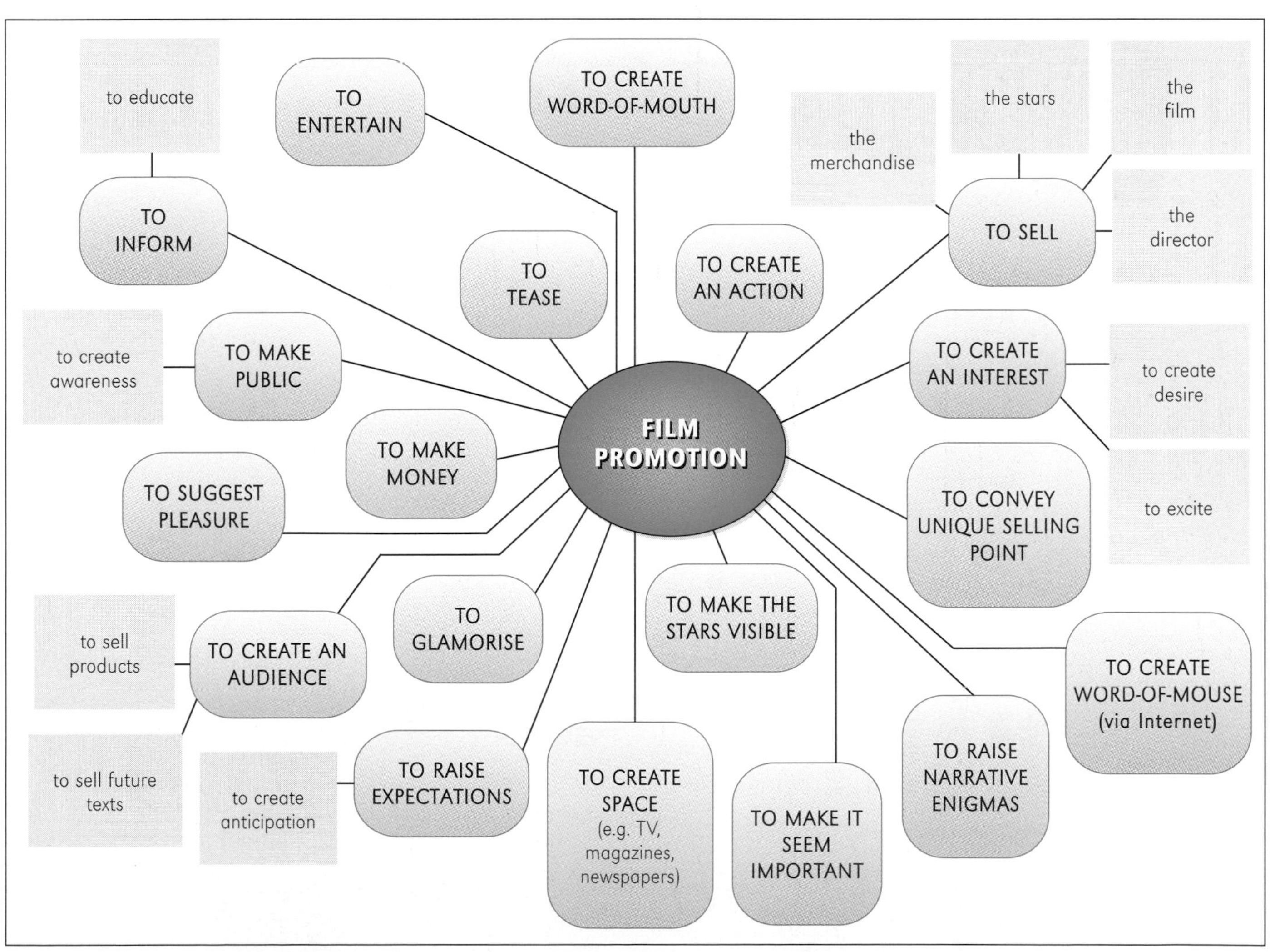
FILM PROMOTION
to educate
TO ENTERTAIN
TO CREATE WORD-OF-MOUTH
the merchandise
the stars
the film
TO INFORM
TO TEASE
TO CREATE AN ACTION
TO SELL
the director
to create awareness
TO MAKE PUBLIC
TO CREATE AN INTEREST
to create desire
TO MAKE MONEY
TO SUGGEST PLEASURE
TO CONVEY UNIQUE SELLING POINT
to excite
to sell products
TO CREATE AN AUDIENCE
TO GLAMORISE
TO MAKE THE STARS VISIBLE
TO CREATE WORD-OF-MOUSE (via Internet)
to sell future texts
to create anticipation
TO RAISE EXPECTATIONS
TO CREATE SPACE (e.g. TV, magazines, newspapers)
TO MAKE IT SEEM IMPORTANT
TO RAISE NARRATIVE ENIGMAS

The poster is an important part of making audiences aware of the film

3 Exhibition

Showing the film to the public at the cinema. This involves showings such as **premières**, **gala performances**, **critics' showings**, **preview screenings** and **first runs** in cinemas for the public.

There are a number of different types of cinema we could visit:

- an **old-style cinema** in the High Street that is showing one, two or three new films
- an independent **art house** cinema that shows films in a repertory system with a mixture of old and new films
- a large **multi-plex cinema** that has a large number of cinemas showing a large number of new films
- an **IMAX** cinema that shows a particular format of film on a very large screen
- a **drive-in** cinema, particularly popular in the USA in the 1950s
- a **temporary** cinema set up in a park, for example

The other major recent aspect of distribution and exhibition is the **secondary** showing of the film in the following ways:

- the first and subsequent showings on **television**
- the showing of the film on **pay-on-demand** on **digital** and **cable** delivery systems
- the creation of a **VHS video** or **DVD disc**
- a **collector's edition** video or disc with extra material, interviews, trailers, documentaries (*The Making of...*) etc
- the 'new' version of the film, such as the **director's cut**
- **anniversary versions** of classic films

FILM AND AUDIENCES

What is an audience?

The simplest answer is: the groups of people who watch the film.

This answer, of course, is a little too simple. Let's consider who the audience may consist of.

Think about a film like *Star Wars* (George Lucas, Lucasfilm, 1977). You might well think that this is a film for everybody, for the whole family to enjoy. What about the following groups of people?

- Those who do not like science fiction
- Those who do not like Harrison Ford
- Those who do not like Hollywood films
- Those who think that *Star Wars* is for children

From this starting point it is not difficult to see that audiences are different in a number of ways:

- Audiences can be very large (billions) or much smaller (thousands)
- Audiences may consist of **subgroups** (smaller groups)
- Audiences can usually be **predicted**
- Audiences can be **targeted**
- Audiences are not passive – they are very **active** during the watching of a film and afterwards

- *Why is it that different people like and dislike different films?*

Let us look at a film like *Saving Private Ryan* (Steven Spielberg, Amblin/Dreamworks et al, 1998). Do you think that an ex-soldier who fought in the Second World War would have a different experience of watching the film than a 15-year-old boy or girl?

The point is that a viewer brings many things to a text when he or she watches it and they affect how the viewer interprets or experiences the film.

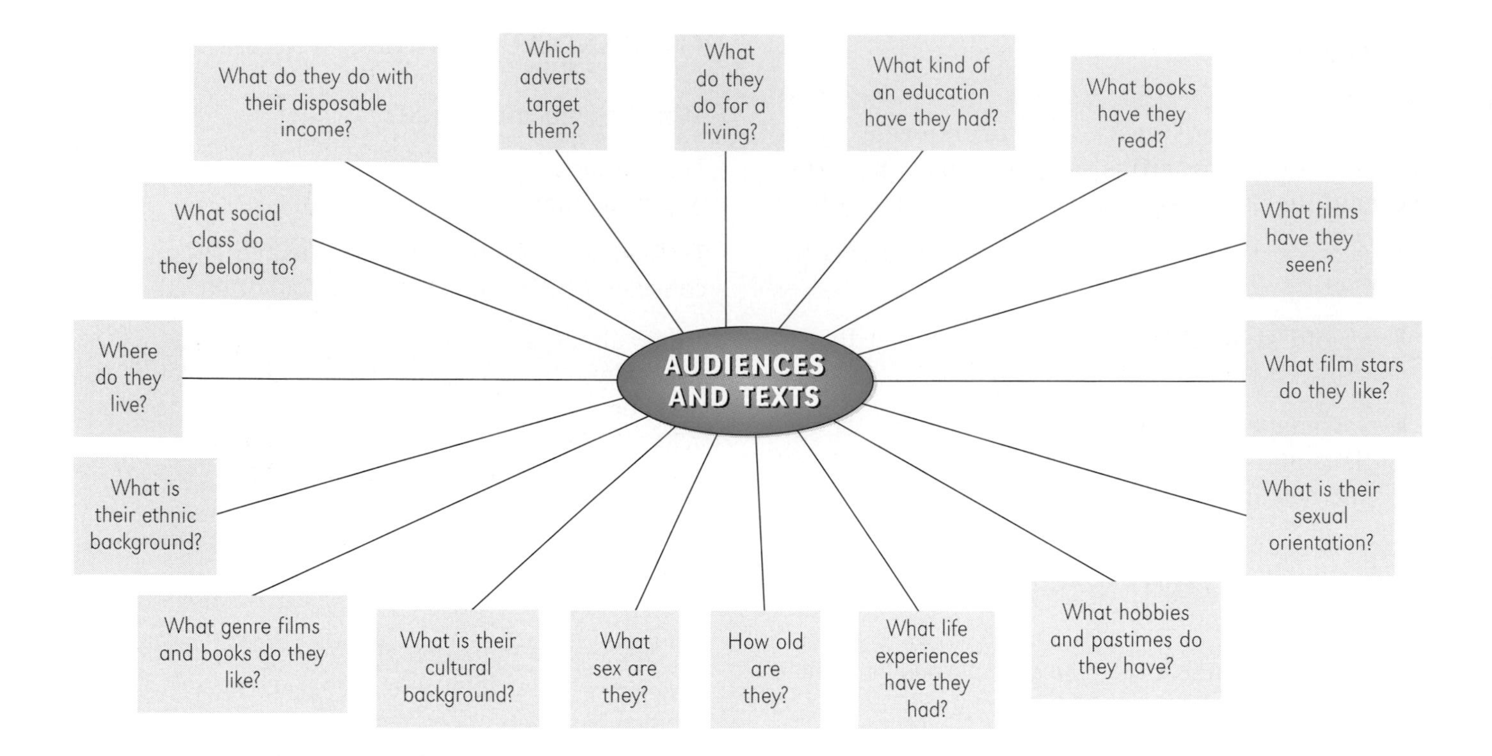

- *What do these questions tell us about audiences and texts? Consider some specific films that you have seen.*

Different types of audience

Hollywood is particularly good at giving young people what they want – it frequently targets a particular age group. This is called the **target audience**. The target audience for a large number of Hollywood films is 18 to 26 years of age, or sometimes 14 to 26 years of age. This is because a large number of people in this age range have a high **disposable income**, that is, most of the money they earn goes on things which they can choose to spend it on, such as leisure activities.

An audience that is large and covers a wide variety of different types of people is called a **mainstream audience**. Most Hollywood films are mainstream films for mainstream audiences. The reasons for this are so that they can:

- Create maximum chances to get a **return on their investment** by attracting a film-going audience – this age group will spend more of their money on socialising than older groups. If you spend a large amount making a film then you must get a large mainstream audience to make a profit

ACTIVITY 6

- Think about the films you have watched recently and copy and complete the following table:

NAME OF FILM	*COUNTRY OF ORIGIN*	*STARS*	*GENRE*	*LIKE OR DISLIKE*

- Compare answers – what are the differences and similarities and why?
- Would you expect other groups of people to have the same or different views from you?
- Ask your parents to provide you with information for their own lists. What are your conclusions?

- **Persuade advertisers** to use ad slots that are associated with this film, now and in the future (e.g. when they are on television)

If you look at the main ingredients in the average Hollywood blockbuster you can identify a number of aspects that are designed to attract this group, for example:

- **Humour** – it makes the audience laugh with jokes that are more likely to be appreciated by this group
- **Spectacle** – action films with car chases, explosions, disasters etc
- **Sex** – bodies on display etc
- Designer **goods** on display
- A **lead character** fits this age group, such as a **heroic** character who may be seen as a role model for the target audience
- All the main characters fit this age group
- The **soundtrack** – music that will appeal to this age group

Spectacle is important in modern blockbusters – a scene from *Titanic*

Audiences that are very small and quite particular are referred to as a **niche audience**. For example, audiences who enjoy obscure vampire films such as *The Fearless Vampire Killers* (Roman Polanski, Cadre Films / Filmways, 1967). Again, these films can enjoy a small audience as they have a small **budget** and low **production values**. An interesting and unexpected exception to this was *The Blair Witch Project* (Daniel Myrick / Eduardo Sanchez, Haxan, 1999), which cost $35,000 to make yet took over $140 million at the **domestic box office**.

An expensive film does not guarantee a large audience or a profit as it is not possible to predict the success of a film. *The Avengers* (Jeremiah Checkik, Warner Bros, 1998) is an example of a film that **flopped**.

- *Advertisers are also interested in the 16–25 age group. Why?*
- *What is the link between films and advertising in terms of target audiences?*

What does an audience get for its money?

When we buy products in shops in most cases it is clear what we are getting for our money. If we look at film as a **product** to be sold we can see some similarities and begin to ask some interesting questions.

Just as our customer gets pleasure from his or her chocolate bar, a member of the audience receives **pleasures** from a film text. But what exactly are the pleasures on offer?

The three main strands of this approach are:

- entertainment / spectacle
- culture
- stories

The one aspect of our pleasure from the text that ties these together is:

- emotion

Most mainstream audiences expect some form of **emotional involvement** with the texts. If we don't get it we feel let down, disappointed – in short, we have not received enough pleasure from the text in

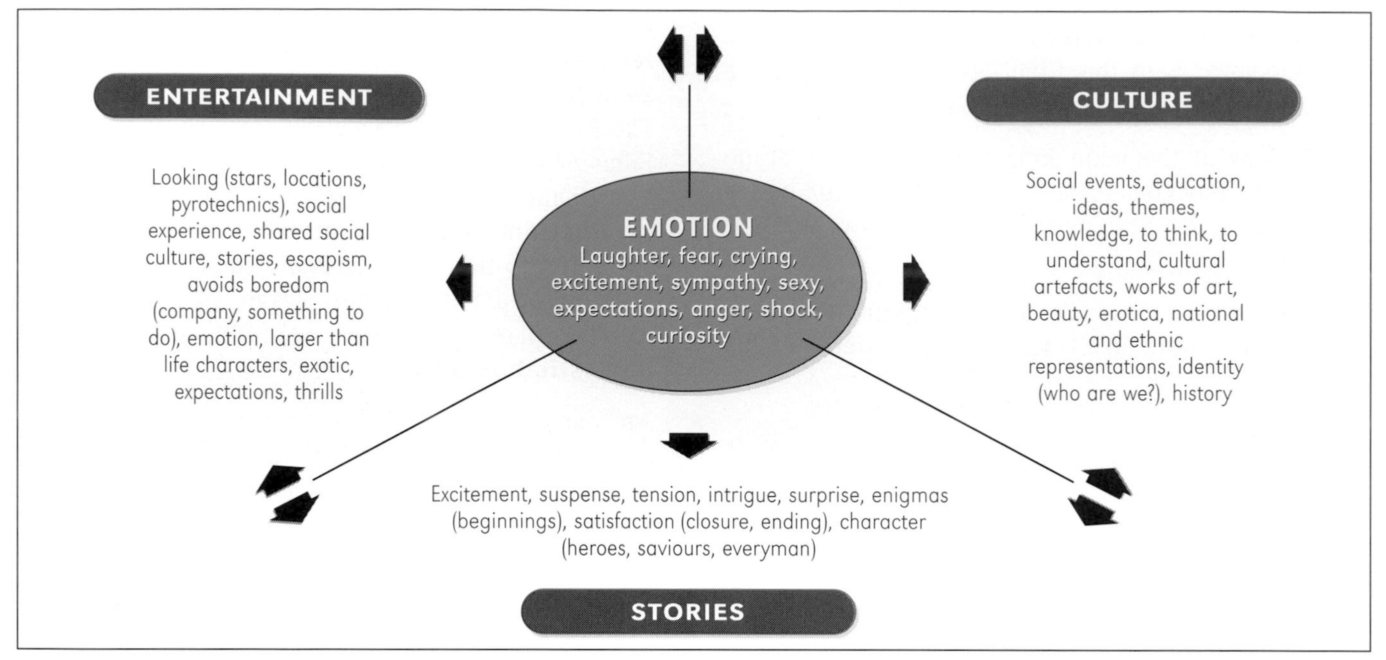

Pleasures of the text

relation to what we have paid in **money** and in **time**. This is one of the reasons that film-makers frequently try to get us to **identify with** or **relate to** the major character(s), as it is likely to increase the chances of emotional involvement if we feel a tie with sympathetic characters, e.g. Jim Carrey in *The Truman Show* (Peter Weir, Paramount/Scott Rudin, 1998).

- *Name some films that have let you down and give reasons why.*
- *Name some films where you have felt sympathetic towards a major character. How was it achieved?*

Let's not forget, however, that one of the main functions of film is to **entertain**. We use film to **escape** boredom, to escape from real life, to provide thrills – this often affects our initial judgement of a film. It is also true that some films we don't think of as great works of art do score high on entertainment value, e.g. *Naked Gun* (David Zucker, Paramount, 1988).

- *Name some films which in your opinion are highly entertaining. Why is this so?*

When we begin to rank one film higher than another we must be aware that we are making **value judgements** and that it is primarily our **opinion**

Jim Carrey in *The Truman Show*

which we are expressing. Critics get paid simply to express their opinion. The fact that we all like and dislike different films is part of the enjoyment of the art form – it celebrates the **diversity** of human beings.

Audiences and texts

When people first began to study the media in relation to audiences they considered the audience as a **passive** entity – that is, they thought that the audience did not actually *do* anything. Modern thought and research in this area have tended towards seeing the audience as far from passive – in fact, they are now considered to be highly **active** – that is, they are doing something, they are **engaged** in activities.

What is actually going on when someone watches a film? Many points have been made about this above (e.g. take pleasure, identify with, relate to, be sympathetic towards) but we need to consider this in a little more detail. It partly depends upon *where* it is seen and *who* you are seeing it with. In showings of *A Few Good Men* (Rob Reiner, Castle Rock, 1992), some audiences became partisan – some supporting Tom Cruise and some cheering for Jack Nicholson, as if they were actually watching a sports event. When *Braveheart* (Mel Gibson, Icon/Ladd, 1995) was first shown in Glasgow the audiences went wild at certain Scottish patriotic moments.

Our experience of the text can involve: talking, cheering, laughing, shouting, crying, groaning, screaming. When we see a film at home we may be more likely to do something else at the same time than we would in a cinema. But in a cinema we may feel that it is more of a social experience. Experiences of watching film can stay with a spectator for years.

When an audience come to a film they bring many things with them. We saw earlier what some of those things are. For example:

UPBRINGING	ATTITUDES	KNOWLEDGE
LIFESTYLE	EDUCATION	TASTE
CULTURE	EMOTIONS	EXPECTATIONS

In short:

THEIR
LIFE
EXPERIENCES

With these life experiences we create **mental models** which we use to work out what is going on when we watch a film. For example, if we have seen *Goldfinger* (Guy Hamilton, UA / Eon, 1964) we are likely to work out instantly the genre of *The World is Not Enough* (Michael Apted, Eon / MGM / UA, 1999) – we will have **expectations** of this **subgenre**.

Mel Gibson in *Braveheart*: did you get involved?

MEDIA LANGUAGES AND CATEGORIES

FILM AND GENRE

What is genre?

Genre is a type of film. It is a way of **classifying** a film to help us to identify it so that we can:

- **create** it – e.g. for a director of a film
- **choose** it – e.g. for a member of an audience
- **understand** it – e.g. for a student of film

The easiest way to see this is to give a few examples:

Animation / Cartoon

PRISON DRAMA

FANTASY

CHILDREN'S FILM

SCIENCE FICTION

COMEDY

HISTORICAL

CRIME

SPORTS MOVIE

THRILLER

HORROR

DOCUMENTARY

WESTERN

Action / Adventure

WAR

LOVE STORY / ROMANCE

GANGSTER

MELODRAMA

LITERARY ADAPTION

BIOPIC

The major genres of film

There are three types of genre:

Major genre	A dominant, important category – it should be relatively obvious and easy to define and / or spot, e.g. *Unforgiven* (Clint Eastwood, Warner, 1992) is a western.
Subgenre	A minor category or subdivision that is very closely related to its major genre by being a specific type in its own right, e.g. James Bond films, such as *The World is Not Enough*, are a subgenre of the spy genre.
Hybrid genre or Generic hybrid	A combination of major genres that sometimes creates another type of film, e.g. *The Quick and the Dead* (Sam Raimi, Columbia Tristar, 1995) is a horror / western.

How do we use the concept of genres?

Different groups may use this idea depending upon whether they are **producers** or **audiences** or critical **analysts**.

The following list gives an indication of the variety of ways of looking at this concept:

- particular **audiences** like certain types of films
- it helps us to **analyse** films and to see how they are **constructed** and marketed
- to give a film an **identity**
- to **attract** a **mainstream** audience
- to **target** a specific **niche** audience
- to inform an audience of the type of **storyline** or **characters** or **stars**
- to **sell** the film
- to play with variations on a **formula which works**
- to **deliver** an audience to **advertisers**
- to give audiences what they **expect**

- to create **historical progression**, i.e. directors make films of genres they have enjoyed
- to define, create and utilise **stars**
- to assist **writers** to sell it to producers (i.e. the pitch)
- to make it **safe** or easy for a specific audience
- to **avoid disappointment**

How do we recognise genre?

We identify genre by looking for **generic codes** and **conventions** – these are the **signifiers** that have been established through time and should be recognised in the ***mise-en-scène***, the **characters** and the **storyline**.

Signifiers are the physical aspects that we see or hear in a film, such as the clothes or gunshots. We interpret these signifiers to create **meaning**.

The *mise-en-scène* is that which we see in the **frame** of the film – it is that which is 'put into' the picture. So this would include the **set**, the **props**, the **costumes**, the **landscape** in **the world of the film**.

The two major questions to ask are:

1. **What do we see?**
2. **What does it mean?**

Signifiers (what we **see** or **hear**):

We see: saloons, horses, ten-gallon hats, six-shooters, sheriffs, bartenders, call-girls, ranches, tumbleweed, railroads, cacti, cattle, cowboys and Red Indians.

We hear: cows mooing, gunshots, piano players, horses galloping, arrows flying, guitars, harmonicas, signs creaking as they swing.

Signified (what we think it **means**):

Genre: because we know the visual and aural **codes** and **conventions** we know that it is a western.

ACTIVITY 7

- *Consider the following table. How would you complete it?*

GENRE	WESTERN	GANGSTER	SCI-FI	CHOOSE ONE
WHAT WE SEE	cowboys, horses, saloons, gunfights, sherifs	?	alien creatures and landscapes, spacecraft	?
WHAT WE HEAR	cows mooing, horses galloping, guns firing, piano-playing	?	?	?
TYPICAL CHARACTERS	lone gunman, honest sheriff, innocent townsfolk	Al Capone – gang boss Elliot Ness – honest lawman	?	?
TYPICAL STORYLINE	Evil man wants to take over town – good man fights him	?	?	?
THEMES MORALS IDEAS	good v evil right v wrong one man can make a difference	?	we can learn from other cultures, civilisations	?
EXAMPLES	*High Noon* *Pale Rider* *Unforgiven*	*The Untouchables*	?	?

Genre and signifiers

Notice how there are other significant features of a genre that we expect to see:

STORYLINES
(or narratives)

and

CHARACTERS

We'll be returning to these later when we do a proper analysis of a scene in a film. Before this, let us consider genre and audiences.

Genre and audiences

Genre is an important aspect of **targeting an audience**. You will frequently find producers making similar genre films at certain **periods** when there is a huge surprise hit, e.g. *Star Wars* – look at the number of cheap sci-fi films which followed this in the late 1970s and early 80s. Studio executives don't want to be left out if there is a seeming bonanza on the way.

Similarly some producers and directors specialise in certain genres: John Ford mainly directed westerns; Broccoli and Saltzman almost exclusively produced the James Bond subgenre.

So what does this tell us? Genre is one way of **packaging**, **presenting** and **selling** a major film. Fans of a particular genre are on the lookout for their type of film and in some cases producers can predict quite accurately who the audience for a particular genre might be by age and gender, for example:

Horror:	young people
Western:	older people
Romance:	women
War:	men
Cartoons:	children

These are, of course, **generalisations** – it is perfectly possible for older people to enjoy horror films or for women to want to see war films. The point is that producers need to get a return on their investment and as long as they have a target audience who are dependable then they will hope to **break even** at least. The producers will often use **market research** to find out exactly which type of audience is watching which type of genre film.

The **real audience** for a film is, of course, much bigger. Films like *Saving Private Ryan* and *ET* (Steven Spielberg, Universal, 1982) had quite a wide audience. In fact, Hollywood producers frequently try to market a film to as wide an audience as possible. Remember, we refer to these films as **mainstream films** for a large **mainstream audience**.

One way of doing this is to mix genres together to create hybrid genres. Take, for example, *Star Wars*: there is evidence that this film contains the following genres:

- Science fiction
- Action adventure
- Comedy
- Historical
- Romance
- Western
- War

This probably explains why the film was so successful: box-office returns for the franchise have reached $3 billion!

The *Star Wars* franchise with the French version of the logo

- *Find the proof from the signifiers, mise-en-scène, storyline and characters that these genres are evident in* Star Wars.
- *Can you think of any other films that are hybrid genres?*
- *Why do you think that certain people like certain genres?*
- *Which genres do you like or dislike and why?*
- *Are some storylines in some films predictable? Do you think there is a formula that some writers write to?*

Genre and stars

Another important aspect of genre is that frequently certain star names become attached in the public's mind to certain genres because a particular actor has been successful in the part. We sometimes hear of actors becoming **type-cast** when they find it difficult to be cast in any other type of role or genre. Examples include: John Wayne in the 1940s and 50s (western); Sean Connery in the 1960s (James Bond); Jean-Claude van Damme in the 1980s (action adventure). These actors have a **star persona** which audiences expect to see.

Connery was for a while seen only as James Bond, but by taking a wide variety of different roles he managed to break free from the public's image of him, especially as he became older. More recently, actors like Jim Carrey surprised audiences after years of crazy slapstick comedy to star in *The Truman Show*; some people were disappointed that they didn't get the Carrey they expected, or indeed the genre.

This can also apply to directors: if you went to see a Hitchcock film (1920s to 1970s) you were likely to get some form of thriller. Spielberg, however, took years to be established as a director of serious, mature work such as *Schindler's List* (Amblin, 1993). People began to expect easy-going action adventures such as *Raiders of the Lost Ark* (Lucasfilm, 1981).

FILM STRUCTURE

One of the most important aspects of media texts we must realise as students is that they are man-made – they are not natural products – they are **constructions**.

The cornerstone of the construction is laid by the writer (possibly and probably in conjunction with the director and / or producer).

The starting point is the **idea** – what is the film about?

This can be a major **theme** or a **character** or a **storyline**. This then develops into a **screenplay** format and / or storyboard format. The writer may even have a brief **pitch** for the film where he can tell an executive the selling points as quickly as possible. For example, the pitch for *Alien* (Ridley Scott, Brandywine, 1979) could be: '*Jaws* on a spaceship.'

The three basic aspects of screenplay and film construction are:

1 What happens? ⇨ **storyline**

2 Who does it happen to? ⇨ **characters**

3 What is it about? ⇨ **themes**

Each of these can be part of the original big idea that began the creation of the text.

A simple way of seeing this is:

Storyline = events or happenings or incidents

Characters = people

Themes = ideas or beliefs or values

Probably the most important aspect of the initial structure of a film is the way the story is told. The word we use to cover all aspects of the storytelling is **narrative**.

Narrative

The narrative of a film is, in simple terms, the story. The story is made up by the people who made the film, e.g. writer, director and the viewer's life experiences.

When we watch a film we make sense of what we see, so we can be said to be mentally active. We bring to the viewing all of the aspects of our lives that make us what we are: our upbringing, our education, our backgrounds, our life experiences, including other film and media texts that we have consumed. The interaction of all these things makes us unique, so it is hardly surprising that when they in turn interact with the film text we watch, we may all have different experiences. This helps to explain why we make different judgements about films.

Film grammar

In the last section we discovered that film has a language of its own. There are other aspects of grammar we could look at too when we ask the question:

What can we do with the camera?

When we pick up a camera to make a film the first thing that occurs to us is: 'What do we do with it?' Film is a medium that uses **space** and **time**. The camera tells us where to **look**.

The possibilities are numerous and the history of film-making shows that directors have continually played with the medium trying constantly to find new ways of making films, from the first short films shown in early cinemas (nickelodeons) through to *Citizen Kane* (Orson Welles, RKO, 1941) and the films of today such as *Titanic* and *Antz* (Eric Darnell / Lawrence Guterman et al, Dreamworks, 1998).

One important aspect of Hollywood historically is that it created a way of making films – of putting them together. A film, as we have seen, is made up of thousands of little bits, and a director has to pay attention to the little details when making each shot, and keep in mind the overall aims of the project. We are now going to look at the details in a practical way by considering the major **techniques** of camera usage.

When we put letters together to create words, and words together to make paragraphs, we call this **grammar**. Just as we do this in writing we also do it in films: we put bits of film together to make scenes, and scenes together to make the whole film. We also call this grammar as it is the way in which we use **film language** to make **meaning** and **sense**.

Let's take an example: if we film someone from above, is this different from filming him or her from below?

Look:

Two shots: from above and below

- *What is the difference in effect of this switch in angle?*

Because the way in which he or she films things has very particular meanings it is important for the director to consider carefully the **choices** that he or she makes.

The first aspect of film grammar is equivalent to a letter in the alphabet: it is the **single shot** of an object, person or action. If we **freeze** it for a moment we may also call it the **frame** so that we can see what the director has placed in the rectangle of the screen. Clearly a shot consists of many frames; in fact, a feature film is usually shot at about 26 frames per second. The shot also can vary in time: some shots are for a split second, others can take minutes, e.g. *Rope* (Alfred Hitchcock, Transatlantic, 1948) is entirely made up of 10-minute shots.

The term shot can also be referred to as a **take**, especially during the filming process itself where each time a shot is filmed the take is given a number, e.g. 'Take 3' or 'Take 97'! This enables the editor more easily to identify each different piece of film.

Let us consider the major options available to most directors.

Distance

How far away is the person from the camera and how does it appear in the frame? Consider the following table:

TERM	DRAWING	COMMENTS
ELS Extreme Long Shot		This shot can be: • a horizon shot • an infinity shot • an establishing shot • a landscape • a small figure in relation to a large building
LS Long Shot		This shot: • shows a whole figure, but closer to the camera • shows them in relation to their surroundings • can also be an establishing shot
MLS Medium Long Shot		This shot: • shows more details of the character • retains the setting quite clearly in the *mise-en-scène* • shows the whole body
MS Medium shot		This shot: • is roughly from knees or waist to just above the head • is sometimes called a 'mid-shot' or 'three-quarter shot' • is similar to MLS
MCU Medium Close Up		This shot: • is from the mid-chest to the top of the head • it shows much more detail of a character • it can contain two people talking
CU Close Up		This shot: • shows head and shoulders • is very detailed • is used to show emotion and feelings / reactions
ECU Extreme Close Up		This shot: • shows small part of a face or object • can also show extreme fear or emotion if tightly on the eyes

Storyboarding – camera shots in relation to distance

Why would we use different shots? Well, the main answer is that it adds great variety to the film, but of course it does much more than this. It gives the director his **first layer of meaning**. By having these different shots available he can suit the shot to the content and have better control of what the audience see and the way in which they see it.

- *Why would a director use a medium shot? A long shot? A close up?*
- *Can you think of examples from films that you have seen?*

Framing

The director also considers where he places the people and objects in the frame: are they to the left or the right or dead centre? Are they at the top or the bottom? Are they near or far away?

Remember that the director is putting together different elements in the frame and shot and is, in a sense, composing what we see. We can therefore also refer to this as **composition**.

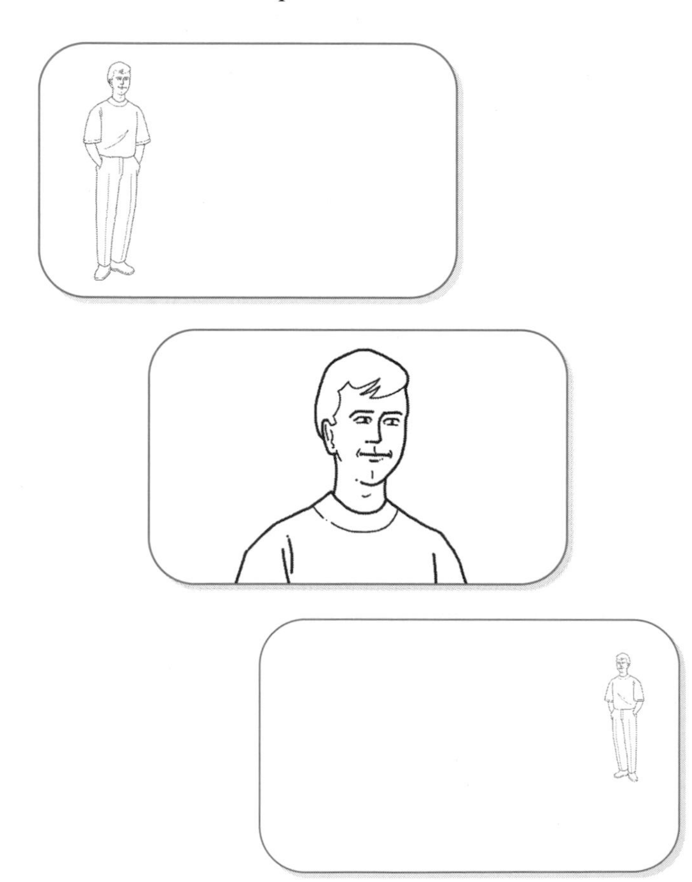

Three different frames

- *Which of these shots makes the character look the weakest? Which the strongest?*
- *Do you know why you might feel this to be true?*

Angle

If we film from above we can make individual characters look weak or, conversely, film them from below and emphasise their size so making them appear stronger. We refer to these positions as **high angle** or **low angle**. You may also come across terms such as **bird's-eye-view** or **worm's-eye-view**. If the high angle shot is filmed from a helicopter or aeroplane it is referred to as an **aerial shot**; these are particularly useful for establishing shots or chase sequences.

Movement – the lens

These shots do not, of course, have to remain the same. We can go from a long shot to a close-up in one move without cutting to another shot by using the lens of the camera. This is called a **zoom** – it can either zoom in or zoom out.

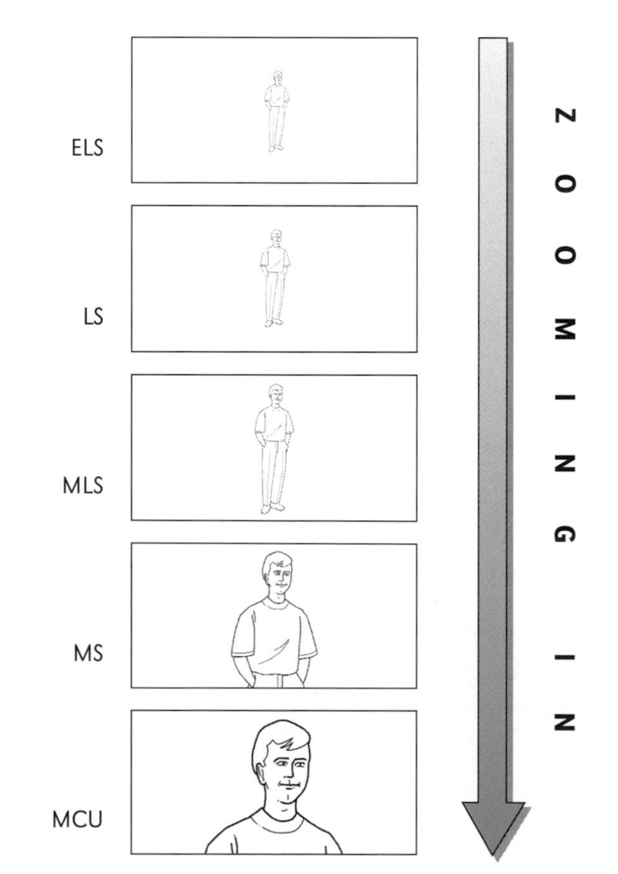

Zoom effect

Movement – the camera

We can move the camera in a number of different ways. Remember that the real world is experienced in **three physical dimensions** and the **fourth one of time**.

The camera is usually on some form of tripod that allows it to **pivot** around on the spot; we can therefore move the camera to the left or the right, just as we use our heads when looking at something. This movement is called a **pan** or **panning**.

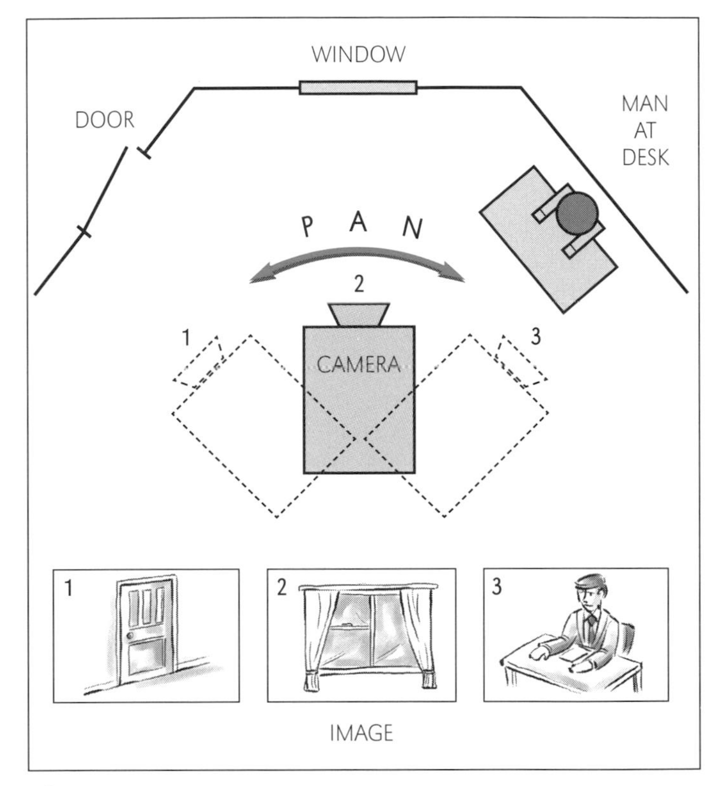

Pan movement

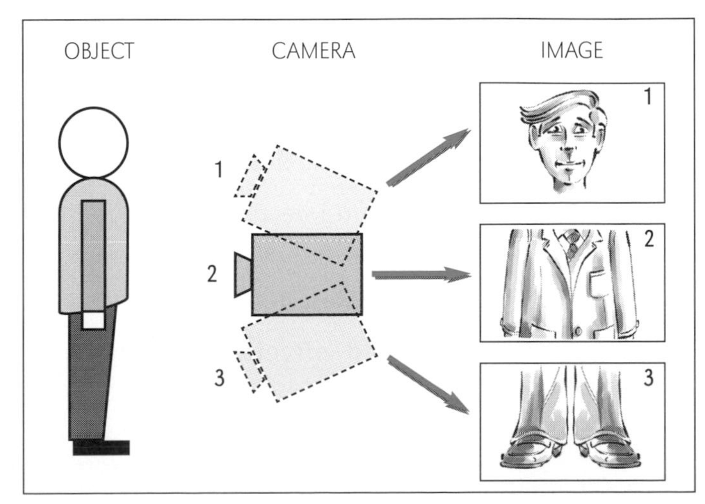

Tilt movement

Similarly, it can be made to look up or down; this is known as a **tilt**. It can be involved in the angle of a shot that we referred to earlier.

We can also place it on tracks that are rolled along the ground so that it can follow someone walking or running. This is called a **tracking shot**. It can also be moved by placing it on a vehicle such as a van or car. A sophisticated variation of this is created by using a special camera called a **steadicam** which can follow the action quickly but still keeps the camera steady so that it can flow over the terrain. This is frequently used in thrillers or horror films.

We can even put it in a helicopter and have an **overhead shot** which follows a person or an object, sometimes called an **aerial shot** or a **bird's-eye-view shot**. Another variation of this is to place it on a crane so that it can start on ground level but can then be lifted up into the air to quite a high point; this is called a **crane shot**. Look at the last shot in *Much Ado About Nothing* (Kenneth Branagh, Renaissance, 1993) to see a particularly clever use of both steadicam and crane in one long shot.

Time

The shot can last a split second or 10 minutes. Shot **duration** is very important as it allows the director to change the **pace** of the action if he or she wants to.

Time can also be played around with in a narrative by suggesting flashbacks, etc.

ACTIVITY 8

- Look at some of the exciting sequences of your favourite films to see how many shots can be fitted into 20 seconds.

Editing

Finally, the director has control over the way in which shots are put together in a sequence to form a **scene**. This process of **cutting** the film and **splicing** it together is known as **editing**.

One aspect of editing is the way the director takes us from one scene to another. He or she can use:

- **Fade**: one scene fades away to black and the next fades in, or possibly cuts in straight away
- **Dissolve**: one scene fades out as another simultaneously fades in
- **Wipe**: one shot is literally wiped off the screen by another.

These devices are used to suggest a **change in place and / or time**. They tend to suggest a greater passing of time than a straight cut would, as most cuts are reserved for the bulk of the edits in a scene.

The way in which the film is put together at the editing stage is one of the most creative aspects of film-making, so much so that many film directors insist on being thoroughly involved in the editing process. Some poorly directed films have been made to look much better as a result of the editing process.

TEXTUAL STUDY

When we study a film we need to look at the text in a number of ways. Our study could involve the following:

- **Description** – what do we see and hear?
- **Interpretation** – how do we make sense of what we see?
- **Analysis** – how can we look closely at its structure and analyse what is going on or how it was made?
- **Critical perspective** – what do other people say or write about this text?

Although all of these are important, at GCSE level you are likely to be asked by your teacher only to describe and interpret, and occasionally to analyse.

We are now going to examine a scene from a major film to see what the director was doing. Films we study like this we refer to as case studies as we analyse them to learn what happens in the construction of a film.

Case study: The Untouchables

We will look at the **mid-act climax** of *The Untouchables* (Brian de Palma, Paramount, 1987): a very famous scene that borrows its set-up from a film called *Battleship Potemkin* (Goskino, 1925), directed by an important figure in the development of film, the Russian Sergei Eisenstein.

The structure of a film does not just depend upon the storyline leading up to one final climax. The end might indeed be dramatic, but if we had to wait two hours for this we might well become bored and uninvolved. To prevent this most stories have climaxes at different parts of the film.

The story so far – the **context**: in Chicago of the 1930s Elliot Ness (Kevin Costner) has been trying without success to get enough evidence together to convict Al Capone (Robert de Niro) of murder and extortion. Two of his men have already been killed, but he has now been given a lead to locate and arrest Capone's book-keeper in the hope that this will secure the crucial evidence against the gangster. Ness, with his one remaining ally Stone (Andy Garcia), arrives at Chicago Grand Central Station to make the arrest, knowing that it will not be an easy job and that blood may be spilt.

De Palma's set piece is fraught with **directorial** problems, but it is a **masterpiece** of technique. Here are some of his concerns:

- How do I create **tension** in this scene?
- How do I give the right amount of **information** to the audience?
- How do I **visually** show the size of the problem facing Ness?
- How do I give the audience **satisfaction**?
- How many **cameras** do I need and what do I do with them?
- How do I create the ***mise-en-scène***?
- How will I use **sound effects** and soundtrack **music** and / or **silence**?
- How can I **close** the scene **dramatically**?

Let us look at some of the details of his answers.

Before the two men enter the station, Stone asks Ness what time train the book-keeper will be catching. The answer is five minutes past midnight. But this **information** is not for the storyline itself, but **for the audience to be informed**. The audience are more likely to feel the tension in the scene if they are aware of the timescale. They are more likely also to have expectations of something dramatic happening if they know that the hero will meet the villains at a specific moment.

When they do enter the station we see in LS (long shot) the whole scene which emphasises a large clock at the top in the centre so that the audience may now see the seconds ticking away to the moment of **confrontation** itself. De Palma can now **use time creatively** in this scene and he will cut back to the clock in CU (close up) at certain moments.

The **establishing shot** (one which establishes where we are) of the station steps themselves dwarfs the two men: they seem insignificant amidst all the stone, concrete and marble as they are placed in the weakest part of the **frame**. Their job is a difficult one: they might not make it. Tension begins. Putting characters in frames which dwarf them or surround them with space is always likely to create a sense of weakness as they look small relative to what is around them.

The director also uses this shot as his **master shot**. This is the shot that shows the whole scene and can be used as a **safety shot** during the editing process. When the director and editor cut the scene in **post-production** they will always have the option of including the master shot if they feel that any of the close-ups are insufficient. (See the section on editing on page 39.)

Stone needs to check out the platform in case the gangsters are already there so he leaves Ness to guard the entrance: our hero is now on his own. The audience is already thinking that this could be a mistake.

At this point de Palma has to decide how to ratchet up the tension a few more notches and comes up with a simple but powerful **device**: he introduces a young woman trying desperately to wheel her baby in a pram up the staircase. As our hero watches her trying to do this he realises that she may be unwittingly placing herself in the midst of a bloodbath. Our hero now faces a major moral **dilemma**: WHAT WILL HE DO? He is, of course, a very moral man, as we have seen throughout the film, so he must act according to his **character** and do the right thing: he will go down the steps to help the woman and baby.

De Palma uses a variety of shots, for example:

- **Long shots** of the whole station
- **Close-ups** of Ness showing the tension in his face
- **Bird's-eye-view shots** as he looks down on the woman and baby
- **Point-of-view shots** so that we can see the situation through Ness's eyes, or **perspective**
- **Pan shots** to the left and right
- Increasing **zoom shots** on the clock

He also plays with **sound**:

- The footsteps of people walking on the marble floors
- The baby crying
- The doors of the station entrance banging
- The music effects of tension – e.g. cello
- The musical chimes of a lullaby

Can you see how de Palma has given himself many **tools** to use in creating the whole scene? There is very little said in this scene: it is a mixture of **pictures** and **sounds** that enables de Palma to create this tension. Some of the sounds are in **the world of the film** (footsteps, announcer, gun shots) and some are not (sound effects, lullaby, soundtrack).

The critical moment approaches: the gangsters arrive. Ness must make a crucial decision: will he shoot first, thereby having the advantage but endangering the baby, or will he let the gangsters go thereby losing his advantage and endangering his partner, Stone?

The **turning point** occurs: Ness uses violence to defeat them as he makes the first move. This is an important point in the film in relation to character: he is acting against his nature but he has learnt from Malone (Sean Connery) that he must fight fire with fire. It is Malone's death that has motivated him to act this way – it is also what the audience wants as we like to see evil being defeated.

At this crucial point de Palma switches to **slow-motion** after five minutes of **real time** have built up to this critical moment. This **technique** has some advantages:

- It gives the audience time to savour the **spectacle** of the shoot-out, which in real time would be over in a few seconds
- It gives de Palma the opportunity to **show off** some spectacular effects
- It **surprises** the audience
- It helps in the editing so that the director can **cheat** a little with space and time

A bloodbath does ensue: the audience's **expectation** is fulfilled, but not necessarily the way they expect it. Just look at the **closure** of the scene: we think the scene is more or less over when the **dramatic tension** is increased with the **stand-off** between Ness and the gangster holding the book-keeper. We can, of course, remember that Stone was a crack shot at the academy and it is inevitable that the villain will lose this particular encounter. A very satisfying and **dramatic finale** for a mid-act climax. **Quick cut** into the middle of the next scene to **advance the narrative** quickly.

ACTIVITY 9

- Try to analyse a scene from a film for yourself. Opening scenes are ideal as there is usually quite a lot to be established by the director. Look at the opening of *Batman* (Tim Burton, Warner Bros, 1989), including the **title sequence**. How does the director establish:
  - the hero
  - the world of the film
  - tension
  - enigmas (questions that the audience ask)
  - the film's genre

  Remember to look at how the director:
  - uses the camera
  - uses the *mise-en-scène*
  - tells the story
  - sets us up for what happened next

MEDIA MESSAGES AND VALUES

FILM AS IDEAS

Earlier in this chapter we referred to films having themes. These are the ideas that are present in the film and answer the question: what is the film *really* about?

The main reason artists create their art is because **they have something to say**. Film is an art form that can be seen by the audience as primarily an entertainment, but this does not mean that it is without other qualities. Many writers and directors are using film to say something about the world we live in or the nature of being human. These themes could be conveyed in a novel or a play or a poem, but some artists find the medium of film to be the right one to use. Film is **powerful**, it can reach a **very large audience** and it can **last a long time** in the **popular imagination**.

Ken Loach, in a film called *Kes* (Woodfall, 1969), created such a film. Although it may seem dated now, especially to a young audience used to widescreen colour film and very lively Hollywood blockbusters, it still says something today about society and individuals. The character of Billy Caspar still exists.

A modern example to look at is *Billy Elliot*. Can you see how this film can have these same qualities?

- *Think about some recent films that you have admired. What are the major themes in these films? Do you think they say something about society today?*

Billy Elliot: a modern *Kes* – but are the ideals the same?

FILM AND REPRESENTATION

When we watch a film it will present to us a story, people and ideas. The way in which a film deals with its content is very important as it seems to portray the real world and can consequently **reinforce**, **contradict** or **change** views or attitudes, which we may or may not already hold. So we must always realise that films do not present the real world exactly as it exists but one which is constructed by a creative group of people who have **their own views and attitudes** towards the world in which we live.

So when we talk about the way film portrays groups of people, for example, we can talk about how it re-presents them, and this leads us to the concept of **representation**.

Consider the following simple model of **mass communication**:

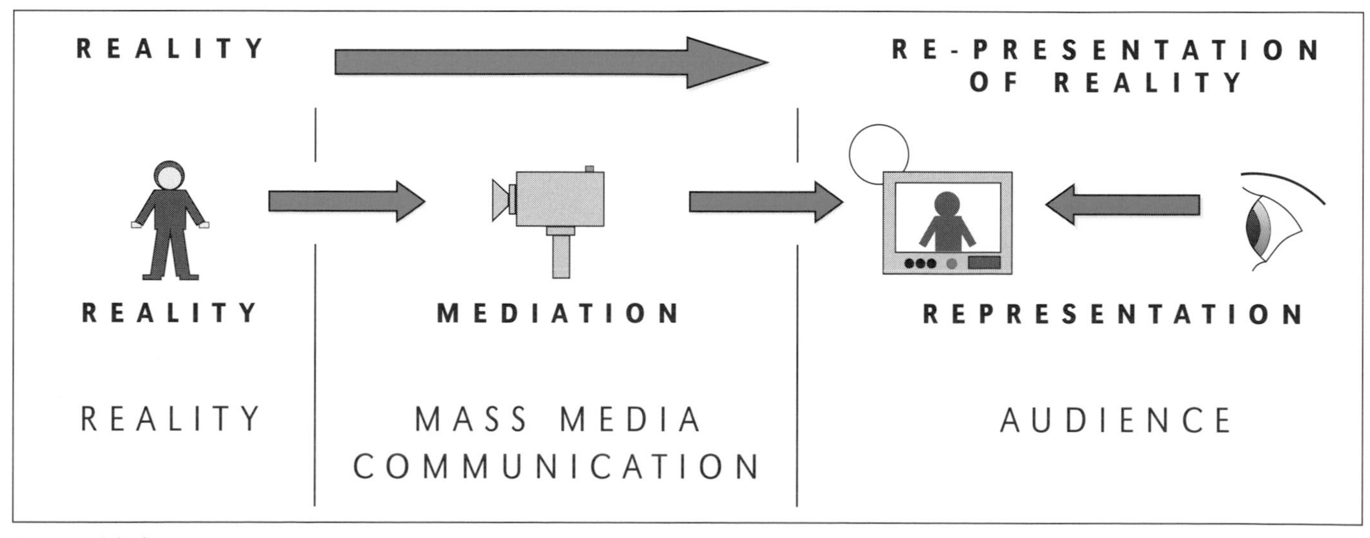

Basic model of representation

Because the writers, directors and producers want to say something about the world, their films are usually **encoded** with ideas and attitudes. We have sometimes to think very carefully about what those ideas may be or why they are important. We have, in turn, to **decode** these **messages** and **values**.

A film such as *Saving Private Ryan* may show the horrors of war and may make people understand what it was like to be going through such a terrible episode in world history. But this is not all that the film might be saying: as a representation of America it could be interpreted as a statement about the superiority of the American nation or an even blunter statement that they won the war. Some British or European viewers may disagree with this view of a true historical incident, even though some British films may have given an equally **biased** representation of British soldiers during the war.

The four major representations

The four major representations are:

1 Gender

2 Age

3 Race

4 Social class

Through these four major ways of looking at a media text we can begin to understand what is really going on. To show you how we do this we are going to look at one specific area: **gender**. This refers to the sexual categories of male and female, and the sexual orientations of heterosexual and homosexual.

Representation and masculinity

CASE STUDY: James Bond 007

We are going to look at **masculinity** and the movies and at the **subgenre** of the James Bond films. How does the hero portray what it is like to be that particular kind of man?

Look at any of these films, from *Dr No* (Terence Young, Eon, 1962) to *The World is Not Enough* and see what we can identify about the construction of the hero, James Bond.

This hero possesses a number of qualities:

- he is physically very fit
- he is highly intelligent
- he is resourceful
- he is good-looking
- he is sexually active
- he is attractive to women
- he is admired by other men
- he is a connoisseur of taste
- he is brave
- he is loyal to his country

So, what questions do we ask to begin to analyse this representation?

- Are all of these qualities unquestionably **positive**?
- To what degree is this portrayal a **stereotype**?
- To what degree is he merely a **fantasy** or a piece of male or female **wish-fulfilment**?
- Is there anything serious in the **messages** he sends out?
- Is he in any way a **role model** for young boys / men?
- Is any of this important?

- *Compare him with other* ***super-heroes****. How do they compare?*
- *What similarities might you see?*
- *What conclusions can you come to about masculinity in this type of film?*
- *Compare the films of Arnold Schwarzenegger and Leonardo di Caprio. What kinds of men do they portray? How do they represent masculinity?*
- *Look at the way girls or women are represented in films. Are there any significant differences? Can you think of reasons for your observations?*
- *Can you think of any films in which women act heroically? How are they portrayed?*

SUMMARY

- Film was the new art form of the twentieth century – it is conditioned by technology and the imagination of those who make and consume films.
- Film is a construct that is carefully put together by very creative and artistic people.
- Film is a multi-billion-dollar industry.
- Film is a product to be sold and marketed just like any other.
- Film is a medium with a message – it has something to say and it represents our world.
- Film has a structure, a language and a grammar.

GLOSSARY

camera obscura principle – when light enters a dark chamber through a small hole it projects a picture of the outside, inverted and upside down, on to the surface opposite the hole

dailies / rushes – footage shot each day

editing – cutting and splicing pieces of film to create the finished product

footage – filmed scenes

genres – types of film e.g. horror movies, Westerns

mainstream audience – audience composed of large numbers of different types of people

mise-en-scène – setting, props, costumes, landscape we see on screen

movie mogul – owner or manager of a film studio

niche audience – small audience with a special interest or enthusiasm for a particular minority genre

pitch – original idea for a film script

print – finished product

product placement – when a particular product is showcased in a film as a means of advertising

signifier – what we see or hear in a film, allowing us to recognise its genre and interpret its meaning

soundtrack – musical score for a film

steadicam – camera that is strapped to the body; a sophisticated series of gyroscopes allows the camera to remain steady on the horizontal even if the operator runs with it

take – piece of film encompassing a single shot

trailer – sequence of shots to advertise a film's imminent release and whet the appetite of the prospective audience

type-casting – actors become closely identified with a certain type of role and play similar parts again and again

unique selling point – the aspect of a film that sets it apart from its competitors

vertical integration – when one company owns / controls all the stages of production including the means of distribution (e.g. cinemas) for its own product (e.g. films)

(See pages 36–40 for technical terms relating to camerawork.)

2 Television

VIVIENNE CLARK

Coming up

In this chapter we will be looking at:

- the role of television in our lives
- the history of television
- how programmes and channels are paid for and regulated
- ways of studying television
- how and why programmes are divided into genres

INTRODUCTION

PART OF THE FURNITURE?

This chapter will explore a familiar piece of furniture in our homes. Often decorated with family photos, a china ornament or the family cat, the television set has become a piece of furniture like a sideboard or a set of shelves. We hardly notice it is there, but we look at it many times a day. It is no longer classified as a luxury item, but as a necessity for modern living.

In the 1950s, early television cabinets were made of wood and were polished and cherished like a treasured heirloom. They were expensive and out of reach of most people, as early sets cost as much as a family car.

For hundreds of years, living accommodation was designed so that people could sit around an open fire to cook, keep warm and talk. But what did they actually do and what did they look at before television?

As television became widely available, this new piece of furniture took people away from cinemas. Before the invention of television, people went to their local cinema several times a week for newsreels and films. Most towns of reasonable size had a cinema. But as television spread, they preferred instead to stay in the comfort and convenience of their own homes.

ACTIVITY 1

- Do some research, either using books or by talking to family members over 60 years old, to find out how people spent their time before television arrived in the home.

Television has been called the new 'hearth of the home', around which busy families talk, eat and share opinions. Ordinary television sets are relatively cheap, with a wide range of sizes available. Indeed, today, many homes have more than one television set with additional sets in the kitchen and bedrooms.

In the 1980s, with the availability of videocassette recorders for us to play videotapes of films, the concept of **home cinema** was born. This home entertainment concept was updated in the 1990s and into the 2000s with larger screens, high-definition and widescreen television sets with digital Nicam stereo sound to rival the cinema experience.

Widescreen televisions with digital stereo sound, perfect picture quality and larger screens mean that we can now watch our favourite films and programmes in the comfort of our own homes – like our own mini cinema. Or in the words of a fashionable phrase: 'Staying in is the new going out'!

But when the very first widescreen digital television sets and plasma flat screen TVs came out in the late 1990s, they were, once again, the price of a family car and were out of reach of most people. However, as always, technology becomes more affordable as new advances are made. Before too long, most people will have a flat screen digital television in their homes.

SWITCHED ON

Think about your home and where and when you and your family watch television:

- *How many television sets do you have at home? Where are they?*
- *Where and how do you like to sit when you watch television?*
- *What do you like to do when you watch television?*
- *Who watches with you?*
- *Who decides what you watch?*

TV ADDICTS?

When television became a popular pastime in America in the 1950s, some people warned of its strange and terrible powers, believing that it would rot our brains and turn us into zombies!

It was called the 'goggle box', the 'boob tube' ('boob' being an American slang word for idiot) and the 'plug-in drug'. Warnings were also issued to people about the dangers of sitting too close to the set and getting their eyes and brain 'fried' by the radiation rays produced by the television tube.

Today, some people are also concerned that we are breeding a race of 'couch potatoes' and that the increase in teenage obesity in the USA and Europe is due to the amount of time young people spend inactive in front of the television, rather than out pursuing sport and exercise. In the title of a book by Neil Postman, an American writer on culture and media, are we in fact *Amusing Ourselves to Death*?

This kind of language suggests that television has a hypnotic, narcotic and sedative effect on viewers, that some people cannot do without television and are dependent on it, in the same way that a person may become dependent on drugs.

- *Do you agree with this view?*

In the 1999 Channel 4 television series, *The 1900 House*, where a family had to live as they would have done in 1900, the main aspect of their contemporary lives missed by the children was the television.

- *Could you do without your television set? What would you do instead?*

At regular intervals, commentators have suggested that television will make us more violent, less capable of reading and writing accurately and will reduce family communication. However, the research evidence for this is inconclusive. Study of television was made a compulsory element of Britain's National Curriculum for English from 2001.

Furthermore, books about television and film and novelisations (the book of the film / television programme) are amongst the most popular titles in the booksellers' best seller charts. Every time a classic drama serial is aired, the sales of the original book, and tie-in books, increase, suggesting that television may in fact stimulate book sales.

Two recent popular TV adaptions of classic novels

A WINDOW ON THE WORLD?

Polish writer Stanislav Lec said:

> "The window to the world can be covered by a newspaper."

(*Unkempt Thoughts*, 1959)

An early commentator adapted this and called *television* a '**window on the world**'. The phrase caught on and there was even a British television documentary series of the same name in the 1960s. The glass television tube is still thought of as a window through which we can see how people live in parts of the world that we can only dream of visiting or have never even heard of.

However, the transparency of the glass television screen has led us falsely to believe that what we see is **unmediated**, i.e. a direct recording and reflection of how life is. Media Studies contradicts this old belief and is concerned with **deconstructing** (analysing the components of) the images and ideas we are shown.

Television has always shown us how other people live, here and in other countries, all in the safety and comfort of our own homes. Our curiosity about real animals, real places and real people means that wild-life **documentaries**, travel programmes and **docu-soaps** (a combination, or **hybrid**, of a documentary and a soap opera, such as *Airport* or *Paddington Green*) regularly attract high **ratings** (figures measuring how many people watch programmes).

The success of Channel 4's *Big Brother* in the summers of 2000 and 2001 showed just how fascinated we are by reality programmes, or '**real TV**' as it has been dubbed, watching how ordinary people live together, 24 hours a day. An American film, *The Truman Show* (Peter Weir, 1998), anticipated this fascination with the story of Truman Burbank, played by Jim Carrey, who was filmed and watched by millions from the day he was born, under the controlling gaze of the television director, Christof (Ed Harris).

The poet T. S. Eliot also anticipated 'real TV' with his comment:

> "Today nobody's home is his castle - it's a potential TV studio."

Our memories contain images and sounds of famous events, advertising jingles and favourite television moments. Television nostalgia is big business, with many of the cable and satellite channels devoted to television from the past. **Re-runs** (or repeats) of old programmes cost nothing to make and exist in television companies' archives to be re-sold to other television channels and on video. Television archives have become valuable business assets, as demand has increased for ready-made programmes to fill the rising amount of airtime.

In September 2000 the British Film Institute published its Top 100 British Television Programmes (from 1955–2000), after having surveyed 1600 programme-makers, critics and executives. The results showed that 72 of the 100 programmes were made by the BBC. The highest ranked recent programme was *Who wants to be a Millionaire?* (ITV) at number 23.

- *What classic TV moments would you choose for your top 10?*
- *What would your class or family's top 20 TV programmes (British and American) be?*

Famous TV moments – Queen Elizabeth II's coronation in 1953 and a clip from the 1970s sitcom *Fawlty Towers*

OUR FAVOURITE WASTE OF TIME?

Some television audience facts:

- A 1990s *Radio Times* street survey found that 15% of the people questioned would not give up their television sets for a million pounds.
- The 1997 edition of *Popular Cultural Trends* found that in 1995 the British watched television on average for 25.2 hours per week (with women watching three hours more than men!).
- A 1994 BARB (Broadcasters' Audience Research Bureau) survey showed that the age group that watches the most television per week is the over 55s, with an average of 33.6 hours per week, compared to 4–15- and 16–24-year-olds who watch 18.5 and 19.6 hours per week respectively.
- 'Watching television' was the reply that most people in the UK gave when asked in a recent leisure survey what their favourite hobby was.
- However, another survey (*Henley Centre 'Media Futures'*) reported that three fifths of its interviewees said they 'would rather be out *doing* something, than watching TV'.

This last statistic suggests that we know we are wasting time, but perhaps we cannot be bothered to do anything else. Or, in a busy post-industrial, high-speed, technological life, perhaps we *need* to waste a little time and relax in front of the 'telly' to survive?

Many people now come home from work or school, sit in front of the television with the remote control and a cup of tea and just 'zap' aimlessly, to unwind from another hectic day by consuming 'eye candy'. Or, as Fred Allen, an American wit, put it in the 1970s:

> " Television is chewing gum for the eyes. "

In 1972 a group of sociologists defined four major categories of need which the media serve to gratify. This is now referred to as the **uses and gratifications** theory. It might be useful to think about it here, to consider *why* we watch television and *what* we get from it.

Audience uses and gratifications

These four needs were:

1. **Diversion** – an escape from the routines of daily life, from the burden of our problems, as an emotional release, as relaxation, fantasy
2. **Personal relationships** – to help companionship and social interaction with others, discussion of shared experiences and interests
3. **Personal identity** – to explore new experiences and points of view, to reinforce our personal ideas, values and beliefs about life
4. **Surveillance** – to supply the need for information in our complex world, to keep up to date with events

SEE FOR YOURSELF – AUDIENCE RESEARCH

- *Can you think of any other reasons you have for watching television?*

ACTIVITY 2

- Keep a television journal for one week, recording when and what you watch and for how long, and, more importantly, what you think about what you watch.
- Create a questionnaire that collects data from your friends, relatives, teachers and other year groups about what they watch, to display or use in the section on television audiences. Collate the data to draw conclusions
- Why not start a web site to collect data from an even wider field of television viewers?

So what is television for its audience?

- *Just part of the furniture?*
- *A dangerous drug?*
- *Our window on the world?*
- *Our favourite leisure activity?*

Suppliers of home entertainment want their customers to stay at home

THE HISTORY OF TELEVISION

Television, as an invention, has been around for many centuries. As early as 1666, Sir Isaac Newton (who formulated the theory of gravity) experimented with light and a glass prism, anticipating the processes that produced the cathode ray tube, an essential stage in the scientific development of television. But the history of its development as a mass medium of communication is fairly recent and rapid, occurring only within the last 60 years.

If we understand *how* television has developed historically, it will be easier for us to understand *why* we have the kinds of television we have today. From the information below, you can see how television has developed from a one-channel system to a multi-channel one. Following are some key moments in the history of television. Notice how long ago many programmes and **genres** (a type or category of programme, such as soap opera, sit-com, documentary, chat show), which are still popular today, started.

KEY DATES

1922 In Britain, the British Broadcasting Company (later Corporation) broadcasts its first radio programmes

1924 John Logie Baird's patent for a 30 line television transmission system is accepted in Britain

1925 Charles Jenkins demonstrates a similar system in the USA. Other experiments are conducted in Japan, Hungary and Russia and an international race begins

1928 The first transatlantic television transmission is made by Baird. The BBC is granted its Royal Charter to make it a public service

1929 Baird transmits with the BBC to an audience of 29 television sets in London

1935-36 Regular transmissions of a 180 line system are made in Germany including the Berlin Olympic Games

1936 The world's first regular high-definition television news service starts from the BBC. Competing companies, Baird (with a 240 line system) and Marconi-EMI (405 line system), broadcast alternately from Alexandra Palace, in North London. Marconi-EMI wins and becomes the company which supplies the service

1937 The coronation procession of King George VI is broadcast to 2000 television sets in Britain

1939 Because of the fear that the lights from the BBC at Alexandra Palace would attract enemy planes seeking to bomb London, all UK transmissions cease due to the Second World War, but 20,000 sets are in use in London. Regular transmissions start in Germany and the USA

1940 Twenty-three television stations are in existence in the USA

1946 BBC resumes its television service after the war

1951 There are now one million television sets in Britain. *What's My Line?* is Britain's first game show

1953 56 per cent of Britain's population watch the coronation of Queen Elizabeth II. Twenty million people watch it on only 2.5 million television sets. People cram into public places, or save up to buy a television for their street, to get a glimpse of the new Queen on this new invention

1954 The Independent Television Authority (ITA) is set up to oversee the introduction of a new commercial television network (ITV) to run alongside the BBC

1955 Independent Television (ITV) starts in London and the South East. Independent Television News (ITN) is formed by the ITV companies. The first ever British television advert to be broadcast is for Gibbs SR toothpaste. *The Groves* is Britain's first television soap opera. *Emergency Ward 10* is ITV's first soap opera. Over five million television sets are now in use in Britain

1956 More than 500 stations are in existence in the USA. In Britain, ITV becomes available in the Midlands and the North

1958 Twenty-six countries now have broadcast systems. In Britain 80 per cent of the population can receive both BBC and ITV. *Blue Peter* begins on BBC1

1960 There are now 10 million sets in Britain. The average viewer watches television for almost two hours per day. Granada Television's *Coronation Street* starts on ITV and goes on to become Britain's longest running television soap opera

1961 Britain's first satellite is launched into space. Morecambe & Wise's comedy show begins on ITV

1962 ITV becomes available to the whole of Britain

1964 BBC2 goes on air (625 lines). *Top of the Pops* starts on BBC1

1965 BBC begins trials with Philips colour television cameras

1966 The first world-wide televised event is broadcast jointly by BBC and ITV: the World Cup final from Wembley, London, goes out to an estimated international audience of 400 million. The popular US import *Batman* begins on ITV

1967 In Britain, BBC2 begins Europe's first colour television service to a small number of colour television sets

1969 The landing of the US astronauts on the moon is watched live by an enormous international audience. BBC1 and ITV provide 625 line colour services in Britain. Despite their high cost, there are 100,000 colour sets in use. Three years after its debut in the USA, the science-fiction series *Star Trek* begins on the BBC

1972 In Britain, 1.6 million colour sets are in use. The first domestic video recorder by Philips is made available in Britain. During the 1970s, Sony develops the VHS video system and JVC develops the Betamax video system. Sony's VHS system wins and Betamax becomes obsolete for domestic use. In Britain, the ITA, which looks after the running of ITV, becomes the Independent Broadcasting Authority (IBA). The soap opera *Emmerdale Farm* starts on ITV

1973 Over three million colour sets are in use in Britain

1975 The sit-com *Fawlty Towers* starts on BBC and police drama *The Sweeney* on ITV

1981 2 per cent of British homes have video recorders. The sit-com *Only Fools and Horses* starts on BBC

1982 Channel 4 and its Welsh counterpart S4C start. *French & Saunders* comedy series starts on BBC. The soap opera *Brookside* begins on Channel 4

1983 Breakfast television starts on BBC1, followed by ITV two weeks later

1984 Sky Channel is launched on satellite and by cable

1985 *EastEnders* starts on BBC1 and goes on to become *Coronation Street's* main rival in the soap audience ratings

1986 The BBC offers the first daytime television service, followed by ITV in 1987

1988 The Australian soap opera *Neighbours* begins on BBC1

1989 97 per cent of all homes in Britain have television sets. 56 per cent of British homes have video recorders. 56 per cent of all British homes have more than one television set

1990 A new Act of Parliament governing broadcasting, the Broadcasting Act 1990, is passed. *The Simpsons* begins on Sky TV

1991 The IBA becomes the Independent Television Commission (ITC). The USA's CNN (Cable News Network) becomes the leading international news source due to its coverage of the Gulf War and has a significant influence on all news broadcasts from now on

1993 The new ITV licensees begin their 10-year licences on January 1

1996 The BBC's Royal Charter is renewed. Channel 5 starts broadcasting

1997 A new Broadcasting Act is passed

1998 Sky Digital and On Digital services are launched

ITV reschedules its flagship news programme, *News at Ten*, to widespread criticism. Following an ultimatum from the ITC, this decision is overturned in 2000

The quiz show offering the highest prize money in the world, *Who Wants to be a Millionaire?*, starts on ITV, presented by Chris Tarrant

Source: Dick Fiddy, *Television: An Introductory Guide to its History*, MOMI Education / BFI

2000 DVD players become more affordable and are set to replace VCRs and VHS tapes

Big Brother, transmitted on Channel 4's web site and in daily TV bulletins, represents a departure in so-called reality TV – a documentary crossed with a game show – and gives Channel 4 record ratings in the usually quiet summer period

The British Film Institute releases its list of the 100 best all-time television programmes, which is topped by *Fawlty Towers* (first shown on BBC in 1975) at No. 1, *Cathy Come Home* (BBC, 1966) at No. 2 and *Doctor Who* (BBC, 1963–89) at No. 3

The new Director-General of the BBC, Greg Dyke, announces his vision for the BBC – an array of five television and five new radio channels

On Digital and Sky Digital start an Internet service, with a keyboard that connects to the television set, for access to the World Wide Web and e-mails via the television

The BBC moves its *Nine O'Clock News* programme to 10 pm

TiVo, the personal video recorder, becomes available in the UK. By personal programming, viewers would be able automatically to record and store favourite programmes and cut out what they did not want to watch – adverts, for example

2002 The ITV companies' licences come to an end in December; eight companies renewed their licences early in 1999. New licences start from January 1, 2003

2006 The BBC's 10-year Royal Charter due for renewal

TELEVISION PRODUCERS

POWERFUL VISIONS

Even in five years' time we will be astonished at the shape of television; perhaps no television set any more, but a flat screen on your wall the thickness of a thin sheet of plastic, linked to your PC. Your PC could be programmed with your personal preferences, which will in turn select what you like and filter out what you don't like, such as adverts or programmes you don't want to watch. TiVo's arrival (a personal video recorder) in 2000 was the first of many such personalised services. Truly 'Me TV'. We can already order goods and pay bills through interactive television services.

Rupert Murdoch's daughter, Elisabeth, when still working for BSkyB, offered her interpretation of the future of television at the Edinburgh Television Festival in 1998:

> "TV will continue to be the dominant medium for 'lean-back' leisure rather than 'lean-forward' interaction. Both pieces of technology will happily sit together in the home of the future, fulfilling different needs for their owners."

POWER GAMES

The power and popularity of television today cannot be denied. But television is far more than just entertainment. If Media Studies is the study of the power of money and the power of ideas, television combines both. Television has made people's careers and fortunes, either as stars or as shareholders of successful companies.

Television (and newspapers) made Rupert Murdoch, owner of News Corporation and BSkyB, the sixth most powerful person in Britain (*The Power 300 List: The Observer*, 24 October 1999). The broadcaster and writer, Melvyn, Lord Bragg, became a multi-millionaire when his shares in LWT boomed after the 1991 ITV licence contest.

With one brief close-up, endlessly replayed, television made soccer star David Beckham the most hated man in British sport for a year or two after the 1998 World Cup (he was ranked the 68th most powerful person in Britain in 1999). It may have helped to make Tony Blair Prime Minister in May 1997 and June 2001 and the most powerful man in Britain. Incidentally, his Media Secretary, Alastair Campbell, was identified in 1999 as the fifth most powerful man in Britain, not through elected status or financial standing, but because of his manipulation of and liaison with the media.

Top players in the power game – Tony Blair (top), Rupert Murdoch (bottom)

If the media and political power go together we also need to consider power in terms of economics and global communications technology. Bill Gates, the Chairman of Microsoft, was identified in 1999 as the second most powerful person in Britain. **'New media'** (multi-media, personal computers and the Internet) **barons** (a ruler, a person who is powerful in industry) have replaced many of the television, press and film barons in the annual *Power 300* list. It is only a question of time before the screen industries and cultures of film, television and information and communications technology all become one.

The process of the coming together of more than one media form is called **convergence**. In other words, the capabilities of digital technology mean that all media can be communicated and accessed by the same means; we can now use laptops for editing our own videos or watching DVDs and surf the net using our WAP phones.

NOKIA
9110i
Communicator
"I can take care of business while waiting for a flight, with the Nokia 9110i Communicator. I check my email, write a note in the calendar, answer a few calls, access mobile Internet
"Email at the airport."
services using the WAP browser. I can also access the Internet with the WWW browser. During the flight, with the phone turned off, if the airline allows, I write replies which are sent automatically when I turn the phone back on. It's fast with the large display and key-board. With the new Nokia 9110i Communicator I connect on the move."
WAP
NOKIA
CONNECTING PEOPLE

Surf and go: portable communication

So might the term **Screen Studies** come to replace Media Studies in the future, when we receive most of our information and entertainment via a screen?

Many people believe that government elections, in Britain and overseas, are won or lost through the medium of television, the power of the photo opportunity and the **'sound-bite'** (a brief but memorable phrase easily included in a television or radio bulletin). Also, in times of war or invasion, the opposing side always tries to take over television and radio stations in order to control the flow of information, to steal an advantage over its enemy. Senator Hiram Johnson could not have anticipated how appropriate his words were in 1917 during World War I:

> "The first casualty when war comes is always the truth."

In the case of modern warfare, if you control the medium, you control the message; television, radio and the press are powerful tools of propaganda and morale. This is a paraphrase of a famous quote by Marshall McLuhan, a communications professor in the USA, on the power of television. He went further, to declare that:

> "The medium is the message."

(*Understanding Media: The Extensions of Man*, Marshall McLuhan, 1964)

This quote suggests that television itself is the most powerful commodity – regardless of what is on the television, we are still watching it.

So what is television?

- A magic tool for making people famous, notorious, or even Prime Minister?
- A major source of business and personal wealth?
- A way of shaping our views of the world around us?

THE DIGITAL FUTURE FOR TELEVISION

Radio and television broadcasters have so far used an **analogue** transmission system that converts sound and pictures into **radio waves**, which are conveyed to our rooftop aerials from **terrestrial** (or land-based) transmitters, or by satellite via dishes or via cable.

Digital television and radio converts sound and pictures into **digits** (noughts and ones). In order to decode the digital signals you need a **set-top box decoder** or a television set with an in-built decoder.

Digital television and radio are much more efficient methods of transmission as a digital system can squeeze many more television or radio channels into the space currently used to carry a single analogue channel. Not only is it more efficient, but the system is more robust, improving picture and sound quality and reducing interference.

This creates opportunities for many more television and radio channels than at present. Before too long, the old analogue terrestrial transmitters will be switched off and all television and radio will be digital. Initially, Britain was slow to take up the new digital services, but the high-profile campaigns advertising free set-top boxes by On Digital and BSkyB boosted the numbers of people currently using digital **platforms** (outlets used by television companies for showing their programmes and services).

Digital television also has the potential to offer other services to the viewer, such as high-definition or widescreen pictures, CD-quality sound, 'video on demand', and interactive home services, such as home banking, shopping by connection to the Internet. Soon, digital radio sets will give the added feature of screens for us to see details of what we are hearing.

Digital television

MEDIA PRODUCERS AND AUDIENCES

TELEVISION PRODUCERS

We think very little indeed about how the programmes we watch are made, by whom or how much money changes hands in the television business. But this look behind the channel and company logos that start and finish every programme will help us to understand the part that our favourite programme plays in the broader picture of television economics and politics.

In *Tomorrow Never Dies* (1997, UIP/MGM), Commander James Bond (Pierce Brosnan) faced a new kind of villain, a power-crazed media tycoon, Elliot Carver (Jonathan Pryce); so perhaps we ought to keep a closer eye on the media barons of this world!

Like all media industries, the television industry changes on a daily basis. For the most up-to-date information on the financial, audience and structural details of each television company, it is best to consult their web sites where you will get the opportunity to look at their annual reports, including financial statements. The following is a summary of the main television companies currently operating in Britain.

BBC

Popular BBC sitcom *Men Behaving Badly*

The BBC developed from its origins in 1922 as an information service on radio for the military services into the main provider of television for Britain, a position it has been struggling to maintain in recent years. In 1999, the BBC's share of the total television audience was 40.2 per cent (BARB).

TELEVISION AUDIENCE SHARE IN 1999	
BBC (1 & 2)	40.2%
ITV	32.9%
CHANNEL 4	9.9%
CHANNEL 5	4.6%
CABLE/SATELLITE	12.4%

(*Source*: ITC)

This current position is rather different from its early days as the sole provider of television. The BBC was intended to be a national utility, or **service**, for information and entertainment, like the Royal Mail, gas, electricity, water and transport, which were all originally national public services and not required to be run for profit. This is where the term **public service broadcasting** came from.

The first Director-General of the BBC was Lord Reith. He believed that the BBC should '**Educate, inform and entertain**'. This phrase has been used as a mission statement for the Corporation during its history. It has been recently modified to '**Entertain, educate, inform, innovate and enrich**' in order to reflect the Corporation's vision for the twenty-first century.

The BBC has always been funded by the licence fee. It does not have shareholders to deliver profits to, as the commercial companies do. The payers of the licence fee are really the shareholders as all revenue generated is used to develop the BBC's service to the public. However, it has other ways besides the licence fee of generating income; by selling programmes abroad, on video and DVD, to digital and satellite services, by film production and sales from several subsidiary companies, such as BBC Worldwide and UK TV. The BBC also has its own film production arm, BBC Films.

With this income it had, until 2001, provided the following terrestrial services accessible to all: national services on BBC 1, BBC 2, Radios 1, 2, 3, 4 and 5, BBC World Service radio, as well as 12 regional television services, each with its own regional news programme, and BBC Local Radio.

Since the 1990s, the BBC's sole right to the licence fee has been contested on two fronts; on the one hand, by viewers, who claim they have never watched the BBC since they bought satellite or cable; on the other, by some commercial television executives. This is why the BBC's battle to retain a major share of the total television audience is so crucial.

The other battle the BBC has had to face in changing times has been the desire of audiences to have a wider choice of programmes to watch. With only two terrestrial channels (BBC 1 and 2), compared to the hundreds of channels now available on satellite, cable and digital, the BBC experimented during the late 1990s with new services to answer the competition. In 1998 it introduced BBC News 24, a seven-day, 24-hour news service, and various new channels on cable/satellite and digital.

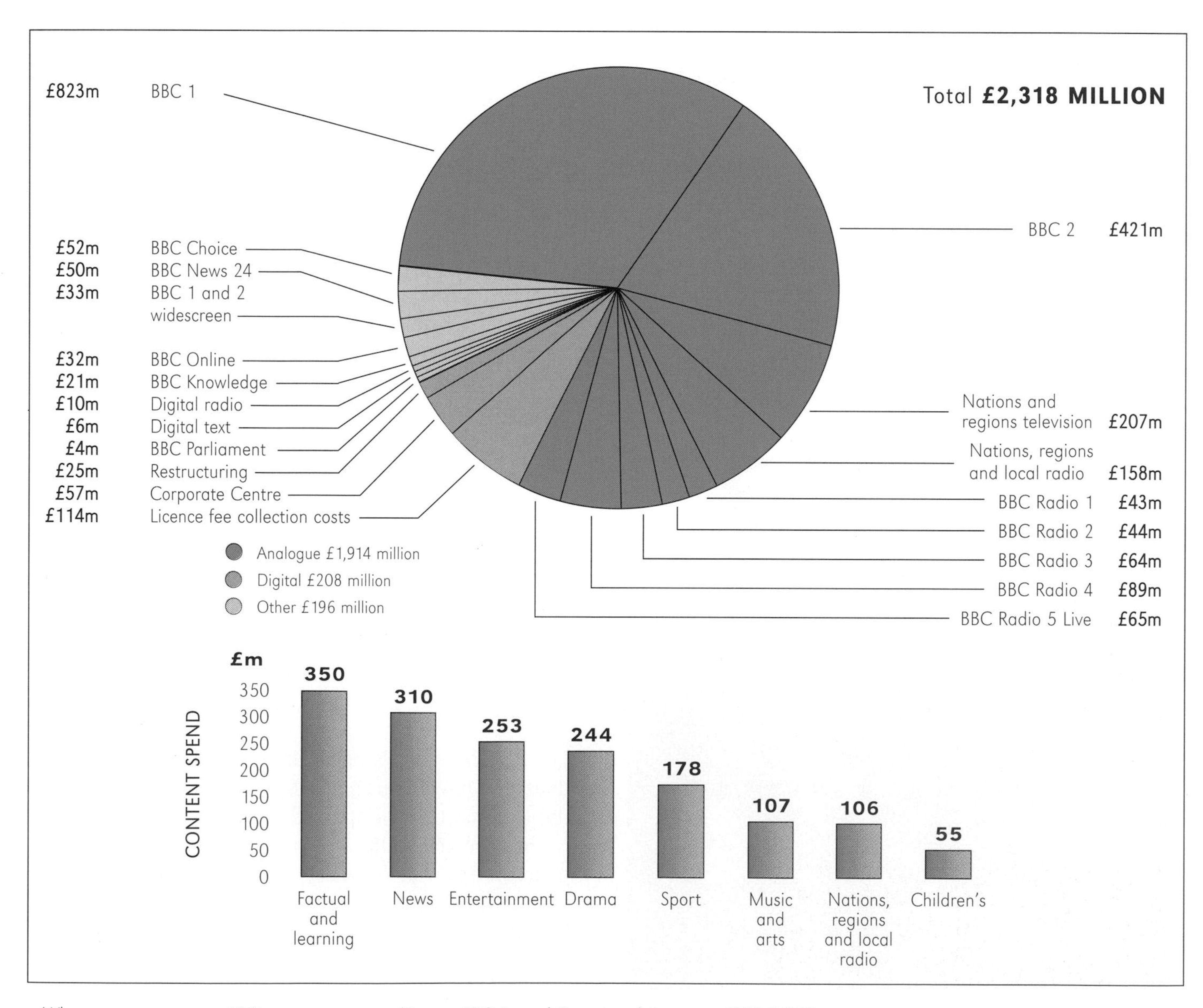

Where our money goes: BBC programme costs (*Source*: BBC Annual Report and Accounts 1999–2000)

The most radical vision for the BBC, unveiled by Director-General Greg Dyke, was proposed in August 2000. From 2001, the BBC would be providing five terrestrial channels (BBC 1, BBC 2, BBC 3, BBC 4 and BBC News 24) and had plans for five new radio channels.

To survive in the **multi-channel** environment of the twenty-first century, the BBC will have to balance two main objectives:

- 'universality' – making its programmes available to the widest possible audiences, especially if it wishes to retain the licence fee, by delivering mixed programme genres to mass audiences
- to deliver what has been termed **genre** or **niche** television, due to the increase in single genre commercial channels (those specialising in one kind of programme, such as films, sport, news or films). These are aimed at particular groups of viewers, for example, gardeners, sports fans or ethnic minorities.

The BBC is principally a **producer broadcaster** – it makes and broadcasts its own programmes. It has its own studios and production facilities. However, in addition, like ITV, it is required by the Broadcasting Act to use **independent producers** (programme-making companies which are not also broadcasters) for 25 per cent of its total programme output. The process by which a broadcaster asks a production company to make a programme on its behalf is **commissioning**, so the BBC may also be called a **commissioner**, or **publisher broadcaster**.

The BBC operates under a Royal Charter which runs for 10 years. The current one will be due for renewal in 2006. The BBC is accountable to its independently appointed Board of Governors. They, in turn, appoint a Director-General who is responsible for the day-to-day running of the Corporation.

(*Source*: BBC)

ITV

Recent ITV hit quiz show *Who Wants to be a Millionaire?*

Independent Television was started in 1955 to provide an alternative to the BBC for viewers, to break the BBC's **monopoly** (the dominance of a market by one supplier).

There are now 15 regional Channel 3 licensees and one national breakfast-time service. There is also ITV2 on cable, satellite and digital. Each licensee produces a regional news service and a range of other regional services. Together, the Channel 3 companies form the **ITV Network**. Currently no company may have more than 15 per cent of the total audience through its ownership. But it is likely that these rules will soon be relaxed and, as major players such as Carlton and Granada gradually take over the commercial television map, there is speculation that ITV will soon be dominated by one or two companies. The companies consist of two types of broadcaster: publisher/commissioner and producer broadcasters.

In order to produce and broadcast programmes on commercial television, the companies need a **licence**. They apply to the ITC (see below) for a licence to supply a television service to a particular region. The licence period is 10 years.

The ITV licences were held in 2001 by the following companies (see the ITC web site for changes):

1. Anglia Television – owned by United News and Media
2. Border Television – Border Television and Cumbrian Newspapers Group (18%)
3. Carlton Television – Carlton Communications
4. Central Broadcasting – Carlton Communications
5. Channel Television – Channel Islands Communications

6 GMTV – Walt Disney (25%), Granada Group (20%), Scottish TV (20%), Carlton Communications (20%) and Guardian Media Group (15%)

7 Grampian TV – Scottish Media Group

8 Granada Television – Granada Group

9 HTV – United News and Media

10 London Weekend Television – Granada Group

11 Meridian Broadcasting – United News and Media (76%), Carlton Communication (20%)

12 Scottish Television – shareholders include: Flextech (5.95%), Flextech Investments (13.9%), *Scottish Daily Record / Sunday Mail* (19.81%), Chase Nominees (5.38%), FMR Corp (4.94%)

13 Tyne Tees Television – Granada Media Group

14 Ulster Television – owned by Ulster Television

15 Westcountry Television – owned by Carlton Communications

16 Yorkshire Television – owned by Granada Media Group

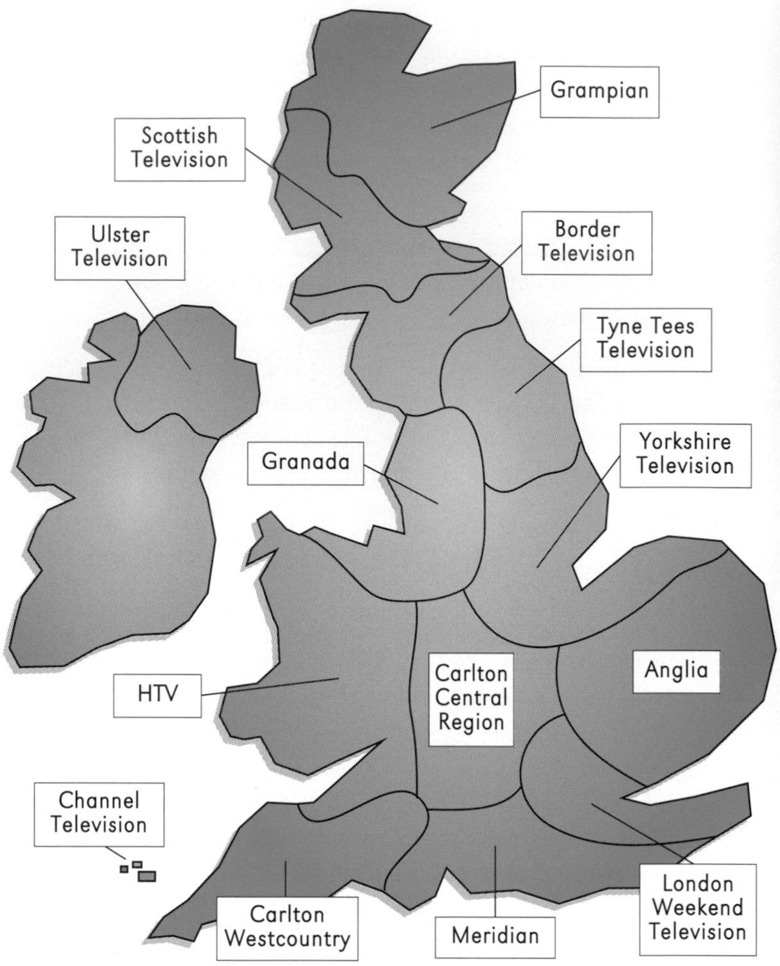

The ITV regions

ACTIVITY 3

- Which area do you live in? Look at some regional listings in a newspaper or TV magazine – how different is your regional service from another's?
- Why do you think that a newspaper company (United News and *The Guardian*), a leading children's entertainment company (Disney) and a leisure and entertainment company (Granada) would wish to hold shares in a television company?
- Try to find out what other companies the major shareholders own.
- What do you think the television companies gain from their partnerships with these major shareholders, in addition to their initial investments?

The Broadcasting Act of 1990 increased competition between television companies, in order to create more choice for the viewer and wealth for the Government; however, many people believe that our choice of programmes has in fact decreased.

In 1991 the Independent Television Commission (ITC), the body established by the 1990 Act to regulate commercial television, had to judge which companies should be awarded each of the regional licences and the national breakfast licence. It looked first at which companies planned to produce the best range of programmes, the **quality threshold**. From those companies, it chose the highest bidder, the one which promised to pay the most money to the Treasury.

After the competition, some companies disappeared from our screens, such as Thames TV (although Thames TV still produces programmes such as *The Bill*) and TVS, and new ones were born, for example Carlton and Meridian. The term 'Channel 3' was introduced in the White Paper on Broadcasting (1988) which preceded the Broadcasting Act 1990. However, the name ITV is still commonly applied to describe the Channel 3 service and is used as a **brand name** for marketing.

The ITV companies have to pay the Government Treasury Department an annual sum of money in return for their licences. The amount that a company may earn in a year's broadcasting is potentially very large and the sum it pays to the Treasury is, in effect, a kind of tax, which creates income for the Government to spend on the running of the country.

ITV is BBC1's main rival for mass audience viewing and the **audience share** each achieves fluctuates each year with a special battle for **ratings** occurring every Christmas when these two channels compete for our attention between presents and food.

On ITV, many films and programmes are **networked** (they are shown at the same time in every ITV region). For example, the ITV network might buy a major film to show over the whole network. Or, the ITV companies, or independent producers commissioned by ITV Network Centre, will make programmes for the network. *London's Burning* and *Coronation Street* are examples of networked dramas.

ACTIVITY 4

- Look at the end credits for ITV programmes and see which companies appear most often. See which ones also make programmes for the BBC.

HOURS OF VIEWING, SHARE OF AUDIENCE AND REACH

Including Timeshift

Channel	Average Weekly Viewing (Hrs:Mins) per person	Share of Total Viewing %	% Reach Average Daily	% Reach Weekly
ALL/ANY TV	23:58	100.0	75.8	93.7
BBC1	7:22	30.7	56.3	87.3
BBC2	2:35	10.7	36.3	75.6
TOTAL/ANY BBC	9:56	41.5	62.2	89.3
ITV (incl. GMTV)	5:59	24.9	49.8	82.6
CHANNEL 4/S4C	2:25	10.1	32.8	72.2
CHANNEL 5	1:19	5.5	18.2	46.8
TOTAL/ANY COMM. TERR. TV	9:43	40.5	59.7	88.1
Other Viewing	4:19	18.0	24.5	38.2

BBC1 Millions Viewing
(Including Timeshift) - w/e 08/07/2001

	Programme	Total	1st Showing	2nd Showing
1	EASTENDERS (THU/SUN)	14.24	10.61	3.63
2	EASTENDERS (TUE/SUN)	13.91	11.21	2.70
3	EASTENDERS (MON/SAT)	12.52	10.56	1.96
4	AIRPORT (THU 2001)	8.15		
5	WAKING THE DEAD (MON 2059)	7.33		
6	ONLY FOOLS & HORSES (FRI 2004)	7.11		
7	WAKING THE DEAD (TUE 2100)	6.93		
8	ULTIMATE KILLERS (SUN 2029)	6.59		
9	VICAR OF DIBLEY (SAT 2015)	6.45		
10	WIMBLEDON 2001 (FRI 1345)	6.08		

BBC2 Millions Viewing
(Including Timeshift) - w/e 08/07/2001

	Programme	Total	1st Showing	2nd Showing
1	WIMBLEDON 2001 (MON 1743)	4.32		
2	TODAY AT WIMBLEDON (WED 1735)	3.72		
3	TOP GEAR (THU 2030)	2.84		
4	MASTERCHEF (TUE 2030)	2.82		
5	HAMPTON/FLOWER SHOW (MON2101)	2.77		
6	WIMBLEDON 2001 (SAT 1701)	2.76		
7	PORRIDGE (WED 2101)	2.64		
8	WIMBLEDON 2001 (FRI 1930)	2.57		
9	GARDENERS WORLD (FRI 2030)	2.49		
10	DADS ARMY (THU 2101)	2.37		

ITV Millions Viewing
(Including Timeshift) - w/e 08/07/2001

	Programme	Total	1st Showing	2nd Showing
1	CORONATION STREET (MON/WED)	12.20	11.66	0.54
2	CORONATION STREET (WED/THU)	12.18	11.62	0.56
3	CORONATION STREET (SUN 1929)	12.03		
4	CORONATION STREET (FRI 1931)	11.46		
5	WHERE THE HEART IS (SUN 1959)	8.69		
6	EMMERDALE (FRI 1901)	8.56		
7	EMMERDALE (TUE 1900)	8.32		
8	EMMERDALE (THU 1900)	8.19		
9	TOUCH OF FROST (SUN 2103)	8.17		
10	BAD GIRLS (TUE 2100)	8.15		

CHANNEL 4 Millions Viewing
(Including Timeshift) - w/e 08/07/2001

	Programme	Total	1st Showing	2nd Showing
1	BIG BROTHER (MON 2202)	4.88		
2	BIG BROTHER (FRI 2235)	4.59		
3	BIG BROTHER (TUE 2202)	4.39		
4	BIG BROTHER (THU 2202)	4.25		
5	BIG BROTHER (WED 2201)	4.21		
6	BROOKSIDE (FRI/SAT)	3.54	2.22	1.33
7	BROOKSIDE (WED/SAT)	3.51	2.35	1.16
8	BIG BROTHER (FRI 2030)	3.46		
9	BROOKSIDE (TUE/SAT)	3.03	1.97	1.06
10	FRIENDS (FRI 2102)	2.81		

CHANNEL 5 Millions Viewing
(Including Timeshift) - w/e 08/07/2001

	Programme	Total	1st Showing	2nd Showing
1	GHOSTBUSTERS (SUN 1705)	2.03		
2	AVENGERS (TUE 2103)	1.85		
3	THE LAKE-FILM (WED 2104)	1.83		
4	BATMAN [FILM] (SUN 2102)	1.83		
5	DEATHE WISH V (SAT 2200)	1.68		
6	CSI (SAT 2101)	1.62		
7	CRIMINAL INTENT (MON 2103)	1.59		
8	BORDERLINE (THU 2100)	1.54		
9	WWW.SEX (THU 2303)	1.51		
10	MOTHER/SLEEP/DANGER (FRI 2103)	1.49		

BARB (Broadcasters' Audience Research Board) produces weekly ratings for television programmes and channels. These are the ratings for the week 2-8 July 2001.

At other times, the regional broadcasters have the freedom to **schedule** (to give a programme a particular time-slot when they think it will reach the right audience) when they want.

ITV has a news service supplied by ITN, Independent Television News. ITN also supplies the news for Channel 4 and Channel 5. Each ITV regional licensee produces its own regional news programme.

(*Source*: ITV Network Centre and ITC)

Channel 4

Channel 4 became a public broadcasting service in January 1982. It has a legal duty to provide information, education and entertainment; to appeal to tastes and interests not generally catered for by Channel 3; to encourage innovation, diversity and originality and to have a distinctive character of its own. Channel 4 now sells its own advertising; but in its early years it was funded by ITV, in return for selling its advertising.

Its former Chief Executive, Michael Jackson (who is a Media Studies graduate himself), spoke of his determination to take the channel beyond the alternative margins of British television:

> “Channel 4 is no longer a minority channel for minority audiences. Its future lies in being the channel of contemporary culture (which is) ahead of the mainstream.”

(*Source*: *Guardian Media Guide 2000*)

Channel 4 is a publisher / commissioner broadcaster; it does not have its own studios or production facilities but commissions other companies to make its programmes (look at the logos at the end of each programme to find out which they are). In 1997, Channel 4 started a cable / satellite / digital service, Film Four, paid for by monthly subscription from viewers, which shows a wide range of films, uncut and uninterrupted by advertising breaks. It also has a film production arm, responsible for such successes as *Four Weddings and a Funeral* (Mike Newell, Channel 4 TV et al, 1994), *Trainspotting* (Danny Boyle, Channel Four Films et al, 1996) and *Brassed Off* (Mark Herman, Channel Four Films et al, 1996).

(*Source*: *Guardian Media Guide 2000*)

Channel 4's film production company made hit film *Four Weddings and a Funeral*

S4C

S4C is the Welsh Channel 4 service, which started in 1983. It broadcasts an average of 34 hours per week in Welsh and 10 hours provided by the BBC. The analogue output carries over 70 per cent of Channel 4's output, around S4C's commitment to scheduling programmes in Welsh at peak time. S4C Digital broadcasts via On Digital in Wales and on satellite for the UK and broadcasts in Welsh for at least 12 hours a day. S4C International is responsible for the channel's commercial activities. Its flagship programme is *Pobol Y Cwm* (*The People of the Valley*), the only *daily* soap opera on television in the UK.

(Source: Guardian Media Guide 2000)

Channel 5

Channel 5 began broadcasting on 30 March 1997, with a launch led by The Spice Girls. As with Channel 3, it must meet the positive programme requirements of the ITC. After the early few months of restricted availability and poor reception quality, Channel 5 is close to reaching 100 per cent of the British population and is paid for by advertising revenue. ITN produces its news service.

Its decision to schedule a nightly film at 9.00 pm is considered to be responsible for the rescheduling by ITV of *News at Ten* and the BBC's subsequent decision to move the *Nine O'Clock News*.

(Source: Guardian Media Guide 2000)

Welsh soap opera Pobol Y Cwm

The Spice Girls launch Channel 5

Satellite and cable

These services were encouraged to challenge the **duopoly** (the dominance of a market by two suppliers) of the BBC and ITV. This was meant to create competition, which was intended to benefit the viewer, and to further the technological developments of television. By 2001, more than 50% of families with children in Britain had either cable, satellite or digital terrestrial, and these accounted for about 20% of all TV viewing.

Satellite and cable companies are funded by a combination of advertising revenue; **subscription**, where a monthly payment is made to the company; and **pay-per-view**, where one-off payments are made to the company for special sporting and music events or film premières.

The top cable companies are currently Telewest and NTL. In 1999 there were 137 franchises with 4.239 million homes connected to cable television and / or telephone services. In 1999, Microsoft bought 5% of NTL and observers are waiting to see precisely when Bill Gates' company will make a significant move into the cable market. Here the concept of **media convergence** suggests that Microsoft could, before too long, completely control the home PC, Internet and television market.

The most successful satellite television company is BSkyB. It started as a rival to British Satellite Broadcasting but the two companies soon merged. It has subscribers in more than 5.4 million British and Irish homes and its current annual turnover is in excess of £1.94 billion. Rupert Murdoch's company Sky Global Networks owns 36.7% of BSkyB and the French media conglomerate Vivendi owns a 22% stake.

COMMERCIAL TELEVISION FUNDING – ADVERTISING

So where do commercial television companies get their money? We already know that the BBC takes all of the annual television licence fee. In addition to programme sales and investments, the main source of funding for ITV and Channels 4 and 5 is the sale of advertising airtime. For satellite, cable and digital services, additional funding comes from subscription and sponsorship.

The ITC has set down rules of how many minutes per hour may be devoted to adverts and the rules by which advertisers have to abide.

ACTIVITY 5

- Look at the ITC's Code of Advertising Standards and Practice on its web site to see what can and cannot be done.

A great deal of money is spent by advertisers on television **spots** (an advertisement in a break) due to the considerable **reach** achieved by television (how many people will see it). Look at these figures for 1997:

MEDIUM	*PERCENTAGE OF TOTAL BUDGET*	*AMOUNT (£ MILLION)*
TELEVISION	31.5	3,651
PRESS (display adverts)	33.8	3,860
PRESS (classified ads)	26.8	3,107
OUTDOOR	4.3	500
RADIO	3.4	393
CINEMA	0.8	88

How advertisers spent their budgets in 1997.
(*Source: Guardian Media Guide 2000*)

The aim of the broadcasters is to raise as much money as possible from companies who want to advertise their products, in order to pay for new programmes. They publish their advertising costs on a **rate card**. Companies pay television broadcasters in order to have their products advertised at time-slots when potential customers for that product are watching. They can pay for either an advertisement spot or to **sponsor** a programme.

There are several stages of an advertising campaign (see below). Chapter 5 Radio has further information about advertising in general and on radio, which you can apply to television.

Advertising is a **cross-media** form, because it uses more than one medium to communicate with its audiences.

Advertisers want either a mass audience or a niche audience:

- a **mass audience** is a large and mixed audience
- a **niche audience** is a small and selective audience

Peak time (6 pm to 10.30 pm) is when the largest audiences can be guaranteed to be watching television. Therefore the more expensive spots will fall during this time of day, with the most expensive spots occurring between 8 pm and 8.30 pm. Peak-time spots are expensive because the sellers of the spots can guarantee high audience statistics (the **TVR** – target viewer ratio) that will appeal to someone wishing to sell a product.

The current problem for television companies is that there are now so many more commercial television channels to attract advertisers, as well as a new medium, the Internet, to increase the competition between media for advertisers and their precious revenue.

For example, on average, 15 million people watch *Coronation Street* on a Monday evening (September 2000 – BARB). It is the advertisers' hope that a number of that 15 million might, by seeing their advert in the break, be encouraged to consider buying their product instead of their rivals': buy a Nissan not a Renault Clio the next time they want a car, for example, or pop into Tesco's rather than Sainsbury's.

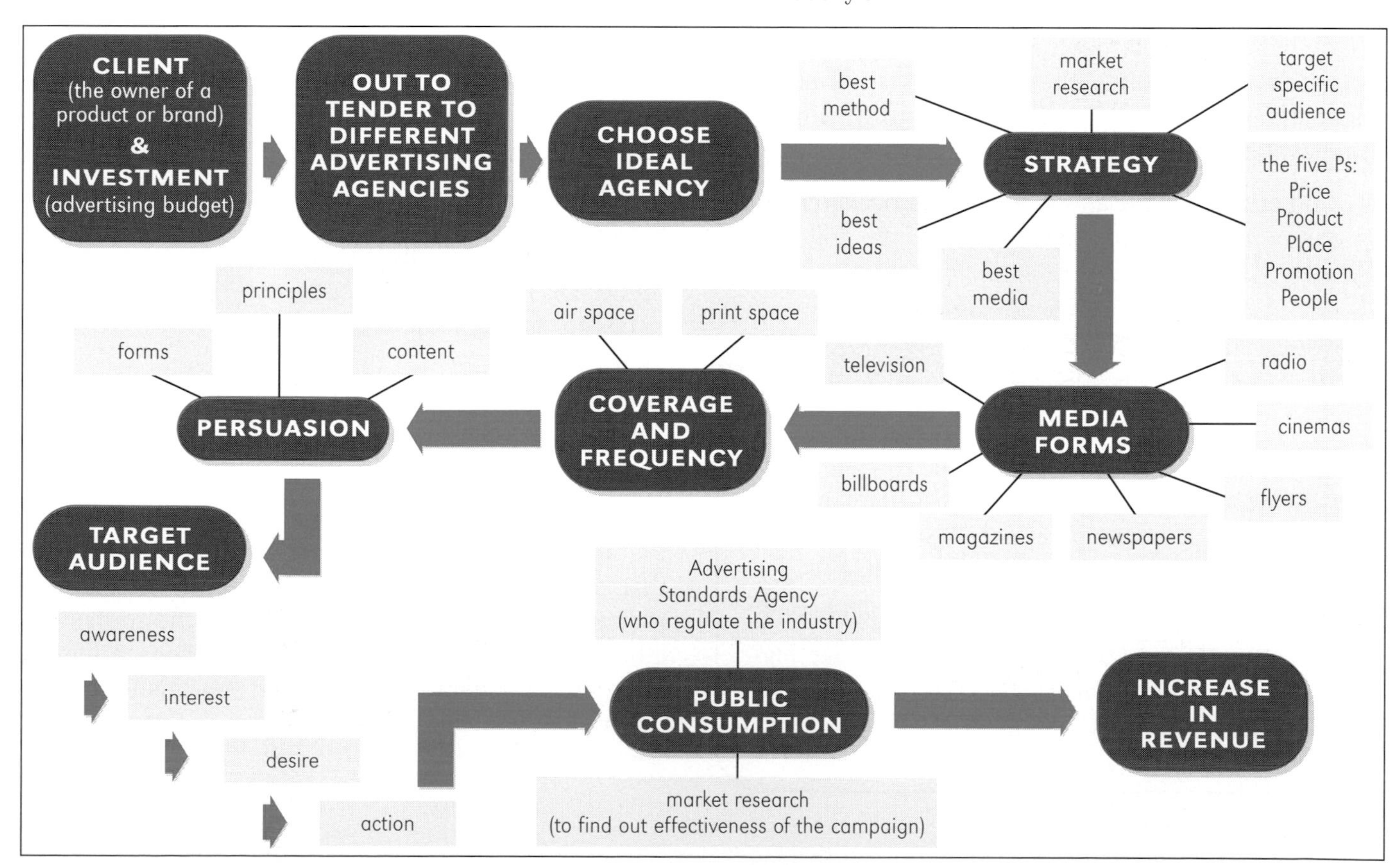

The stages of an advertising campaign

It is also common sense that advertisers would want to know not just *how many* people are watching, but *who* is watching so that they may target their advertisements more precisely. Therefore, knowing more about their audience, or their **classification**, is vitally important to them.

Advertising is a hugely speculative, or risky, business. Advertisers may not even be sure whether or not it works, but they cannot afford to risk *not* advertising their products. We might see their advert, or we might have popped out to the toilet or to get a cup of tea and miss it. Also, we are not robots, we cannot be guaranteed to obey the advertisements, especially as we all strenuously deny being influenced by advertising if we're ever asked!

TELEVISION AUDIENCES

Consumer classification

Audience classification is how we, as individuals, may be grouped by the things that we have in common with other individuals, for the convenience of advertisers and programme-makers.

We are each a 'one-off', a unique individual; we rarely enjoy being 'lumped together' with other people. But all kinds of businesses need to see us as groups of people to sell their goods and services to. So what do we have in common with other individuals?

To find out a bit more about who might be watching a programme with you, have a go at the following Activity:

ACTIVITY 6

- Look at any television listings guide, in a newspaper or the *Radio Times* or *TV Times*, and try to work out what type of people will be watching particular programmes at different times of day. What products might they be interested in buying?
- Look at the adverts around any programme and guess from the products advertised who might be watching.

To assist in the accurate **targeting** of audiences by broadcasters and advertisers, viewers are classified by economic status, media consumption and lifestyle preferences. These statistics are called **audience demographics** (statistics on people by age, gender, social group etc) or **psychographic profiling** (information about people's lifestyles and values).

Group	*Description*
A	**Upper middle** - Business / professional, upper management
B	**Middle** - Professional, middle management
C1	**Lower middle** - Supervisory, trades
C2	**Skilled** - Skilled manual workers
D	**Semi- / Unskilled** - Manual workers
E	**Subsistence** - Pensioners on state support only, unemployed

Audience demographics categories

In the new, more competitive market, commercial channels may have to reduce their advertising charges. This could mean less money to pay for new programmes. So, the advertising 'cake' must now be sliced even more thinly if there is to be enough to go round. On the other hand, advertisers may just have to pay for more media spots.

Peter Bazalgette (Creative Director of Endemol Entertainment, which made Channel 4's *Big Brother*) predicted that the number of sponsorship **stings** (e.g. Ericsson for *Frasier* and Domino's Pizza for *The Simpsons*), which currently make up 2.5 per cent of the advertising 'cake', would rise even more. Also, that **product placement** (the currently prohibited practice of placing name brands within the context of a programme) would grow. But what other strategies are there to generate income from advertising or for programme-making?

"Broadcasting is getting narrower all the time. Witness Channel 4 and Sky's successes in delivering more focused audience groups to advertisers. And it will get narrower still, in the broadband, online world, the advertisers may well become broad / narrowcasters themselves. The likes of Ali G might be directly funded by Nike and available exclusively on Nike's channel."

(Peter Bazalgette, quoted in *Media Guardian*, September 2000)

So perhaps by **targeting** smaller audiences more precisely, programme-makers can reach smaller but more identifiable audiences of particular interest to specific advertisers and so charge more money to companies as they can guarantee a specific audience.

ACTIVITY 7

- Have a look at a **niche** cable or satellite channel, and see how specific the adverts are to the interests of those likely to be watching that channel.

The cost of making new drama is very high indeed. Television news reporting is also very expensive and whenever there is a major international conflict or natural disaster, television news services have to put enormous amounts of money into their operations in order to stay one step ahead of the competition, and retain or attract more viewers.

Using the BBC's 1999 Annual Report as an example, we can see the cost of programme-making and consider the connection between the cost of a programme or genre and its position in the schedules:

TELEVISION GENRE	COST PER HOUR OF BBC-ORIGINATED PROGRAMMES (£000)
Drama	531
Entertainment	222
Factual	139
Continuing education	134
Political / current affairs	123
Arts & music	106
Sport	90
Children's	88
Schools	85
News	54
Daytime	34

Breakdown of the BBC's programme-making costs by genre
(*Source*: BBC Annual Report 1999)

NEWS

News is a cross-media form – it uses more than one medium to communicate with audiences. However, the processes of **newsgathering** (collecting news stories) and **treatment** processes (**editorial** – who decides which stories / information are included and **presentation** – the use of sound and image to present the programme and stories) are much the same for every news medium.

Television news is **picture-driven** and needs a continuous flow of pictures to keep us interested as news producers fear that we will become bored by static images or a shot of a newsreader. There is useful information on news in Chapters 3 and 5 on Newspapers and Radio, that may be adapted for television. The diagram on the following page shows the two main processes of news production: **input** and **output**.

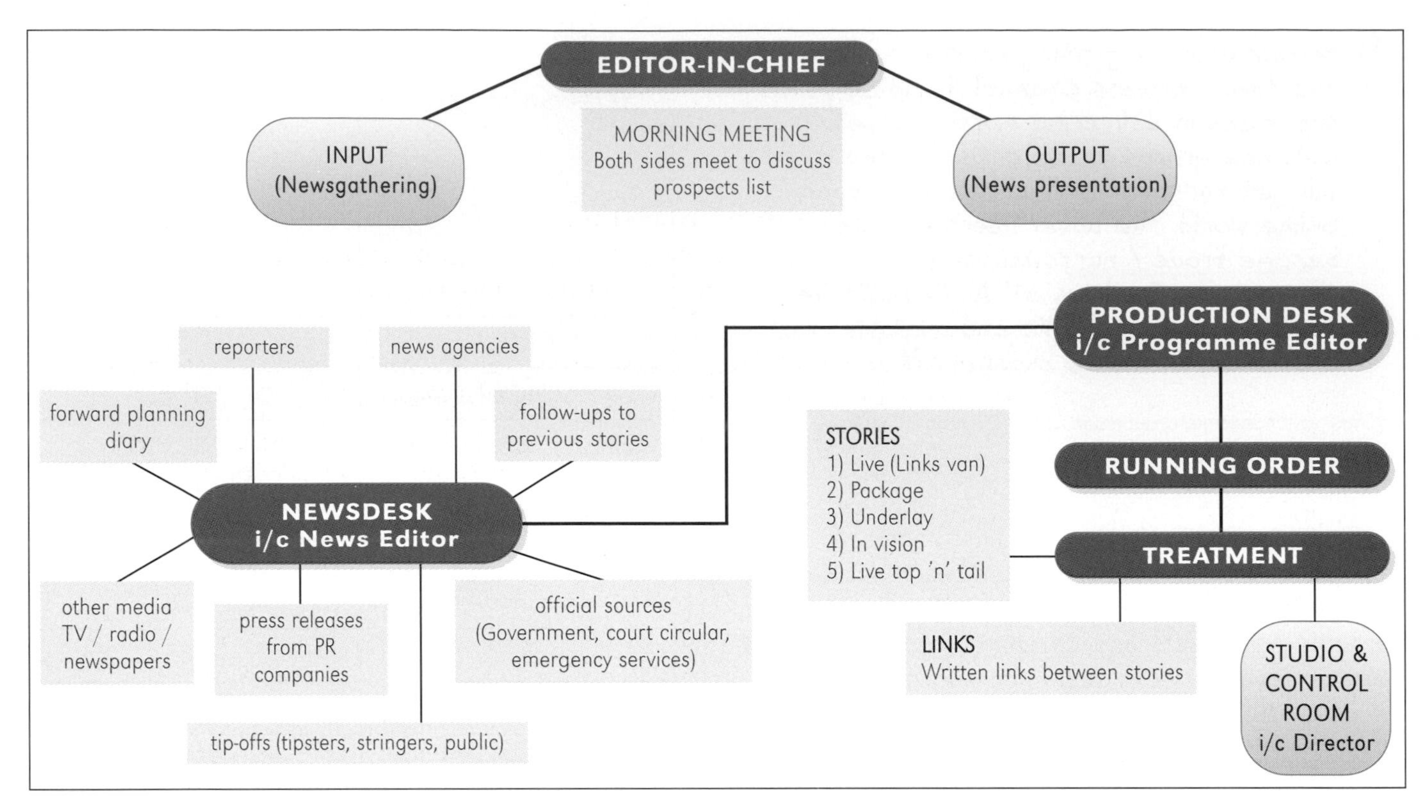

The newsgathering and presentation process – common to TV, radio and newspapers

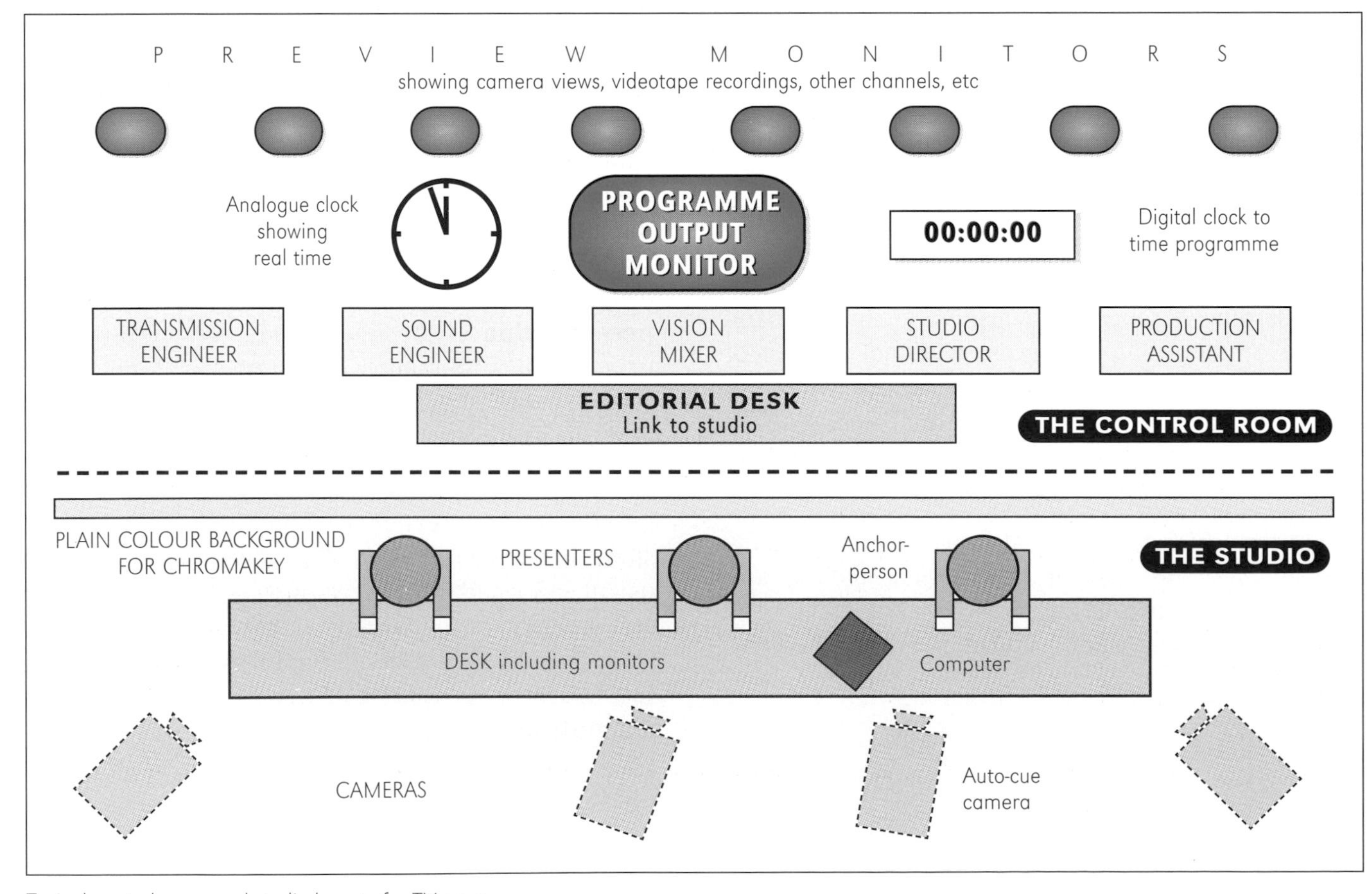

Typical control room and studio layouts for TV news

For any news programme, whatever time it is broadcast, the process of newsgathering and presentation is a 24-hour job

- The main work starts with a **morning meeting** between the **senior news editor** (in charge of how news is gathered) and the **producer** (in charge of how the news is presented) and the **editors** from various **news desks**, such as forward planning (this desk keeps a diary of all scheduled events such as a royal visit or film première), sport, entertainment, politics, finance etc.
- They consider a range of stories from their various **sources** (see diagram on page 68) and discuss the most important stories for their programme that day, or at a particular time, and who are the most appropriate **reporters** to cover them.
- The producer puts together a working draft of a **running order**, a schedule of the order in which stories will be presented. New stories will occur during the day and the producer may need to rearrange the order of stories in the running order.
- Reporters arrive and receive their **roster** of duties for the day from the news editor and their computer.
- When the draft running order has been decided, reporters are dispatched to cover particular stories, often accompanied by a **camera operator** and **sound recordist** (often, reporters will act as their own sound recordists).
- Meanwhile news editors on the various news desks sift through information from various sources, including television, newspapers and the Internet, together with the stream of news stories and photographs coming from **news agencies** to which they subscribe.
- During the day, the **subeditors** on the production desk are given stories by the producer to write up for the programme's running order. As well as the stories in the bulletin themselves, they also write the **links** and **trails** read by the presenters throughout the day.
- Meanwhile, as the bulletin broadcast time approaches, **programme editors** will be working on the final running order with the editor.
- **Video** and **sound editors** work on editing video footage of items produced by the reporters at an event and sent back to the base by courier, or from existing footage from the library or news agencies, to create **packages**. **Graphics**, such as maps, and **captions** will also be prepared. If time is short, some video footage will actually be **edited** in the **links van** (an outside broadcast vehicle that contains its own editing facilities sent to cover important stories).
- There are different types of news **presentation**. A **news package** is an edited tape of sound and pictures ready to go into the programme. **Underlay** is the use of a voiceover that strings stills or video footage together to make a story. A **sandwich**, or **top and tail**, is a story that begins with a studio introduction, the middle being a **live link** to a reporter or a pre-recorded package and finishing with the reporter linking back to the studio.
- During the day, the **news presenters**, or **anchors**, prepare and rehearse their scripts in advance, but there are frequent occasions when they have to rely on last-minute information and instructions from the director via the **talkback** link in their ear. This is a vital link, because, as news broadcasting is always **live**, there might be problems with upcoming video tapes, non-arrival of interviewees or even **breaking news** that needs to be included. They read a script from the **autocue** and often have a hard copy (on paper) and a computer at their desk as well.
- The **technical crew** is managed by the **director** who oversees all of the work on tape and in the **studio** from the many television screens in the **gallery / control room**. They work on the production of the sound and images we will see in the broadcast of the bulletin itself. The crew consists of a **vision mixer** (who mixes all vision sources, from the studio, outside broadcasts, adverts, video tapes), **sound mixer** (who mixes all audio sources), **vision engineer** (in charge of the studio lights, autocues and cameras) and **production assistant** (who times each part of the bulletin and checks that it does not overrun).
- And then the process starts all over again, with **night editors** monitoring news stories during the night for the next day!

ACTIVITY 8

- Study the ITN news bulletins on one day, on all three channels (ITV, Channels 4 and 5), and examine what the differences are in **presentational** as well as **editorial treatment**
- Analyse the **branding** (or labelling) of each bulletin from its **ident** (or identity logo) and the construction of its opening titles.
- What do these differences tell us about who is watching each of these channels (the **target audience**)?
- Study the advertisements either side and in the middle of the bulletins to find out more about the target audience.

TELEVISION FINANCE

- *Look up the annual reports of other TV companies to discover their income and expenditure details.*
- *How, then, can broadcasters save money?*
- *Where can they get programmes from if they don't make them themselves?*
- *Which types of programme are less expensive than others?*
- *How might these economic factors have an impact on what we watch?*

Commercial terrestrial companies, as well as the BBC, can also raise money from selling programmes abroad, to cable and satellite channels for repeats or to release on video. They can also link up with another producer, at home or abroad, to fund jointly a programme made by both of them, called a **co-production**.

Not only do commercial television companies have to pay the Treasury and fund, or buy, new programmes. They also have to produce a reasonable return for their shareholders who expect to make a profit in return for their investment in the company.

ACTIVITY 9

- Look at the stocks and shares page of a newspaper to see how the various TV companies are doing.
- Look at the annual reports of one of the commercial companies to see how much money it is making.
- Look at the ITC web site and the *Guardian Media Guide* to see how much each television company has to pay the Treasury each year.

SCHEDULING

Each television channel has a **scheduler** for the channel, network or corporation as a whole. The job of the scheduling department is to decide what time to show a programme. The schedules are mostly **ratings-driven** – they are announced at the start of each new season and are an important tool in the battle for achieving better ratings than the competitor. In particular, the Christmas schedule is a key period for clever scheduling, as it is the time that most of us watch the most television.

All television channels have a schedule and they are printed in daily newspapers and specialist listings magazines, such as the *Radio Times*. The purpose of creating a television schedule is to match the programme with an audience, to ensure healthy viewing figures.

The schedules tend to reflect our lifestyles, so children's programmes are on after 4 pm when most schools finish. Pre-school children's programmes are on during the day. Adult programmes, which may contain strong language, sex or violence, are on after the **watershed** at 9 pm.

Another way of looking at the purpose of scheduling, certainly in commercial terrestrial, cable, satellite and digital channels, is that its main job is not to put programmes on when *we* want to watch them, but *to deliver audiences to advertisers*. Many people would argue that this is the *sole* function of the television schedules.

- *Think about why this might really be the case.*

Here are some terms used to describe different types of scheduling:

- **Hammocking**: Putting a less popular programme between two popular ones to try to boost its audience. Not a reliable strategy any more, as we are more than likely to reach for the remote control.
- **Inheritance factor**: Putting a new programme after an established one to build its audience.
- **Trailing**: Advertising a programme at the beginning or end of a programme that the audience watching the main programme is likely to be interested in, either straight afterwards, later that day or on another day.
- **Stripping**: Showing the same programme, or type of programme, at the same time, every day, every week – for example, news, sport, soap operas, chat shows.
- **Time-shifting**: Scheduling by the audience – recording a programme to watch later. The new personal video recorder TiVo could be the ultimate in time-shifting.
- **Zones**: Programming a series of similar programmes one after the other, for example, art, music or comedy zones.

ACTIVITY 10

- Look at the schedules to see if you can observe patterns that match audiences' ages and lifestyles.
- Look at the schedules for a niche channel and a mainstream channel to compare which kinds of audiences are being targeted.

REGULATION

The BBC is regulated by its Board of Governors.

The Broadcasting Act of 1990 gave the ITC the power to regulate ITV, Channel 4, Channel 5 and cable, satellite and commercial digital companies.

PUTTING VIEWERS FIRST

The ITC has a **Programme Code**, which gives details of how it monitors commercial television. It includes requirements for:

- offensiveness
- taste and decency
- accuracy
- impartiality

Failure to observe these requirements can result in warnings, fines or the removal of a licence.

(*Source:* ITC)

AUDIENCE RESEARCH

BARB

BBC and ITV agreed in 1980 to have a common source of television audience research and BARB (the **Broadcasters' Audience Research Board** Ltd.) was created. The company represents the major UK broadcasters and the Institute of Practitioners in Advertising (IPA).

It is responsible for the **TV Audience Reaction Services**, which produces **qualitative** (about *what* they watch) data based on what a regional panel of 3,000 adults (over 16 years of age) watches on television. There is also a Children's Panel of 1,000 children aged 4–15. BARB also provides the **Audience Measurement Service**, the purpose of which is to provide **quantitative** data (about *how many* watch).

BARB could not possibly monitor what we all watch, so the sample of households is chosen to reflect the age, gender, race and earning power of viewers in the 23+ million households throughout the UK.

In each of the 4,485 households in the sample, all television sets, video cassette recorders and cable, satellite and digital decoders are electronically monitored by a specially designed 'people-meter' system. The meter system automatically identifies and records the channel to which each television set is tuned whilst the set is switched on, and monitors all possible viewing, including video recording and playing of retail, rental or home-recorded off-air tapes of programmes to watch later (time-shifting).

Each resident or visitor registers their presence via a special handset before they watch television or videotapes. At the end of every day, the data is collected by the processing centre and collated by BARB for distribution to broadcasters and advertisers. We can find out the ratings information from some television listings guides, newspapers and the BARB web site (www.barb.co.uk).

(*Source*: BARB)

- *Why do you think this information might be useful to a) broadcasters and b) advertisers?*

MEDIA MESSAGES AND VALUES

The questions in the **key concepts** section of the Introduction can be used to study the **messages and values** in the programmes that we watch. Just as we have our own personal system of ideas, values and beliefs (**ideology**) and apply our own judgements about all aspects of life, we can see the value systems of others operating in the programmes they make.

Television, whether fiction or non-fiction, constructs images and narratives of all types of social groups, which are often defined by the following characteristics:

- age
- gender
- race
- religion
- nationality
- regionality
- disability
- social class
- sexuality

Constructions that stand for a person, or social group, are called **representations** and are often based on **stereotypes** (a simplified generalisation). Stereotypes are quickly and easily recognisable and are used frequently in advertising and comedy as messages that may be quickly conveyed and understood by the audience. Stereotypes are often considered to be unfair and unjust, as they tend to focus on negative aspects of a particular social group that may disadvantage them in real life, as some people tend to judge real people by the stereotypes that they see in the media. But they may also be constructed to convey positive representations.

No representation is neutral, its construction and selection is always informed by the messages and values of the producer. We act as our own editors, as we have our own ideas of which photographs we like of ourselves (or of a boyfriend or girlfriend) and **edit** (select) which ones we show to other people. We often say, 'It's not a very good photo' if for some reason we decide that it is not really an accurate representation of us, or of how we would *like* to be represented!

ACTIVITY 11

- One photograph of you does not tell the full story! Make a self portrait collage – in an attempt to represent *all* aspects of your personality and experience. Choose photographs, objects, poems, song lyrics, sections from books, photos of people or things you like, labels, drawings; anything that can build up, or construct, a three-dimensional representation of yourself.
- Perhaps you could make two – one for your public face and one for your private one (you don't have to show anyone this one!).
- Keep them carefully and look at them as you get older to see how your representation of yourself has changed.

NOTABLE ABSENCES

Another important question to think about is the degree to which *all* members of the British population are represented, either in terms of their visibility (or invisibility) on the screen, or in terms of representations of their points of view, culture or interests.

- *Look at any programme and analyse how social class and gender are represented.*
- *Look at how representations of ethnic minorities are used, by using qualitative (what kind) and quantitative (how many / often) analysis.*
- *How would you represent your own school or community in a news programme?*
- *Analyse the representations of people and places, as well as the messages and values, in your school or college prospectus or web site.*

CASE STUDY: Advertising

Advertising is an excellent source of short texts for analysis. A **textual analysis** (a detailed study, or deconstruction, of how a media text is constructed) of how **television language** is used can lead to a study of how and what kinds of messages and values are communicated through media texts.

Advertisers use a variety of techniques to sell us their products, but they may be divided into two kinds: **psychological** and **creative**. They can often be identified as using one of two **categories** of advertising: hard-sell and soft-sell.

Hard-sell is where the advertisement gets straight to the point; for example, 'Ronseal: it does what it says on the can.' **Soft-sell** is where we may not be too sure what is being advertised. The advertiser creates an attractive image or mood to link with the product, but might not actually give many details or facts about the brand being sold. Advertisements for banks, cars and telecommunications companies tend to use a soft-sell approach; for example, breathe.com's campaign had images of breathing, waves and arty clouds, and said, 'It's amazing what happens when you breathe.' But what it said about the actual product was rather vague.

Advertisers often try to appeal to our **aspirations**: who we would like to be and what we would like to own. We do not really *need* most of what is advertised, but, in economically secure societies, we can afford to consider the luxury of **consumerism**, buying and owning for its own sake, rather than to satisfy practical needs. So adverts often stress that a product is: fast, convenient, luxurious, safe, rare, expensive, value for money, stylish, unique, original, the best, traditional, fashionable, ethical, the latest etc.

Advertisements try to appeal to our values, what matters to us, in order to sell us something; for example, 'I'll buy this because it is important to me to: save time / support organic farming / be fashionable / keep my home hygienic / have the latest technology.'

In doing so, advertisements can be an interesting historical record of what is important to a society at one time or another.

ACTIVITY 12

- Try to look at collections of old print or television advertisements to see what they reveal about social values at the time they were made.
- What has changed? Why?

They also may reveal what messages we create or accept about how we live, the opinions we hold and how we treat other people.

ADVERTISING TECHNIQUES

Advertising employs a variety of techniques and these must be appropriate to the **product** being advertised and the **medium** used. There are **two** main kinds of techniques:

- **Presentational** (the use of a visual design concept, graphics, actors, images, colour, layout, editing, music, sound effects)
- **Psychological** (the use of different methods of persuasion through choice of words and images)

PERSONAL OR HOME HYGIENE PRODUCTS

Presentational techniques

- **Design concept** – a view of a designer or family bathroom or kitchen, depending on the price of the product and its image, with props that are recognisable as being in fashion or popular at the moment
- **Colours** – depending on desired image, pastel colours such as pink or blue, or bright fresh colours such as lime green and lemon yellow, whites and reds for hygiene, or blues and metallic steel and silver greys, especially if for men
- **Graphics** – computer animation and diagrams of molecules or active ingredients are often used for products making scientific claims, such as face cream, shampoo and toothpaste; cartoon or comic figures / shapes if for children

Psychological techniques

- Suggestions of hygiene, dependability and safety to protect the family, especially children (if a disinfectant or cleaner); luxury; advanced technology to improve appearance; sexual attractiveness; comedy; insecurity about standard of housekeeping (cleaning products)

COMPUTER SOFTWARE OR HARDWARE

Presentational techniques

- **Design concept** – views of a world united by advanced technology, with images of many countries and cultures or emphasis on the advanced nature of the technology, or visions of hi-tech processing power, increasing speed and efficiency in one's work
- **Colours** – multi-coloured, for different nationalities, or hi-tech colours such as luminous yellow, green, silver
- **Typography** – often minimalist, sans serif fonts in lower case, to reduce formality and increase a sense of accessibility
- **Graphics** – digital images of digits or of nets, suggesting the global nature and power of the Internet
- **Music** – classical / operatic, choral world music or sci-fi sound effects or tones

Psychological techniques

- A human figure may be used as the friendly face of the product to reduce fear of technology
- Children are often used to indicate the future generations who will benefit most from technology or to present an optimistic face in global unity, which is again linked to the product, as if to suggest that the project promotes or will facilitate world unity
- Invitations to join a technology community as something that is amazing and fun, rather than making us anxious about falling behind – more likely to be successful than making us feel inadequate (opposite of cleaning product psychology!)

ACTIVITY 13

- Take an advertising campaign for any product.
- Deconstruct these aspects of the campaign:
  - the overall concept or creative idea
  - the use of *mise-en-scène*
  - camera techniques
  - editing techniques
  - the use of words
  - the use of music
- Is it hard- or soft-sell?
- How does it depict the product?
- What values does it suggest that we have if we wish to buy the product?
- What messages does it reveal about how we live and regard other people?
- How are these messages constructed?
- Who is present? Who, or what, is absent?
- How do you personally respond to this advert and its messages and values?

MEDIA LANGUAGES AND CATEGORIES

TELEVISION LANGUAGE

The similarities between books, plays and poems, on the one hand, and television programmes and other mass media, on the other hand, are obvious. Media Studies regards them all as **texts** to be read and enjoyed, as well as **products** of media industries; they each have a specific **language** and record human experience, real or imagined. They also bear the fingerprint, or **style**, of the producer.

If a writer wishes to tell a story in a novel, she has the language of words to use. This language is made up of verbs, adverbs, nouns, adjectives and so on. Each type of word gives us information on what is being written about.

For example, a verb tells us what is happening or being done (in the past, present or future) and an adjective gives us more detailed information about a person, object, place or emotion by describing them.

These words are put together according to the rules of grammar that dictate in which order the words need to be within a sentence, so that they make sense. Sentences are then structured in paragraphs, in order that the readers may see easily that the writer is moving from topic to topic.

Television also has its own specific language, originally adapted from **film language** (see also Chapter 1 (Film)). Like novels, television creates fictional and non-fictional stories. For a television programme, a story starts with a script but it has to be turned into **moving images** and **sounds** in order to make sense to us. There are many kinds of moving images and sounds and they make up the language of television. In addition to a pen or word-processor, the producers need the following to construct, or produce, their media text:

- cameras, film or videotape, lights, microphones
- talent (people who appear on television)
- sets, locations, costumes, props and make-up
- production personnel and crew
- transport, food
- insurance, royalty and copyright payments
- plenty of money to pay for all of this and everyone's wages!

This is just the start. There are four stages of television production: **Research and Development**, **pre-production** (planning the programme, securing finance and personnel), **production** (making the programme) and **post-production** (editing the programme).

This is a very extensive process, beyond the scope of this book. There are specialist books on television production and behind-the-scenes programmes and web sites that are useful for learning about this aspect of television.

Details of camera terms are provided on page 36–40 in Chapter 1 (Film).

TELEVISION CATEGORIES

Different kinds of stories are called **genres** (a French word for type or **category**) as they share certain features and rules (**codes** and **conventions**). Genre is a very important aspect of studying television, as well as other media. It is useful for the audience, to

ACTIVITY 14

- Keep an eye out for behind-the-scenes programmes, books and videos of how a particular programme was made.
- Create a production package for a new local news programme. Design your own ident and storyboard the opening titles. Try to take your own photographs for it with a conventional or digital camera. How can you convey a sense of authority, speed of newsgathering technology and appropriate scenes of the local area? Create or find an appropriate 10–30-second piece of music. If you have access to a video camera, now shoot and record your opening titles on video.

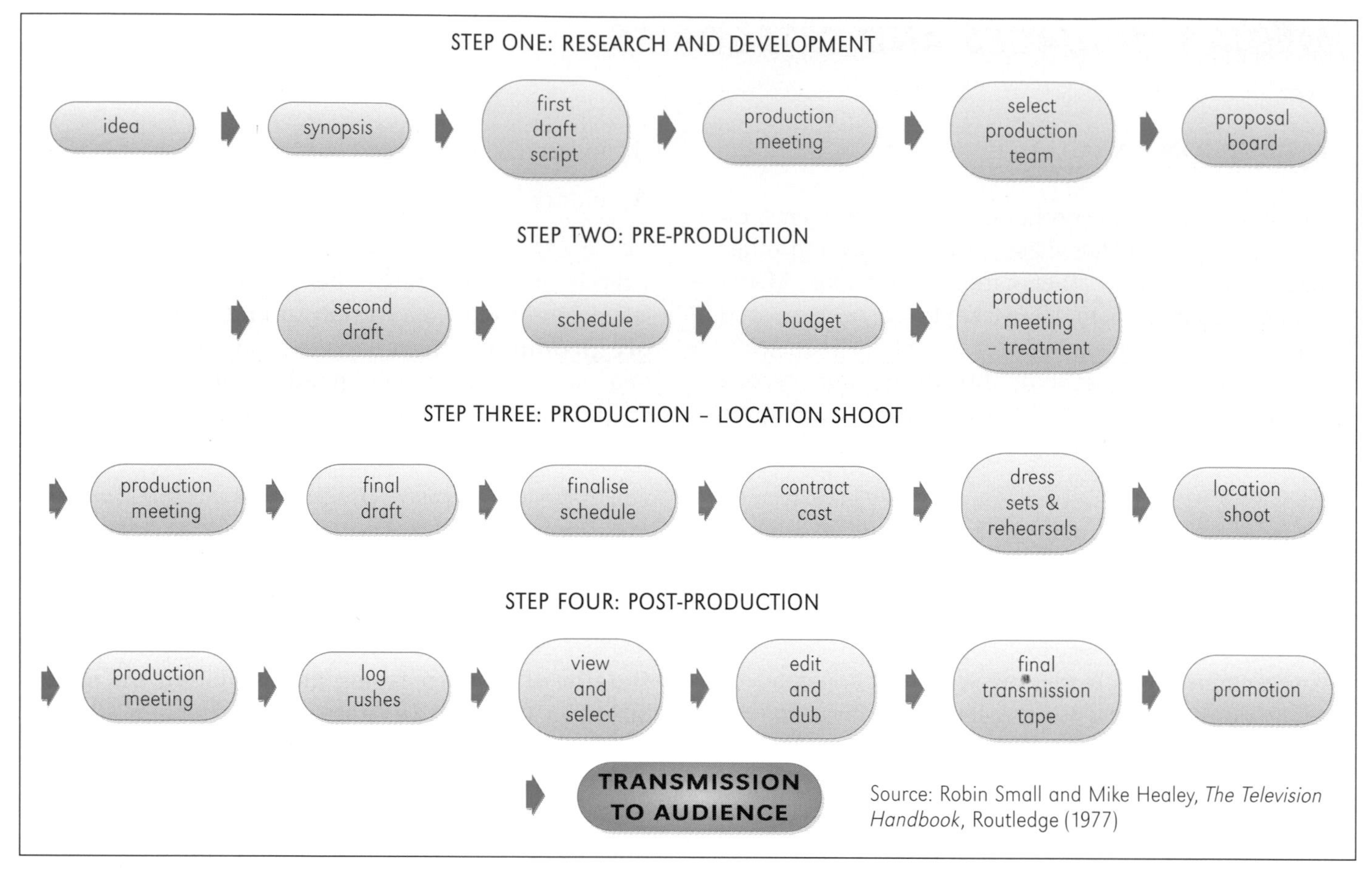

The four stages of television production

help us to decide whether we want to watch something or not. It helps producers and broadcasters to decide which programmes to make, how to make them (using which codes and conventions) and when and where to show them. Most television genres originally came from either books, films, theatre or music hall entertainment.

- *Look at the opening titles of a programme – what clues are there to its genre?*
- *How typical is your chosen programme of its genre? Or how and why is it atypical?*

A **generic hybrid** is a combination of more than one genre. They can be more interesting for audiences and they are beneficial for producers as they can aim their programmes at more than one kind of audience. For example, *Ready, Steady, Cook* is a cookery programme and a game show.

Codes and conventions

A **code** is a sign, or system of signs, such as dress, speech or music, that make sense when arranged by a set of rules, or **conventions**, e.g. by **narratives** (structured storylines) or **themes** (controlling ideas). You will find that even if not all soap operas, sit-coms, news programmes or crime dramas appear to be the same, they share features.

Codes and conventions help us to find our way around a text. When we watch a programme or film, or read a book, we may recognise some features which provide us with the **pleasure** of familiarity. We may sometimes **predict** what happens next, which also causes pleasure, especially if we are right.

ACTIVITY 15

- Use the checklist opposite to identify the codes and conventions of different television genres.
- Research the history of television genres – you'll find that many have been adapted from American television formats from the 1950s and 1960s.

Sometimes we might be surprised by something we did not expect; writers call this **violation of expectation**. This may be enjoyable, because our television viewing pleasure is often poised between enjoying what is familiar and what is new, or unexpected. This delicate balance between prediction and surprise is very important as producers need to prevent one particular response in an audience: boredom. Our boredom may result in the very thing broadcasters dread: we may change channels.

A genre is like a recipe or formula that most programmes tend to follow, or even delight in departing from sometimes. When you are trying to identify a programme's genre, whether fiction or non fiction, you need to look closely at the following 'ingredients' of a programme, the codes and conventions it typically uses. The soap opera genre has been used as an example:

Generic codes and conventions	*Sample genre: Soap opera*
Character types – major and minor	• Individuals – the main characters who are more 3D than the others • Stereotypes – villains, domestic archetypes (mothers, 'good' wives), sexually attractive (dangerous) women, authority figures (police, clergy etc) – sometimes played against type to become an individual character • Minor characters – the chorus
Casting choices	• Family favourites, from comedy or light entertainment • Young new talent
Performance or presentation style	Depending on the type of soap opera or character: • Realistic, natural, low-key styles *or* • Heightened, exaggerated performances, almost like pantomime
Mise-en-scène – setting, props, extras, lighting etc	• The recreation of realistic settings and locations, lighting and weather, attention to detail in costume, make-up and props • Key communal settings for dialogue to take place (a café, pub, club, shop, home)
Camerawork and editing	• Camerawork that does not usually draw attention to itself, some dramatic devices occasionally used, such as hand-held, crane shots and slow motion • Editing that is discreet, establishing shots, reverse shots and close-ups
Music	• Ambient music – on a car radio or someone's house • Background music – which is overlaid influencing the mood or effect of a scene (i.e. comic, romantic, tragic or sad)
Storyline or narrative	• Open-ended, continuous storylines that run all year • A hook at the start – dramatic irony, a revelation, a set-up etc • A cliff-hanger at the end
Themes	Two extremes: • Conflict – within or between families, between friends, lovers or enemies, motivated by class, crime, betrayal etc • Unity – within communities and families

These are the main genres appearing on television:

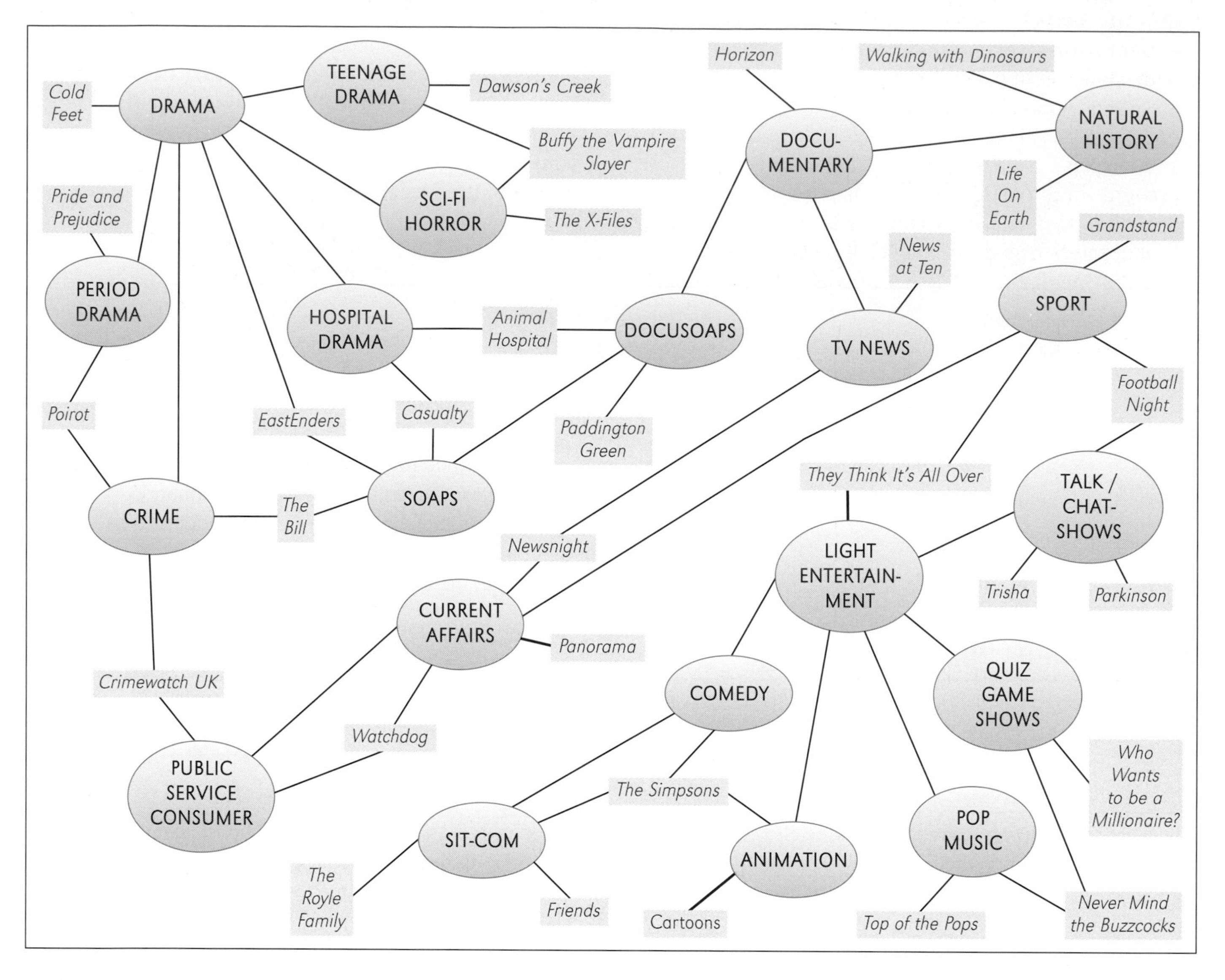

Television genres and hybrids

ACTIVITY 16

- Search the schedules and make a list of programmes under each genre.
- Are there any that are difficult to place? Why?
- Can you identify different combinations of genre hybrids?
- Choose one or more programmes and consider what pleasures they offer to the audience.

SUMMARY

- British television has changed from one company, the BBC, to many companies and its expansion will continue in the twenty-first century.
- Television is a **democratic medium** – it is available to, and affordable by, most people in Britain.
- Television has a major part to play in how we view the world, and indeed, how powerful decisions are made.
- Television is an important aspect of our daily life, playing a part in our memories of historical moments and shared viewing experiences.
- Television is a fiercely competitive and profitable business, in which successful companies and individuals stand to make millions of pounds every year.
- Television can be studied by applying the three key concepts of Media Studies: **Media Languages and Categories**, **Media Producers and Audiences** and **Media Messages and Values**.
- **Media Languages and Categories**: Television texts can be deconstructed to identify how the languages of media texts create meaning, by recognising the use of codes and conventions and the categories to which they belong.
- **Media Producers and Audiences**: Television companies and programmes may be studied in detail to discover information about the processes used to construct media texts, the institutions that produce them and the audiences that consume them.
- **Media Messages and Values**: Television texts may be studied in detail to learn how social messages and values are constructed and the nature and effect of their meanings.

GLOSSARY

broadcasting / narrowcasting – communicating to mass or niche audiences

convergence – the coming together of several media via one, in this case, digital communication

digital – the conversion of sound and visual information into digits for transmission via decoders

director – the person principally responsible for decisions on how to shoot the script and how to direct the actors / presenters

editor – the person(s) responsible for the post-production of a programme

post-production – the editing of sound or vision of a programme, including the addition of graphics, titles, special effects and extra sound, such as music, to make a finished programme

pre-production – developing and planning a programme

producer – the person(s) responsible for the financing of a programme

production – recording a programme on film or video

public service broadcasting – the production of programmes for entertainment, education and information, principally for the sake of public service, rather than to serve commercial interests

ratings – measurements of how many people are watching a programme

regulation – checking that no company departs from agreed procedures or codes of practice for television programmes and advertising

revenue – income raised from sales of advertising airtime or programmes

scheduling – deciding the day and time to show a programme

terrestrial – land-based transmission of radio and television

3 Newspapers

EILEEN LEWIS

Coming up

In this chapter we will be looking at:

- the history of newspapers
- different types of newspapers
- news photographs
- who produces the newspapers
- who reads the newspapers
- how news is selected
- what newspapers tell us about the world

INTRODUCTION

Newspaper sales in Britain are falling. Daily sales of the major UK newspapers fell from 15 million in 1988 to about 13.5 million in early 2001 – a drop of nearly 10 per cent.

Those who own and produce newspapers worry that this decline will continue. As part of their struggle to survive, newspapers have got bigger, with supplements on sport, lifestyle, media, fashion and business. In the twenty-first century competition will increase from the Internet and the growing number of television channels, local radio stations and free newspapers.

However, in a recent survey, 34 per cent of those questioned agreed very strongly that they would miss their daily newspaper if forced to do without one. Newspapers are portable and can be read anywhere. They have played an important role in our lives in Britain for over 300 years.

ACTIVITY 1

- Find out which sources of news 10 people among your friends, family and teachers prefer.
- Why do they read certain newspapers or certain sections of newspapers?
- Do they ever buy a newspaper for the free gift or competition it offers?
- Would they miss newspapers if they disappeared?
- When you have completed this survey, compare your findings with those of others in your class. See how many findings you have in common. What do they tell you about newspaper reading habits?

Britain's major daily newspapers

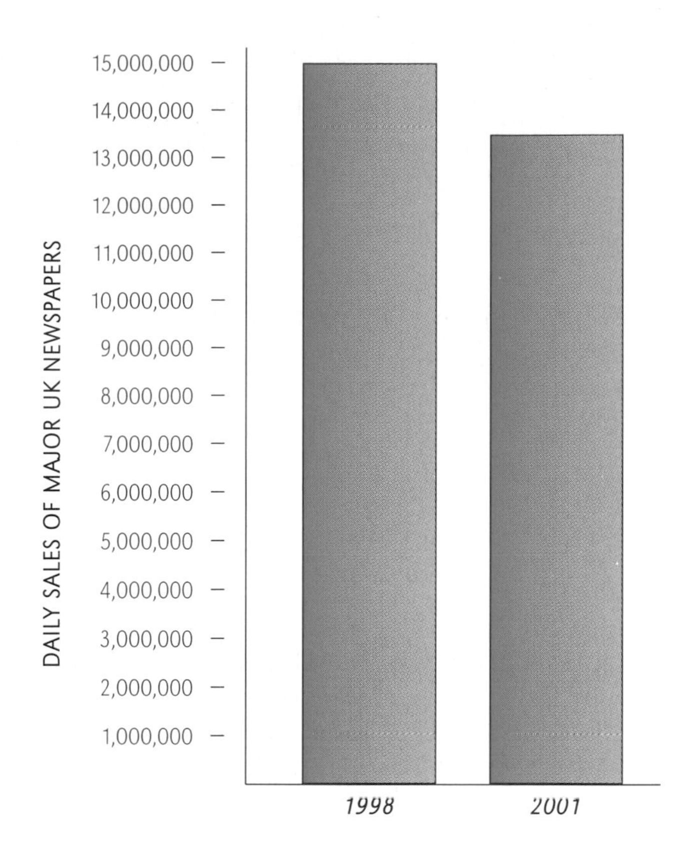

Daily newspaper sales have fallen by nearly 10 per cent since 1988

THE HISTORY OF NEWSPAPERS

The Chinese produced the world's first newspapers for those with wealth and power in the eighth century. In Europe, most news was carried by word of mouth, through travelling minstrels, players, messengers and town criers, until the eighteenth century.

CONTROLLING THE NEWS

In 1474, William Caxton set up the first English printing press. However, books and printed texts were for the ruling classes and clergy only. It was in the interests of the ruling classes to control the printing presses in order to prevent the lower classes gaining knowledge which might make them dissatisfied. The lower classes were further controlled by the fact that they were not taught to read or write.

Weekly news **pamphlets** – unbound news sheets sympathising with one side or the other – began to be produced during the English Civil War (1642–49), which overthrew King Charles I. The anti-royalist Long Parliament tried to control what was published through the licensing of all printing presses in 1644.

The poet John Milton, a great believer in individual freedom, wrote the first defence of the freedom of the press, attacking government control of the presses in a speech to Parliament the same year. The principle of the **free press** – acceptance that our newspapers will be biased (see page 98) – is still strongly defended by journalists today.

- *Does the public always have a right to know or should the government in certain circumstances restrict what may be published?*

Oliver Cromwell became the focus of attempts to rid the country of the autocratic King. He accused the King of waging war against Parliament and the people, and assembled a special court which sentenced the King to death.

Despite Cromwell's efforts to suppress them, accounts of the execution of Charles I in 1649 were published and sold all over the country. These accounts were **biased** – they were either strongly in support of Charles I or against him.

ACTIVITY 2

Write a brief modern newspaper article on the death of Charles I, using the information below. Make your article EITHER strongly biased in favour of Charles I OR against him.

The execution of Charles I

Charles I was tried by his political enemies, led by Oliver Cromwell, as a 'Tyrant, Traitor and Murderer, and a public enemy to the Commonwealth of England'. He was sentenced to death. The execution took place on 30 January 1649.

Charles wore two shirts so that he would not shiver and be thought afraid. His hair and beard were grey from months of captivity. His spaniel, Rogue, tried to follow him as he walked across St James's Park, but was sent back.

At two o'clock he walked out of the Banqueting Hall at Whitehall on to the black scaffold where two masked executioners stood. The scaffold was surrounded by soldiers, some on horseback, in case the waiting crowd tried to intervene.

Charles protested his innocence, calling himself 'the Martyr of the people', and forgiving his enemies. He gave a jewel to Bishop Juxon, saying, 'Remember.' The executioner cut Charles's head from his body in one blow and held the head up, crying: 'Behold the head of a traitor!' The crowd was quickly cleared from the street by the soldiers.

The Execution of Charles I, an etching by Jan Luyken

FREEDOM OR CONTROL?

In 1702 the *Daily Courant* (from the French phrase *au courant* – up to date) became the first daily newspaper. The struggle to control the press – and with it public opinion – continued. The Government introduced Stamp Duty in 1712, a tax which meant that only the wealthy could publish newspapers. Reporting on Parliament was illegal, but newspapers continued to publish these reports.

BIRTH OF THE TIMES

Britain's longest surviving newspaper, *The Times* (founded in 1785 as the *Daily Universal Register*) first appeared under its new name in 1788. The choice of name showed editor John Walter's determination to provide a *reflection* of 'the times' he lived in. It mainly

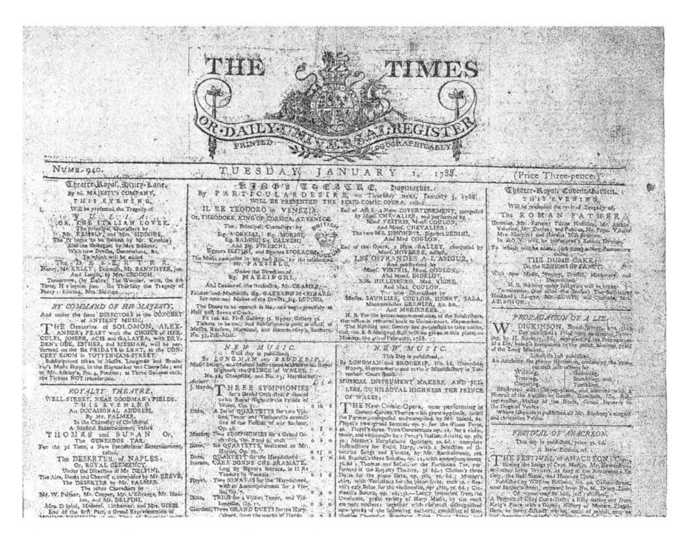
THE TIMES

OR DAILY UNIVERSAL REGISTER

NUMB. 940. TUESDAY, JANUARY 1, 1788. (Price Three-pence.)

The Times first appeared in 1788

carried foreign news, parliamentary reports and advertising for books, theatre shows etc and was paid by the Government to publish information favourable to the party of King George III.

However, the deal backfired in 1789 when Walter was sent to Newgate prison for 16 months for publishing gossip about George III's sons. Like the tabloid editors of today, Walter had tried to use **scandal** to make *The Times* more popular. Three days after Walter's **libel** trial started, the French Revolution began, marking a return to serious news reporting.

> **scandal** – gossip or rumour, spoken or published
> **libel** – illegal, published defamation of character or reputation

THE UNDERGROUND AND RADICAL PRESS

In 1802 the fight for press freedom entered a new phase with William Cobbett's *Political Register* and *Twopenny Trash*. These were **radical** (anti-Establishment) newspapers, for the working classes who had no vote. These papers carried revolutionary ideas, arguing for the need for a free press. They were seen as threatening by those in government, who often tried to close them down. Some newspapers avoided paying Stamp Duty and went '**underground**' (operated in a secret, illegal fashion).

- *Do you think there is an 'underground' press in Britain today?*

THE PETERLOO MASSACRE

In 1819 a peaceful trade union meeting in Manchester was broken up by mounted police who killed or wounded more than 400 people. This terrible event was reported not only by the radical papers but also by *The Times*, where an eyewitness report damaged the reputation of the Government. This resulted in the Government tightening the laws on libel and increasing taxes on newspapers. This made newspapers very expensive, but people still managed to read them by sharing them.

GROWTH OF THE POPULAR PRESS

In the second half of the nineteenth century, many more people learned to read. The invention of the steam-driven press and the abolition of Stamp Duty made it cheaper to produce newspapers. Many more newspapers appeared, featuring crime, sport and fashion, appealing to a popular audience. '**Human interest**' stories (covering **newsworthy** events in famous and ordinary people's lives) became common. Many of today's **news values** – criteria used to decide which stories and photographs are worth using (see page 89) – can be traced back to this period.

BIG BUSINESS BARONS

As the industry grew larger and sales of newspapers increased, so it attracted more **advertising**. Advertising revenue made newspapers more viable financially than the **cover price** alone could (see page 103). This meant that businesses found it profitable to invest in newspapers.

By 1937 four peers, Lord Beaverbrook, Lord Rothermere, Lord Camrose and Lord Kemsley, owned more than half the national and local daily papers and one third of the Sunday papers. They came to be known as the **press barons** – leaders of business who had a stake in important news outlets as well. Rupert Murdoch is their modern equivalent.

This **concentration of ownership** (many newspapers owned by very few people) continues to increase at the beginning of the twenty-first century.

COMPETITION FROM RADIO AND TELEVISION

Once radio began broadcasting in the 1920s and television in 1936, newspapers had to face competition. Radio was much faster at **newsgathering** than newspapers. At first, there was concern that people would no longer buy morning newspapers if they could hear radio news bulletins the previous evening.

Radio became the main source of news during the Second World War (1939–45), when print was rationed. After the war, newspapers coped with the competition from radio and television by offering a more detailed presentation of news, with more in-depth analysis. Newspapers (see *The Guardian* below) also took the lead in stories of scandal and corruption, partly because newspapers were (and still are) less tightly controlled by the law than broadcasters.

Pinter
His life and work

Whose sperm is it anyway?

With 22 pages of jobs
Education
Universities: one cash crisis too many

45p

The Guardian

Disgraced former minister and lobbyist abandon £10m case at last minute

A liar and a cheat

New evidence halts MP's libel suit

Comment
A pattern of corruption and deceit

Questions for cash. . .

Inside: 5 | 12 | 19 | 26

The Guardian (1 October 1996) denounces MP Neil Hamilton following the 'cash for questions' scandal.

WAPPING POST

A TIDAL WAVE OF SUPPORT FOR STRUGGLE

SATURDAY 24th JANUARY 1987 PRICE 25p

Mikes message

I SEND this special message to all readers of the Wapping Post. My appeals against conviction and sentence have been turned down in the Court of Criminal Appeal.

In giving judgement Lord Chief Justice Caulfield referred to "the notorious Wapping dispute". That remark betrayed the *real* outlook of Judges.

They are part of the Tory State and can be relied on by all the Murdochs of this world to deliver verdicts which favour the bosses against the working class.

Now that the appeal is over I am reinforced in my view that the judgements of my fellow workers are the true voice of justice and democracy.

I would rely on the common sense of any one of the ordinary workers in the Wapping dispute, who have stood by their principles, rather than the mumbo jumbo of a thousand Judges.

Just think about it. The highest in the land have been conned into believing that the police at Wapping do not wear watches and have no way of giving accurate timings of events.

If the police can't tell the time why did the inspector say that my alleged offence was at 9 o'clock. If there was a problem why didn't he use his radio communicator to report the alleged assault. The report would have been timed and logged?

No. The police were caught out in a fit up and the Judges have covered it up for them.

Why is it that an internationally known millionaire-class snooker star is fined £200 for head-butting a man yet I am sentenced to 12 months?

And how is it that the courts do not jail the vice-chairman of the Tory party for being three times over the legal alcohol limit whilst driving?

Readers of the Wapping Post will know what conclusions to draw. The decision of the Court in my case is intended as a punishment and a warning to all who have the guts to challenge Murdoch and his like. So don't give up!

I thank you for all your support. I am in good spirits partly because of your splendid letters. It is essential for the TUC to fight wholeheartedly for the printers. Our campaign for jobs is not narrow or selfish. It is for every worker.

There is no time for moaning and whining. Get stuck in as I know you will. Only by lifting the struggle can we win and I am confident this will be done.

See you when I'm released, hopefully on February 23.

Until then heads up — defeat is no part of our language.

Yours in solidarity

B 82649 Michael Hicks

UNITED WE ALL STAND

Those who stood back and watched will look back in shame when they remember 1986

AFTER 12 long, bitter months of struggle once again thousands of supporters march on Fortress Wapping to demonstrate their solidarity with the sacked printworkers. Despite the hardships, tragedies and jail sentences — and the virtual media blackout imposed on the dispute, a tidal wave of encouragement and declarations of support has flooded in this week to reaffirm that the vast majority of the labour movement and other members of the general public are solidly behind us in the fight to claim trade union rights and to work.

One trade union President told the Wapping Post that in the opinion of his members the printworkers had now become the spearhead of the workers battle against the pernicious ambitions and objectives of Thatcherism and the multi-nationals.

Courage

This week has seen the dispute open a window on the world. Television viewers in Russia, Poland, Germany, France, Australia and America have all seen for themselves the courage and determination which has been so evident throughout the year.

Oppression

They have seen, too, that we have political prisoners here. A fact which our own media steadfastly ignore whilst pointing accusing fingers at political oppression of workers in other countries.

Nearer home there is increasing evidence that more people in the UK are becoming concerned at the ruthless activities of Murdoch and the injustice with which the sacked printworkers are being punished by the State.

Threat

The reiterated threat by the EETPU scab in chief Hammond on TV this week that he would leave the TUC if he didn't get his way must have convinced any doubters that he is using our organisation purely for his own ends and his strike-breaking members.

There have been many victories along the hard road we have all travelled over the past months. The repeated rejection of Murdochs contemptuous offers by the sacked printworkers has evoked admiration throughout the labour movement.

First Anniversary Issue

It has also bewildered most sectors of the media. One TV producer asked the Wapping Post why the offers had been turned down. We told him to come down to Wapping and ask the pickets. It was only after he did so that he was convinced that we were not going to go away.

The successful lobby of Congress started a chain of events which has not yet run its course. The crimes against all workers that Hammond has perpetrated will be punished in the long term.

Salute

We have lost comrades along the way it would be invidious to single out any one here. We salute them all.

Murdoch said on radio yesterday that the scabs were now settled in and working well. Readers of the Wapping Post know otherwise.

For 365 days, 24 hours each day they have had to face our picket. Each day to them is another crisis of conscience. Many have given up and discovered that it really is better to be a picket than a scab.

Those who have stood by whilst their comrades and their families were brutally beaten up by Thatcher's riot police on May 3 and many other occasions and who have watched whilst Congress decisions have been wilfully flouted will look back on 1986 with shame.

Frighten

The jailing of 4 sacked printworkers is now widely seen as an attempt by the authorities to frighten and discourage trade unionists from demonstrating for their democratic rights. That, and the behaviour of the police at Wapping and elsewhere has raised issues and questions which must be resolved now before they become accepted as established practice and all the trade union rights, fought for and won over a century are swept away.

In solidarity lies strength. Peaceful demonstration is a cherished right in Britain and it must not be removed by allowing the thuggish activities of a capitalist like Murdoch to prevail. March on to victory in 1987.

In this issue

- Tony Benn
- Fired From Afar
- May 3 – What it Meant
- Search – the facts
- Why we must win
- Women of Wapping

WE ARE NOT GOING AWAY WE ARE NOT GOING AWAY

Wapping News – a weekly newspaper published by the unions during the printworkers' strike, 1986–7

COMPUTER TECHNOLOGY

As newspapers became cheaper to produce because of computer technology, printworkers took industrial action to try to safeguard their jobs. In 1986 *The Times* proprietor Rupert Murdoch took the opportunity to dismiss the printworkers when he moved all of his newspapers from Fleet Street (where most newspapers had been based for 200 years) to Wapping in London's Docklands.

A year-long dispute followed, marked by violent clashes between pickets (lines of union officials and members trying to stop people going to work and 'breaking' the strike) and police. The printworkers were defeated and other newspapers moved to Wapping.

THE FUTURE

Perhaps surprisingly, computer technology has not so far led to an opening up of the newspaper market. Six national newspapers have been launched since the Wapping dispute, but the only serious daily newspaper to survive is *The Independent*. *Sunday Business* was launched in February 1998, but has the lowest circulation of all the Sunday newspapers.

Newspapers have responded to competition from the Internet and the growing number of television and radio channels by setting up their own web sites and putting their newspapers online. This means they can offer readers a constantly updated and interactive service, which is closer to live broadcasts. But despite these changes, with the cost of newsprint likely to rise and the possibility that income from advertising will go down, all newspapers face a difficult time in the future.

CROSS-MEDIA OWNERSHIP

The business corporations that own our newspapers have interests in many other media, such as radio, television, film, cable and publishing. This **cross-media ownership** means that if one part of the business is not doing well, other parts of the business will help it to get through that period.

Rupert Murdoch can afford to price *The Times* at 10p for a limited period, because of his ownership of:

- *The Sun*
- *The Sunday Times*
- *News of the World*
- *The Times* and its supplements
- 36.7% of BSkyB satellite TV
- global media interests, including hundreds of newspapers, a number of magazines, television stations, publishing interests and Twentieth Century Fox Film Corporation

ACTIVITY 3

In groups, decide whether you agree or disagree with the following statements:

- It doesn't matter that control is concentrated in the hands of a few owners; we can make up our own minds about the news.
- I don't like having so much of the media controlled by a small number of owners.
- We need to have as wide a range of views as possible.

KEY DATES

- **868** First printed book in China
- **1474** Caxton sets up first English printing press
- **1649** Cromwell tries to suppress all coverage of the death of Charles I
- **1702** *Daily Courant*, first daily newspaper, launched
- **1785** *Daily Universal Register*
- **1788** *The Times* (originally *Daily Universal Register*)
- **1791** *The Observer*
- **1817** *The Scotsman*
- **1821** *The Manchester Guardian* (later *The Guardian*)
- **1822** *The Sunday Times*
- **1827** *The Standard* (later *Evening Standard*)
- **1843** *News of the World*
- **1855** *The Daily Telegraph*
- **1881** *The People*
- **1888** *The Financial Times*
- **1896** *The Daily Mail*
- **1900** *The Daily Express & Morning Herald*
- **1903** *The Daily Mirror*
- **1915** *Sunday Pictorial* (later *Sunday Mirror*)
- **1918** *The Sunday Express*
- **1961** *The Sunday Telegraph*
- **1962** *The Sunday Times* magazine
- **1969** Rupert Murdoch's News International acquires *The Sun* (previously *Daily Herald*) and The *News of the World. The Sun* becomes tabloid
- **1971** *Daily Mail* becomes tabloid
- **1978** *Daily Star*
- **1981** Murdoch acquires *The Times* and *The Sunday Times*
- **1986** Murdoch moves all his national newspapers to Wapping
  The Independent
- **1990** *The Independent on Sunday*
- **1998** *Sunday Business*

MEDIA LANGUAGES AND CATEGORIES

CATEGORIES OF NEWSPAPERS

According to their size, newspapers can be roughly divided into two different types or **categories**: **broadsheets** and **tabloids**. Broadsheets – literally, 'wide' pages – measure approximately 60 x 37 cm while tabloids – 'tablet-like' pages – are approximately 30 x 37 cm.

- *Analyse these newspapers' names and discuss in groups why they are called what they are. What image does each name represent?*

The Guardian

The Sunday Telegraph

The Observer

DAILY EXPRESS

Tabloids

Some would argue that we can divide national newspapers further – into three categories – by distinguishing between the mid-market tabloids the *Daily Express* and *Daily Mail* and the 'red-top' tabloids *The Sun*, *The Mirror* and the *Daily Star*, so called because of the red background to their **masthead**, or title. However, these distinctions are becoming increasingly blurred, as the most popular titles move up-market to capture an increasingly middle-class readership and the mid-market papers use down-market ploys to attract more readers (see page 102).

Other differences

We can identify other differences between categories of newspapers by looking at the content, price, layout, use of photographs, design, vocabulary and news values. In order to attract their target audiences newspapers create their own identity through their **mode of address** – the way they 'speak' to their readers (see Headline language on page 90).

> "Typography is an instant message."

> "Typefaces are the clothes words wear."

A–Z of Typography, Channel 4

One of the ways in which newspapers 'speak' is through **typography** – the kind of typeface they use.

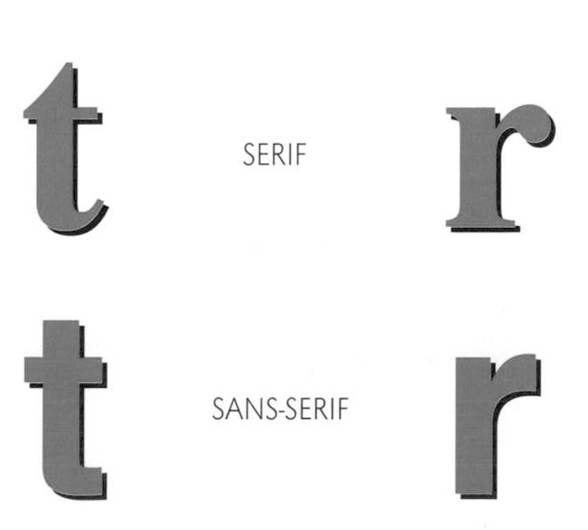

Subeditors can use CAPITAL LETTERS, *italic*, **bold type** or underline to emphasise certain words. The broadsheets and the mid-market tabloids tend to use a more traditional typeface then the red-top tabloids, using **serifs** – a bar across the arms of the character. *The Mirror* and *The Sun* deliberately use a simpler, more modern typeface without serifs – a **sans-serif** typeface. This has a big effect on the overall look of the paper and is part of the mode of address.

ACTIVITY 4

In pairs, look carefully at the mastheads on this page.

What impressions of the newspaper are conveyed by the following:

- the title
- the typeface
- the **logo** or symbol, if there is one
- the price
- the strip underneath or above the masthead, called the **puff** or the **teaser**
- any other information?

How does each newspaper try to attract and address its audience?

News values

> “News is what somebody, somewhere, wants to suppress. All the rest is advertising.”

Lord Northcliffe (1866–1922)

Perhaps more than anything else, **news values** are what set different papers apart. News values are the qualities which explain why photographs and events are selected as newsworthy. Johan Galtung and Mari Ruge (1965) were amongst the first theorists on the media to define news values. The following list is adapted from their work. Use it whenever you are analysing news stories.

News values

1. **Immediacy** – Has it happened recently? Is it new?
2. **Familiarity** – Does it mean something to us in Britain? Do we relate to it?
3. **Amplitude** – Is it a big event? Does it involve many people?
4. **Frequency** – Is it something that happened fairly quickly?
5. **Unambiguity** – Is it clear? Are the results / effects obvious?
6. **Predictability** – Is it predictable? Do we expect it to happen?
7. **Surprise** – Is it a rare or unexpected event?
8. **Continuity** – Has it already been defined as news? Is it a **running story**?
9. **Élite nations and people** – Which country has the event happened in? Does it concern well-known people – stars, or the royal family?
10. **Personalisation** – Is it a personal or human interest story?
11. **Negativity** – Is it bad news?
12. **Balance** – Is it a home news story which has been used to balance coverage of foreign news?

ACTIVITY 5

Find out how easy it is to identify the differences between *The Independent* and *The Sun*. In pairs, look carefully at their front pages.

- Write down as many news values as you can find in the images and the headlines.
- Number them in order of importance for each newspaper.

THE Sun

BOOKS FOR SCHOOLS TOKEN IS ON PAGE 14

32p

SURF THE NET FREE

FREE ODEON CINEMA PASS

Blair: I WON'T send in ground troops

EXCLUSIVE

IN BED WITH POSH

TODAY The Sun gives you an exclusive peek inside Posh Spice and David Beckham's new home.

THREE PAGES OF EXCLUSIVE PICTURES INSIDE

- What differences and similarities are there between the two newspapers?
- What kinds of audience do you think these newspapers are aimed at?

THE AWARD-WINNING NEWSPAPER

THE INDEPENDENT

MANDELSON: THE FIRST INTERVIEW

PETER MANDELSON ANSWERS YOUR QUESTIONS

This atrocity is still a mystery to Nato. Perhaps I can help...

ROBERT FISK

When you stand at the site of a massacre, two things happen. First, you wonder about the depths of the human spirit. And then you ask yourself how many lies can be told about it. The highway of death between Prizren and Djakovica – on which the Serbs say Nato slaughtered 74 Kosovo Albanian refugees in a series of bombing raids – is no different.

Only hours after I slipped on a dead man's torso near an old Turkish bridge, less than a day after I stood by the body of a young and beautiful girl – her eyes gently staring at me between half-closed lids, the bottom half of her head bathed in blood – I watched James Shea, Nato's spokesman, trying to explain yesterday why Nato still didn't know what had happened on Wednesday.

GARNET POINT

THE LANGUAGE OF NEWSPAPERS

Headline language

The Guardian was one of the first newspapers to use puns in headlines. Headline writing was transformed further by Kelvin MacKenzie who was Editor of *The Sun* from 1981 to 1994. His style was highly influential: often crass and simplistic, but undoubtedly eyecatching, MacKenzie's puns and jokes helped to make *The Sun* the best-selling newspaper in Britain.

THE Sun

LES DAWSON WIFE DIES OF CANCER See Page 7

Wednesday, April 16, 1986 18p TODAY'S TV IS ON PAGE 14

THRILLED TO BLITZ!

Bombing Gaddafi was my greatest day says US airman

Gaddafi ... escape

By KIERON SAUNDERS

JUBILANT American bomber pilots were walking on air last night after the revenge mission aimed at wiping out Libya's "Mad Dog" Colonel Gaddafi.

One airman described the hit-and-run raid as the "greatest thrill of my life." But another crewman said he regretted the crazed dictator had escaped with his life and that "we didn't nail the bastard."

The raid early yesterday was spearheaded by 18 F-111 bombers based in Britain—backed by 15 jets from U.S. carriers in the Mediterranean.

The attack was ordered by President Reagan as a reprisal against outrages by Libyan bomb squads.

One airman, relaxing in a bar near his base at Mildenhall, Suffolk, said: "We were not told until the last minute we were taking part."

The fuel tanker flier added: "Gaddafi is a schizo. How else do you deal with a guy like him?"

Gaddafi's 15-month-old adopted daughter Hanna died in his Tripoli HQ, Libyan doctors claimed. His two youngest sons were also injured.

Reports early today put the death toll at about 100. Newsmen were shown 15 corpses at a civilian hospital.

Two F-111s failed to return from the strike.

A search was going last night for one lost in the Med. A second landed in Spain with engine trouble.

SUN NEWS SPECIAL See Pages 2,3,4,5 and 6

Mission accomplished ... smiling Americans at Lakenheath, Suffolk, yesterday after the raid

The Sun, 15 April 1985

Headlines have to be written to fit the space available. The tabloids have less space than the broadsheets, so if they wish to use a large typeface they tend to have much shorter headlines which use shorter words. Shorter words are also used for greater impact. Just before England football coach Glenn Hoddle was dismissed from his job in February 1999, *The Sun* chose to fill almost the whole of its front page with the single word: 'GO!'

Headline-writing techniques

Some common techniques used by headline writers:

- **Alliteration** – repetition of the same sound at the beginning of two or more words: 'BIRD-BRAINED BEEB BOOBS'
- **Assonance** – repetition of the same vowel sound in a phrase: 'SO ALONE'
- **Cliché** – phrase which has been so over-used it is almost meaningless: 'balanced on a knife edge' or 'walking on a tightrope'
- **Colloquialism** – conversational language: 'THE BOY DUN GOOD' is conversational and puns on the name of jockey Richard Dunwoody
- **Exclamation** – 'NO WAY JOSÉ!'
- **Hyperbole** – exaggeration. A slight problem or difficulty is described as something far worse: 'Nightmare search for good pub food'
- **Metaphors** – direct comparison between two unconnected people or things. Boxing metaphors are often used in disputes when one side 'throws in the towel' or is 'saved by the bell'. Metaphors can be misleading: 'DINNER LADIES TO GET CHOP'
- **Parody** – a slight change to a well-known phrase or song: 'Who do you think you are kidding, Mr Milosevic?', a *Mirror* headline run during the NATO bombardment of Yugoslavia, is a direct reference to the Second World War song 'Who do you think you are kidding, Mr Hitler?' This is in keeping with the overtly patriotic, or **jingoistic,** values of the newspaper and makes a direct link between Milosevic and Hitler
- **Personalisation** – use of first names and nicknames: 'VOTE FOR MAGGIE', 'CLOBBA SLOBBA'. Although these abbreviations are used to save space, they also narrow the gap readers and politicians or celebrities and often portray the person in the news in a negative way
- **Puns** – 'WHAT'S THE BIG IKEA?'
- **Repetition** – 'Spend, spend, spend'
- **Rhyme** – 'WE SPANK THEIR TANKS' and 'DEATH BY STEALTH' are headlines from *The Sun* and *The Mirror* in the same week, both referring to the NATO bombing of Yugoslavia

ACTIVITY 6

The following headlines relate to the release of the Bridgewater Three – three men who had been held in prison for 18 years for a crime they did not commit. See if you can guess which newspapers the headlines come from and try to identify the techniques used:

1 'For long lonely years we wept in despair...now we're free'

2 'Bridgewater Three walk free'

3 'Threedom'

Techniques

1 *The Guardian* uses a quotation from one of the freed men, Jim Robinson. This technique relies on authenticity and reinforces the tone of the article – which concentrates on the appalling miscarriage of justice which has taken place. The quotation uses **alliteration** (see above) in order to reinforce the injustice even further in the phrases: 'long lonely' and 'we wept'.

2 *The Daily Telegraph* also uses **rhyme** with the words free and Three. This is a departure from their more usual headlines which are longer, informative and serious in tone; in this case, perhaps the intention is to deliberately lighten the tone of the whole report and to demonstrate *The Daily Telegraph's* commitment to seeing justice done.

3 *The Mirror* uses the most common tabloid technique – **a pun** – with the word 'Threedom'. The pun relied on the fact that there had been a great deal of coverage of the case in the few months before the men's release and it was consistently referred to as the case of the Bridgewater Three. This is a common journalistic convention; any news story with more than one protagonist is referred to in this way. Two pigs which escaped from a lorry taking them to the abattoir in 1998 were referred to as the 'Tamworth Two'.

News language

The expressions below are commonly used by the press, particularly in tabloids. Most of them are short, to save space, but notice also how they can change the **tone** – the overall impression – of the report:

aid (*help*), axe (*reduce / dismiss*), bid (*attempt*), blast (*explosion*), blaze (*fire*), blitz (onslaught, *bombing*), boom (*sudden increase*), boost (*lift*), breakthrough (*development*), bug (*disease*), clash (*argument*), curb (*restrict*), dash (*rush*), deal (*agreement*), dice with death (*escape*), drive (*campaign*), facelift (*improvement*), given a green light (*permitted*), grilled (*questioned*), gutted (*upset*), heads will roll (*sackings*), horror, leak (*unofficial release of information*), loom (*approach*), minefield (*complicated situation*), mob (*group*), ordeal, plea (*request*), plummet (*sudden fall*), quit (*leave*), rap (*criticism*), red faces (*embarrassment*), saga (*a long-running story*), squeeze (*control, usually financial*), scenario (*situation*), slam (*criticise*), slap on (*price increase*), soar (*rise*), tragedy, trauma (*difficult experience*), vow (*declare*), walk free (*release*), watchdogs (*monitoring groups*), wed (*marry*), whitewash (*cover-up*), woo (*try to appeal to*).

Recognising tone

When you are analysing newspapers, ask yourself if the tone of the report is:

- sensationalist
- hyperbolic
- emotive
- patriotic
- sentimental
- ironic

Writing the story

Remember the five Ws:

“Who? What? Where? When? Why?”

Include the most important information in the first paragraph – usually one sentence of no more than 30 words. Give additional details in the following paragraphs, perhaps with a quotation in the fourth paragraph. Remember that if your article is cut, it will be cut from the bottom, so it has to contain all the important news at the start.

ACTIVITY 7

Use the headline-writing techniques and some of the words in the news language list to rewrite the following article for a red-top tabloid newspaper and to make the tone sensationalist rather than formal. Try to tell the story in no more than eight paragraphs with one or two sentences in each.

Alan Jepson: 'It's classic drama'

Student watches The Sweeney for his degree

A GRADUATE is studying for a masters degree by doing a thesis on the 1970s television police series The Sweeney.

Alan Jepson will watch all 53 episodes to produce his 20,000-word dissertation, entitled: Social Realism in The Sweeney.

He hopes it will earn him his Master of Arts degree in Television Studies on his postgraduate course at Aberystwyth University in mid-Wales. 'I am getting a lot of mixed reactions from people,' said the 24-year-old from Blackpool. 'A lot of the students are very cynical when they hear what I am studying. But The Sweeney is an important part of our popular culture.'

He was too young to see the series – starring John Thaw and Dennis Waterman as Flying Squad officers Jack Regan and George Carter – first-time round, but became hooked after watching repeats. It takes its title from Sweeney Todd, the rhyming slang name for the Flying Squad.

'It is classic TV drama,' said Mr Jepson, who previously gained a BA in Communications at the University of Lincolnshire and Humberside.

'A lot of people write it off as nostalgia, but that is unfair. Yes, they wore flared trousers and kipper ties and some of the terminology sounds a bit dated. But it was a ground-breaking show.

'It broke the mould of cosy police series like Z-Cars and Dixon of Dock Green.'

His thesis will cover areas such as Regan's 'abrasive' relationship with his mild-mannered boss Haskins and Regan's friendship with his younger protege Carter.

'Regan and Carter were really the Batman and Robin of TV police drama,' said Mr Jepson.

Daily Mail, 7 April 1999

The language of photographs

As you can see from looking at the front page of the first issue of *The Times*, 1 January 1788, on page 83, early newspapers contained large sections of type with tiny headlines and few or no illustrations.

Today all newspapers carry colour photographs on the front page. In the tabloid press, news photographs can stand as a story in their own right and can fill the whole of the front page. These changes have occurred partly because of advances in technology and the growth in popularity of television news, but mainly because of the increasing dominance of the visual image at the start of the twenty-first century – the **visual imperative**.

ACTIVITY 8

In pairs, look at these famous news photographs. Try to find out the answers to the following questions for each photograph (the date of each event has been included as a starting point for your research):

- Who is in the photograph?
- What is the event?
- Where did the event take place?
- What news values did the story hold – why was the event considered newsworthy? (You will find a list of news values on page 89.)

1

11 February 1990

2

29 September 1938

3

20 July 1969

4

22 January 1901

5

8 June 1972

6

5 June 1989

1

- Nelson Mandela and his then wife Winnie
- Mandela was released after the white South African government had imprisoned him for 27 years for campaigning against apartheid and racism
- Victor Verster prison, South Africa
- Amplitude, unambiguity, predictability, continuity, personalisation

2

- Neville Chamberlain, Prime Minister
- Chamberlain returned from a meeting with Hitler with a signed agreement that Germany and Britain would not go to war. He said: 'I believe it is peace for our time.....Go home and get a nice quiet sleep'
- Chamberlain waved the statement as he stepped off the plane from Germany
- Immediacy, familiarity, amplitude, continuity, élite

3

- Neil Armstrong
- 'Man takes first steps on the moon'. As he stepped on to the surface of the moon, Armstrong said: 'One small step for man: one giant leap for mankind'
- The Sea of Tranquillity on the moon
- Immediacy, amplitude, continuity, élite nations

4

- Queen Victoria
- 'The Empire Mourns Its Loss': the grief of every member of the Empire at the death of Queen Victoria
- Queen Victoria died at Osborne House on the Isle of Wight
- Immediacy, familiarity, amplitude, frequency, unambiguity, predictability, élite, negativity

5

- Nine-year-old Phan Thi Kim Phuc and other Vietnamese children
- The children were running from a napalm attack (a mistake by the South Vietnamese air force) on their village during the Vietnam War. Kim Phuc's clothes were burnt off her in the attack. The photo-journalist, Nick Ut, drove her and other injured villagers to hospital before he made sure the film was safely developed. Kim Phuc survived
- Vietnam
- Immediacy, amplitude, surprise, continuity, personalisation, negativity

6

- 19 year old student, Wang Weilin
- Wang defied a line of government tanks after the Chinese government had attacked unarmed pro-democracy demonstrators with machine guns
- Tiananmen Square, Peking
- Amplitude, surprise, continuity, personalisation

Ways of seeing

Photographs such as those in the Activity above offer us ways of interpreting – or seeing – the world. They can be highly influential in changing opinion. One of the best-known examples of this is Photograph 5 of the children fleeing a napalm attack during the Vietnam War, taken by photo-journalist Nick Ut. This became a symbol for the anti-Vietnam War movement which gradually gained strength in America and Europe from the end of the 1960s.

Early photo-journalists, like Matthew Brady in the American Civil War (1861–65), could photograph only the build-up and the aftermath of battles, because the equipment took so long to set up. As technology developed, photo-journalists like Robert Capa, famous for his pictures of the Spanish Civil War (1936–39), could take top-quality photographs of rapidly changing situations. In 1947, photo-journalists founded their own international agency, Magnum, with the objectives of high-quality photography, independence, objectivity and control.

During the Vietnam War photo-journalists like Nick Ut, Philip Jones Griffiths and Don McCullin were able to get quite close to the conflict. However, despite the fact that Don McCullin was highly respected for his pictures of hardship and war all over the world, he was refused permission to cover the Falklands War in 1982 in favour of less experienced photographers. This suggests that governments have become more aware of the negative effects of powerful images of misery and suffering on public relations.

The power of the photograph as a way of understanding the past is reinforced every time it is reproduced. The photograph can also take on new **connotations** in different contexts. Many of the photographs and documentary footage taken during the Second World War and the Vietnam War have been used by film-makers like Steven Spielberg in *Saving Private Ryan* (1999) and Oliver Stone in *Platoon* (1986) to create 'authentic' looking sequences. The continuing circulation of these images increases their symbolic importance.

Photographs as propaganda

However, we should remember that photographs are a highly **subjective** view of an event and that news photographs are carefully manipulated through camera angles, **framing**, lighting, **cropping**, **context**, and **anchorage** through the caption. This manipulation **positions** the audience to read the photograph in a particular way, or with a particular **bias** – they are encouraged to accept the **preferred reading**.

Dorothea Lange's photo *Migrant Mother*, 1936

anchorage – the way in which a picture editor uses a caption to 'fix' or limit the meaning of a photograph

bias – a particular slant or angle on a story which is favourable or unfavourable to certain people, places, events or issues

connotation – a critical term meaning additional / associative meanings and values in stories and images

context – the articles, advertisements, images which surround the photograph or news story

cropping – a newspaper term meaning to cut away part of a photograph to emphasise a particular aspect, create a particular meaning or fit a given space

denotation – the main message of a story or image

framing – a technical term meaning how the subject matter of the image is placed within the frame

polysemic – an image or text which carries several possible meanings

positioning – the way in which audience is placed in a position by the picture editor where they are likely to accept a 'preferred reading'

preferred reading – the interpretation that the producers of the text would prefer audiences to accept

propaganda – the careful construction of a photograph or news story to support or attack a person, group or cause

subjective – from a particular point of view

A famous example of manipulation is Dorothea Lange's *Migrant Mother*, taken in 1936 as part of the work of the American Farm Security Administration. This photograph of a mother with her three children, first published in the *San Francisco News*, came to symbolise the enduring courage of Americans caught up in the Depression of the 1930s. It was used by John Ford to help recreate the look for the film version of John Steinbeck's book *The Grapes of Wrath* (1940).

But it was later revealed that other members of the family (there were seven children) had been cropped out of the image so that the Farm Security Administration could represent the family in the most sympathetic light. The photograph had been carefully constructed in order to portray the kind of suffering and poverty with which people in other parts of America would sympathise. The photograph can therefore be termed propaganda, especially as the 32-year-old mother, Florence Thompson, felt that she had been exploited.

Layers of meaning

Photographs can also be **polysemic** – interpreted in different ways according to the caption and the context in which they are presented. Audiences will also interpret photographs according to their own values and may not accept the preferred reading.

ACTIVITY 9

Look at the photograph of a demonstration against the poll tax (1990). Write two different captions for the photograph:

1. a caption which sympathises strongly with the Conservative Government which introduced the poll tax and the police's attempts to deal with an angry crowd of demonstrators
2. a caption which sympathises strongly with the demonstrators who believed that the poll tax was an attack on individual freedom and civil liberties.

Crop the photograph if it helps you to convey your preferred reading.

MEDIA PRODUCERS AND AUDIENCES

WHO OWNS THE PRESS?

The following information on newspaper owners and editors was correct at August 2001:

News Corporation

News International

Owner: Rupert Murdoch

The Sun (Est. 1969) Editor: David Yelland

The News of the World (Est. 1843) Editor: Rebekah Wade

The Times (Est. 1785) Editor: Peter Stothard

The Sunday Times (Est. 1822) Editor: John Witherow

Other interests

All *The Times* supplements

BSkyB, Times Books, Harper Collins

TV Hits, Inside Soap, Sky

Shares in Pearson

Twentieth Century Fox

Star Asia

National and regional newspapers world-wide

Daily Mail and General Trust

Associated Newspapers Ltd

Owner: Fourth Viscount Rothermere

Daily Mail (Est. 1896) Editor: Paul Dacre

Mail on Sunday (Est. 1982) Editor: Peter Wright

London *Evening Standard* (Est. 1827) Editor: Max Hastings

Other interests

Northcliffe Newspapers

A stake in Westcountry TV, Teletext, Classic FM, Channel One cable, 13 local radio stations

Mirror Group Newspapers

Trinity

Chief Executive: Philip Graf

The Mirror (Est. 1903) Editor: Piers Morgan

Daily Record (Est. 1847) Editor: Peter Cox

Sunday Mirror (Est. 1915 as *Sunday Pictorial*) Editor: Colin Myler

The Sunday People (Est. 1881) Editor: Neil Wallis

Other interests

Share in Scottish TV

Share in Newspaper Publishing

Scott Trust

Guardian Media Group

Chair: Hugo Young

The Guardian (Est. 1821) Editor: Alan Rusbridger

The Observer (Est. 1791) Editor: Roger Alton

Other interests

Manchester Evening News

Some local newspapers

Shares in some TV and radio companies

The Scott Trust ensures that all profits from *The Guardian* go back into the business and that editorial independence is guaranteed

Northern & Shell

Express Newspapers

Owner: Richard Desmond

Daily Express (Est. 1900) Editor: Chris Williams

Sunday Express (Est. 1918) Editor: Martin Townsend

Daily Star (Est. 1978) Editor: Peter Hill

Other interests

Over 100 regional newspapers

14 Spanish newspapers

300 magazines including *Exchange and Mart*

Shares in the Press Association

30% Channel 5, Anglia TV, HTV, Meridian

Hollinger Inc

Owner: Conrad Black

The Daily Telegraph (Est. 1855) Editor: Charles Moore

Sunday Telegraph (Est. 1961) Editor: Dominic Lawson

Other interests

The Spectator (Est. 1711)

Newspapers in Canada, USA, Middle East, Australia

Pearson

Chief Executive: Marjorie Scardino

Financial Times (Est. 1888) Editor: Richard Lambert

Other interests

The Economist magazine

Longman, Ladybird, Pitman, Penguin, Puffin

Newspapers in France and Spain

Other publishing interests

Independent Newspapers

Owner: Tony O'Reilly

The Independent (Est. 1986) Editor: Simon Kelner

Independent on Sunday (Est. 1990)

Editor: Tristan Davies

Other interests

A range of Irish newspapers

WHO CONTROLS THE PRESS?

ACTIVITY 10

- In pairs, look at the chart on page 101 on circulation figures showing the circulation of the main daily and Sunday newspapers.
- Now look back at the names in *Who owns the press?* and work out who owns the best-selling newspapers.
- Name the three companies that control around three quarters of the national daily and Sunday circulation.

This is an example of increasing **monopolisation** – a small number of corporations controlling the entire newspaper market.

As we can see from the information in *Who owns the press?*, there are few truly independent newspapers. Most, including regional and local newspapers, belong to larger companies with many other media interests.

Control by owners

The tradition of a free press in Britain means that we accept the principle that our newspapers will be biased. Newspaper owners like Beaverbrook, Northcliffe and Maxwell all interfered in the day-to-day running of their newspapers, sometimes ordering editors to rewrite their editorials. They also gave (and some still give) large donations and written support through their newspapers to the political parties of their choice.

Robert Maxwell

Robert Maxwell, owner of *The Mirror* from 1984 to 1991, 'turned the paper into a family album', according to John Pilger in *Breaking The Mirror* (1997). Maxwell used the paper to publicise himself and to promote his business interests. He even had his own personal *Mirror* photographer, Mike Maloney, to photograph him with heads of state, celebrities and politicians.

"When Maxwell was at the Mirror I used to have a list on the wall of his friends - and they covered a wide section of British industry. Immediately a story came in about one of those people, I had to be completely on my guard."

Mirror columnist Paul Foot, quoted in Keeble, Richard, *The Newspapers Handbook* (Routledge, 1998)

When Maxwell drowned in November 1991 the front page of *The Mirror* declared him a hero: 'THE MAN WHO SAVED THE MIRROR'. Three weeks later it was discovered that he had stolen millions of pounds from *The Mirror* pension fund. The headline read: 'MILLIONS MISSING FROM MIRROR'. The fact that Maxwell had been able to keep this secret shows just how powerful newspaper owners can be.

REGIONAL AND LOCAL PRESS

Britain has a strong regional press. Three out of four adults regularly read a regional or local newspaper. Most daily regional newspapers are evening papers, like the London-based *Evening Standard* with sales of around 450,000. The best-selling regional is the Glasgow *Daily Record*, a morning paper with sales of around 715,000.

There are about 90 regional dailies, 10 Sundays and 430 weeklies. There are also about 950 freesheets, funded by income from advertising.

Increasing monopoly

The ownership of the regional press reflects that of the national press. After a number of changes in the ownership of regional newspapers in the mid-1990s, two newspaper companies: Northcliffe (owned by the

Local newspapers are normally produced for a town and its surrounding community

Regional newspapers are produced for large areas or cities

Daily Mail and General Trust) and Newsquest own more than 36% of all British regional newspapers.

This greater concentration of ownership in fewer hands worries some critics who argue that this limits the freedom of newspaper editors.

On a more positive note, increasing monopolisation means that national advertisers are more interested in using regional newspapers to advertise their products. The money from this advertising will help regional newspapers to thrive.

Why are the local and regional press thriving?

Unlike national newspaper sales, the circulation of regional newspapers is stable, while sales of local newspapers are going up. Roy Greenslade (*Media Guardian*, 15 March 1999) suggested that this was because:

- the emphasis is on providing local news
- local and regional newspapers have a more traditional look and are not sensationalist, so they appear more trustworthy
- they mix positive stories with negative, with the emphasis slightly more on the positive
- national newspapers are too remote and out of touch with their readers
- local and regional newspapers use the Internet to boost advertising

ACTIVITY 11

In groups, conduct a survey of readership of your own local newspapers. You can work out your questions using the points above and find out how far your community supports its local press.

HOW ARE NEWSPAPERS PRODUCED?

Who does what?

editor: writes **editorial** (the column voicing the newspaper's opinion on issues of the day); responsible for whole newspaper, including circulation and advertising

subeditor: writes headlines; corrects and restructures or **rejigs** copy; checks **house style** (guidelines on style and language to maintain consistency throughout the newspaper); checks for legal problems; works out layout of stories on computer

news editor: decides which stories to follow up and what angle to take on them; assigns stories to reporters and photographers

copytaster: makes first selections from press releases and other stories

foreign news editor: selects all foreign news stories

features editor: selects **soft news** – longer articles on less immediate stories and special series

reporters: write up and research stories they have been assigned

picture editor: controls the photographic team; selects, enlarges or crops photographs

photographers: take photographs required

designers: produce graphics for advertisements and features

Sources of news

Most news stories come from routine sources, such as **news agencies**, political parties, court cases, press conferences, the police, companies and charities. Many of these organisations will send press releases – usually a single sheet of A4 with the basic information on events or news, often with a quotation from a spokesperson.

Newspapers are rarely the first to distribute news: news is most often 'broken' on the Internet, on radio bulletins or on TV broadcasts.

News agencies – companies which sell their stories to news producers all over the world. Associated Press, Reuters and United Press International are the three main international news agencies, while the Press Association is the main British news agency. They have their own reporters, photographers and broadcast crews who pride themselves on speed and accuracy. The Press Association transmits on average 1,500 stories and 100 pictures every day.

WHO READS THE NEWSPAPERS?

The best-selling newspapers in Britain – those with the biggest **circulation** figures – are the red-top tabloids, with *The Sun* selling over 3.5 million papers a day and *The Mirror* selling almost 2.5 million a day.

However, as we can see from the chart below, sales for more than half the UK's major newspapers dropped between early 2000 and early 2001. Only the market for the *Financial Times* and *The Scotsman* showed appreciable growth.

	January 2001 (excluding bulks)	*January 2000 (excluding bulks)*	*% change*
DAILIES			
The Sun	3,624,563	3,555,661	1.94
The Mirror	2,113,705	2,241,730	-5.71
Daily Record	593,138	616,710	-3.82
Daily Star	637,826	593,753	7.42
Daily Mail	2,441,398	2,317,964	5.32
Daily Express	943,898	1,006,925	-6.26
The Daily Telegraph	975,890	997,550	-2.17
The Times	686,618	695,215	-1.24
Financial Times	458,292	417,880	9.67
The Guardian	400,708	397,458	0.82
The Independent	197,075	196,519	0.28
The Scotsman	87,879	74,733	17.59
SUNDAYS			
News of the World	4,024,011	4,137,813	-2.75
Sunday Mirror	1,801,843	1,980,041	-9.00
Sunday People	1,458,535	1,599,227	-8.80
Sunday Mail	696,576	739,488	-5.80
The Mail on Sunday	2,330,545	2,282,687	2.09
Sunday Express	841,873	926,493	-9.13
The Sunday Times	1,378,710	1,350,375	2.09
The Sunday Telegraph	763,889	791,789	-3.52
The Observer	410,262	402,428	1.94
The Independent on Sunday	215,229	218,989	-1.72
Scotland on Sunday	96,610	105,982	-8.84
Sunday Business	37,595	56,008	-32.88

National newspaper circulation (Source: Audit Bureau of Circulations, February 2001)

ACTIVITY 12

Why is the circulation of the national press falling?

In pairs, look at the following statements and decide which you agree with:

- It is a result of making profits the main concern of newspapers, rather than reporting the news
- *The Sun*'s coverage of television programmes and stars, its human interest stories, often with sexual content or 'sleaze', and its bingo competitions have been so successful that other newspapers have been forced to compete on the same terms
- It is a result of Murdoch's price war, begun in 1993, when Murdoch halved the price of *The Times* and doubled its circulation

The price war

All newspapers have been affected by Murdoch's price war. Some have been directly drawn into it.

- In 1993 Murdoch cut the price of *The Times* to 10p
- Since 1993 sales of *The Times* have nearly doubled to around 750,000
- Since 1993 sales of *The Independent* (price 45p) have fallen from nearly 400,000 to around 225,000
- In 1996 *The Guardian* offered *Independent* readers a week's free subscription to *The Guardian* and *The Observer*
- In September 1997 *The Independent* relaunched with a week of price-cutting to 20p
- In 1999 the Office of Fair Trading warned Murdoch that he would have to offer a detailed explanation before any more price cuts were allowed

BLURRING THE BOUNDARIES

Broadsheet or tabloid?

Clear-cut differences between categories of newspapers are disappearing. Stories are often broken by the tabloids and followed up by the broadsheets, sometimes in a style that looks more like that of a red-top tabloid than a broadsheet. Compare the reports about Catholic bishop Roderick Wright in *The Guardian* and *The Mirror*.

> " It's very dangerous if you get into the mindset that there are broadsheet subjects and tabloid subjects. What there has to be is unity of tone, and that's how you define broadsheet values. "
>
> Alan Rusbridger, Editor of *The Guardian*, 3 October 1996

- *What does Alan Rusbridger mean by 'unity of tone'?*

Some see this as a move away from serious reporting, while others would argue that it is a more humanised, people-centred approach. No one disputes that it sells more newspapers.

Changing class

Class boundaries were changing throughout the twentieth century.

Figures from the National Readership Survey show that there is a growth in the AB middle class grades and a larger growth in the C1 lower middle class. A decrease in the C2DE working classes helps to explain the falling sales of the red-top tabloids and the success of the *Daily Mail*, whose circulation has grown by almost 50% since 1992. Both *The Mirror* and *The Sun* are considering going 'up market' to attract new readers, but they will take care to keep their C2DE audience. For more details on **audience demographics** (profiling readers by social group, occupation etc.) see page 66 of Chapter 2 (Television).

DAILY Mirror
THE PAPER FOR WINNERS
Who won our £2,000 a week for 10 years
HONESTY, QUALITY, EXCELLENCE
Weeping mother's TV bombshell
I HAD SEX SCANDAL BISHOP'S LOVECHILD
FULL AMAZING STORY: Pages 2, 3, 4 &

Sport96
Friday Review
The Guardian
The bishop's secret son
Mother rocks Catholic church by revealing Bishop Wright has teenage boy
Maxwell goes free: so who did steal the £400m?
Inside

The strange genius of pop
Mark Lawson: why I chose sex over celibacy
The Guide
WEEKEND EDITION
The Guardian
Cardinal describes nightmare Catholics dreaded for years
Betrayed by the bishop
Yeltsin at risk in heart surgery
I.Q. of 145 and Can't Remember?
Murdoch fears writer's block means she will never write again
The new-look Saturday Guardian: five sections giving you everything you could want for your Saturday reading

DAILY Mirror
INSIDE TODAY
8 FREE £50,000 SCRATCH CARDS
HONESTY, QUALITY, EXCELLENCE
COMING NEXT WEEK
2 TICKETS FOR 1 AT ODEON
PLUS: 3 FREE GOES IN £10m MIRROR LOTTO SYNDICATES
NEW BISHOP SENSATION
RANDY ROD: TWO MORE LOVERS
Blair will defeat us – Norma
Mirror EXCLUSIVE
Woman, 73 dies after rape attack

Daily Mirror and *Guardian* front pages, 20 and 21 September 1996

Changing politics

Traditional political loyalties of newspapers have also blurred since 1997. It is increasingly difficult to place newspapers in categories according to their politics.

In 1992 *The Sun* clearly supported the Conservative party.

After the Conservative victory *The Sun* boasted 'IT WAS THE SUN WOT WON IT'. *The Guardian* and *The Mirror* were the only two newspapers to support Labour.

Yet in the 1997 General Election there was a huge change; this time few newspapers openly supported the Conservatives. Even the *Daily Mail*, traditionally a strong Conservative supporter, abstained.

In a surprising about-turn, *The Sun* openly supported Tony Blair and New Labour. Despite complaints, *The Sun* did not lose readers.

ACTIVITY 13

In groups, decide whether you agree or disagree with the following statements:

- Newspapers should stick to supporting one political party
- I don't think newspapers affect the way people vote in general elections
- I don't think that it's right for owners to put their business interests and profits before the interests of their readers

ADVERTISERS AND AUDIENCES

We cannot judge the success of a newspaper by its circulation figures alone. The money made by newspapers comes from the **cover price** – the price of the paper – and from the **advertising fees** – the money paid by businesses to promote their products.

Newspapers *need* advertisers; broadsheets, regional and local newspapers rely on advertising rather than sales for profit. Careful advertising to its target audience by the *Financial Times* helps to explain how the newspaper thrives while other papers with a bigger circulation struggle to survive.

THE Sun

PHOTO FINISH

Thursday, April 9, 1992 25p

TENNIS HERO ASHE HAS AIDS

Health

If Kinnock wins today will the last person to leave Britain please turn out the lights

ELECTION DAY SPECIAL

IT'S D-day folks – the day you make the big decision about who you want to run our great country.

You know our views on the subject but we don't want to influence you in your final judgment on who will be Prime Minister! But if it's a bald bloke with wispy red hair and two K's in his surname, we'll see you at the airport.

Goodnight and thank you for everything.

The Sun, 9 April 1992

THE Sun

MAY 1st

An historic announcement from Britain's No1 newspaper

Tuesday, March 18, 1997 28p THE PAPER OF THE PEOPLE

THE SUN BACKS BLAIR

Give change a chance

THIS is the election for the millennium.

The Sun, 18 March 1997

Newspapers are able to publish freesheets because they are financed by the advertising. Generally, the smaller the circulation of a newspaper, the more space is given to advertising.

When editors increase the number of supplements in their newspapers they are aiming to reach a wider audience for advertisers as much as trying to gain more readers for the newspaper.

We can learn about audiences from looking carefully at advertisements. Advertisers try to define the type of readership of newspapers by looking at age, gender and social group. However, as we have seen, changes in class and politics are making it more difficult to place readers in categories.

ACTIVITY 14

In groups, choose four daily newspapers.

- List the following:
  - any special offers to encourage readers to buy the newspaper
  - any advertisements on the front page and on three other pages of the newspaper
  - any competitions
- Look carefully at the items for sale, the prices quoted and the ways in which these items are sold. Try to identify the target audiences for your newspapers as closely as possible, thinking about age, gender and social class.
- How different are the target audiences for your chosen newspapers?

AUDIENCE EXPECTATIONS

This is another way of examining the differences between newspapers. The news values of different newspapers are directly linked to the expectations of their target audiences.

An article on the Budget in *The Guardian* might be 1,000 words long, while an article on the same subject in *The Sun* would run to no more than 500 words.

ACTIVITY 15

- In pairs, choose one tabloid and one broadsheet newspaper.
- Measure the space given to the written text, images and advertisements on the front page.
- Work out the word to picture ratio.

'Gatekeeping' – how is news selected?

Journalists decide in a number of ways whether items of news will be used or not. News conferences take place (sometimes as many as six in one day for the national newspapers), where journalists discuss **copy** – possible news stories. They draw up the **news list** – the stories they intend to cover.

Galtung and Ruge (see page 88) referred to these decisions as **gatekeeping** – the process by which certain stories are selected and others rejected. All those involved in producing the news act as **gatekeepers**. Their decisions will depend to an extent on the news values on page 89, the priority they give to those news values and the expectations of their readers.

News values and audience

The photograph of the murder suspects coming out of the 1998 inquiry into Stephen Lawrence's murder was seen as having high news value by journalists as it was the first photograph of the five suspects which had not been carefully posed.

The photograph was published in most of the daily newspapers, with headlines like: 'The Mask Slips'.

But the photograph did not make the front page of *The Times*. It was displaced to an inside page by the photograph of David Beckham receiving a red card during the 1998 World Cup quarter-final.

- *What does this tell you about news values?*
- *How does this decision relate to the expectations and interests of the audience?*
- *Do you think this was the right decision?*

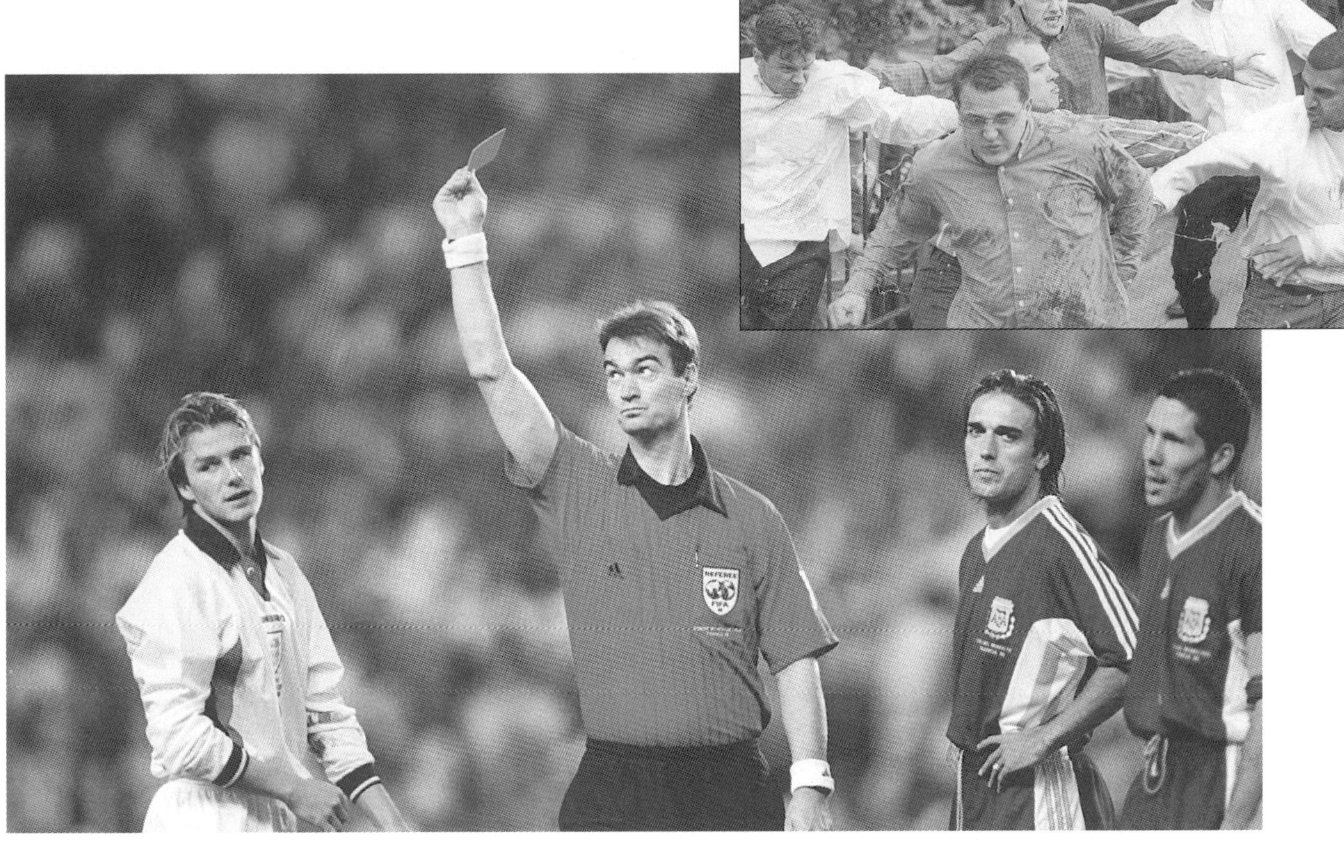

David Beckham's offence upstages the Stephen Lawrence murder suspects (*The Times*, 1 July 1998)

ACTIVITY 16

Working in groups, choose to be EITHER tabloid OR broadsheet journalists.

- Look at the following 12 news stories. Choose EIGHT of the stories for the news list for your newspaper.
- Put your news stories in order of importance, according to the news values of your newspaper and the expectations of your readers.
- Identify your front-page stories.
- Write headlines for your front-page stories.
- Explain your choices to the rest of the class.

News stories

1. Tourists report sighting of Loch Ness Monster
2. Scientific report proves that genetically modified food is dangerous
3. Indonesia invades East Timor
4. Search continues for kidnapped toddler
5. Anniversary of nail bomb attack in Soho
6. Senior citizens who robbed bank with toy pistol go on trial
7. Henry, the Prime Minister's cat, goes missing again
8. Soap star dies suddenly
9. 'Air Rage' drunken airline passenger jailed for three years
10. European Court refuses to ban Orange Day parade in Belfast
11. Fighting continues between India and Pakistan on Kashmir frontier
12. Madonna starts World Tour

MEDIA MESSAGES AND VALUES

BIAS

bias – a particular slant or angle on a story which is favourable or unfavourable to certain people, places, events or issues.

We looked at **bias** when we saw how the execution of Charles I could be reported in different ways, and when we looked at images which could take on different connotations according to how they were constructed and the caption they were given.

But bias is by no means always the result of a conscious attempt to favour or discredit the subject matter of a news story. It is the result of a whole range of influences.

Completely `objective' news does not exist. We have seen how the political bias of a newspaper can change, perhaps in an attempt to boost sales, or to ensure that other business interests are secure.

Bias can come from:

- a need to boost sales
- the political beliefs of the owner or editor of the newspaper
- the business interests of the owner of the newspaper
- the news values of the news team
- the need to fit in with readers' expectations

REPRESENTATION

As we can see, newspapers tell us about the world in different ways and not all newspapers will cover the same stories. The same person, group or event can be **represented** in very different ways in different newspapers – different messages can be conveyed about that person, group or event depending on which newspaper we read.

STEREOTYPING

stereotyping – the process of categorising a social group, place, or issue according to previously held beliefs. Stereotyping involves making a value judgement which is often negative.

Stereotyping is a kind of shorthand for understanding the world. However, as it is a way of generalising about the world, it is an oversimplification which allows for little or no change and can have harmful effects.

POWER AND CONTROL

Whilst this may be unintentional, stereotyping often involves power and control over the group which is being stereotyped. Tabloid journalists are particularly likely to stereotype as the process means instant recognition and can often create humour.

In this section we look at the messages journalists give us about:

- gender
- politicians
- groups and places
- nations
- race

MESSAGES ABOUT GENDER

There were many changes in the twentieth century in the ways both men and women were represented in the media. Most of the recent changes came about because of the **women's movement** – a campaign to achieve equal opportunities for women. There are now many positive representations of women in the media and a range of representations of men which have become possible only since the 1970s.

However, stereotypes like the 'dumb blonde' do still exist and are often to be found in the tabloids, even if they are less obvious than in the past.

An experiment at Coventry University in April 1999 demonstrated that women with platinum blonde hair are still more likely to be rated as significantly less intelligent by both women and men than women with natural blonde, brown or red hair.

MESSAGES ABOUT POLITICIANS

Newspaper reports on the Government used to rely on the **lobby system** – daily Government briefings for journalists. The journalists then wrote reports referring to 'Government sources' without mentioning names. Tony Blair ended the lobby system in November 1997 when he announced that tape recorders could be brought to briefings and spokespeople could be named.

Spin doctors

All politicians are now associated with '**spin doctors**' – public relations experts whose job is to put the best **spin** (angle or interpretation) on the news for their party. This is an open acknowledgement of attempts to control the messages we receive about politicians in the media.

CASE STUDY: Hillsborough – stereotyping groups and places

When 96 Liverpool football supporters died in the Hillsborough disaster of 15 April 1989, Kelvin MacKenzie, the Editor of *The Sun*, represented the fans as villains. His headline read: 'THE TRUTH. Some fans picked pockets of victims. Some fans urinated on the brave cops. Some fans beat up PC giving kiss of life'.

By representing the Liverpool fans in this way MacKenzie was supporting the police – a value or **ideology** which he expected would later be justified by the inquiry. He was also reinforcing negative stereotypes of Liverpudlians.

MacKenzie's representation backfired when the inquiry by Lord Justice Taylor laid the blame on crowd control mistakes made by the South Yorkshire Constabulary. The misrepresentation of the Liverpool fans cost *The Sun* £10 million a year in income as the people of Liverpool **boycotted** – refused to continue buying – *The Sun*.

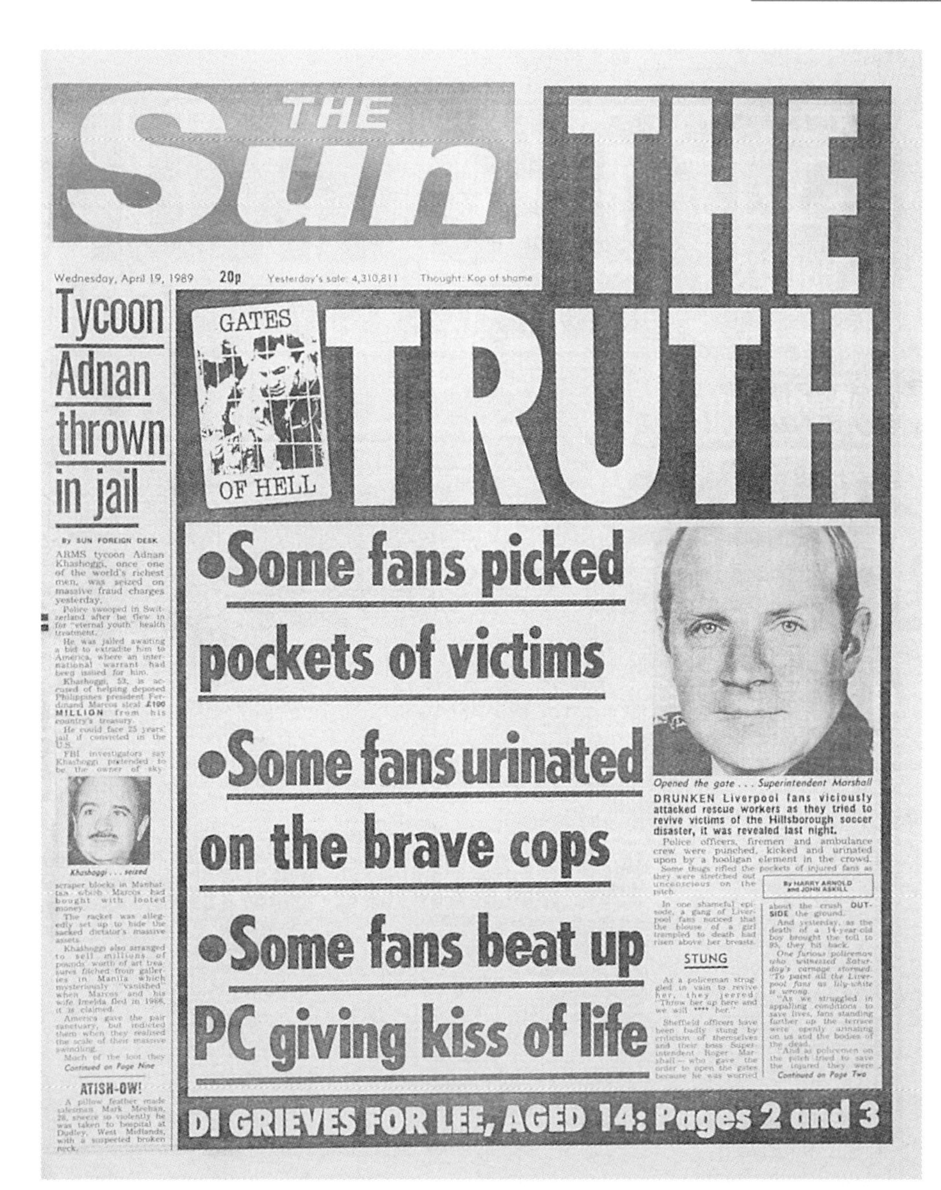

THE Sun

Wednesday, April 19, 1989 20p Yesterday's sale: 4,310,811 Thought: Kop of shame

THE TRUTH

GATES OF HELL

•Some fans picked pockets of victims

•Some fans urinated on the brave cops

•Some fans beat up PC giving kiss of life

Opened the gate . . . Superintendent Marshall

DRUNKEN Liverpool fans viciously attacked rescue workers as they tried to revive victims of the Hillsborough soccer disaster, it was revealed last night.

Police officers, firemen and ambulance crew were punched, kicked and urinated upon by a hooligan element in the crowd.

Some thugs rifled the pockets of injured fans as they were stretched out unconscious on the pitch.

By HARRY ARNOLD and JOHN ASKILL

In one shameful episode, a gang of Liverpool fans noticed that the blouse of a girl trampled to death had risen above her breasts.

STUNG

As a policeman struggled in vain to revive her, they jeered: "Throw her up here and we will **** her."

Sheffield officers have been badly stung by criticism of themselves and their boss Superintendent Roger Marshall – who gave the order to open the gates because he was worried about the crush **OUTSIDE** the ground.

And yesterday, as the death of a 14-year-old boy brought the toll to 95, they hit back.

One furious policeman who witnessed Saturday's carnage stormed: "To paint all the Liverpool fans as lily-white is wrong.

"As we struggled in appalling conditions to save lives, fans standing further up the terrace were openly urinating on us and the bodies of the dead.

"And as policemen on the pitch tried to save the injured they were

Continued on Page Two

Tycoon Adnan thrown in jail

By SUN FOREIGN DESK

ARMS tycoon Adnan Khashoggi, once one of the world's richest men, was seized on massive fraud charges yesterday.

Police swooped in Switzerland after he flew in for "eternal youth" health treatment.

He was jailed awaiting a bid to extradite him to America, where an international warrant had been issued for him.

Khashoggi, 53, is accused of helping deposed Philippines president Ferdinand Marcos steal **£100 MILLION** from his country's treasury.

He could face 25 years' jail if convicted in the U.S.

FBI investigators say Khashoggi pretended to be the owner of sky-

Khashoggi . . . seized

scraper blocks in Manhattan which Marcos had bought with looted money.

The racket was allegedly set up to hide the sacked dictator's massive assets.

Khashoggi also arranged to sell millions of pounds' worth of art treasures filched from galleries in Manila which mysteriously "vanished" when Marcos and his wife Imelda fled in 1986, it is claimed.

America gave the pair sanctuary, but indicted them when they realised the scale of their massive swindling.

Much of the loot they

Continued on Page Nine

ATISH-OW!

A pillow feather made salesman Mark Meehan, 28, sneeze so violently he was taken to hospital at Dudley, West Midlands, with a suspected broken neck.

DI GRIEVES FOR LEE, AGED 14: Pages 2 and 3

The Sun, 19 April 1989

This is one of the most damaging examples of negative stereotyping in the history of the tabloids. The negative effect of the messages about the Liverpool fans, which MacKenzie later admitted he had invented, is made even more obvious when compared to the approach of the regional newspaper, the *Liverpool Echo*. Editor Chris Oakley described *The Sun's* front page as 'a disgrace to journalism'.

Other national newspapers had also published highly intrusive photographs of the dead and the dying at Hillsborough. These photographs had been taken with long-range lenses. Oakley, unlike the editors of the national press, decided not to publish these distressing photographs: 'We were well aware that the people who were victims were likely to be the sons and daughters, the fathers, the brothers of our readers and we really didn't want them to open the *Echo* and see their loved ones in their last agonies.'

(Quoted in *Hard News,* 20 April 1989)

The unethical reporting of the disaster in the national newspapers led to an increase in demands for tighter controls on the press.

Liverpool ECHO

HOME EXTRA

33,872 WEDNESDAY •• APRIL 19, 1989 20p

BRITAIN'S REGIONAL DAILY NEWSPAPER OF THE YEAR

SPEAKING UP FOR MERSEYSIDE

We challenge the London papers and Sheffield police:

PRODUCE YOUR EVIDENCE

- and for the memories of the innocents who died

A POISONOUS smokescreen is being put up around the Hillsborough disaster.

The smokescreen is a vile attempt to divert attention from the stark fact that inadequate crowd control led directly to the deaths of 95 innocent Liverpool supporters.

It seeks to smear the name of Liverpool fans and is an unforgiveable insult to the memory of the dead.

And it will not work — because the one thing lacking from this pathetic package of inuendo is *EVIDENCE.*

Where, for instance, are the pictures?

We have seen hundreds of pictures of Liverpool fans gallantly aiding their stricken friends. We have seem them on TV and in the newspapers.

Where are the pictures of them urinating over the police officers?

Not even the Sun, whose front page coverage today is a disgrace to journalism, has managed to dredge those up.

If so many fans were seen by police picking the pockets of the dead, stealing and looting, where are the arrest figures?

When are the ghouls coming up in court?

If, as the chairman of the South Yorkshire Police Federation claims, there was mass drunkeness among the 3,000 fans milling around the Leppings Lane entrance, how many were arrested?

And lastly, if the purveyors of smears want it both ways, can they say why the gates were thrown open and the so-called drunken hordes allowed on to the ground to imperil all the other spectators?

WE HAVE NOT SEEN EVIDENCE TO BACK UP ANY OF THESE SLURS.

But it has not stopped South Yorkshire police officers seizing the chance to get themselves off the hook by using Liverpool

● Turn to Page 3

The Sun ... it would not know the truth if it walked into Wapping

The Star ... a gutter newspaper that is going down the drain in a tide of lies

COMMENT

Despicable, say Mersey officers

By Bob Burns, Chief Reporter

MERSEYSIDE policemen have attacked South Yorkshire officers for branding Liverpool fans as thugs in the wake of the Hillsborough tragedy.

They also criticised Mr Irvine Patnick, Conservative MP for Sheffield Hallam, who broadcast allegations made to him by the Sheffield policemen.

The Merseyside officers say the comments of the South Yorkshire Police are "despicable" — and especially hurtful to them because a son of one of the Liverpool inspectors is lying in a coma in hospital.

Bill Braben, secretary of the Merseyside Police Federation, which represents almost 5,000 local officers, today telephoned the head of the national federation urging him to gag the Sheffield policemen at such a sensitive time.

He pleaded: "Let us bury our dead. Now is not the time to be pointing the finger of blame."

Mr Braben revealed that Stephen Devine, the son of a Merseyside police inspector was battling for his life in a coma following the Saturday's tragedy.

He added: "The Merseyside Police Federation disassociates itself entirely from the appalling comments made by the MP concerned and the South Yorkshire Police Federation.

"We have an affinity with the people of Merseyside and we are a part of them as they are a part of us.

"To make such statements at such a sad time is the height of distaste."

Heartbroken families hit back: Pages 2-7

Our title joy is muted by our mourning

THE Liverpool Echo has been named as Britain's regional daily newspaper of the year.

Judges for the prestigious UK Press Gazette awards said: "We can't imagine a better paper for its readership."

Editor Chris Oakley said "We are proud to have won this important award. The Echo speaks for Merseyside.

"Our pleasure is only diminished by sharing in the city's mourning."

The award was presented at the Cafe Royal in London yesterday by Home Secretary Douglas Hurd.

Judges said the Echo was: "A really great newspaper. Every page has something good to read. Probably the most active display and layout of any newspaper we have seen.

Awards

"We can't imagine a better paper for its readership."

Two individual awards were also presented to Echo journalists.

Keith Kendrick, 25, won the Young Journalist of the Year title for "an impressive range of work which featured themes of clear interest to the regional readership of the paper, but treated them in the broadest possible manner."

Tom Dowling was commended in the Specialist Writers' Category for his campaigning column for disabled people "I Can Do That."

The award comes hard on the heels of a number of international, national and regional honours

Liverpool Echo, 19 April 1989

Control of the press – self-regulation

Journalists were concerned to avoid tighter controls and drew up the **Code of Practice** – a set of guidelines which journalists should follow.

The Code contains guidelines on the use of long-range lenses and bugging devices. Lord Wakeham, head of the Press Complaints Commission, argues that it is a 'tough' code and that reporting has improved since the Hillsborough disaster. However, the Code does not instruct journalists to follow the guidelines, but merely suggests that they should do so. Journalists can argue that the Code need not be followed if the news story is 'in the public interest', a matter of public concern that might require action from the authorities.

Although journalists are still criticised for intruding into people's privacy, many of them are concerned that there are too many restrictions on their activities.

MESSAGES ABOUT NATIONS

In 1996 during the European football championship, *The Mirror* ran an anti-German campaign, stereotyping Germans as losers, with references to the Second World War: '*Mirror* declares football war on Germany'.

This stereotyping provoked a number of complaints, resulting in a warning from Lord Wakeham. Journalists consequently took more care over the reporting of the 1998 World Cup.

MESSAGES ABOUT RACE

The idea of categorising groups of people according to race was invented in the eighteenth century by white Europeans. Yet today we assume that clear differences exist between different racial groups. This offers journalists another convenient way of labelling people. The National Union of Journalists has drawn up guidelines on race reporting, but these are not always followed by all journalists.

There are still very few black journalists in Britain. Black groups and issues therefore have less access to the news media.

CASE STUDY: Stephen Lawrence

The story of the black teenager Stephen Lawrence, who was murdered by a white gang on 22 April 1993, was an exception. It eventually gained a very high profile in the national press. The original style of reporting: 'Race murder stabbing of perfect pupil' (*The Sun*, 24 April 1993) gradually changed to a broader and more significant debate on race issues and the police: 'Anger after race case collapse' (*The Guardian*, 26 April 1994).

Vitamin B6 — should you take it? Health, G2 pages 13-16

Can England beat Argentina? David Lacey in the Sport section

Education: To Sir, with love... With all the best education jobs

45p
Tuesday June 30 1998
Published in London and Manchester

NEWSPAPER OF THE YEAR

The Guardian

Violent protests as suspects deny any part in murder

Lawrence inquiry fiasco

'I'm going to be walking out of here with nothing. We have tried to be as dignified as possible. What's happened here will get us branded as hooligans.'
Neville Lawrence

Eyre report will damn Royal Opera House board

Orangemen vow to defy Drumcree ban

Loyalists intend to stretch forces wide to push march through

'Last stand', page 4; Leader comment, page 17

Inside

Home: A woman who helped her mother to commit suicide was given 12 months' probation and praised for her honesty, courage and devotion. 10

International: Marchers and dancers in the daily parade at Disneyland in Paris have gone on strike in an attempt to win more glamorous roles. 11

Analysis: Peter Mandelson's ambitions and talents are crucial to Tony Blair's plans to strengthen the centre of his government. 15

Finance: The repercussions of the economic crisis in Asia reached South Africa and sent the rand tumbling to a record low. 19

Weather 15; Obituaries 18
Leader 17; Crossword 23
G2: Quick Crossword 18
Radio 19; Television 20

The Guardian, 30 June 1998

While the case had been reported as a miscarriage of justice in black newspapers like *The Voice*, it was not until the *Daily Mail* ran its front page naming the five suspects 'MURDERERS' that it really became a high-profile news story. The *Daily Mail* risked being charged with contempt of court, as three of the suspects had been found not guilty of the murder.

The story had the positive effect of provoking a large number of radio and television debates, and many more newspaper articles. Lord Macpherson was asked by the government to investigate the police's handling of the case and much importance was given to his subsequent report, which criticised the police for 'institutionalised racism'.

The case of Stephen Lawrence was powerful in challenging accepted values and attitudes and in calling for improvements in attitudes to race within the police, the judicial system and society as a whole, including the media.

FLY TO IRELAND FOR £50 See Escape for details. **Plus** safe skiing guide

Sunday 28 February 1999 £1

The Observer

Previews of all the new Hollywood hits IN SCREEN

What Dame Shirley did next BY JAY RAYNER, IN THE REVIEW

Why I care about Aids by Natasha Richardson IN THIS SECTION

Giggs guns for Europe Exclusive interview IN SPORT

Tory plot to topple Hague

Rebel supporters of Clarke will stand against party in European elections

by Patrick Wintour Political Editor

'We are not looking for a gesture. We want to hit Hague so hard we knock his head off'

Anyone for tennis? Lesbians come out for a new gay icon

Police powers to be curbed

Bias against blacks brings pledge of written 'stop and search' records

'SS bank' to help fund new MoD headquarters

The Observer, 28 February 1999

ACTIVITY 17

Research the details of the reporting of the Stephen Lawrence case. How far do you agree with the following statements about the case?

- Newspapers made it clear that a miscarriage of justice had taken place from the beginning
- The case was well publicised because Stephen's parents, Neville and Doreen Lawrence, refused to give up the fight for justice
- The *Daily Mail is* a strong supporter of black rights

SUMMARY

- Newspapers have tried to avoid government control since they began in the seventeenth century as news pamphlets.
- There is increasing monopolisation in the ownership of both national and regional newspapers.
- Sales of national newspapers are falling; regional newspaper sales are stable; sales of local newspapers are increasing.
- Journalists and newspaper owners act as gatekeepers - they select news stories according to the news values of their newspaper and the expectations of their readers.
- National broadsheets, regional and local newspapers make most of their money through advertising.
- Advertisers target audiences for different newspapers carefully in order to sell their products.
- Different messages about people, groups, places and issues are conveyed by different newspapers.
- Different types of newspapers use different types of language and have different modes of address.
- The meaning of a news photograph can be changed by adding or altering a caption.
- It is difficult, but not impossible, for widely held beliefs and values to be challenged in newspapers.

GLOSSARY

advertising fees – income generated by selling newspaper advertising space

broadsheet – newspapers with wide pages; extended to describe the serious, 'quality' papers

circulation – number of copies sold

concentration of ownership – many newspapers owned by very few people

copy – news stories

cover price – cost of newspaper

cross-media ownership – business corporations with interests in several types of media

free press – tolerance of newspapers of all political affiliations

gatekeeping – process whereby news stories are selected or rejected

human interest – stories or images with a more personal appeal at the level of the individual

masthead – style of newspaper title

news list – stories for which cover is planned

news values – criteria used in selecting which stories and pictures to use

newsworthy – pictures and stories high in news value

press baron – originally used to describe a group of peers who controlled the major newspapers in the first half of the twentieth century, now extended to cover any media moguls

tabloid – newspapers with small, 'tablet-like' pages; extended to describe the popular, 'trashy' papers

tone – overall impression of a report, e.g. sensationalist, serious etc

typography – typeface selected

underground press – newspapers operating in a secret, illegal fashion, often taking an anti-Establishment stance

visual imperative – dominance of the visual image over text

(See page 95 for technical and critical terms relating to use and editing of images.)

(See page 100 for definitions of people's roles in newspaper production.)

4 Magazines

RICHARD HARVEY

Coming up

In this chapter we will be looking at:

- definition of and types of magazines
- the history of magazines
- who owns what
- advertising and magazines
- case studies of particular magazines
- 2000 and beyond

INTRODUCTION

A poll conducted in 1988 suggested that every person over the age of five had read at least part of one magazine every week of the year. Magazine publication is a multi-million pound business. The top-selling monthly magazine, *Reader's Digest,* sells over one and a half million copies every month. The top television listings magazine, *What's on TV,* sells over one and a half million copies a week and over two million copies of the Christmas edition.

Before March 1991 full information about BBC radio and television programmes was allowed to be published only in *Radio Times,* which at that time had the highest **circulation** (sales) for any magazine, averaging over three million copies weekly with an estimated **readership** (the number of *readers,* as opposed to *purchasers*) of over ten million. The largest sales were for the 1989 Christmas edition with 11,037,139 copies sold.

After March 1991 television listings were deregulated, which meant that full information could be published in other magazines. The top-selling television listings magazine is now *What's on TV* with *Radio Times* close behind. The two together sell more than three million copies every week.

The 1989 Christmas edition of the *Radio Times* saw record sales

Magazines that come under the heading 'Women's Interests' sell more than five and a half million copies every week. This category includes magazines such as *Chat* and *Woman's Own*. 'Women's Lifestyle' magazines, which include *Cosmopolitan* and *Marie Claire*, sell over three and a half million copies every month. 'Men's Lifestyle' magazines, which include titles such as *FHM* and *Loaded*, sell over two and a half million copies every month.

But the magazine market is changing. Over a period of only four years there has been a significant drop in sales of what were once top-selling women's magazines and FHM has overtaken them all in sales and rankings (see graph on this page and rankings on page 123).

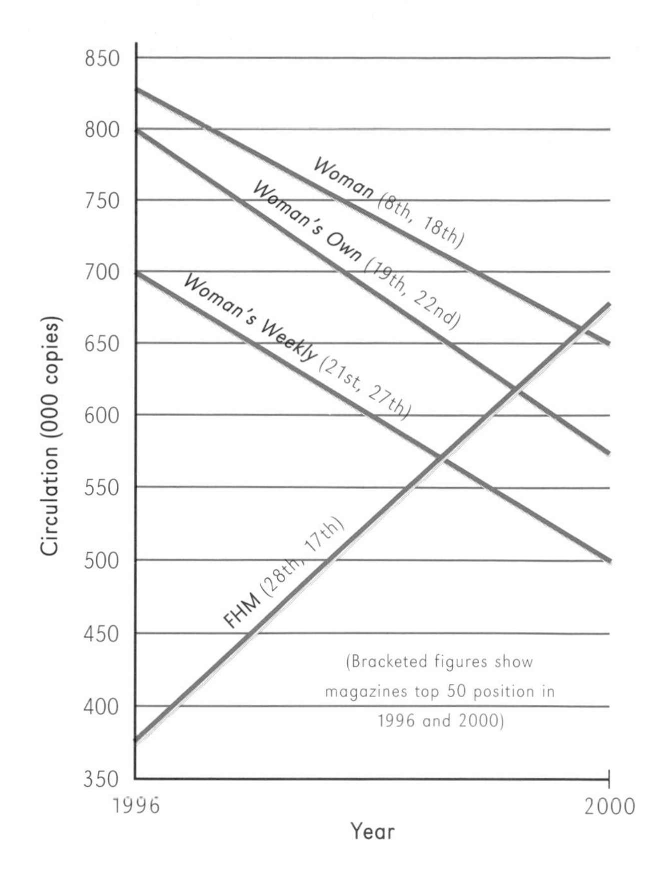

FHM sales have outstripped the most popular women's interest titles (*Source*: *ABC*)

ACTIVITY 1

- Compile a list of the magazines that you, your family and your friends read.
- List the features that the magazines have in common and things that are different. Discuss in small groups whether you think any of the magazines you have listed may be called 'lifestyle' magazines.
- Go on to discuss how 'lifestyle' magazines may be considered different from those which are concerned with men's or women's 'interests'.

The categories and sales figures above are produced by an independent organisation called the **Audit Bureau of Circulations (ABC)**. This is an independent body which provides certified circulation figures for newspapers and magazines.

WHAT IS A MAGAZINE?

A magazine can be defined as a collection of articles and stories, published at regular intervals and mainly designed for reading as a leisure or recreational activity. Most magazines also include illustrations and photographs. Magazines are sometimes referred to as periodicals, particularly in the USA. They are called periodicals because they are published with specific periods of time between them. Magazines dealing with academic subjects are often called **journals**.

The word *magazine* comes from the Arabic word *makhazin*, which means storehouse: a magazine being a publication that collects together a variety of useful things – a storehouse of information and stories.

Because magazines appear at regular intervals they are called **serial publications**. The other major serial publication is newspapers. The main differences are that newspapers are printed on pulp (low quality) paper and have relatively large, unbound pages. (See Chapter 3 (Newspapers) page 87.) Magazines generally appear on finer paper with smaller, bound or stapled pages and appear at less frequent intervals. Magazines are usually published weekly or monthly and are designed to be kept for longer than newspapers.

KINDS OF MAGAZINES

Magazines can be divided or classified into categories or **genres**.

> ### ACTIVITY 2
>
> - Write down as many names of different magazines as you can.
> - Look at the content of the magazines. Discuss in groups what common elements (**codes and conventions**) you think some of the magazines have.
> - Using your findings try to arrange the magazines into genres of magazine.

There are magazines called trade and technical magazines that are directed at business, industrial and professional groups. Many of these magazines are bought by subscription or distributed free. There are over 5,000 titles in this category, but few are ever seen by members of the general public.

The magazines that you see on the news stands in shops are called **consumer magazines**. These are defined by the **Periodical Publishers Association** as those which 'provide people with leisure time information and entertainment'.

Trade journals – read by a select few

> **The Periodical Publishers Association** is the trade association for magazine publishers, representing nearly 200 companies producing 80% of the magazine industry's revenue.

Some magazines are more difficult to categorise. Some news magazines look like magazines but their content is similar to that of newspapers.

Newsweek

Some magazines are linked directly with television programmes but are sold in newsagents.

BBC publications

Some magazines are not sold through shops but are available only by subscription. Two examples of these are:

- *France,* a quarterly targeted at those people who take regular holidays or even own property in France
- *New Internationalist,* a magazine dealing with a range of world issues such as human rights, hunger and genetic engineering

Subscription magazines

Increasing numbers of magazines are published with material of interest to particular ethnic or racial groups. *Chic* was the first glossy magazine targeted at black women.

Magazines of ethnic interest are on the increase

THE HISTORY OF MAGAZINES

BEGINNINGS IN THE SEVENTEENTH CENTURY

It is very difficult to be certain when the very first magazine appeared but the magazine, as we would recognise it now, began only after the invention of **printing** in Europe.

> **Printing** as we know it today began in Europe in the mid-fifteenth century, first from wood blocks and then from movable type cast in lead. The inventor of European printing methods was Johann Gutenberg of Mainz in Germany.

Among the earliest magazines were the German *Edifying Monthly Discussions* (1663–68) and the English *Philosophical Transactions of the Royal Society of London* (1665). These were essentially scholarly collections of summaries on developments in art, literature, philosophy and science.

The lighter type of magazine, or **periodical of amusement**, can be dated from 1672 which saw the appearance of the French *Le Mercure Galant*. This contained gossip about the King and his court, anecdotes and short pieces of poetry. It was followed in 1688 by a German magazine with what is probably the longest title of any magazine ever published.

It was called *Entertaining and Serious, Rational and Unsophisticated Ideas on all Kinds of Agreeable and Useful Books and Subjects*! In England, a penny weekly, *The Athenean Gazette* was first published in 1690. Soon after came *The Gentleman's Journal* (1692–94) and in 1693 the first magazine specifically for women, *The Ladies' Mercury*, was published.

THE EIGHTEENTH CENTURY

Literacy increased in the middle and upper classes in the eighteenth century, especially among women. People were eager to read about new ideas and the circulation of magazines became larger and they were more securely established. The most famous of the early magazines were *The Tatler* (first published 1709–11) and *The Spectator* (first published 1711–12). These were like newspapers in the frequency of their publication but they were more like magazines in content. Political articles appeared on foreign and home affairs and did much to influence the ideas and tastes of the age.

The first publication actually to be called a magazine was published in 1731 by the English printer Edward Cave. This mixture of reading entertainment was called *The Gentleman's Magazine*. It was originally a monthly collection of articles taken from other publications.

Until the use of the word magazine in this context, such publications had been called periodicals or journals. The word magazine became commonly used in rival titles such as the *London Magazine* (1732) and the *Scots Magazine* (1739). Among the increasing number of women's periodicals was the *Ladies' Magazine* (1739). The *Gentleman's Magazine* outlasted all of its rivals, being published until 1907.

THE NINETEENTH CENTURY

Early in the nineteenth century monthly or quarterly periodicals were introduced with articles by famous authors or politicians. They were usually linked with political parties of the time. Of these, two stood out from the rest. *The Edinburgh Review*, founded in 1802, was published to support the Whig Party. This had among its contributors **Sir Walter Scott**. *Blackwood's Edinburgh Magazine* (1817) supported the **Tory Party** and included satirical comment on Scottish affairs and serialised novels.

Whigs – This was the name of a political party traditionally opposed to the Tory party. The name Whig was originally a term of contempt and came from the word 'whiggamore', the name for horse-drovers in the west of Scotland. The party came into being in the full sense after 1784 and represented the ideas of non-conformity, dissent and reform. From 1815 the Whig Party gradually became the Liberal Party.

Tories – The term Tory was also used originally as a term of abuse. The word came from old Irish and meant fugitive or outlaw. Throughout the eighteenth century the term was used to apply to those who supported the landed aristocracy and the Church of England. During the early 1830s the Tory Party became more commonly known as the Conservative Party. The term is still, however, used as a synonym for Conservatives.

Sir Walter Scott was a very popular Scottish novelist. He wrote, among other novels, the adventure *Ivanhoe*.

In the second quarter of the nineteenth century popular weeklies and monthlies were published. Some were illustrated and sold for only a few pennies each. Among these were *The Mirror* (1822–49) and *The Cornhill Magazine* (1860–1939). *Bentley's Miscellany*, published in 1837, had Charles Dickens as its first editor and *Oliver Twist* as one of its first serials. Several magazines selling for only one penny were published. Of these *The Family Herald* (1843) and *The London Journal* (1845) were the first magazines to achieve what might be called a truly mass market circulation.

The Family Herald achieved sales of 175,000 copies in 1850. As the population in the United Kingdom was only 13 million in 1850 compared with 60 million in 1999, this was a significant achievement. The success of these magazines helped develop the magazine publishing industry in London. In 1846 there were 14 one-penny magazines, three half-penny titles and 37 novels being published in serial form in magazines. The first person in Britain to recognise the impact of illustrations on magazine sales was a Nottingham newsagent called Herbert Ingham. He moved to London in 1842 and began publishing the *Illustrated London News*, a weekly magazine of 16 pages of **letterpress** and 32 **woodcut** illustrations.

letterpress (relief printing) – a form of printing in which the image is raised in relief and the ink is then applied to this raised surface. The image is taken off by pressing the paper against it. Although gradually dying out, this system is still being used 500 years after its first introduction.

woodcuts – designs and pictures are cut into the surface of a plank of wood. The parts of the design to remain white are cut out, leaving the parts to be black as raised wood.

The *Illustrated London News* was very successful from the start. Its illustrations were originally drawn by well-known artists, but were not drawn from life. They were what the artist *imagined* the event looked like. Later on the magazine sent artists, employed by the magazine, all over the world to make drawings on the spot. Drawings like this were made during the first **Boer War**, sometimes at great risk, and were a very popular feature of the magazine.

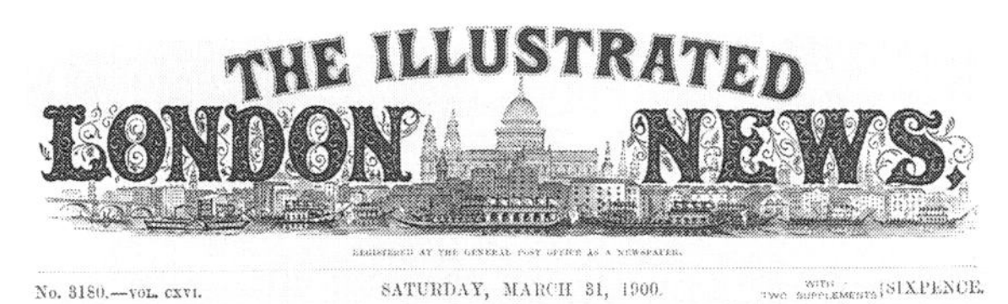

Boer Wars – two wars fought by the United Kingdom against the Boers (Dutch settlers in South Africa) 1880-81 and 1899–1902.

The invention of photography began to transform this type of magazine from the 1890s onwards, with the artist being replaced by the camera.

Cartoons, however, remained a popular feature of magazines – see Chapter 7 (Cartoons), pages 217–225. The weekly humorous magazine *Punch* (founded in 1841) is still famous for its cartoons.

An early *Punch* cartoon showing Queen Victoria dissolving Parliament, which is represented as a pack of cards

ACTIVITY 3

Collect political cartoons from a variety of newspapers or magazines. What do you think might be considered funny about them? Who or what are they poking fun at? Think about how comedians on television, such as Rory Bremner and Ben Elton, and programmes such as *Drop the Dead Donkey* carried on the tradition of making fun of politics and politicians.

The potential market for magazines had greatly increased by the last quarter of the century as the public was eager for light entertainment and information. This was mostly as a result of rapid improvements in literacy. Until this time literacy was restricted mainly to the upper and middle classes. The Education Act of 1870 provided for a school to be within reach of every child in the country. Schooling became compulsory in 1880 and free in 1891. The effect was quite dramatic. In 1850, according to census reports, 40% of the population could not sign their name. This figure had dropped to 20% by 1881.

For young people the *Boy's Own Paper* was published in 1879 and the following year the *Girl's Own Paper* appeared.

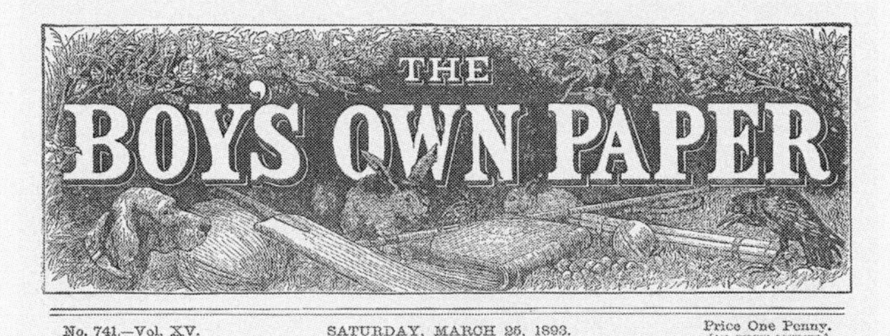

THE BOY'S OWN PAPER

No. 741.—Vol. XV. SATURDAY, MARCH 25, 1893. Price One Penny. [ALL RIGHTS RESERVED.]

TOM, DICK, AND HARRY.

"Bracketed top with Dicky."

The first man to discover the great desire in the population for an entertaining as well as an informative magazine was George Newnes who liked, as a hobby, snipping out paragraphs that appealed to him from different publications. In 1881 he turned his hobby to great advantage by publishing a penny magazine called *Tit-Bits from all the Most Interesting Books, Periodicals and Contributors in the World*. This rather long and awkward title was soon shortened to *Tit-Bits*. It was restyled in 1968 and called *Titbits*.

It was a great success and from this beginning Newnes developed a publishing empire that was to include *Country Life* (founded 1897) and the *Strand Magazine* (1891–1950). The *Strand Magazine* became enormously popular and was famous for publishing the Sherlock Holmes stories by Arthur Conan Doyle.

Two of the staff of *Tit-Bits* went on to build publishing empires of their own. Alfred Harmsworth, later Lord Northcliffe, became the proprietor of one of the largest newspaper groups in the United Kingdom. Harmsworth left *Tit-Bits* and launched a rival publication in 1888 called *Answers to Correspondents*. This was the first magazine to be promoted with competitions – an idea that proved to be very popular.

Harmsworth formed the publishing group that now includes the *Daily Mail* group and Northcliffe Newspapers which is the second largest group of local newspapers in the United Kingdom with a total circulation of over eight million.

Another employee of *Tit-Bits*, Arthur Pearson, launched *Pearson's Weekly* (1889–1927) and started a publishing empire that today includes the *Financial Times* and *The Economist* magazine.

All three entrepreneurs recognised that by keeping the price down and offering contents that reflected the interests and problems of the average reader, very high sales were possible.

THE TWENTIETH CENTURY – ADVERTISING AND POPULAR MAGAZINES

Although a few advertisements appeared in magazines after an Advertisement Tax had been abolished in 1853, most publishers were still reluctant to use advertisements in their magazines. In this same year *The Atheneum* magazine said, 'It is the duty of an independent journal to protect, as far as possible, the credulous, confiding and unwary from the wily arts of the insidious advertiser.'

> The *Reader's Digest*, with its massive circulation, admitted advertisements to its American edition only in 1955.

The twentieth century, however, saw a rapid increase in advertising and today no popular magazine is free from its influence. No magazine could survive without substantial income from advertising.

It was the United States which first showed what magazines could achieve by looking for advertising revenue. In 1897 the publisher of *Ladies Home Journal*, Cyrus Curtis, used profits from this magazine to buy the *Saturday Evening Post* which was failing badly. By 1922 Curtis had built its circulation to two million and with this came an advertising income of $28 million. High advertising rates could be charged and justified by high **circulation figures**, i.e. the numbers of copies sold for a publication. Once high circulation figures became all-important, advertisers wanted to be able to make sure that they were accurate. The Audit Bureau of Circulation – an independent organisation which calculated circulation figures – was created in the United States in 1914.

Increased advertising also had an effect on the appearance of the magazines. At the turn of the century, advertisements began to move forward from the back pages into the main part of the magazine.

Advertisers were increasingly able to put pressure on magazines concerning the editorial content. In 1940, for instance, *Esquire* magazine in the United States lost its piano advertisements after publishing an article recommending the guitar for musical accompaniment. The magazine won the advertising back again only after publishing a prominent apology.

Magazines today insist that they have **editorial independence**, that is, the editor of a magazine will want to have as much say as possible about what goes in the magazine. However, advertisers will have some power to object if they feel that content of a magazine may affect their sales. Because of this tension something like a balance of power exists between advertising and editorial.

> In the USA, in 1900 advertising might form up to 50 per cent of a popular magazine's content: by 1947 the proportion was more often 65-70 per cent.

Advertising in the United Kingdom

The advertising revolution began in Britain at the same time as in the USA, but did not develop as rapidly. Britain's Audit Bureau of Circulations was not set up until 1931, and its membership remained small until the 1960s. It was then that consumer spending, and therefore advertising, really began to grow at an enormous rate. This was particularly reflected in a boom in women's magazines.

Women's magazines

Several American women's magazines came out in British editions, such as *Vogue* (1916), *Good Housekeeping* (1922), and *Harper's Bazaar* (1929) – amalgamated with *Queen* in 1970 as *Harper's and Queen*.

The fortnightly *Woman's Weekly* (1911), and the monthly *Woman and Home* (1926) were joined by such popular weeklies as *Woman's Own* (1932), *Woman's Illustrated* (1936-61) and *Woman* (1937). During the Second World War some of these magazines gave practical advice on how to cope with shortages.

In post-war Britain, magazines began to be distributed through shops – mostly supermarkets – other than newsagents. The main example of this was *Family Circle* (1964) – an Anglo-American publication. A similar publication, *Living*, arrived in 1967.

The trend towards a younger market was shown with

Early editions of women's magazines were full of practical advice

the launch of *She* in 1955, *Honey* (1960), *Annabel* (1966) – targeted particularly at younger married women, *Petticoat* (1966–75) – for girls aged 14–19 – and *19* (1968), which became a market leader.

The birth of the colour supplement

The second half of the twentieth century saw the death of many of the old general magazines. This was due to the availability of cheap paperback books and the increasing popularity of television. The decline of illustrated weekly magazines left room for a new opportunity for advertising revenue. The first to seize this opportunity was Lord Thomson, who in 1962 brought out a colour magazine to go with *The Sunday Times*.

So successful was it that *The Observer* and the *Daily Telegraph* produced their own colour supplements. (The *Daily Telegraph's* magazine was eventually removed and produced with its sister publication, the *Sunday Telegraph*.) By the early 1980s all the major Sunday newspapers had their own magazine.

Now, national newspapers have magazine supplements on other days of the week. Saturday editions rival the national Sundays with a variety of magazine supplements.

In October 1999 *The Mirror* launched a magazine for women. Its advertising was directed to keep its own readership with a 'free' magazine and to increase its circulation in the competitive world of national newspapers. More than two thirds of the front page on Tuesday, 19 October 1999 was dedicated to the promotion of this venture. On page three, a direct attack was made on some of the most popular women's monthlies and weeklies.

With this venture the line between newspapers and magazines is becoming more blurred. Total magazine sales have been increasing and newspaper circulations have been declining over the last few years, so newspapers have adjusted their content to suit the demands of their potential readership. Even local and regional newspapers offer free magazine supplements. Westcountry Publications offers a free magazine for 'the over 50s' with all its local titles.

Colour supplements have blurred the line between newspapers and magazines

74 DAYS TO 2000 AD

The Mirror

Tuesday October 19 1999

THIS PAPER COSTS JUST 20p

www.mirror.co.uk

FREE INSIDE TODAY

A brilliant new glossy mag for every woman

YOUR copy of our fantastic FREE new magazine M is inside today's Mirror.

M has 44 glossy, packed pages of health, relationships, beauty, home-style, sex, shopping, food, travel and lots more. It's the first time a newspaper is giving away a brilliant women's magazine completely FREE.

Free today and every Tuesday. It's the only mag you need.

The real reason you're not losing weight

How old does your naked body look?

'Why I dumped my millionaire lover'

fashion beauty sex interiors food shopping travel

Brady's 19-day hunger strike

By BRIAN ROBERTS

MOORS murderer Ian Brady was slowly starving to death last night as he entered the 19th day of a hunger strike.

Experts say the child killer, who is only taking black tea and coffee, is unlikely to last more than two months without food.

Brady, 61 – who has no plans to end his strike – has told in a letter how he is protesting at being forcibly moved to another

TURN TO PAGE 4

NOT AGAIN

By DAVID PILDITCH

New 'red light' train crash

A COMMUTER express that ploughed into the back of an empty train last night may have gone through a red light.

One person was slightly injured in the smash. He was treated at the scene for whiplash injuries, cuts and bruises.

One shaken survivor said: "How the hell could this happen again?"

Two weeks ago, more than 30 people died when a rush-hour train went through a red signal at Paddington and collided with an express.

Last night's incident came at 7.19pm when a Connex London Victoria-Hastings service carrying 10 people hit the back of an empty Seaford-Brighton train at low speed. Ambulances dashed to the scene outside Lewes, East Sussex, to find passengers suffering from shock. None was seriously injured.

Last night an investigation was under way. British Transport Police said it was "possible" the Connex train went through a red signal. Asked whether that had happened, Connex spokesman Peter Kendall said: "I do not think that is something anyone could say at this stage."

Shadow Transport Minister Bernard Jenkin said: "I trust the Government will set up a suitable inquiry."

Speaking at the scene, Lewes Lib-Dem MP Norman Baker said he would raise the crash in the Commons today. He added: "The need to be extra vigilant is not being fully observed."

FULL STORY: PAGE 7

THE MIRROR, Tuesday, October 19, 1999 PAGE 3

Why buy any of these..

..when you can get this FREE

FREE inside today's Mirror is our fabulous new magazine, M.

M's 44 packed, glossy pages come completely free with The Mirror every single Tuesday which makes us ask why ever pay up to 70p for a weekly magazine again?

In M, you'll find fantastic real-life stories and investigations, everything you need to know about men and sex and the hottest fashion.

M gives you the truth about beauty products – what works, what doesn't – and the latest health advice from top medical experts.

All this, plus travel, careers, food and interiors – brought to you in a modern, stylish package. TV and radio star Sara Cox agrees with us that you'll find it compulsive reading.

She said: "This is great. A proper women's magazine – free!

"I read every word of the first M and I loved it. I'll be looking forward to it every Tuesday."

The fact is, unlike other magazines, M isn't crammed with ads, which means there's more for you!

Once you see M, you won't just want to throw out your regular weekly magazines, you'll wonder why you ever paid more than £2.50 for a monthly mag.

In M you get just as many must-read pages – it's just spread over four weeks.

M – *it's the only magazine you need.*

M-ARVELLOUS: DJ Sara Cox loved reading the first M

The Mirror promotes its new women's magazine, 19 October 1999

KEY DATES

- **1663-68** Earliest magazines in Germany
- **1690** First English magazine
- **1693** First women's magazine – *Ladies' Mercury*
- **1709** First woman editor of a women's magazine – *The Tatler*
- **1711** *The Spectator* first published
- **1731** First publication to be called a magazine
- **1820** First popular weeklies
- **1843** Penny magazines first mass circulation publications
- **1842** *Illustrated London News*
- **1879** *Boy's Own Paper*
- **1881** *Tit-bits*
- **1890** Photography in magazines for the first time
- **1911** *Woman's Weekly*
- **1916** *Vogue*
- **1922** *Good Housekeeping*
- **1929** *Harper's Bazaar*
- **1932** *Woman's Own* and *Woman and Home*
- **1955** Advertisements first appear in *Reader's Digest*
- **1960** Teen magazine, *Honey*
- **1962** First colour supplement – *The Sunday Times*
- **1964** *Family Circle*
- **1966** *Annabel*
- **1967** *Living* magazine
- **1968** *19* published
- **1969** *Shoot!* magazine
- **1970** *Harper's Bazaar* amalgamates with *Queen* as *Harper's and Queen*
- **1991** Deregulation of TV listings magazines
- **1994** *Sugar*
- **1995** *Loaded*
- **1998** IPC Magazines sold by Reed Elsevier
- **1999** *Mirror*'s magazine for women, Attic Futura's *Shine*, Eve Pollard's *Wedding Day*

MEDIA PRODUCERS AND AUDIENCES

THE PUBLISHERS

There are almost 3,000 consumer magazines on the market today but all these publications are produced by relatively few companies. Five publishers have over 50% of the market share of consumer magazines sold in the United Kingdom.

It is calculated that the consumer magazine industry in the United Kingdom is worth £2.2 billion. Over the last 10 years the number of magazines published has increased by over a third. In 1997 alone 180 new titles were launched.

Reed Elsevier was the largest of the magazine publishing houses until January 1998, when it sold IPC Magazines for £860 million to a management team.

By far the largest publisher is IPC Magazines. Others include EMAP, National Magazines, D.C. Thompson, Condé Nast, H. Bauer, Reader's Digest and G&J of the UK.

ACTIVITY 4

Research which magazine titles are published by EMAP. You can do this simply by looking at the editorial pages of magazines or you can access the publisher's web site on the Internet. The web site also shows what other media companies are owned by EMAP. The reference sections of public libraries can also help you with investigations.

ACTIVITY 5

- List two or three magazines that you enjoy reading.
- Look to see who publishes them.
- What magazines are in the same genre?
- Try to find out who publishes these magazines. Discuss why you prefer one magazine to another.

The following table shows the top UK magazines by circulation.

1	*AA Magazine*	4,246,863
2	*Skyview*	2,299,295
3	*Cable Guide*	2,067,752
4	*Safeway Magazine*	1,944,359
5	*Boots Health & Beauty*	1,909,500
6	*What's on TV*	1,741,156
7	*Somerfield Magazine*	1,413,900
8	*Asda Magazine*	1,363,354
9	*Radio Times*	1,334,908
10	*The National Trust Magazine*	1,319,122
11	*Take A Break*	1,218,915
12	*Voilà*	1,200,000
13	*Reader's Digest*	1,131,273
14	*Saga Magazine*	1,019,629
15	*TV Times*	790,603
16	*Debenhams*	742,350
17	*FHM*	674,836
18	*Woman*	653,045
19	*TV Quick*	638,855
20	*Birds*	579,876
21	*Bella*	564,104
22	*Woman's Own*	552,916
23	*IN2Film*	525,500
24	*That's Life*	521,650
25	*OK!*	491,586
26	*Chat*	490,516
27	*Woman's Weekly*	483,722
28	*Best*	461,851
29	*Cosmopolitan*	460,970
30	*Candis*	450,443
31	*Hello*	436,523
32	*Marie Claire*	422,995
33	*Prima*	413,196
34	*Sugar*	385,812
35	*Now*	390,812
36	*Good Housekeeping*	384,541
37	*People's Friend*	383,149
38	*Sainsbury's*	382,161
39	*National Geographic*	378,976
40	*Loaded*	353,640
41	*Top of the Pops*	349,813
42	*Motoring and Leisure*	337,731
43	*Official Playstation*	337,186
44	*Know Your Destiny*	332,755
45	*Auto Trader*	326,388
46	*Computeractive*	325,751
47	*My Weekly*	324,216
48	*BBC Gardeners' World*	312,252
49	*Yours*	309,906
50	*Maxim*	304,663

Source: Audit Bureau of Circulations, June 2000

ACTIVITY 6

- Using the Top 50 listings investigate which of these titles are paid for and which are free.
- Organise the titles into genres and calculate which genres are the most popular.

Although the circulations of magazines have their ups and downs, the top women's magazines – *Cosmopolitan, Woman's Journal, Company, Options, She, Woman* and *Woman's Own* saw their combined circulation fall from 3.4 million in 1987 to 2.1 million in 1997. The circulation figures for *Woman's Journal* continued to fall throughout 1998 but *Company* and *Cosmopolitan* managed small rises. During 1999 the total circulation of women's monthly magazines increased by 4.2 per cent.

The more encouraging recent figures for women's magazines are insignificant when compared to the astonishing increases in circulation of the new breed of men's lifestyle magazines. Magazines like *FHM, Loaded* and *Esquire* have flourished. The market leader, *FHM,* has seen an increase of over 100,000 year on year and in July to December 1998 reached a circulation of 751,493, almost 300,000 more than the top-selling women's monthly, *Cosmopolitan*. It also outsold the top-selling women's title, the weekly *Woman,* which had sales of 731,764. This produces revenue for a single edition of almost £2.5 million and advertising revenue of more than £6 million.

There are many theories as to why men's magazines have had such extraordinary success. In *The Media Guide: A Guardian Book* it is suggested that 'perhaps it's just that modern blokes are more in need of the make-you-feel-better consumer formulae which magazines peddle so well'.

ACTIVITY 7

- Discuss what you think is meant by the above quotation from *The Media Guide*. You might like to consider the way in which the letters, jokes and subject matter of the advertising and articles relate to the readers of these magazines.
- Discuss what you consider to be other reasons for the continued success of men's lifestyle magazines.

Extension activity

- Select one magazine that you enjoy reading. Write down as many reasons as you can for why you enjoy your magazine. Compare your reasons with those of at least two other people in the class.
- Draw up a chart of reasons you found you had in common.

Advertising in magazines

Without advertising no magazine could survive. (See pages 119–120 on the history of advertising in magazines.) Some readers think that there are too many advertisements in magazines but the cover price of most magazines would be three or four times greater without advertising. *Sugar* would cost approximately £7 and *Cosmopolitan* could cost as much as £10.

Not everyone dislikes advertisements in a magazine. For some readers the advertisements are an attraction.

ACTIVITY 8

Class discussion

- Do you think that there are too many advertisements in magazines?
- What enjoyment can you get from looking at the advertisements in the magazines you have studied?

Advertisers can include free samples in magazines

The income for a magazine is from both the sales of an issue and advertising. A magazine with a small circulation is more dependent upon advertising than one with a very large circulation. Advertising, even with the most popular magazines, accounts for approximately 70 per cent of their income.

Magazines are very popular with advertisers because they target their audience very carefully and can offer much more detailed information about products that cannot be seen in a short television commercial. Magazines are also able to include small free samples attached to an advertisement. It could be for cleansing tissues or even perfumes.

Sugar can offer its advertisers a target audience of 1.3 million 11–19 year olds and 864,000 15–25 year olds. (*Source*: NRS Jan–Dec 1998)

It is calculated that *Sugar* readers spend:

- £6 million per week on toiletries and cosmetics. (£1 in every £3 spent by teenagers on toiletries and cosmetics is spent by a reader of *Sugar*.)
- £12.50 on clothes every week.

Sugar readers are also responsible for buying almost a quarter of the total number of tapes and CDs purchased by teenagers in any given month.

Analysing advertisements

You can use the same technique to analyse advertisements as used in analysing the front covers of magazines (see case study on *Sugar*, page 133). Most of the time you can clearly identify the advertisements, but some look like features. There may be a romantic story entitled 'How can I get him to notice me?' but as you look more closely it becomes clear that it is an advertisement for hair colouring or shampoo! These are called **advertorials** because they are a mixture of editorial content and advertising.

ACTIVITY 9

- Using a copy of *Shine*, calculate the income from sales based on 120,000 copies sold.

  (This was approximately the sales figure for its first edition in March 1999.)

Advertising rates for single pages in *Shine* are quoted as:

Outside back cover	£5,600
1st or 2nd right-hand page	£5,600
Inside back cover	£5,100
Run of magazine	£4,200

Run of magazine means all places through the magazine other than those specified above. Fractions of a page are calculated on the same basis as the full-page rate. So a half-page in the main part of the magazine would cost £2,100. To guarantee the advertisement is on the right-hand side in the run of the magazine costs an extra 10 per cent.

There are other ways in which advertising revenue can be obtained. An advertiser can pay to have its own printed advertisements sent out with the magazine. Single sheets can be included at a rate of £35 per thousand. A perfume strip can be added for £55 per thousand.

ACTIVITY 10

- Using the advertising rates for *Shine* quoted above calculate what income your copy of *Shine* would have received from advertising.

ACTIVITY 11

- Collect a selection of magazines with promotional material and make a display for the classroom.
- Discuss how successful you think the different items are in persuading readers to buy the magazine.

Advertising rates for different magazines are often published on the Internet. You could undertake the same activity but with a magazine of your choice.

Promoting magazines

As well as advertising the products of others, magazines also need to sell as many copies as possible in a very competitive market. The most common method of promotion is the gift attached to the front cover. This will always be a product aimed especially at the target audience of the magazine. In the past *Total Football* has given away a video of an interview with Alan Shearer together with a compilation of his best goals; *Red* offered a free sunglasses case 'worth £8.99'; *Prima* gave away a beach bag 'worth £7.99' and *Empire* regularly gives away videos.

Top of the Pops magazine's March 2001 edition gave away pop badges

CASE STUDY – IPC Magazines

IPC Magazines is firmly established as the market leader in publishing consumer magazines. Since a group of its managers bought the magazine publishing division from its parent company, Reed Elsevier, in January 1998, IPC has formed a working joint venture with the market-leading Australian magazine publisher, Australian Consolidated Press (ACP). This working relationship enables the two companies to market their own titles in the other's country. This has helped IPC to continue to develop its range of magazines in Australia. IPC has also bought Link House publishers, adding *Hi-Fi News, Superbike* and *Mountain Biker* to its ever increasing list of titles. IPC now has almost 100 different titles, including 26 in the top 100 sellers list. Some of its most successful titles are *What's on TV, Woman's Own, Marie Claire, Country Life* and *Loaded*. Eight of its titles were launched over 100 years ago.

Although IPC is one organisation its publications are divided into six different publishing companies, each with a different identity:

IPC Connect Ltd publishes six weekly women's magazines and one bi-monthly publication. The total sales for all six magazines are over three million and the combined **readership** exceeds 12 million.

> The **readership** of a magazine or newspaper is not based upon sales alone. Publishers calculate that for each copy of a magazine or newspaper sold three or four people will read it. This could be friends or members of the purchaser's family. Readership is therefore calculated as being the total number of sales multiplied by three or four. This is very important when selling advertising space.
>
> More accurate estimates of readership are provided, on a subscription basis, by the **National Readership Survey (NRS)**. This is an organisation that sets out to provide estimates of the number and nature of the people who read UK newspapers and consumer magazines.

The six weekly titles are:

Woman ● *Woman's Own* ● *Woman's Weekly* ● *Woman's Realm* ● *Now* ● *Chat*

Woman is the best-selling weekly women's magazine with sales of almost 700,000. IPC Connect has annual revenues of over £88 million from sales and advertising.

IPC tx Ltd publishes IPC's television-related magazines:

What's on TV ● *TV Times* ● *TV & Satellite Week*

These titles account for 57 per cent of the market share in the extremely competitive television listings magazine market. *What's on TV* is the top-selling listings magazine with sales of over 1,780,000. Its nearest rival is *Radio Times* with sales of just over 1,400,000.

The latest addition to this group of magazines is *Soaplife*, published monthly and featuring news, interviews and storylines from the most popular of all the television genres. This was published for the first time in June 1999 and achieved sales of 175,000 within the first six months (see pages 130–131).

IPC SouthBank Publishing Company Ltd publishes 18 magazines targeted specifically at the female population of the United Kingdom. The company claims that every month one in three women in the UK reads a SouthBank magazine. The various magazines are designed to appeal to women at every stage of their life whether teenager, bride or mother and of varying levels of income. SouthBank's publications can be classified under the genre of women's lifestyle magazines, but can also be divided again into subgenres:

Fashion & beauty
e.g. *Marie Claire*

Home interest
e.g. Ideal Home

Women's lifestyle group
e.g. *Woman & Home*

Women's special interest
e.g *Wedding and Home*

Young women's interest
e.g. *Mizz*

ACTIVITY 12

- Discuss why you think that IPC sees a need for two different publishing groups for women's magazines. You should begin by looking closely at the IPC magazines published by IPC Connect.
- Discuss what the contents – articles, and advertising – tell you about the target audience for these magazines.
- Do the same with examples of the magazines from IPC SouthBank.

IPC Country & Leisure Media Limited is the largest in terms of number of publications, with 37 titles. Its turnover is in excess of £60 million and it employs over 400 people. The publications are in the specialist leisure areas of Country Lifestyle, Wine, Equestrian, Boating (power and sail), Shooting, Photography, Angling, Aviation, Rail, Rearing and Care of Birds (Aviculture), Gardening, Outdoor and Caravaning Holiday Guides and Collecting.

According to the National Readership Survey advertisers can reach over a million adults classed in social groups ABC1. This can be done though a single contact in this leisure group, instead of having to reach each different title.

Attached to this division is also **FHG (Farm House Guide) Publications**, which publishes 13 annual holiday guides from its base in Scotland.

IPC Music & Sport Ltd publishes 30 magazines with a combined turnover of over £55 million. This company specialises in mainly male interest magazines across a range of markets which include men's lifestyle, music, football, rugby, golf, cycling and motor sports.

Music & Lifestyle

Loaded (a complementary, electronic version of this magazine was launched in 1995, which attracted a large audience in its own right. A spin-off from *Loaded* was launched in 1998. Called *Loaded Fashion*, it is published twice yearly.)

Other titles include *New Musical Express* and *Melody Maker*

Sports

This subgenre includes titles such as *World Soccer, Shoot! and Cycling Weekly.*

Motoring

The Link House Motoring group publishes eight titles that come under the control of Music & Sport Ltd and include highly specialist magazines for enthusiasts in motoring.

IPC Magazines NMP (New Media Publishing) works with the publishing branches to develop all aspects of electronic publishing, from CD-ROMs, through the development of electronic programme guides for digital television to World Wide Web Internet sites.

nme.com is one of the most frequented of the UK offering news, reviews and gossip with the style of the paper version.

Electronic sites to supplement *Loaded* and *Yachting and Boating World* have already been mentioned and early in 1999, *Country Life*, one of the UK's longest established magazines, launched its own web site.

IPC has been a pioneer in the development of electronic programme guides (EPGs), developed for digital television. The electronic version of *TV Times*, developed for the Cambridge interactive TV trial, was the first UK live digital EPG.

Target audiences

As we have seen above, IPC produces many magazines, all aimed at different readers. In the terminology used in the study of the media these readers are often referred to as the **target audience**, the group of people to whom publishers want to sell their product.

Many of the IPC brands reach readers world-wide through the publication of licensed editions of titles such as *Homes & Gardens* in Germany and *Essentials* in Romania. There are 21 international magazine licences, covering 13 titles in 14 countries.

audience – usually used to refer to people who watch a performance in a theatre or watch a film at the cinema. However, with reference to the media it is a term used for the people who 'receive' any media text whether it is a film, a television programme, a newspaper, a magazine or a web site.

mass audience – for a magazine, a readership on a large scale in terms of geographical area or numbers of people reached.

niche audience – as mass media audiences have become more fragmented, publishers, who have to try to sell as many magazines as possible, have produced more magazines for a narrower group of readers called niche market magazines.

ACTIVITY 13

- Choose some of the titles published by IPC and discuss whether you consider them to be mass or niche publications.

  Is it possible to have a formula that will define a mass or niche publication?

Extension activity

- Some theorists suggest that mass audiences must span age, gender, class and race. How many of the magazines that you have discussed fit this definition?

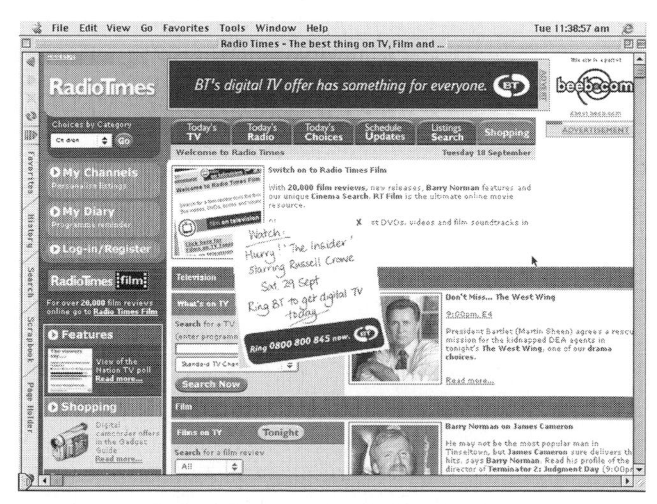

Magazine websites: World Soccer, nme.com, Country Life and Radio Times

CASE STUDY – Soap magazines

With viewing figures regularly exceeding 17 million the two most popular soap operas, *Coronation Street* and *EastEnders,* cannot really be considered niche market television. It is surprising that magazine publishers took some time to realise the full potential of this market. Interest was obvious, given the amount of coverage of soap operas in the tabloid newspapers. Many magazines featured articles about the main soaps and their stars, but until the summer of 1999 only one title was dedicated to the interests of soap addicts. This was the fortnightly *Inside Soap,* published by Attic Futura, selling over 250,000 copies for each edition. By the end of 1999 there were three. In June 1999 IPC tx , the television division of IPC (see above), launched *Soaplife.* This monthly publication claimed sales of 175,000 within three months of launch. IPC's magazine undercut the price of *Inside Soap,* offering its monthly at 99p against *Inside Soap's* £1.10. The intention was to attract some of the year-on-year success achieved by *Inside Soap.* Circulation figures had increased by over 20 per cent each year. IPC used the popularity of its listings magazine *What's on TV* to help launch its new title.

In October Attic Futura, aiming to keep its dominance in this range of publications, produced *All About Soap.* Priced at 99p it is in direct competition with *Soaplife.* (An Australian monthly called *TV Soap* is also available at some newsagents.)

When IPC tx launched *Soaplife,* its managing director said that she saw the publication as a natural extension of its other titles (see above). Soaps always featured strongly in *What's on TV* but it was clear that there was a strong market for magazines dedicated to the on- and off-screen stories from the soaps.

Soap opera fans watch much more television than the average viewer and are interested in the characters and the actors and actresses who play them. There is a great curiosity as to what they do and what their interests are.

The link between IPC television publications and soap operas expanded in May 1999 when *What's on TV* sponsored the first British soap awards. This programme was watched by more than 10 million viewers – a 48 per cent share of the total viewing public.

Soaplife, April 2001

All three magazines consider their target readership to be young women. This is clear from the content. They are full of interviews with young female soap stars and pin-ups of male leads. *All About Soap* refers to male stars as 'gorgeous soap dishes'.

Sometimes it is difficult to distinguish between the coverage of the actors' real lives and that of their fictional characters. Detailed descriptions of plot lines are mixed with interviews with stars about their hopes, fears, clothes, hair, make-up and love life.

There are guides to fan clubs and web sites as well as fan-sites where comments can be exchanged on the latest plot developments. There is even a site for fans of *Eldorado,* the failed BBC soap set in Spain. This soap was taken off the air more than six years ago.

When the actor Ross Kemp left *EastEnders* in October 1999 he featured on the cover of issues of *Soaplife* and *Inside Soap,* which also provided special souvenir pull-out posters. *All About Soap* had a double-page spread called 'Ross Kemp: This is Your Life.'

ACTIVITY 14

Soaps like *EastEnders* and *Coronation Street* regularly attract audiences of more than 17 million and so can certainly be said to appeal to a mass audience. Soap magazines sell, at most, just over a quarter of a million.

- Discuss why, given the huge audiences for the television programme, the magazines do not sell more copies.

Extension activity

- In small groups discuss what you think might be the reasons for the relationship between young women, soap operas and soap magazines.

ACTIVITY 15

Practical task

- Think of an important event that is happening in either *Coronation Street* or *EastEnders* at the moment. Design a front page for one of the soap magazines mentioned above featuring the event. Look closely at past and current editions of the magazines for ideas about how the front covers look.
- Apart from soap operas there are other very popular television genres. See Chapter 2 (Television), page 78.

  Choose one of these genres and design the front cover of the first edition of a magazine that will be dedicated to just television programmes of the one genre: for example, programmes that are based upon the medical profession. The programmes could be both American and British.

CASE STUDY – Shoot!

Shoot! was launched in August 1969 and became an immediate success. The first issue sold nearly 300,000 copies. It remained the market leader for more than 25 years. Its circulation is now down to 56,624.

When it was first launched the articles were very much related to a readership that went to see their favourite teams play and the articles were written by fans who stood on the terraces and understood the language of the game. Questionnaires were very popular and top players were eager to be included in the magazine. The magazine launched a 'Big Match' verdict where experts would give points to every player on each side. Sticker albums were used as a way to promote the magazine. With one album launch the magazine reached a record sale of 525,000 copies.

ACTIVITY 16

- *Shoot!* is targeted, according to IPC, at males between nine and 16 with an average age readership of 12. In its 30th birthday issue *Shoot!* published a poll which voted Michael Owen the second best player of the last 30 years, coming just behind George Best. Discuss how the result of this poll relates to the target audience of the magazine.
- Compare the content of *Shoot!* with another football magazine of your choice. Are the articles about the same topics or can you see any differences? What do you think is appealing about the front covers of the sports magazines that you have looked at?

Extension activities

- Look at a variety of sports magazines. Discuss who you think the magazines are aimed at. What is there about the magazines that suggests their target audience?
- Look at a football fanzine. Discuss in small groups what you think are the main differences between a fanzine and a football magazine such as *Shoot!* Consider both content and style.

Articles in early editions had columns by Alan Ball, Bryan Robson and Gerry Francis. Then, as now, these articles were very often **ghosted** by football journalists or members of the staff of *Shoot!* This means that the football star gives his name to the column but does not actually write it. Many autobiographies of sporting stars are ghosted in the same way.

The aim of the magazine was to promote the game of football and be positive about the image of the game and its players. The pieces were kept short and simple with as much illustration as possible. Action shots were particularly important. In the early days of the magazine it had easy access to the top players but now the top players have their own agents who run their affairs and it is more difficult to reach players directly.

IPC suggests that 'the magazine aims to bring young readers closer to the game and is strongly biased towards Premier League clubs and their top stars.'

ACTIVITY 17

Practical task

- Choose a sport, other than football, and design a front cover of a magazine especially for this sport, that you think would attract a target audience of boys and / or girls aged 10–17.

  You could choose a game played mainly by girls such as netball or games played by both girls and boys such as tennis or basketball. If you wanted to be more adventurous you could try to design a front cover of a magazine for the growing number of young women who are now playing rugby.

  You may choose a multi-sports magazine if you wish.

MEDIA MESSAGES AND VALUES

REPRESENTATION OF GENDER

Representation is how we communicate with each other using words or images. To be able to communicate with each other we need images and words that we all understand. When we first learn to read, simple words are written underneath images or pictures. There might be a picture of a cat with the word 'cat' underneath. Both the word and the picture represent the idea of a cat. As individuals if we see the word 'cat' we may have in our mind very different images or pictures of a cat. It may be your family pet or a picture that you have seen of a cat.

The words that we use to describe people can lead to assumptions being made about them. Even what appear to be the simplest of words encourage us to think in a particular way. Words associated with gender, for example, male, female, boy, girl, masculine and feminine all have attitudes associated with them and values placed upon them by society.

From an early age people are 'trained' to conform to an idea of how males and females behave. Baby boys were traditionally dressed in blue, baby girls in pink. The way in which these differences in the characteristics of the genders were seen is reinforced throughout society by peer groups, parents, teachers and the media.

It is generally accepted by society as a whole that there are certain characteristics more associated with either masculine or feminine ideals. At times these views may be challenged by some people because they consider them to be unfair. In the 1960s several women's movements challenged assumptions about the place of women in society. They argued that women should be treated according to their individual merits rather than just being categorised as 'women'.

The following table lists gender characteristics or ideals still commonly thought to relate more to males or females.

Masculine characteristics	*Feminine characteristics*
aggressive	affectionate
ambitious	caring
competitive	compassionate
dominant	easily flattered
forceful	gentle
independent	loyal
individualistic	shy
leadership qualities	sensitive
sporty	understanding

ACTIVITY 18

Class discussion

- How far do you think that the characteristics described above are appropriate?
- Can you think of any other stereotypical views of masculinity and femininity?
- Discuss where in the media you think that these ideals are shown.

Extension activity

- Compile similar lists to contrast stereotypical views of teenagers and senior citizens.

Practical task

Group (or Individual) - Over two or three weeks collect as many cuttings of words and images as you can from magazines that show a particular representation of masculine or feminine ideals. Stick them on to a large sheet of paper and display in the classroom. Describe to the class your reasons for choosing your selection and where you found the items. You may choose to keep to a stereotypical view or you may select words and images that show an alternative view of men and women.

CASE STUDY – Sugar

Sugar is published by Attic Futura, a division of PMP Communications which publishes magazines in Australia, Germany and the UK. *Sugar* was launched in 1994 and was an instant success. Its circulation for January to June 1998 was 451,696 copies per issue, making it by far the most popular teenage magazine on the market and among the 10 top-selling consumer monthly magazines in this country.

In its information pack the publisher suggests that 'the *Sugar* reader is an ordinary teenager who is changing physically and growing emotionally. She is developing a sense of her own identity and forming her own opinions for the first time. She loves being young but can't wait until she's older. Most of all she wants to have fun.' The typical *Sugar* reader is described as 'living at home with her parents (and probably arguing with them). She is studying at school and has ambitions to go to university and have a career. While she gets pocket money she wants to be independent so she has a part-time job.'

Sugar - the most popular teenage magazine

ACTIVITY 19

Class discussion

How does the description of a typical *Sugar* reader compare with the feminine ideals that you have already studied?

Extension activity

Stereotypes are often criticised as being false. Are there any stereotypes that you think are true?

ACTIVITY 20

- Look at a copy of *Sugar*. Study the contents of the magazine, including the advertisements. What is there that would appeal to the typical *Sugar* readers described above?

Extension activity

- Describe two or three girls who *you* would think would be typical *Sugar* readers.

Sugar gives details of two girls who are typical readers:

Sam age: 14
star sign: Virgo
lives: Eire
studying: '10 GCSEs but I keep changing my mind about what I want to do.'
favourite shop: TopShop
favourite music type: Boy bands
the worst record ever is: Ant and Dec's *Let's Get Ready to Rumble*
chilling out is: 'Chocolate, mates, and getting ready to go out to parties.'
I wish I had the guts to: 'Talk to more people I don't know.'

Jo age: 15
star sign: Scorpio
lives: London
studying: 'GCSEs. I would like to be a vet.'
favourite shop: Benetton
favourite music type: Dance and Indie
the worst record ever is: *Macarena*
chilling out is: 'Doing my nails and trying out new make-up with my friends.'
I wish I had the guts to: 'Ask someone out.'

In the information that the publishers of *Sugar* give to potential advertisers they point out that the typical reader is an active purchaser of make-up, toiletries, fashion, CDs and videos. They say that 'you name it, if it's cool, she wants it!'

According to readership surveys *Sugar* has a readership of almost 1.3 million 11–19 year olds.

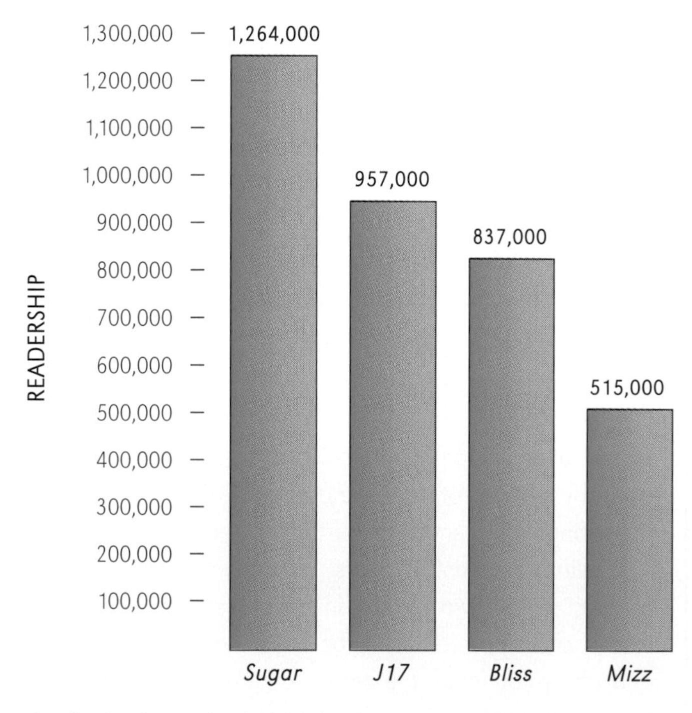

Readership figures for the UK's leading teenage magazines

Relationship between the magazine and its readers

An amazing 93 per cent of all teenagers read magazines and, as we have seen, magazines target very specific groups. What is it that a teenage magazine like *Sugar* offers its readers?

The magazine tries to offer:

- A close relationship between the reader and the magazine. It becomes like an extension of the reader's friendship group.
- A sense of trust. Advice given in the magazine is considered to be trustworthy.
- Something that is interactive. Readers can do quizzes, enter competitions, etc.

It is accepted that girls who read *Sugar* want questions answered, for example how to look and feel good, how to be popular (with both boys and other girls). It is thought that teenage girls find it difficult to discuss their concerns with parents or teachers. Their magazine becomes a trusted source of information and relaxation. They can read without embarrassment about matters that concern them, but in privacy. They can then discuss the articles with their friends or laugh about some of the features in the magazine and feel reassured.

Sugar prides itself that its content will appeal to its target readership. It says it is full of 'wearable fashion, reassuring advice, easy-to-follow beauty tips, celebrity gossip and compelling real life stories. *Sugar* provides its readers with an irresistible package. It speaks to them in their own voice, without using embarrassing patronising "teen speak" and gives them something they can feel proud and excited to be a part of. Irreverent and cheeky, it's a magazine that laughs at celebrities as much as it admires them, and in turn helps the readers take themselves a little less seriously.'

ACTIVITY 21

- Look closely at the content of any copy of *Sugar*. Discuss, in small groups or as a class, whether you think that *Sugar* does fulfil what it promises to give to its readers.

As you can see, the magazine aims to be fully a part of the life of its readers. It also tries to establish a sense of loyalty within its readership. One in five readers read only *Sugar* and over half its readers read *Sugar* on a regular monthly basis. These are higher proportions than any other lifestyle magazine.

A sister publication of *Sugar* is called *B*. It is targeted at 18–25-year-olds who are either in their first or second job, or at a college. This overlaps neatly with *Sugar*, targeted at 13–19-year-olds.

ACTIVITY 22

- Look at the content of a copy of ***B***. In class discuss how far you think that the content shows us a stereotypical view of women.

In March 1999 Attic Futura launched a new magazine called *Shine* on to the market. Its first issue sold more than 120,000. Its broad target audience is stated as being ABC1 women of 20–35 with its core target market of ABC1 women aged 25–34. The average age of its readers is considered to be 26–27. Its main editorial focus is beauty, health, fashion and fitness.

ACTIVITY 23

- Look at the content of a copy of *Shine*. Compare the contents of this magazine with ***B***. In class discuss what view of women is being presented.

Magazines for women represent not only views about the qualities and attitudes of women but also women's views and attitudes to men.

ACTIVITY 24

- Look at articles in *Sugar* and other magazines targeted at a female audience and discuss what views of males are represented in them.

Essay

Describe the ways in which magazines aimed at a female audience reflect gender stereotypes.

Teenage girls' magazines are often read by a younger age group than that suggested as the main target readership by the publishers of the magazines. This is because the contents of the magazines offer representations that the readership can aspire to, that is, hope to become. The reverse is often the case with older women who may read magazines targeted at a younger readership.

ACTIVITY 25

- In class look at two magazines targeted at a young teenage readership and two magazines targeted at young women. Discuss what there is in each magazine that you think might appeal to an age range outside the suggested target readership given by the publishers.

MEDIA LANGUAGES AND CATEGORIES

HOW TO ANALYSE A MAGAZINE

The first step in analysing any visual media text is simply to look to see what is there. You should describe in detail what is, for instance, on the cover of a magazine or on any of the pages inside. This process of description is called **denotation**. Here is a checklist of questions that you can use to carry out a careful and detailed description of the front cover of a magazine:

1. What is the magazine called?
2. What other words or phrases are on the page?
3. What colours are used?
4. What images are on the page? (When describing the images make sure that you describe all the detail. For instance, on the front page there may be the image of a girl, aged approximately 15. She may be blonde, with blue eyes, and she may be smiling.)

At this stage you do not need to explain what the words and images mean or how you react to them. If there is a picture of a person who is smiling do not at this point write that 'they are happy'.

ACTIVITY 26

- Look closely at the front cover of a magazine of your choice and make notes on your responses to the questions above in relation to this magazine.

When you have all the details carefully listed you should consider them separately and together in order to discover what the details might mean. The possible meanings of this content are called the **connotations**.

If you were to see a picture of a red flag then this denotes simply 'a flag' and its colour is red. It could, however, have different connotations. It could connote 'danger' or 'left-wing politics', such as communism.

When you have detailed answers to the four questions above, ask yourself *why* they are used – what meanings do they offer?

1 Why is the magazine called .....?
2 What does the style of language tell you about the readership of the magazine?
3 How do you react to the language?
4 Why are the colours used chosen?
5 What meanings do they have?
6 How do you react to the colours? How do they make you feel?
7 Why do you think the images are arranged as they are?
8 How do you react to the images?
9 What are the people like in the magazine? You could consider age, gender and race.

You will notice that the questions asked about the meanings or connotations of what you see are much more How? and Why? This is when you are beginning to analyse the text in more detail. It will take time. It is not something that can be done very quickly. Think through as many ideas as you can, no matter how absurd they may seem. Discuss your ideas in small groups.

When you have looked at the different parts of the front cover consider the impact of the cover as a whole. Ask the following questions:

1 Who is the magazine's target audience?
2 How does the front cover suggest this?
3 How does it attract its audience?
4 How effective is the cover in attracting its target audience?

ACTIVITY 27

- Make notes on your responses to the questions above in relation to your chosen magazine. You will now have notes on both **denotations** and **connotations** in relation to your chosen magazine. Using your notes write a complete analysis of the front page of your magazine.

When you have extracted as much information and meaning from the front cover the same process can be used to consider any part of the content of the magazine, including the advertisements.

Once you have studied the magazine in detail you should consider what the main areas of interest are in the content as a whole.

There are some further questions that you should consider.

1 Who produces the magazine?
2 What other titles do they produce?
3 What is the competition?
4 How successful do you think that the magazine is in fighting the competition?

Finally you should ask:

1 Does the magazine fulfil the expectations of its readership?
2 What pleasures do the target audience gain from the magazine?

CASE STUDY – Textual analysis of front cover of April 2001 edition of Sugar

Fig 4.21

The title of the magazine is referred to as the **masthead** in the same manner as newspapers.

The words and phrases giving information about what is inside the magazine are called **plugs**, **cover** or **sell lines** or **teasers**.

The reference to 'Britain's best selling girls' magazine' which appears under the price and dateline is called a **puff**, because it 'puffs up' the image of the magazine.

The title of the magazine is *Sugar* which **connotes** sweetness. A common but rather old-fashioned description of girls was 'sugar and spice and all things nice'. 'Sugar' has also been used as a term of affection for girls.

The title is partially covered by the model, which shows that the magazine is sufficiently popular to be recognised without the full title showing. The model is linked with the title, becoming part of its structure which suggests that she is also sweet.

Individual words are used to attract attention – such as 'exclusive', 'cool' and 'FREE'.

The 'true stories' teaser offers stories that are sensational but the story about mugging will have practical significance for the target readership.

In keeping with the view of *Sugar* that it is a 'girl's best friend', terms are used that will connect with the readers. Words such as 'sussed' and 'snog' make the tone chatty and casual.

ACTIVITY 28

- Discuss in small groups other wording on the front cover.
- Why do you think that these references to the contents were used?
- Look at another edition of *Sugar*. Compare references to the contents on the front page with the full contents listings.
- Discuss why you think these items were chosen for the cover and not others.

Although you cannot judge them here, the colours used on the front cover are predominantly bright and cheerful. Yellow connotes sunshine. The background is deep pink, with connotations of femininity. The background for the free gift is bright Day-Glo orange, which has direct impact. The lettering for some of the teasers is also in the same colour, which contrasts with the gentler colour of the overall background. The overall impression the colours give is of a young, bright, lively, fresh and fun-loving magazine.

To accentuate some of the lettering, a black edging is given to part of each letter. This is called **shadowing**. The shadowing on the title is rough-edged, which gives *Sugar* a friendly casual look.

The image on the front cover is a head shot of a young, attractive girl with a casual hairstyle. This makes the image almost the same size and proximity as a person talking directly to you and reinforces the image of the girl as a friend. Her make-up is not overstated and she has a wide friendly smile. Her gaze, which welcomes you as a friend, is directly at the reader. Her eyes are a continuation of the title, so the girl becomes part of the title itself. Her top is casual giving the front cover a relaxed feel.

If you add together all the components of the front cover, the magazine attracts its potential readers by giving the impression that it is a friendly magazine, interested in the same topics of gossip and sensation. The girl on the cover invites you to be like her and to like her: and by implication like and buy the magazine.

INTO THE NEW MILLENNIUM

According to the consumer magazine circulation figures released by the Audit Bureau of Circulations in June 1999, women's and men's lifestyle magazines were struggling to sustain their readership.

The men's market appeared to have reached saturation point as two thirds of the magazines of this genre reported falling sales for January–June compared with the same period in 1998.

The market leader, EMAP's *FHM*, saw sales fall by 9.6 per cent (the equivalent of 74,000 copies). *Loaded* slipped back by almost 16 per cent.

Magazines related to computers, games and the Internet, on the other hand, had been very successful. This group of magazines as a whole saw an increase in sales of 14 per cent from June 1998 to June 1999.

Women's monthly magazines had seen even bigger setbacks, with all but two titles showing decreases in sales. IPC's *Marie Claire* saw an increase of 5 per cent and Attic Futura's *B* an increase of 11 per cent over the same period of time.

ACTIVITY 29

- Using the information from the chart above, discuss in class reasons why you think that the magazines have lost sales. What methods could they use to help increase sales?

Competition from other media and the increase in the number of magazines on the market have led to the loss of sales. Magazines are also targeting ever tighter audiences. The publishing companies may sacrifice some readers from one magazine and attract them to another. Attic Futura may have lost some of its *Sugar* readers when it launched *B* in 1997, but it substantially broadened the appeal of the two magazines put together.

The magazine market in Britain continues to be extremely volatile. There is ever increasing competition from newspaper supplements and e-zines. New magazines are being launched more often, yet, in spite of all this activity, paid-for circulations have dropped by nearly 40 per cent in the last five years. Magazine sales tend to follow fashion and the magazines that have done best are comics, those dealing with men's fashion, the countryside, teenage interest, motoring, computers and the Internet, and TV listings. This last category may well come under fire when Web-based programme guides are directly accessible from TV sets.

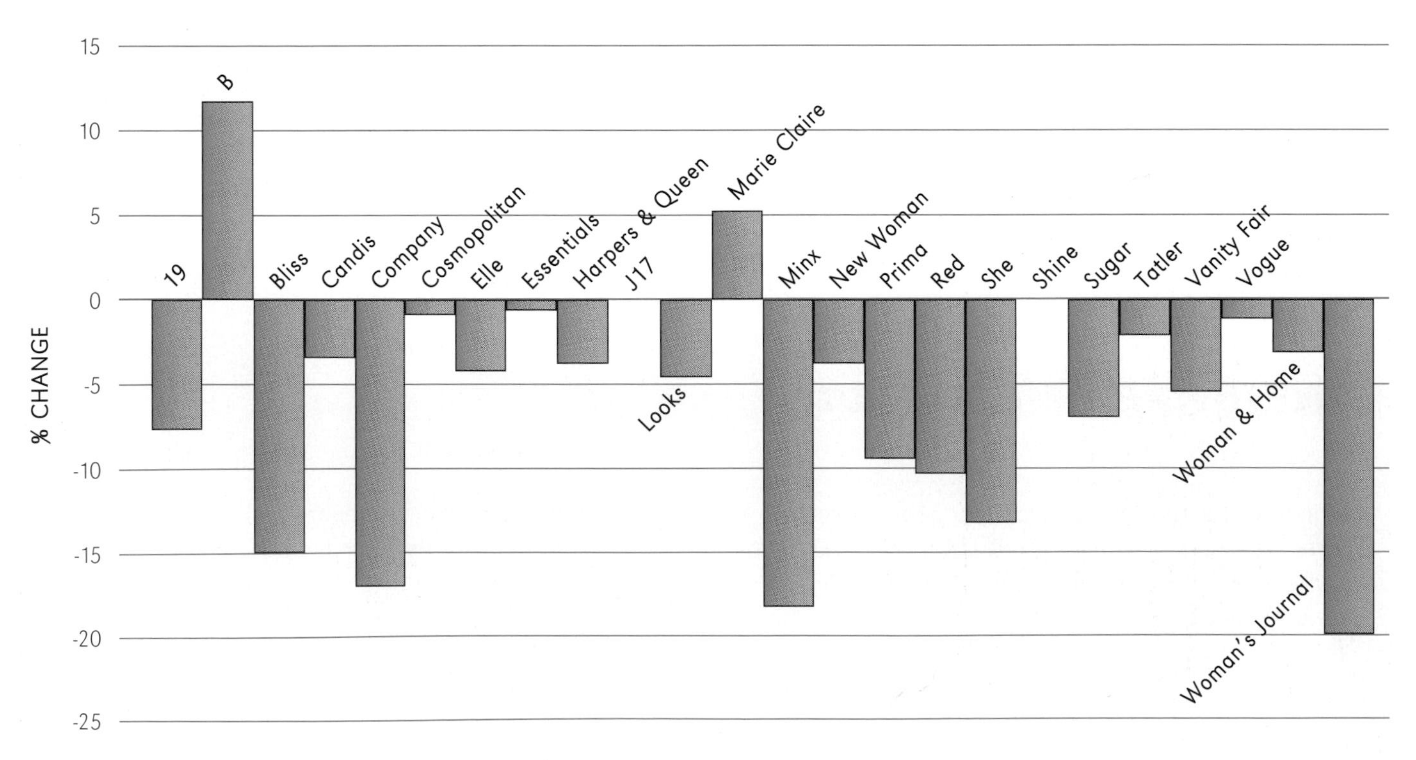

Source: ABC

SUMMARY

- A magazine is a collection of articles and stories published at regular intervals.
- Kinds of magazines can be divided into categories or genres; for example, women's lifestyle magazines or gardening magazines.
- With increased literacy in the eighteenth century magazines began to flourish.
- In the nineteenth century many popular writers such as Dickens and Sir Walter Scott serialised their novels in magazines.
- The early twentieth century saw the rapid advance of advertising in magazines. Between 1910 and 1939 some of the most popular and enduring of the women's magazines were published for the first time in Britain – *Vogue, Good Housekeeping, Harper's Bazaar, Woman's Weekly, Woman and Home, Woman's Illustrated* and *Woman*.
- The younger women's market was targeted in magazines such as *She, Honey, Annabel, Petticoat* and *19*, from 1955–1968.
- The largest publisher of magazines is IPC Magazines with 20 per cent of the market share. EMAP has 13 per cent of the market share.
- Magazines are more and more being targeted at specific audiences. Many magazines fail. But there are always more around the corner waiting to be published.
- Competition from newspaper supplements and Internet-based e-zines has caused magazine sales to fall.

GLOSSARY

audience – people who 'receive' any media text, whether it is film, television, radio, newspaper or magazine

Audit Bureau of Circulations (ABC) – independent organisation which calculates the circulation figures for newspapers and magazines

connotation – the meanings that images or sounds can suggest

consumer magazines – those which provide people with leisure time information and entertainment

cover lines – information about major articles given on the front page

denotation – describing what can be seen or heard

genre – category, or type

letterpress – form of printing with raised image

magazine – comes from the Arabic word meaning 'storehouse'

mass audience – readership on a very large scale

masthead – the title of a magazine or newspaper; usually placed at the top of the front cover

National Readership Survey (NRS) – organisation that sets out to provide information on the number and nature of readership of magazines and newspapers

niche audience – narrow group of readers, for example for a magazine about antiques

Periodical Publishers Association – trade association of magazine publishers

plugs – information about the contents given on the cover

puff – words or phrases on the cover of a magazine to boost its status

readership – not just 'who buys' a magazine or newspaper, but total number of people who are likely to read the publication

representation – how we communicate with each other using words or images

teasers – short phrases on the front cover to tempt a reader to buy the magazine

5 Radio

RICHARD HORSMAN

Coming up

In this chapter we will be looking at:

- the nature of radio
- the development of radio from a hobby to a mass medium
- how radio is paid for
- how the battle for listeners affects what we hear
- how a radio newsroom operates
- how radio commercials are produced

INTRODUCTION

This chapter will look at a medium which is so successful, it's taken for granted – a medium which is consumed by nine out of 10 adults in the UK every week.

Hundreds of stations exist in the air all around us, generating output which is received free by listeners, and which is also comparatively cheap to produce.

Radio is older than television, but it's still a young medium. All the major developments in UK radio broadcasting have taken place within living memory. All Britain's national independent stations (Virgin, Talk Radio and Classic FM) have come on air since a typical GCSE student started school. Radio is constantly evolving to serve new audiences in new ways, using new technology to improve the quality and variety of output available for listeners to enjoy.

Radio is the most portable medium there is. No other medium can reach us at work and at home (even in the shower), in the car and on the bus, in the town and in the countryside. We can listen alone or in groups, on a Walkman or on a factory PA system.

Radio is the most personal medium there is. No other medium can reach inside the theatre of your mind, creating scenes and characters which are different for each individual listening, even though thousands of people have heard exactly the same broadcast. Radio DJs seem to be speaking to us all one at a time, whilst still reaching audiences of millions.

Radio is the fastest popular medium there is. When news breaks, radio can get the full story on the air within moments. Television is hampered by the need to process pictures. And in comparison with radio, newspapers are lumbering dinosaurs, unable to react to big developments until the next edition, or maybe even the next day.

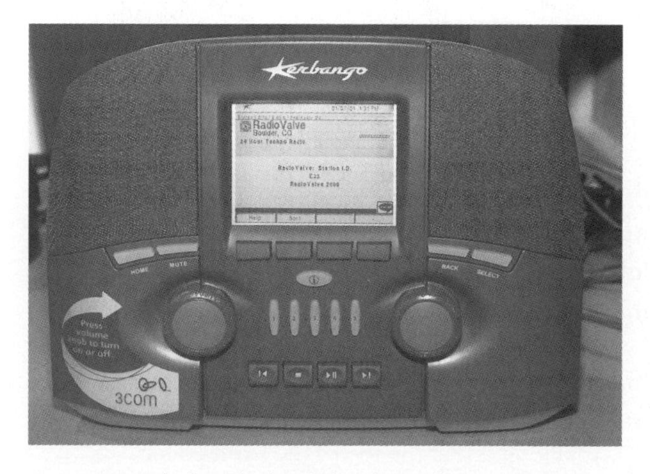

An internet radio launched in 2001 - the medium is constantly evolving

THE HISTORY OF RADIO

Radio broadcasting has been with us for just over a hundred years. In 1895 Italian scientist Guglielmo Marconi found a way to send radio messages in Morse code which could be received a few kilometres away. Marconi moved to England, where he set up a company to develop the system, and in 1901 he managed to send a radio message across the Atlantic Ocean from England to Canada. Marconi was awarded the Nobel Prize for Physics in 1909 in recognition of his achievements.

Another name for radio is **wireless telegraphy**. Early radio receivers were called 'wireless sets', as unlike telephone or telegraph systems there were no wires physically connecting the person sending the message to the person receiving it. In conversation, listeners would say they had heard something 'on the wireless' rather than 'on the radio'.

- *Do your grandparents or older friends remember listening to 'the wireless' when they were young?*

Until the 1920s radio listening was a hobby enjoyed by a few enthusiasts, mainly those interested in electronics, with above-average technical knowledge. They often built their own receivers from component parts. Audiences were tiny, but enthusiastic. Purpose-built radio receivers (like the first home computers) were a luxury, often regarded as toys for people with money to spare. As with the growth of the Internet today, it was the equipment manufacturers who first realised the mass audience potential of broadcast radio.

ACTIVITY 1

- Find out what a '**crystal set**' was.
- Why do you think early radio receivers were big, and shaped like ornate pieces of furniture?

Guglielmo Marconi – inventor of radio signalling

View through the back of an early radio

BIRTH OF THE BEEB

The BBC was originally set up as a private firm – the British Broadcasting Company – to create demand for radio sets by providing programmes for listeners to tune their receivers in to. As audiences began to grow, politicians realised the potential value (and power) of the radio medium, and the BBC was granted a Royal Charter to become the British Broadcasting Corporation, with a duty to provide a range of radio programmes for all listeners in the UK. Unlike newspapers and magazines, which reflect the political opinions and personal interests of their owners, the new BBC was required by law to be impartial in its coverage of controversial topics. This obligation continues to this day, and has been extended to independent television and radio through the various Broadcasting Acts.

- *Why is it important to keep radio independent of any political party or other powerful interest group ?*
- *Why should radio be regulated more tightly than newspapers ?*

RADIO AT WAR

During the Second World War (1939–45) both Allied and Nazi forces used radio as a powerful tool in their military and propaganda campaigns. The young General Charles de Gaulle broadcast to occupied France from London, urging his fellow countrymen to form a resistance movement against the German occupying forces. The BBC then broadcast coded messages to resistance groups in Europe who were planning sabotage attacks against the occupying Nazi armies. The German dictator, Adolf Hitler, used radio to broadcast to Britain in English. These gloomy messages about casualties and sunken navy ships were designed to sap public morale and persuade the British to surrender. Millions heard the broadcasts, and the Irish broadcaster William Joyce who read them out became known as 'Lord Haw-Haw'. Later BBC correspondents went out with the troops during the Allied invasion of France in 1944, sending back graphic accounts of the fighting from their primitive portable recorders.

ACTIVITY 2

- Do your grandparents or older friends remember listening to 'Lord Haw-Haw'?
- What other wartime broadcasts can they remember?

CHOICE OF LISTENING?

Before 1967, listeners in the UK had an extremely limited range of radio programmes to choose from. The BBC held a **monopoly** position in the market (it was the only broadcaster), and although there were some regional programmes for Scotland, Wales and a few English regions there was no local radio in the sense of stations serving individual towns, cities or communities. Most programmes were produced in London for national distribution. There were very few regional accents on the air.

Listeners had the choice of the BBC **Home Service**, a speech-based news and talk station aimed at the British 'home' market (as opposed to the **World Service** not generally received in the UK, which was aimed at overseas listeners) or the **Light Programme**, a music-based service including comedy and 'serials' – long-running light dramas which were the forerunners of modern-day soaps. The **Third Programme** offered classical music, opera, discussions and heavyweight drama whilst the **Study Programme** provided educational output.

PRESSURE FOR CHANGE

In the 1950s and early 1960s music on the BBC's Light Programme consisted mainly of easy listening rather than rock and pop, with much of the output produced by the BBC's own 'dance orchestras' rather than played off commercial recordings. The presenters still had the role of 'announcers', identifying artists and song titles, rather than being personalities or entertainers in their own right. This style tended to alienate younger listeners, who found the output boring and out of touch. These younger listeners were excited by singers like Elvis Presley and Cliff Richard, and new sounds from bands like The Beatles and the

Rolling Stones – as well as US artists. They looked for alternatives, and found them.

Radio waves can easily cross from one country to another, and some legal foreign-based broadcasters were able to reach an untapped market in Britain by providing a more popular music service, with commercials, presented in English. The best-known of these was **Radio Luxembourg**.

BEWARE PIRATES!

Other would-be broadcasters tried to beat the British authorities by operating from ships equipped with powerful transmitters, anchored offshore in international waters just outside the UK's territorial limit. These became known as '**pirate radio stations**', taking their name from the armed ships which used to rob and plunder merchant vessels at sea. The term 'pirate radio' survives, as a term to describe all illegal broadcasts. The best-known and most popular 'pirates' included **Radio Caroline**, **Radio London** and **Radio North Sea International**. The British government eventually defeated the pirate ships by making it an offence for anyone to supply them with food or fuel, or to advertise on their programmes.

The September 28, 1967 edition of *Radio Times* announced the launch of Radio 1

ACTIVITY 3

- Can you name some popular broadcasters still working in radio and TV who started their careers with 'pirate' radio stations?

ACTIVITY 4

- Who was the first voice on BBC Radio 1?
- Can your parents or friends remember listening?
- Who else do they remember on the station?

AUNTIE'S NEW IMAGE

In 1967 the BBC set about modernising its national services, numbering them Radios 1, 2, 3 and 4. The former Light Programme became Radio 2 and the old Home Service became Radio 4. The Third Programme kept its numeric identity as Radio 3, and a brand new service – Radio 1 – was launched to serve the market identified by the pirate stations. Popular presenters who had proven the demand for a new style of radio eventually came ashore to work legitimately as DJs (**disc jockeys**) on the new BBC station, and later on independent radio.

LOCAL VOICES

November 1967 also saw the launch of real local radio in the UK with the opening of BBC Radio Leicester. This was the first station in the BBC's local radio network, with the job of providing 'the missing link of communication ... talking to the citizens about their town, bringing them into contact with each other ... telling the running serial story of local life'. Seven other local stations followed in the first wave of development. The aim was to create 70 local stations covering the whole country, but unable to meet the costs out of licence fee income, the BBC eventually settled for 38 stations covering 90 per cent of the UK population.

ACTIVITY 5

- Find out which BBC local radio station(s) serve your area. When did they come on air?

COMMERCIAL COMPETITION

The world of UK broadcasting changed forever in 1973 with the birth of **independent radio**. Would-be commercial broadcasters had long argued that the BBC's monopoly in radio should be scrapped, pointing to the success of Independent Television (ITV) established in 1956 as a rival to the BBC's television service. Radio in the United States had been run on commercial lines from the earliest days.

INDEPENDENT LOCAL RADIO

The first commercial stations – known as ILR, or Independent Local Radio, went on air in 1973. The London Broadcasting Company (**LBC**) was first on air with a news and speech-based service for London. It was followed shortly by **Capital Radio**, a music-based station also serving London.

Chris Tarrant has been a DJ at Capital Radio since 1984

Nineteen stations were licensed in the first wave of **franchise** awards, with stations obliged by law to include less popular '**public service**' elements in their schedules, such as long news bulletins, arts programmes and religious messages. These obligations resulted in a great deal of token output, such as one three-hour classical music programme a week, broadcast late on a Sunday evening, on a station which otherwise based its schedule on rock and pop. Although each could find a **niche audience**, the arrangement was unsatisfactory for both broadcasters and audiences.

ACTIVITY 6

- Find out which was the first commercial radio station on air in your area.

DIVIDING THE AUDIENCE

The first ILR stations were licensed to use both AM and FM transmitters, and would broadcast the same service on both – an arrangement known as simultaneous broadcasting, or **simulcasting**. The Conservative government in the 1980s became frustrated with the slow growth of commercial radio and, as a spur to increasing choice, allowed existing broadcasters to provide alternative services on AM and FM, with the suggestion that the transmitters could be re-allocated to rival broadcasters if the existing stations failed to do so. This 'use 'em or lose 'em' philosophy saw the rise of so-called '**Gold**' **stations** (often on AM), generally playing hit music from the 1960s and 70s, whilst the FM channels were used for a more contemporary music service.

ACTIVITY 7

- Research out whether your local independent radio station changed its name or its output during the late 1980s or early 90s. How many independent radio stations in your area are owned by the same company? How is their output and image different to appeal to different audiences?

INDEPENDENT NATIONAL RADIO (INR)

Re-organisation of the radio spectrum at national level also cleared the way for the launch of INR – Independent National Radio. The first INR licence was awarded to **Classic FM**, and for the first time the BBC faced a UK competitor in the broadcasting of 'serious' music. The launch of Classic FM in September 1992 prompted an explosion of interest in orchestral and operatic music. **Virgin 1215** was the second national station on the air in April 1993, but its impact has been limited by the fact that in most of the country outside London it is available only on relatively poor quality AM. **Talk Radio** (now rebranded as TalkSPORT) is the most recent INR station, offering a popular speech-based service with a large proportion of phone-ins. It came on air in February 1995.

- *Why do you think Britain's first INR station was Classic FM (playing serious music) rather than Virgin (playing rock)?*
- *What did the launch of Classic FM do for the 'image' of independent radio generally?*

REGIONAL STATIONS

There are also new 'layers' of independent radio. Regional stations, covering areas roughly equivalent to the ITV / Channel 3 TV regions (Yorkshire, Central, Granada etc) serve 'niche' markets with formats such as dance music (Galaxy), or 50 / 50 music and news (Century). These are minority services which, when broadcast over a larger geographical area, can attract a large number of listeners as a small percentage of the total population.

ACTIVITY 8

- Find out what regional independent radio services are on air in your area.
- What specialist audience 'niches' are they serving?

RESTRICTED SERVICE LICENCES – ACCESS FOR ALL?

Community radio, both commercial and non-profit-making, is springing up in very small geographical areas – often taking advantage of **Restricted Service Licences** (RSLs), which provide the opportunity for groups of enthusiasts to broadcast at very low cost.

Each Radio Authority RSL licence allows the holder up to 28 days' broadcasting a year, with no individual or organisation allowed to hold more than two licences. RSLs are often tied to special events (such as an arts festival) or to community activities such as a religious celebration (one example being Fast FM, a station run by Muslims in Bradford during the Islamic holy month of Ramadan).

Another type of RSL station is linked to football or rugby Superleague clubs, broadcasting only on match days, providing fans with interviews, commentary and gossip about their favourite team for a maximum of 28 games during the season. Other small-scale, highly localised radio services can provide information for travellers approaching ferry terminals or airports in their cars.

ACTIVITY 9

- Find out what RSLs are broadcasting (or have broadcast) in your area.

PIRATES STILL EXIST!

Land-based pirate radio stations still exist. Enthusiasts who believe their musical tastes or lifestyle are not reflected in any current 'legal' broadcasts still seek to put themselves on the air, and the technology required to do so is relatively cheap and easy to obtain. However, their unregulated transmissions can interfere with legitimate broadcasters, spoiling the enjoyment of listeners, or block channels reserved for communications in the event of a civil emergency. There are severe penalties for those found guilty of taking part, including the confiscation of their equipment and CDs – and not least a ban on convicted individuals holding a licence to broadcast legally.

KEY DATES

- **1886** Heinrich Hertz produces radio waves using an electromagnet
- **1898** Guglielmo Marconi sends a Morse Code radio message from Dover to a lightship on Goodwin Sands, a distance of 20 km
- **1901** Marconi sends the first Morse Code radio message across the Atlantic, from Cornwall to Newfoundland, a distance of 2,000 km
- **1913** Development of the Triode valve allows first clear broadcast of speech and music by radio waves
- **1915** First spoken words transmitted from Britain to the USA
- **1922** The British Broadcasting Company, a private company, is granted a licence by the government to establish a national network of transmitters
- **1927** The BBC is granted a Royal Charter and becomes the British Broadcasting Corporation
- **1930** The first royal radio message (by King George V) is broadcast by the BBC and is heard by 3 million listeners across the United Kingdom.
- **1939-45** Radio becomes a weapon of war – Nazi Germany broadcasts propaganda to the UK (William Joyce – 'Lord Haw Haw') and the BBC broadcasts coded messages to Resistance fighters in occupied France
- **1950s** Development of FM technology allows clearer broadcasts and potential for many more radio services. BBC begins planning for local radio, prompted in part by perceived 'Cold War' threats to London-based services in the event of a nuclear strike
- **1964** The first 'pirate' broadcasters, Radio Caroline and Radio Atlanta, begin transmissions
- **1966** Government white paper outlines plans for BBC local radio services
- **1967** BBC Radio 1 launched. Marine Offences Act silences the offshore pirate broadcasters. First BBC local station opens – BBC Radio Leicester
- **1971** Broadcasting Act paves the way for legal commercial radio in the UK

  The former Independent Television Authority becomes the Independent Broadcasting Authority (IBA) and assumes responsibility for regulation of Independent Local Radio (ILR)
- **1973** LBC and Capital Radio launch – the first of 19 ILR stations approved in the first phase of development
- **1980s** BBC and ILR local networks grow to cover all major centres of population in the UK
- **1991** Radio Authority takes over responsibility for regulation of commercial radio from the IBA
- **1991** First Restricted Service Licences allow community groups to broadcast for up to 28 days on low power transmitters

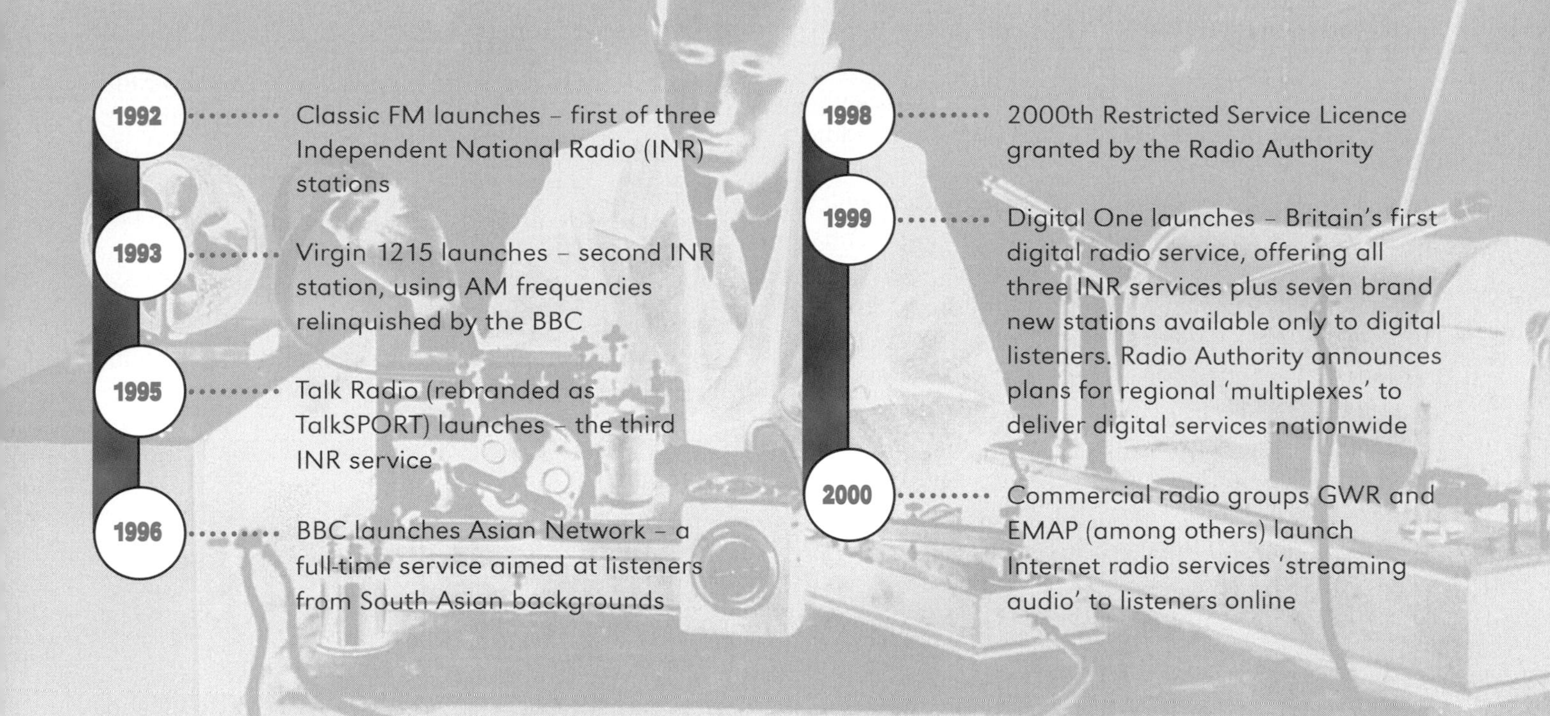

MEDIA PRODUCERS AND AUDIENCES

THE CHOICE NOW

The listener at the turn of the century has a much wider range of radio services available to enjoy. Reorganisation of the radio spectrum has allowed the launch of brand new national services – most notably BBC Radio 5 Live, Virgin Radio and Talk Radio. There are now five BBC national services, three Independent National Radio stations, and a choice (in most parts of the UK) of several local, regional and community services. BBC local radio serves seven million listeners a week, and covers 90 per cent of the UK population. Independent Local Radio now numbers more than 200 stations.

AM TO FM – TECHNICAL DEVELOPMENTS

Well into the 1970s most people listened to programmes in the Medium and Long wavebands, now generally known as **AM** (for **Amplitude Modulated**). Such broadcasts are prone to interference from other stations, especially after dark and in certain weather conditions. The introduction of high-quality **VHF** services (**Very High Frequency** – now known as **FM**, or **Frequency Modulated**) brought about a revolution in technical quality, and the introduction of stereo broadcasts. However, the equipment required to receive such broadcasts was very expensive, and most listeners were reluctant to change their radio sets. The majority of services are now broadcast on FM in stereo. This allows much clearer reception, especially after dark, and with modern transmission systems (combined with accurate tuners) many more stations can be accommodated on the FM waveband.

ACTIVITY 10

- How many UK radio stations can you find on the FM and AM radio bands in your region?
- Which stations still simulcast on both AM and FM?
- What has happened to the national AM slots previously used by BBC Radios 1, 2 and 3?

THE ARRIVAL OF DIGITAL

The introduction of **DAB** (Digital Audio Broadcasting) promises another revolution in radio listening, with even better-quality reception than that offered by FM. Listeners will have the choice of many more stations than ever before, and the potential exists for new interactive services. Radiotext receivers in cars could offer a printout of traffic information for motorists, or money-off coupons at the touch of a button for drivers tempted by an offer in a radio commercial. Radiovision receivers in the home could offer high-quality graphics linked to programme content. However, the provision of such services will depend on demand, and the willingness of listeners to buy the new generation of radio receivers.

HOW RADIO IS PAID FOR

We think of radio as a free medium, and as such it is often undervalued. We think nothing of paying 50 pence or even £1 for a newspaper, which will be thrown away within hours, or at most in a day or two; we may pay £2–3 for a glossy magazine. We must buy a TV licence every year if we have a receiver in our home, regardless of what programmes we choose to watch. Sports enthusiasts and movie buffs are increasingly prepared to accept 'pay-per-view' TV for important events or new releases. We dial premium-rate telephone lines to obtain weather and traffic information. And of course we expect to pay every time we visit a theatre, cinema or concert venue. Yet radio delivers news, weather forecasts and traffic bulletins – free – in a constantly updated form 24 hours a day. Listeners can also choose, free to them at the point of delivery, sports commentary, drama, film and video reviews, rock gigs, classical concerts and much more.

- *How much do you pay out every week for newspapers, magazines, cinema tickets, video rentals, satellite or cable TV subscriptions etc?*

Radio isn't Really Free

Of course there are costs involved in providing radio services. As well as the salaries for DJs, newsreaders, engineers and other station staff there are all the overheads (rent, rates, heat, light and power) associated with any business. Radio stations also face substantial telecommunication charges, both for the normal telephones used extensively in newsgathering and the specialist facilities (**landlines**, **ISDN lines** etc) used for outside broadcasts and for carrying output to transmitter sites.

landline – a phone line laid over land

ISDN line – a phone line with digital quality

Royalties

Every time a record is played on air a **royalty** must be paid to the Performing Rights Society (PRS). This money is distributed to the composer and publisher of the original music, the record company which made the disc, and the performers. Stations must keep an exact and accurate log (to the second) of all music played, and they are subjected to regular checks to ensure their logging is accurate. Although record-keeping is a chore for individual presenters and producers it is essential to ensure musicians receive the payments due to them for their creative efforts. Successful artists and publishers certainly earn vast amounts, but record labels use this income to subsidise their promotion of new bands who otherwise may never achieve public exposure.

Broadcast Rights

Broadcasting of live events costs radio a lot of money. Football clubs charge stations commentary fees for the rights to each game, and some clubs are now charging a premium to give individual stations the **exclusive rights** to cover their matches. Such exclusivity gives the station a competitive advantage in a crowded marketplace, as fans must tune to them in order to follow their team's progress. The bigger fees in turn generate more income for the club. Live broadcasting of music events is also very expensive, both because of the technical requirements and because artists expect to be compensated in their fees for the potential loss of income from record sales. If fans can hear new songs live on the radio (and perhaps tape them) they may be less likely to buy the album when it's released. The broadcaster must meet these costs through different funding mechanisms.

Raising the Cash – BBC Radio

BBC radio is paid for out of the television licence fee, a compulsory levy on every household in the UK with a television receiver, whether or not viewers choose to watch BBC programmes. With almost every home now having a television, and with the fee set by the government, this is effectively a form of taxation. However, unlike other tax-raising measures based on ownership (such as the car tax disc required by drivers) which raise money for general government spending, money raised by the TV licence fee is used only for the specific purpose of funding the BBC. This gives the BBC a guaranteed and predictable income not affected by the general state of the economy and the willingness of advertisers to support individual programmes, or programme channels.

ACTIVITY 11

- Find out how much a TV licence costs.

Those who believe in the idea of **public service broadcasting** also argue that this way of paying for programmes increases the choice and quality available to listeners. Radio services such as BBC Radio 3 and BBC Radio 4 would be impossibly expensive to operate profitably in a purely commercial market, and the introduction of advertising or sponsorship would alter the fundamental nature (and, at a more basic level, the actual sound) of their output.

public service broadcasting – broadcasts for education and information, to serve the public

Programme-makers have a degree of freedom to experiment with new ideas without the need to deliver instant success in the ratings. BBC local radio stations can provide programmes for special interest groups (ethnic minority language programmes, for example, or early-morning news for farmers or specialist music such as folk or gospel) which would never command a big enough audience to make them commercially viable.

- *Is it right that the BBC should offer radio services (like Radio 3) which are listened to by only a tiny minority of the population, but which cost a lot of licence fee money to run?*

Raising the Cash – Independent Radio

Independent radio has no access to any part of the money raised by the TV licence fee, or from any other public source. All the costs of providing the service must be paid for from the station's own resources – the money raised by the sale of **advertising** and **sponsorship**. We make no specific payment to independent radio, but in effect we pay for the service every time we make a purchase. Advertising and marketing costs make up a proportion of the price we pay for most goods. For some, such as designer clothing or cola drinks, these costs can be a substantial proportion of the purchase price. In the UK, radio advertising accounts for only a tiny proportion of total advertising expenditure at around 5 per cent – well below the amounts spent on press ads, TV commercials and posters. However, the proportion is growing fast – and in the United States, where commercial radio has been the norm since its introduction in the 1920s, radio accounts for nearly 20 per cent of the national advertising spend.

Advertising Regulations

When ILR first began in the UK, it was able to offer clients only so-called 'spot' advertising – self-contained messages (usually of 20 or 30 seconds' duration) broadcast within clearly identified 'commercial breaks' which had to be completely separate from the programme around them. No more than nine minutes of commercials could be broadcast in any one hour, DJs were banned from appearing in ads and sponsorship was prohibited. These restrictions severely limited the effectiveness of early radio campaigns, as they worked against the essential nature of the radio medium – its intimacy with its audience. Building barriers around the commercials excluded them from the personal relationship that exists between each listener and their chosen broadcaster.

The Beginnings of Sponsorship

Later modifications to the Broadcasting Acts allowed a much more flexible (although still regulated) approach – particularly with regard to sponsorship of key programme elements such as weather, sport and travel news and allowing presenters to promote sponsored events (such as sports events or concerts) within their own programmes. Some areas still remain off-limits, however, notably the sponsorship of news.

- *Why shouldn't news on independent radio be sponsored?*
- *What problems would have to be faced if it was?*

Alternative Sources?

Other models of funding are set to emerge as radio develops. Small community Restricted Service Licences (RSLs) are often organised by a nucleus of paid staff organising a large number of volunteers. These stations may receive grants from charities or local authorities to promote specific 'good causes' – such as health awareness or adult literacy campaigns. Others may follow the example of the United States, where non-commercial PBS (Public Broadcasting Service) stations organise their own on-air fundraising events, such as phone-in auctions of goods donated by wellwishers.

ACTIVITY 12

- Find out if there's an RSL near you.
- How is it paid for?

WHICH STATIONS DO WE LISTEN TO?

Radio listening is measured by audience research. There is no way stations can ever know exactly how many people are listening at any one time, or how audiences are going up or down over time – unlike newspapers, which record a daily sale. However, audience research is becoming increasingly sophisticated, and over time stations can build up a pretty accurate profile of their listeners and the likely effects of changes to output.

Types of Research

Audience research can take different forms – **quantitative** research, which tries to find out how many people (= quantity) are listening to the station, and for how long; and **qualitative** research, which aims to discover what value (= quality) people place on different elements of the output.

Given that there is no precise method to determine radio audiences, it is difficult for broadcasters, audiences or potential advertisers to obtain objective data on exactly who is listening to what station – and all controllers will always find ways to claim their service is successful.

- *Why do stations want to know more than just how many people are listening?*

RAJAR Audience Measurement

In a bid to create objective figures, the BBC and the independent stations jointly subscribe to a common research agency known as **RAJAR** (Radio Joint Audience Research Limited), which carries out audience surveys by placing 'listening diaries' in homes across the country. These homes are selected to provide a representative sample in terms of age, gender and social type within each survey area. People are asked to complete a diary over the survey period, ticking which station (if any) they were listening to in time segments for each day. The listing of stations is random in each diary so as to avoid any effect from a station being first or last in the list.

National services are surveyed over the whole country. Local and regional stations are surveyed within their declared TSA (Total Survey Area). The survey provides figures for both **reach** (the percentage of people listening to each radio service at any given time) and **hours** (how long these people are tuning in for). From this information it is possible to calculate each station's share of the total radio audience by comparing the total number of listener-hours each station enjoys across a given day, or a week. The basic information for each station in each survey is available to the public (and on the Internet – www.rajar.co.uk), whilst stations paying for the full service receive a much more detailed confidential report, broken down by individual time segments and by localised survey points within their TSA. It is therefore possible for managers to see immediately which presenters or programmes are popular, and how the service is performing in different communities within the area they serve.

QUARTERLY SUMMARY OF RADIO LISTENING

Survey Period Ending 17th September 2000

PART 1 - UNITED KINGDOM

	Survey Period	Adult 15+ Pop (000s)	Weekly (000)	Reach %	Per Head	Average Hours Per Listener	Total Hours (000s)	Share of Listening %
ALL RADIO	Q	48134	43407	90	21.7	24.1	1045718	100
ALL BBC	Q	48134	31168	65	11.2	17.3	537966	51.4
All BBC Network Radio	Q	48134	27085	56	8.8	15.6	422083	40.4
BBC Radio 1	Q	48134	11449	24	2.4	10	114749	11
BBC Radio 2	Q	48134	10233	21	2.8	13.3	136464	13
BBC Radio 3	Q	48134	2012	4	0.3	6.7	13557	1.3
BBC Radio 4	Q	48134	9179	19	2.4	12.8	117293	11.2
BBC Radio 5 Live	Q	48134	5373	11	0.8	7.4	40020	3.8
BBC Local / Regional	Q	48134	9741	20	2.4	11.9	115883	11.1
All Commercial	Q	48134	31148	65	10.1	15.7	487863	46.7
All National Commercial	Q	48134	11095	23	1.7	7.5	83208	8
The New Atlantic 252*	Q	48134	1514	3	0.2	5.2	7820	0.7
Classic FM	Q	48134	6053	13	0.9	7.2	43578	4.2
talkSPORT (Talk Radio)	Q	48134	2053	4	0.3	7	14384	1.4
Virgin Radio (AM only)	Q	48134	2899	6	0.4	6	17426	1.7
All Local Commercial	Q	48134	26510	55	8.4	15.3	404655	38.7
Other Listening	Q	48134	2773	6	0.4	7.2	19889	1.9

Extract from RAJAR Quarterly Summary of Radio Listening to 17 September 2000. (Source: RAJAR / RSL)

ACTIVITY 13

Do-It-Yourself RAJAR!

- We can now try our own audience survey amongst our own friends and associates. Draw up a graph like the one illustrated, with a list of all the radio stations you can hear in your area down the left-hand side, and columns for the hours of the day (from 6 am until midnight) across the top.
- Start off with your fellow students. Put a tick against the stations they listened to yesterday, in the boxes which correspond to the hours they were listening.
- Take the diary home and ask some of your friends or neighbours. Try to include a selection of the following types:

  a older people, especially those who are retired

  b people who go out to work (not at school or college)

  c people who are full-time carers or homemakers
- Use a different coloured pen to record the responses from each group.
- Now examine your graph. You should notice some marked similarities and differences. If you combine your individual results into one big survey for the whole workgroup you may find the trends become clearer.
- When do most people listen? Why do you think this is the case?
- What kind of people listen for longest? Which stations are they listening to?
- Which stations are most popular in each of the categories you identified? (You may include other categories of your own if you wish)

WHEN AND WHERE DO WE LISTEN ?

Radio is an intimate medium – many of us will have woken this morning to the sound of a radio station. The first voice we hear in the morning could be that of a DJ or newsreader. On the road we are reluctant to speak to hitch-hikers or other motorists – but we welcome the voice of the travel news on the radio. Commuters seldom make conversation with strangers on a train – but will happily listen to the radio on a Walkman. We accept radio's routine intrusion into our personal space because we each believe in the deliberately created illusion that people on the radio are speaking to each one of us as individuals.

Radio is a creative medium – it has no pictures, but it can still create vivid images. Dramatists have always known that emotion exists not on a stage, but in the minds of the audience. This is heightened when the audience have no distractions in the form of visual images created by someone else.

This is the 'theatre of the mind' – the empty space we all carry in our heads, waiting to be filled by our own visual images, created by the words and sound effects we hear. On radio, when a monster appears, we each see in our own imagination the monster we fear the most – and we each see a different monster.

MEDIA LANGUAGES AND CATEGORIES

WRITING FOR RADIO

If we are to produce effective radio news, features or commercials we must first realise that radio language is unique and writing for radio is a specialised skill that must be learnt.

Forget written conventions! We must ignore rules such as: 'We use quotation marks to indicate reported speech.' We use CAPITAL LETTERS, **bold typefaces** or exclamation marks! to add emphasis to our words. Can we use question marks to indicate a query? Of course we can. We can also subdivide our text by means of (a) lists (b) indentation or (c) spacing.

None of these devices can be used reliably in radio scripts, when the meaning must be carried by the spoken word alone.

Avoiding Jargon

Writing for the ear – instead of the eye – also means that we must avoid jargon whenever possible, especially jargon which originates from the written page. Listen to police officers speaking on the radio. Even if you switch on in the middle of a report, you will be aware who is speaking not only because of the content but also because of the language used. This is one real-life example:

'We are currently seeking two white males who were seen in the vicinity at around the time of the reported offences. We believe they could hold information which is vital to the investigation. I would therefore appeal for these persons to come forward to assist with the inquiry, as it is important the assailants are apprehended without delay.'

Words like 'persons', 'assailants' and 'apprehended' are seldom used by anyone other than a police officer. They can therefore be included to great effect in the dialogue of a radio play, to indicate (**signify**) that the character speaking is a police officer, even if they have not been introduced as such. However, radio journalists must be very careful not to reproduce such **conventions** in their scripts, which will be read aloud by a newsreader.

Reporting Speech

We must also be very careful with reported speech. A newspaper can make use of written conventions to print without difficulty:

'Sir Toby Fishmonger told the rally, "I tell you now, in my personal opinion, a vote for any party other than the Monster Raving Loony Party is a wasted vote. All other politicians are boring ... trust me, I know what I'm talking about".'

The quotation marks put the words clearly in the mouth of the speaker. Now try reading it aloud. Who is speaking? Who thinks politicians are boring?

Reading the same statement on the radio carries the risk that listeners would believe it was the personal opinion of the newsreader ("I" being the person speaking, "we" being the radio station). The only safe way to report the same comment on radio (other than to broadcast audio of Sir Toby speaking in his own voice) would be to re-write the quote in the third person:

'Sir Toby Fishmonger says that in his personal opinion, a vote for any party other than the Monster Raving Looney Party is a wasted vote. He claims all other politicians are boring ... and that voters should trust him, as he knows what he's talking about.'

Note, however, that the quotes remain in the present tense – radio reports are about what is happening now, not what happened yesterday. A newspaper reporter choosing not to quote Sir Toby directly would switch into the past tense:

'Sir Toby Fishmonger said that in his personal opinion, a vote for any party other than the Monster Raving Loony Party was a wasted vote. He claimed that all other politicians were boring ... and that voters should trust him, as he knew what he was talking about.'

Dynamic Writing

Writing for radio news also demands that we capture the attention of the listener with each story in a bulletin. Newspapers break up the uniformity of words on paper by using headlines to help the reader navigate the page, and we must ensure that the opening lines of radio stories should give the listener a reason to continue listening. This doesn't mean we should use the same clipped journalese of the tabloid newspaper headline writer – 'Police Probe City Vice Scam' or 'Gazza out in England shocker'. These headlines conform to a different convention – that of filling white space on a page with short code words that fit the space available. They sound wrong – unnatural – when read aloud, and should not be used on radio.

TELLING THE STORY ON RADIO

Radio journalists have four basic ways of telling a story, which normally (though not always) run in the sequence:

Copy > Voicer > Cut > Wrap

News copy

The simplest way of telling a story is in the form of **news copy**. A journalist writes the story to be read out on the air by a newsreader, remembering the need to write for the ear and not the eye.

Here are some examples.

```
MORTGAGES...     RH for 27 April

The cost of home loans is going
up again.

The Bank of England has raised
its key base rate by half a per
cent to six and three quarter per
cent.

High street banks and building
societies are expected to follow
suit - meaning borrowers would
pay an extra fifty pounds a month
on a typical 30 thousand-pound
mortgage.

ends
```

```
FIRE...          RH for 4 October

A pensioner has died in a house
fire in Newtown.

Crews were called to a terraced
house in Gasworks Street at
around 6 o'clock this morning.
The man - believed to be in his
seventies - was found in the
kitchen. It's believed he was
overcome by smoke.

His name has not yet been
released.

ends
```

```
FOOTY...         RH for 14 December

City are through to the third
round of the Gungemakers Cup.

They beat United 3-0 in a
thrilling match at Shuntyard Lane
-  two goals from Shortplank and
one in the final minute from
Groinstrain ensuring the
Nitpickers' victory.

They now meet Rovers or Town in
the quarter-finals … their game
finished in a nil-nil draw, and
will be replayed next Tuesday.

ends
```

News copy can be written quickly and altered easily if and when new information comes to hand. However, it can become boring listening to a long piece of copy read aloud, and the newsreader is more prone to making errors. When copy exceeds around 30 seconds in duration, it would be normal to convert it into a voicer.

Voicers

A **voicer** is a scripted report read aloud by a second journalist within a news bulletin. It would normally be pre-recorded, so as to avoid reading errors and to let the newsreader calculate an exact duration for the bulletin. Voicers can however be read live (sometimes from an adjacent studio or directly from the scene of an incident) when a story is developing. Voicers are particularly useful when there is a lot of detail in a report, such as names or numbers. The use of a second voice breaks up the (literal) monotony of the bulletin, and thereby holds the attention of the listener. A pre-recorded voicer gives the newsreader a break during a live bulletin to re-assess her timings and order of stories, especially if she is working within an exact time 'window' which must not be exceeded.

Writing voicers

The first thing to write is the cue for the story, which the newsreader will read out. This will normally be a top line giving the main fact of the story, followed by a line of explanation, with the third line of the cue introducing the reporter.

Here are some examples.

```
MORTGAGE / IQBAL...  RH for 27
                     January

The cost of buying a house is
going up again...

The Halifax has announced a
quarter per cent rise in home-
loan rates - other lenders are
expected to follow suit.


Muhammed Iqbal reports...

MORTGAGE / IQBAL

dur: 22"

o/c: typical family

ends
```

```
SIGNING / REDHEAD... RH for 6
                     October

United have signed Jo Soap from
City in a million pound deal...

The 21-year-old midfielder comes
to Shuntyard Lane after a
spectacular season with his old
club, in which he scored seven
goals.

Joan Redhead has the details...

SIGNING / REDHEAD

dur: 27"

o/c: transfer list

ends
```

The reporter then writes the script that he or she will read, a script that gives the main body of the story. Remember to write the last words (the **out cue**) from the main voicer on to the **introductory cue**, so the newsreader knows when he or she is expected to go on to the next story.

News cuts

A **news cut** is a clip or **soundbite** taken from a recording of someone connected with the story speaking. It can be taken from an interview, or it can be an excerpt from a public speech or comments made within the range of journalists' microphones. Cuts on the radio are like the pictures in a newspaper or magazine. They should be selected to illustrate or amplify the story, rather than to explain it (which is often better done in the form of a voicer).

Cue writing – layout

```
 (1)      (2)      (3)   (4)      (5)
JOBS / SMITH..WRNS/RH for 7 March
                         (6)
                         1000 Embargo

(7)
Five hundred engineering jobs are
under threat in West Yorkshire.

(8)
Workers at Amalgamated Grommets
in Huddersfield are planning
strike action if the company's
new owners press ahead with plans
to reduce staff levels.

Shop Steward Jo Smith says they
haven't been consulted about the
proposals:

(9)
JOBS / SMITH (1)

dur: 13" (10)

o/c: dreadful attitude (11)
```

Notes

(1) SLUG – a name for the story. This strange term comes from the old days of hot-metal newspaper production, when stories were identified as they were moved around the printing works by a 'slug' of lead type in a tray. The slug is normally a single word relevant to the story content, and the same slug must be used for the cue and the tape, cartridge or computer file to which it relates.

(2) WHOSE VOICE – this indicates whose voice is on the audio to which the cue relates, whether that is the voice of a reporter (for a voicer) or the voice of an interviewee (for a news cut). Including a voice ID helps prevent confusion when the newsroom has spoken to more than one interviewee on the same story. It also helps avoid the embarrassing situation when a newsreader takes a voicer they've earlier done themselves into the studio (which of course they could never play in their own bulletin).

(3) SOURCE of the story (WRNS = West Riding News Service)– indicates where the story has come from, if it did not originate within the radio station from which it is broadcast, such as when copy is bought from an agency, or if the story has come from another station. This information is very important when checking agency accounts, or if there's any legal problem with the story.

(4) YOUR NAME or INITIALS – indicates the person who actually wrote the story that went to air.

(5) DATE the story is to be used on air (not the date it was written, unless the two are the same). Vital to avoid stories going out on the wrong day by accident, especially when reporters are busy writing 'overnight' stories for use on air the following day.

(6) EMBARGO, if any – indicates the official time a story may be used on air. Often newsrooms are given important information (such as the monthly employment figures, or the names of people receiving official honours) before it is made public. This device helps journalists prepare material in advance of an official announcement, and should therefore help them explain a story better. Breaking an embargo means publishing such material before the agreed time, and is generally considered to be bad journalistic practice.

(7) MAIN COPY TEXT, separate from heading, double-spaced with at least 2 cm margins to allow for any late corrections and additions by hand.

(8) NEW SENTENCE = NEW LINE – putting all new sentences on a new line helps the newsreader cut the story short if time is a problem by creating 'natural eye breaks' in the text. You should always put the in-line (the line which introduces the audio which follows) on a new line. The newsreader can then easily miss out the line if time is running short, or there is a problem with the audio.

(9) LEAVE SPACE before putting the details of the cut – this stops the newsreader accidentally reading out the slug.

(10) DURATION of the audio – in seconds (or minutes and seconds for longer tapes)

(11) OUT CUE – the last words the newsreader will hear before she is to begin speaking again. A repeated out cue ('I have no faith in the council; I don't trust the council, and I want an apology from the council.') should be indicated by the indicator (x3), i.e.

> PROTEST
>
> dur: 23″
>
> o/c: the council (x3)

Standard out cues

Some stations finish voicers, live or recorded, with their own standard out cue, generally known as an 'S.O.C.' or 'sock':

'Peter Murphy, Westminster'

'Richard Horsman for the Pulse in Sowerby Bridge'

All staff must be aware of the station's current standard out cue, if used – they cannot be made up or modified except by an editorial policy decision. For convenience, they are generally indicated by the abbreviation 'soc':

> CRASH / HORSMAN
>
> dur: 29″
>
> o/c: soc

Wraps

A **news wrap** is the neatest and most complete form of radio reporting. Again generally pre-recorded, it consists of a report in a bulletin read aloud by a second journalist, interspersed with cuts (**audio clips**) which illustrate and amplify the story. The illustrative cuts may be very short, linked with the voice of the reporter who can fill in important details or summarise the arguments. A common style is the '**doughnut**' **wrap**, which showcases a single, powerful illustrative clip (the jam) within an explanation from the journalist (the dough). The **'tennis match' wrap** uses short clips of two or more interested parties, showcased by a reporter effectively saying 'on the one hand ... but on the other' – possibly with the addition of a third party, an independent expert.

The 'Three Par Cue'

Note how each of the above examples makes use of the 'three par cue' – a style of writing a story in three paragraphs. Each paragraph may consist of a single sentence. The first should convey the importance of the story. The second contains additional information, clarification or amplification of the first. The third concludes the story – or in the case of a report which will include an **audio clip** (an extract of someone speaking) it should introduce the speaker.

The art of writing for radio is to be as conversational as possible. Imagine your audience not as thousands (or even millions) of people, but as one person. This can also help overcome feelings of nerves when facing the microphone; you are not speaking to lots of people, but speaking to one person with the message repeated many times over. Few of us would feel nervous repeating the same message to a succession of people coming into the room one at a time; radio does away with the need to repeat it.

Finally, remember the maxim KISS – Keep It Short and Simple. As a general rule, try to confine your radio writing to one idea per sentence.

THE DEVELOPMENT OF A STORY

All news stories develop in a clearly defined order, which journalists instinctively apply. The sequence runs:

Report > Reaction > Analysis > Comment

The **report** stage is telling listeners for the first time that something has happened. It's the equivalent of the old-time town crier standing in the market square ringing his bell. The content is entirely factual.

The **reaction** stage is when the journalist seeks views from people directly associated with the news that has been reported. They may well be opposing views – such as management and union opinion over a factory closure, or Labour and Tory Party spokespeople on a ruling from the European Court.

The **analysis** stage is when the reporter seeks to set the story in context by reference to what has happened before (**historical**) or what happens in other systems, or other parts of the world (**comparative**). This will normally involve speaking to an independent third party with specialist knowledge of the situation – in short, an 'expert'. Experts can range from university academics to retired politicians or actors – anyone with a broad knowledge or experience of the subject in hand.

The **comment** stage is when other interested groups – or the public – are given their say on the issue once the news is well known. One technique often used (some would say over-used) in radio for gathering public comment is the '**vox pop**' – from the Latin phrase '*vox populi*', meaning 'voice of the people'. A vox pop on radio normally consists of a sequence of anonymous comments from members of the public all giving their response to a single question. A good vox pop will include several clearly recognisable accents for variety, and to ensure a good representation of different social groups. It will alternate men and women (for clarity – so the casual listener knows when short comments begin and end), and it will reflect a breadth of different opinions on the issue, ending on a particularly poignant or funny line.

Keeping the story fresh

We expect the news we hear on the radio at lunchtime to be different from the news we heard over breakfast. Our lives have moved on in that time, and we expect the news we hear to have moved on too. The 'shelf life' of a story is normally therefore no more than 2–3 hours.

Repeating stories

The same copy should not be repeated more than twice, ideally it should be re-written between each hourly (or half-hourly) bulletin. The same audio should not be used more than three times, unless it is particularly gripping.

When recording interviews journalists are always listening for alternative cuts (some people call them soundbites) which can be used to keep the story fresh by giving the listeners different audio to listen to each hour. If we have two cuts of an interviewee (Cut A and Cut B), the story can be kept fresh over four hours by rotating the cuts in the sequence A – B – A – B. This means that listeners tuned in for two bulletins hear completely fresh audio in the second bulletin. Very few listeners will stay tuned for the third bulletin in a row.

If we have only one good cut of an interviewee that too can be kept fresh over the same period by reducing the story to copy form in the second hour, and bringing the audio back in the third (so the sequence runs cut – copy – cut – copy).

THE NEWSROOM AT WORK

Radio newsrooms work round the clock

CASE STUDY – Timescale of a breaking story

The following scenario – which is adapted from a real incident – gives us an insight into the operation of a local radio newsroom within the independent sector as it reacts to a breaking story.

10.13 am
It's been a quiet Monday morning until the phone rings. A man's on the line in a distressed state. He says a petrol tanker has run into a house in a village within the transmission area, and several people are dead. The **duty journalist** springs into action – this could be a big story.

- *Could the journalist put the man directly on air?*
- *What risks are there at this point?*
- *What ethical concerns must the journalist be aware of?*

10.14 am
After calming the man down the reporter asks permission to record an interview about what the man has seen. He asks lots of **open questions** (Who? Where? When?) forcing the caller into giving more details, rather than 'Yes' / 'No' responses. This eyewitness account, given moments after the crash whilst the man is still emotional, should provide some gripping audio to use on air. With his microphone shut, the reporter yells the main 'facts' to a colleague – who must check them out.

10.15 am
The second journalist has got through to the police control room. They confirm 'an incident' has taken place involving 'an HGV' in the village named. This is a vital stage in the response – the caller could be a hoaxer, he could be mentally disturbed or may have misunderstood what he has seen. The story must be **'stood up'** (checked for accuracy) with the emergency services.

- *Why would the police be cautious about giving details? What priority will they be giving to calls from the media? Why?*

10.17 am

The **news editor** cuts short a meeting to take charge of the story. She tells the first **reporter** to go out to the scene in the only available **radio car**. He quickly grabs a minidisc recorder, spare discs, and a mobile phone. He checks his equipment carefully, despite the urgency – especially connections and battery levels. He takes a weatherproof coat and buys chocolate and a sandwich from a nearby kiosk as he dashes to the car ... it could be a long day ahead.

- *Why must the reporter be careful to check his equipment before setting out?*

The second reporter is still ringing round for more information. The fire service confirms that a tanker is involved ... but the cargo is not petrol, it's a harmless chemical. They're trying to free the driver. They won't comment on the driver's condition – a sure sign that he's dead, or very badly hurt. Fire crews are also trying to locate an elderly couple who live in the house.

- *Is it yet safe to put the story on air? What assumptions are we making? Why was it a wise decision to hold back from broadcast before?*

The editor must also keep a grip on the rest of the news agenda – the world doesn't stop for one big story. She scans the list of material coming on the satellite from Independent Radio News (IRN). She prints off two stories she will need for the 11 o'clock news, and makes a mental note to record a clip of the Prime Minister talking about job losses which will be sent on the satellite later. There's also a councillor coming in before 11 to be interviewed about a new road improvement scheme – a story which is no longer important, but it's too late to cancel the appointment now.

- *What are the dangers of concentrating on the big story in isolation? What concerns will the editor be feeling at this point?*

10.29 am

The police confirm the driver of the tanker is dead. He was a local man aged 42, but they won't release his name until relatives have been informed. They also reveal that the owners of the house – a couple in their eighties – are trapped in a back room. The husband is pinned down by part of the ceiling which has collapsed: his wife is trying to comfort him.

The editor decides to interrupt the music programme with a newsflash – hoping to get the news out first, and to warn drivers of massive holdups on the road through the village, which is blocked.

10.36 am

The reporter in the radio car phones in to say he's stuck in the traffic jam. The editor tells him to park off the road, then continue on foot to the scene with his mobile phone. He should get there in about 10 minutes. She updates him on the latest developments.

10.40 am

The second journalist back at the studio writes a '**cue**' (an introduction) for the story, which will be the first item in the news. She **pulls a 'cut'** (takes an audio clip) of the eyewitness on the phone describing the scene with the tanker embedded in the front of the house. IRN phones from London – they've seen the story on the Press Association news service, and want to know if the station has any audio they can use in the national news bulletins. The editor sends them the audio clip that's just been taken from the eyewitness interview down an **ISDN line** (a phone line with digital sound quality). She faxes the cue, after re-writing it to remove local references, which would mean nothing for a national audience.

- *What priority will the news team give to national and local audiences? What conflicting priorities will they have to resolve?*

10.47 am

The roving reporter calls in on his mobile. He's at the crash site, and has just seen the old man who lives in the house carried out on a stretcher to a waiting ambulance. The editor tells him to '**file a voicer**' – give his own eyewitness account from the scene, but including the new information about the old man's rescue. The original eyewitness account is now '**dead**' – the newsroom has more accurate and more up-to-date information.

10.50 am

The editor breaks off from the developing story to record the 'cut' she needs of the Prime Minister from IRN. That will now go second in the bulletin after the voicer on the crash. The same feed also includes the station's own 'cut' from the crash, which other stations can now take to use in their bulletins. There's no time at this late stage to update the national story – the first priority is to the local listeners.

The councillor arrives to talk about his road scheme – the studio-based reporter has to break off doing '**check calls**' to the police, fire and ambulance control centres (regular hourly checks for updates on anything new happening) to take him to a studio to record the (now unwanted) interview. It may hold for later in the day.

10.53 am

A stroke of luck – the councillor hears about the crash, and says some residents in the village have been campaigning for heavy lorries to be banned from the main street. He tells the reporter (on tape) that the accident adds weight to their campaign. This is nothing to do with the story he originally came in to talk about.

- *What does this say about the need to adapt quickly to changing news situations?*

10.55 am

The studio-based reporter pulls together a very quick 'cut' of the councillor's comments, and writes an '**add line**' to follow the lead story – the 'voicer' from the reporter at the scene. The station now has reaction to the story, as well as a simple report of what's happened. The Prime Minister is dropped to third place.

10.57 am

The roving reporter calls in to say that the injured pensioner has been officially named as Albert Smith, aged 81. The newsreader makes a hand-written alteration to the 'cue' (introduction) adding the extra information. She makes one last check of IRN before heading for the studio. She must be in her seat by two minutes to the hour, so as to select the pieces of audio she is going to play in on her PC console in good time, read through her scripts to check for errors, and relax – so she is not breathless during the bulletin.

11.00 am

The story is on air, 47 minutes after the first eyewitness called.

In the hour that follows, the priority is to update and improve the quality of what has been achieved so far. The roving reporter will speak to the emergency services and eyewitnesses on the scene, the police, community leaders campaigning for a new road. He will aim to speak to the old woman, who was not hurt, as she is now the accessible human focus of the story. However, he must be careful not to intrude if she is still in a state of shock, or is otherwise unwilling to speak to reporters. Some will want to talk, others won't. Different people react in different ways under such circumstances. He also reports back to the studio the name and telephone number of the tanker firm involved in the crash so they can be approached for comment – and to check their safety record. He will want to know exactly what chemical was in the tanker, and what its effects would be if it spilled. That may involve a call to an 'expert' – probably an academic at a local university or college with a knowledge of chemistry.

The field reporter will knock on neighbours' doors asking for information about the elderly couple – hoping for details (such as a distinguished war record, or recent community activities) which add colour to the report by making the victims appear as rounded human beings – not just statistics. He will make sure he gets back to the radio car in good time to file the material '**at quality**' (in good technical quality, over a UHF radio link, not down a crackling mobile phone line) before the 12 noon bulletin.

EXERCISE – OUR OWN NEWSDAY

We've now seen what tools are available to us as journalists, and how a real radio station would react to a breaking news story. We can now see and feel what it's like by running our own newsday within our workgroup.

The first thing we must do is to decide what sort of station we are going to be. A good starting point might be to imagine we could run an RSL (Restricted Service Licence) from our workplace, serving people within (say) a three-mile radius.

What interests and concerns do our potential listeners share? If it's a very diverse group of people, we might choose to specialise in serving a particular subgroup, such as pensioners, those in education and returning to learning, or a specific ethnic group.

Examples might include:

GROUP	AGE	INTERESTS	CONCERNS
Students	16 – 21	Education	Job prospects
		Music / clubbing	Finding a partner
		Environment	Lack of money
		Fashion	Appearance
		Health / fitness	Transport
Senior citizens	60 +	Community life	Health
		Family	Pensions/Benefits
		How we used to live	Crime
		Holidays	Loss of friends / partners

Draw up a chart like the one above for the group(s) you intend to serve with your radio station.

Give everyone a job – a newsday will work well only if everyone knows what they're expected to do. The main functions are shown in the table below:

NEWSROOM FUNCTIONS		
ROLE	**RESPONSIBILITIES**	**MAIN JOB(S)**
Editor	Legal / Financial	Deciding what stories should be covered
		Deciding who does what story
		Putting stories in perspective
		Deciding if a story goes out
Bulletin Editor	The news this hour	Getting the next bulletin ready
		Keeping stories up to date
		Chasing reporters for their stories
		Checking for updates
Newsreader	The station sound	Checking every script
		Checking all audio before use
		Checking for links between stories
		Delivering error-free reads
Reporters	Gathering news	Getting the stories!

NOW FIND SOME NEWS!

What is news?

News can most easily be defined as anything that happens which is out of the ordinary. Therefore 'man bites dog' is news, whilst 'dog bites man' isn't. A bishop getting drunk at a party could result in a national scandal, whilst a student getting drunk at a party would not excite any interest at all. (Also see News values on page 89, Chapter 3 (Newspapers).)

Diary and off-diary stories

News that can be anticipated (when we know it is going to happen) is a **diary story**; the newsroom will have been told in advance that something is going to happen, and can be ready to cover it on a specific day at a specific time. Examples would include a murder trial starting at Crown Court, or an appearance by a famous person to open a new supermarket.

Off-diary stories are those news events (such as fires, plane crashes or ministers resigning) which happen without any warning. A newsroom must be ready and able to react to a sudden emergency (such as a royal death or a terrorist bomb) whilst also preparing enough 'diary' news to fill the bulletin if nothing unexpected happens.

When something big happens, the Editor must decide which stories are dropped to make way for the important new development. Some of these dropped stories may be kept for another time; others will never go to air at all.

The news agenda

The term '**news agenda**' refers to those possible stories from which journalists can choose the ones they are going to cover according to what they consider important. It's like the menu in a restaurant. What we choose from the menu depends on our own likes and dislikes – and as journalists, we must choose according to what we understand to be the likes and dislikes of the audience we serve.

Where does news come from?

News events happen around us all the time. The job of the journalist is to find out about them. The following table outlines some of the main sources of news:

SOURCE	*EXAMPLES*
Institutional	Council, Parliament, public bodies
Crime	Police, courts
Health	Hospitals, Health Authorities, NHS trusts
Education	Schools, teachers, colleges, student unions
Pressure groups	Interest groups, Greenpeace, unions, gay rights
Business	Share prices, mortgage rates, company results, job creation / losses
Commercial	New products and services, surveys, plugs for products
Seasonal / weather	Christmas, Eid, summer, snow, water shortages
Showbiz / arts	Events, openings, reviews
Personalities	People in the area, home-grown or visiting
Sport	Fixtures, transfers, player fitness reports

RUNNING OUR NEWSDAY

On the day we are to operate as a newsroom we will need:

- All students in on time, dressed smartly for meeting outside contacts. Some may also need to spend time outdoors.
- Access to computers and printers (or typewriters), access to a telephone, portable recorders, editing facilities (if possible) and a studio, or at least a quiet room where the bulletin can be recorded. If we can record directly from the telephone that will be a big help.
- Access to a television with Teletext, a radio to hear other stations' news bulletins, and a supply of recent newspapers – especially local newspapers.

Our job is to put out one five-minute news bulletin at lunchtime, and another in the afternoon (depending on when classes finish). Assuming we start work at 9 o'clock, we should work to the following timetable:

0900 Meeting Appoint jobs for the day – editor, bulletin editor, newsreader and reporters.

0915 Morning Conference Discuss the news agenda for the day. Everyone should suggest at least one story that's happening nationally (or internationally) and one that's happening in the local area. Look at Teletext for ideas. Ceefax on BBC1 or BBC2 page 102 gives an index of national stories; page 160 gives an index of regional stories. On ITV / Channel 3 look at pages 301 and 331. Look at the newspapers. Prepare a list of possible stories we might want to include. We should find at least 30 ideas.

Now let's look again at our station profile – the interests and concerns of our potential listeners. We should cross those stories off our list which will *not* be of interest to our audience. Bear in mind that some will be so important (such as the election of a new US president, or the sacking of a government minister) that they are of interest to everybody at the time when they have just happened (that is, when they are at the report stage, as opposed to the reaction, analysis and comment stages). We will probably cross off about 10 stories.

We also need to delete those stories where we can't speak to anyone involved – the Prime Minister is unlikely to give us an interview, for example. Before rejecting a story, however, we must think hard about local links to a national subject.

A story about foot-and-mouth disease will almost certainly affect a butcher in the High Street, whilst a story about education funding could affect our school or college. A local MP could give us reaction to what the government is doing, whilst a lecturer in international affairs could give us an analysis of the latest world conflict. Students from other courses (or shoppers in the street) can always give comment in the form of a vox pop.

We should end up with a list of around 15 stories that match the perceived interests of the audience - and maybe 10 where we can find a local **angle** for an interview.

We must now decide the most appropriate format (copy, voicer, audio or wrap) in which to present each story. A breaking story, or a national / international story where we can't get an interview, is probably best tackled as copy. A story with a lot of detail, maybe some local interest, but no obvious or available interviewee, would suggest a voicer. A story where we can easily obtain an interview is best presented as an audio clip, and where several interviewees are available you may wish to consider a wrap – although this is the most difficult and time-consuming radio format.

0945 Assign reporters to the stories Depending on group size we may choose to work alone, in pairs or in small groups. If we are going out of our workplace to obtain an interview it's probably better not to go alone, but remember that three or four people turning up together could intimidate our potential interviewee. Choose reporters carefully. If a member of the workgroup has a particular knowledge of the local football team, they are likely to do a better job of covering a soccer story involving that team. Someone's hobby or language skills could also make that person more appropriate for a particular job.

0950 Get to work! The clock is now ticking, and our deadline is 12 o'clock. That means we have two hours to write all the copy, write and record voicers, record interviews, choose clips from those interviews and write the cues for them.

Writing copy stories

Those people writing copy should remember the three par cue layout. Keep reading your work aloud – it's the only way to spot and eliminate tongue-twisters and accidental double meanings.

Writing voicers

Those people writing voicers should remember that the top line (which the newsreader reads out) is the most important. The voicer script itself should flow logically as it explains the story – it should have a beginning, a middle and an end.

Gathering audio

Having decided who we want to interview, we should first telephone that person, and explain what we are doing (making it clear that the interview is for a student project, not a real broadcast). Make an appointment to see them, or if we have the means to do so, ask to record an interview over the telephone. **Remember it is illegal to record a telephone conversation without first getting the interviewee's permission to do so**. Some people may refuse to be interviewed. Real journalists often face the same problem.

Asking questions

When we start an interview it's a good idea to ask a lot of 'open' questions (those which start with Who? Where? When? Why? What? or How?) so the interviewee can't just give 'Yes' or 'No' for an answer. Give the interviewee time to answer. Try not to talk across what they say, to prevent your voice being recorded over theirs. Don't record too much – as a rule, no more than three times the length we intend to use in our bulletin.

1100 Time running out It is now one hour to our bulletin. Most copy stories and voicers should be written, and we must have a good idea which interviews will be ready in time.

The newsreader should be checking through the scripts to make sure they're happy with the writing, and making any necessary changes so it will sound right on air. Remember, listeners will judge the bulletin only by what they hear in the finished product, not by the effort that has gone into newsgathering. Changes must not alter the meaning of a story, but should help it flow better on the air.

The bulletin editor is checking to make sure reporters will meet the deadline. He or she must be very organised, knowing exactly where all the scripts and audio clips are, and how they will be played into the bulletin.

The editor is keeping track of the other news media, listening to radio bulletins, watching local TV news and checking Teletext. He or she may have to divert reporters from stories which are proving difficult (or just too dull) on to new stories which are breaking.

Choosing what audio to use

Listen back to the tape we have recorded. Which phrases stand out as we listen to it? Which indicate best how the interviewee feels about the story? These are the extracts that are likely to be most effective in the bulletin. Remember that good audio will illustrate, rather than explain, the story. Don't include questions in your clip – we should hear the interviewee's voice on its own. The cue should tell us who is speaking, and ideally should be self-standing – it should make sense on its own, in case for any reason we are unable to play the audio clip in the actual bulletin (either because of technical problems, or because of shortage of time).

Editing the audio

If we have the means to do so, **edit** the material so we can play it in cleanly without unwanted bits at either end. We can select material by **splice editing**, where tape (normally ¼ inch audio tape recorded on a portable machine such as a Uher) is physically cut and stuck together with splicing tape; by **digital editing**, where soundfiles are cut and pasted on a PC using computer software such as CoolEdit; or **dub editing**, where a selected portion of tape is copied on to a second tape. When dubbing material be very careful to exclude words before and after the section you want to copy by accurate use of the pause control.

1130 Tough decisions It is now half an hour to the bulletin. All the scripts must now be ready, and all the audio must be in the final stages of production. If we have voicers to include in the bulletin we must decide whether they will be read live (by the reporter going into the studio) or pre-recorded, in which case the reporter will have to prepare a tape or **soundfile** and give it to the bulletin editor. Keep calm – keep organised.

Compiling a running order

A **running order** is a list of stories in the order they will appear in the bulletin. We put our best story – the one that we judge will be of greatest interest to our listeners – first. Then the second-best, and so on. Try to achieve a good mixture of copy, voicers, and audio clips to keep the bulletin sounding fresh. Time each story. We can either use a stopwatch, or make an estimate based on the rule that three words approximately equals one second. We want our bulletin to be five minutes long, as near exactly as we can make it. We may now have to make some tough decisions – if we've found a lot of stories, we may have to leave some out of the bulletin altogether. Others may have to be shortened to fit others in. This may mean we have to leave out some audio.

On the other hand our bulletin may be too short. If so, we will have to re-write some stories to make them longer, use longer clips from our interviews or turn some of our short copy stories into voicers, giving the listeners more detail.

1150 Gate It is now 10 minutes to the bulletin, and **the gate** is closed – no new stories or material can be accepted for the coming bulletin. The remaining time is crucial to make sure the newsreader has all the scripts properly prepared in the right order, and that all voicers and audio clips are cued – that is, set up at the right point and ready to play. Do not be tempted to ignore the gate. If we try to fit stories in late, the bulletin will not flow smoothly and technical problems are much more likely to occur.

1158 Doors closed The newsreader and any reporters reading live voicers are now alone in the studio. The bulletin editor and technical operator are alone in the control area. No one else is allowed to interrupt them. Start the master tape to record the bulletin.

1200–1205 exactly The bulletin is recorded as if going out on air.

Afterwards there may be time for a short celebration – but remember we have another bulletin to do later in the afternoon. In a real radio newsroom the deadline comes round once (or maybe several times) an hour throughout a journalist's shift.

Before the next bulletin, we must decide what went well in our first. What material can be used again, and what needs to be replaced? Remember, in the real world, no story or piece of audio will be used over more than two hours without re-writing. What didn't work? Few bulletins are ever perfect, and there will always be items that could be improved. The editor will also be bringing in new stories, meaning that some material is already out of date. Try to learn the lessons from the mistakes first time round, and make the mid-afternoon bulletin (at whatever time we decide) even better.

Keep copies of the bulletin to play to friends and family. They will probably think it's better than we do, as they won't be aware of the effort that went into its production, and where any mistakes or failures occurred.

TAKE A BREAK – RADIO COMMERCIALS

Radio advertising builds on another of radio's great strengths – the ability to fill the listeners' 'theatre of the mind'. A good commercial requires the skills of a radio dramatist, creating atmosphere, character and a message for the listener – but with the added requirement to do so in a precise time-frame of maybe 30 seconds or one minute.

Several devices are available to the commercial producer that will help create a memorable campaign. (See also Advertising techniques on page 74, Chapter 2 (Television).)

REPETITION

Because radio commercial airtime is relatively cheap compared to television, ads can be repeated more often for the same amount of money. Remember, radio listening is a background activity – this means a good commercial repeated frequently will place the client's name, catchphrase or telephone number in the listener's mind without conscious effort. The downside of this approach is that a bad commercial may irritate listeners, and could prompt a conscious response of turning off (or re-tuning) the radio – and avoiding the advertiser.

CHARACTER

Many radio commercials work effectively by creating larger-than-life characters – **audio cartoons**, which leave a strong impression in the theatre of the mind even if the listener is not giving the broadcast full attention – driving in heavy traffic, for example, or working on a production line.

HUMOUR

Humour is another important ingredient, requiring the skills of a sitcom, sketch or stand-up comedy writer in creating everyday situations that the listener will recognise before adding a twist or punchline involving the client's product. The Hamlet cigar commercials are probably the best-known example of this style, having run on TV as well as radio.

HIGH DRAMA

A TV commercial featuring exotic locations, space flight, natural disasters, expensive props or incredible monsters can cost thousands of pounds to make. The same effects can be achieved in a radio studio using sound effects, microphone and voice techniques at very little cost.

INTIMACY

Commercials also use the theatre of the mind to exploit radio's one-to-one relationship with each listener. Appeals for blood donors and charity campaigns are very effective because they are felt personally by each listener. A good writer can also place the listener at the centre of the appeal by making them imagine their loved ones in need. Characters can also be placed in life-threatening or embarrassing situations (trapped in a burning building, for example, or nude in a crowded shopping centre) with none of the practical difficulties (and expense) that shooting such scenes would present for TV.

MUSIC

Familiar music creates an instant impression in the mind, so that even a few bars of a soap-opera theme or national anthem can transport the listener into that series or country. Hit songs from the 1970s and 80s will immediately remind older listeners of when they were young – which often activates pleasant memories. Even unknown music in familiar styles can also create an instant mood for the commercial – Romantic (soft strings), Dramatic (driving beat), Suspenseful (slow, building to a sudden climax).

JINGLES

A well-written jingle can make an impression on the memory in the same way that young children learn nursery rhymes. The combination of words or numbers with the tune makes it easier to remember. Some jingles date back to the 1930s when Ovaltine bedtime drinks and Bisto gravy were advertised in English on Radio Luxembourg, an overseas station with a big audience at that time in the UK. A more recent example would be the 'Always Coca-Cola' campaign run in the late 1990s.

- *Discuss some radio commercials you have heard recently. Which did you like? Which would be effective in reaching their intended audience? Has the producer used sound effects? Do the voices sound natural, like real people talking, or are they exaggerated, larger-than-life characters? Is there a jingle, or other music?*

Now listen to the commercials again, and then answer the three big questions:

- **WHO** is the commercial talking to ?
- **WHAT** does the advertiser want them to do?
- **WHY** should they do it?

You will probably find that you can do so easily for the ones you like, but it will be more difficult for the ones you don't like.

WHO? asks us to define the target audience for the commercial. For some clients, such as the holiday company Club 18–30, the target audience may be obvious. For others, such as council leisure centres, the targeting process may be more complex. They may want to attract more young parents with toddlers, or perhaps they want more pensioners to use facilities off-peak. These target audiences may change over time and between individual advertising campaigns.

WHAT? asks us to examine the client's objectives. Effective commercials demand a response from the listener. The best commercials avoid confusing the listener with choice ('call in today or phone for a brochure') ... they specify one course of action or the other.

WHY? asks us to give a reason for the listener to respond. We must give a reason for the listener to do what the client wants them to do. Perhaps there is an offer of a free prize draw, or discounts available for a limited period. At a more subtle level we can bring in elements of quality and prestige – the client offers a fashionable or expensive product, therefore listeners see themselves as glamorous or well off if they choose the product.

WRITING A COMMERCIAL SCRIPT

We are now ready to begin the process of writing a script, or several script ideas, for approval by our client. Although it's a good idea to write out rough ideas in a notebook, the finished script should be typewritten or word processed, according to the following conventions:

- The script must be double spaced, with margins of at least 2 cm at each side.
- The elements of the production (voices, music, sound effects etc) are listed in order down the left-hand side of the page. They are normally given in capital letters.
- The actual words to be said, and directions, are written down the right-hand side of the page in upper and lower case characters.The following table gives some of the standard abbreviations used.
- The client's name, a title for the commercial (and/or a reference number) and the intended duration should be written at the top of the script, together with the name of the person who has written it.

ANNO	announcer – formal style read, often used to start or finish a commercial which has 'character' voice-overs within it
ATMOS	atmosphere – used to describe a general effect, such as 'windswept moor' or 'busy office' rather than a specific sound effect such as 'telephone rings'
FVO	female voice-over
FX or F/X	sound effect
GRAM	music ('gram' is an abbreviation of gramophone, or record player)
JINGLE	jingle
JINGLE ENDS or J/E	jingle comes to an end
MUSIC	music
MUSIC BED	music used as a background to a voice-over – often to set a mood, such as 'relaxed music bed' or 'up-tempo music bed'
MUSIC ENDS or M/E	music comes to an end – usually a natural end, rather than an abrupt stop
MUSIC FADES or M/F	music level reduces slowly
MVO	male voice-over
MVO1	first male voice-over (MVO2 = second male voice-over etc)
SFX, FX or F/X	sound effect
VO or V/O	voice-over (gender not specific)

EXERCISE – PRODUCE A COMMERCIAL

IDENTIFY A CLIENT

Our first task is to identify businesses (such as shops or supermarkets), community groups, charities, or local facilities (such as leisure centres) which could benefit from advertising on the radio.

RESEARCHING THE BRIEF

The next job is to arrange a meeting with our client – the store manager or similar person if we are working in the real world, or a tutor role-playing the part of the client if we are simulating this exercise within our workgroup.

It is better to meet the client on their premises, if it is possible to do so safely. Pair up with another student (or go as a group) for this part of the exercise. Partners or colleagues should make notes, not only of answers to direct questions, but of other information which will also be useful when creating our commercial. Ask for copies of any promotional materials (leaflets, brochures etc) given out by the client, and note anything particularly impressive about their organisation – is everybody friendly? Is the showroom warm and inviting? Is there plenty of car parking? Do they have letters on the wall from satisfied customers? These are all details that could be useful when it comes to writing our script, especially if our client has many competitors offering similar products at similar prices.

DECIDE THE BUDGET

Decide how much money the client could afford to spend on commercial production and on airtime. As this is a student exercise, no real money is involved – we will not be selling anything to the client, but we should assess what we would think they would spend from the simplified **rate card** (price list) given on the next page.

DECIDE A LENGTH

We need to discuss what length of commercial is most appropriate for the client. Very short ads (10″) are good for promoting a sale, or 'tagging' longer commercials which will run over a longer period. Long ads (60″ or more) are expensive, but allow for maximum creativity and image-building. Most commercials will be either 20″ or 30″ in duration.

DISCUSS A STYLE

The style we choose will be determined partly by the budget and partly by the mood that the client wants to create in the mind of the listener. A hard, driving music bed may be appropriate for promoting a club or selling a cola drink, where the client wishes to be associated with youth and energy. Such a style would be wrong for promoting soft furnishings or garden products, where the client would rather create a feeling of ease and relaxation. Such a mood can be achieved with soft music or countryside sound effects.

WRITING THE SCRIPT

Feel free to experiment and be creative, but remember the client will have the final say on what is used. We have already decided the length and style of the commercial – now we must make it work. Read the scripts aloud, checking the length against the clock frequently. Radio stations operate to a tolerance of less than one second over or under length. Remember the guideline:

3 words = 1 second

GALAXY 105 RATE CARD

Valid December 2000 – February 2001

Segment Rates

	Timeband	
Weekday Rate	*Timeband Weekend Rate*	*Shoulder Peak*
0500-0700 £43	0500-0700 £16	Breakfast Peak 0700-1100 £185
Daytime 1100-1600 £161	0700-1600 £99	Afternoon Drive 1600-2000 £101
Evening 2000-0200 £53	1600-0200 £37	Overnight 0200-0500 £3
0200-0500 £5		

Package Rates

		Timeband 4	
	Week Rate 8	*Week Rate 12*	*Week Rate*
49 spots 0500-0500	£3425	£3235	£3045
63 spots 0500-0500	£4160	£3915	£3670

FOR SPECIALIST SHOWS; SEPARATE RATE DETAILS APPLY – AVAILABLE ON REQUEST

Package Prices quoted above are per week. Advertisers wishing to purchase less than 49 spots per week should ask for details. Packages are sold on a 7 day even rotation basis; subject to availability.

TIMELENGTHS

All rates quoted are for any length commercial up to 30". For longer lengths please add the following:-

40" +25%   50" +50%   60" +75%

For commercials longer than 60" the rate will be pro rata to the 60" rate.

NON-STANDARD ROTATION

The following premiums and discounts are applicable to any non standard rotation of campaigns.

Early week upweight -10%

Sunday upweight -30%

End of week +15%

Saturday upweight + 30%

Run of week - 5%

CHRYSALIS RADIO UNIQUE GUARANTEE

We will never run more than 16 commercials in one hour

Guaranteed advertiser category exclusivity

Full post campaign details normally sent out within 21 days of completion

CANCELLATION

Bookings may only be cancelled on receipt of written instructions no less than 28 days prior to start date.

DETAILS OF OUR GENERAL TERMS AND CONDITIONS ARE AVAILABLE UPON REQUEST.

A typical radio station rate card

RADIO ADVERTISING REGULATIONS

The Radio Authority's code gives legal guidelines for advertising products such as alcoholic drinks (there must be no encouragement to excessive drinking, or the suggestion that drinking a particular brand makes a person more attractive). Cigarette advertising is banned by law, adverts for toys must not encourage children to demand products from their parents, and advertising for personal products (such as condoms or sanitary towels) must not be in bad taste. You should read a copy of the code for the full details.

TYPES OF COMMERCIAL

Apart from the regulations mentioned above there are no rules about what goes in a radio ad. There are however certain conventional styles, which include:

One straight voice

An actor reads the copy 'dry' (with no music or sound effects) in his or her own natural voice (normally chosen for its attractive qualities) for the exact duration of the commercial. Very direct and powerful if well written, and the cheapest style to produce, but can be boring if the style is used repeatedly in a commercial break. Avoid the temptation to shout a script for greater impact – radio is a personal medium, and you would never shout at close range when speaking to a person you know well.

Two straight voices

Two contrasting voices (often one male / one female) read the copy in sections. Has the advantage of variety – each voice change has the potential to grab the listener's attention. Relatively cheap to make and simple to write, but again can become boring if over used.

Character voices

The voice over reads the script in character – often as a stereotype (country yokel, upper-class twit, granny, thick yob etc). Different voice-over artists have their own 'library' of voices which a producer may call upon. One or more character voices may be scripted together. Cost will depend on the number of voices – but remember, a good character voice-over can 'double up' as a straight reader in the same commercial. Versatile – but beware of overusing stereotypes which have become hackneyed, or reinforcing negative images of minority groups.

Voice over music bed

Like a 'straight' voice-over script, but with appropriate background music to set the mood. Much more expensive as royalties must be paid for using the music. The cheapest source is to license tracks from special libraries (such as the De Wolfe music library) written to exact lengths especially for commercial use. If you want to use a well-known piece, either classical or popular, the fees can be prohibitive.

Sung jingle

For maximum impact there are specialist composers, singers and production facilities that will compose, orchestrate and produce a jingle to the client's specification. For this exercise we will have to substitute a 'choir' of students, but it should still give an idea of the effect.

TEST THE SCRIPTS

It's probably a good idea in our workgroup to prepare several scripts in different styles. Take the scripts back to the client. What is their reaction? Take on board any comments made, and adjust the scripts accordingly. Remember – any alterations we make must still be within the given time limit for the commercial. If we add words in, we must remove others to make room.

MAKING THE ADS

If we have studio facilities, the final stage in the process involves making the ads to the best standard we can manage. If we are using music, take care to edit or dub it cleanly (see page 167). Sound effects may be taken from a record or CD produced for the purpose (most public record libraries will have a selection) or we can record our own. Experiment with ways of making sounds, and different microphone positions to record them to best effect.

CHOOSE VOICE-OVERS

Listen to the different voices of students in the work group. Some will be keen on doing the voice-overs, but don't overlook students who may be shy, but may have an interesting voice. Cast the best voice available for the lines that have been written.

EVALUATE THE COMMERCIALS

Play the tapes of the finished commercials to friends not in the same workgroup. As with the news bulletin, they may well rate these efforts higher than we do, as again they will not be aware of the processes which have gone into the production.

ONYERADIO PRODUCTIONS

Client: Seethru Windows
Script: Smashing Time (SCR 4567)
Duration: 30″
Copywriter: Dave
Salesperson: Ayesha

MVO1: Young boy, not very bright

MVO2: Long-suffering dad, middle-aged

FVO: Bright, young, friendly

ATMOS: Quiet showroom atmosphere under

SFX: Glass smash

MVO1: There's a smashing sale at Seethru windows!

MVO2: Have you gone mad ..?

MVO1: No, but Seethru Windows have! They're smashing ……

SFX: *Glass smash*

MVO1: 30 percent off windows, doors and conservatories for this week only!

MVO2: But Melvyn! That means 30 percent off the price! The Price!!
Not the windows, Melvyn!

MVO1: So I can put me sledge'ammer away, can I dad?

MUSIC: *Bright, strings, upmarket*

FVO: 30 percent off windows, doors and conservatories at Seethru Windows! You'd be mad to miss this smashing sale.

Call 0800 123456, that's 0800 123456.

M/F

This script is copyright © Onyeradio

A sample advertisement

SUMMARY

- Radio is so much a part of our culture, it's taken for granted.
- Radio is still a young medium. All its major developments as a mass medium of communication have taken place within the past century.
- Radio is the most intimate medium there is. It reaches each listener individually.
- Radio is the fastest popular medium there is. Stories can be on the air quickly, without the need to worry about visual images to illustrate the story.
- When writing for radio, write for the ear not the eye. Remember the three par cue model. Always read copy aloud before sending it for broadcast.
- KISS – Keep It Short and Simple. No more than one idea per sentence.
- News runs in the sequence Report > Reaction > Analysis > Comment.
- There are four mechanisms for telling a story on radio: Copy > Voicer > Audio > Wrap.
- Radio news works to the agenda that best suits the station's audience profile.
- Radio commercials make creative use of the theatre of the mind.
- Radio is one of the cheapest media for advertisers, especially in terms of production cost.
- Repetition builds a client's reputation.
- Creative commercials make use of characters, audio cartoons and stereotypes.
- Radio is growing. There is more radio available to UK listeners now from a greater diversity of broadcasters than ever before. It is the most accessible mass medium in terms of work opportunities.

GLOSSARY

diary story – coverage of a planned event e.g. press conference

digital editing – sound files are cut and pasted on a PC using special software

dub editing – a portion of tape is copied on to a second tape

edit – tidy up taped material so it sounds 'clean'

embargo – official time a news story may be used

gate – time at which no new stories can be accepted for the next bulletin

in-line / introductory cue – first words of newsreader's script

news copy – news story read out on air by a newsreader

news cut / soundbite / audio clip – a clip taken from an interview, speech or commentary by someone connected with the news story (**to pull a cut** – to take a clip from an interview etc.)

news wrap – fullest form of radio reporting: consists of a report by a second journalist interspersed with illustrative cuts

off-diary story – coverage of an unexpected event e.g. car pile-up

out cue – last words of voicer, written on newsreader's script so he / she knows when to go on to next story

running order – list of stories in the order they will appear in the bulletin

simulcasting – simultaneous broadcasting on both AM and FM transmitters

slug – name of news story on script

splice editing – audio tape is physically cut and stuck together with splicing tape

standard out cue (soc) – radio station's own particular out cue

three par cue – writing a whole story in three paragraphs, preferably of one sentence each

voicer – scripted report read aloud by a second journalist within a news bulletin (**to file a voicer** – to send an account)

vox pop – from the Latin vox populi, meaning 'voice of the people'; a poll of opinion from members of the public for a news wrap

6 Pop music

TIM LEADBEATER

Coming up

In this chapter we will be looking at:

- the definition of pop music
- the history of pop
- the elements of pop music
- producers and audiences
- what pop music has to say about life, love and the world
- Media Studies key concepts

INTRODUCTION

Pop music is big business. In 2000 world record sales were worth £16.5 billion and although UK sales were worth only seven per cent of that we spend more per person than any other country. On average, we buy four albums a year although students spend over £200 a year on music. However, Oasis manager, Alan McGee, foresees the end of the music business as we know it because young people are more interested in computers (which their parents don't understand) than in pop music (which their parents love).

What is pop?

It is hard to define where pop starts and ends and those in the business are not really bothered. Labels are useful but they don't stop all sorts of interesting musical mixtures. All that counts is whether something's popular – in other words, whether it sells well. We as media students should, however, try to clarify our terms before we start.

- *Are these pop music?*

- *A song in the Eurovision Song Contest*
- Teletubbies Say Eh-Oh
- *A rap to a classical piece (e.g. Sweetbox* Everything's Gonna Be Alright*)*
- My Way *by Frank Sinatra, who has been dubbed 'the voice of the century'*
- *A song by Lata Mangeshkar, a singer in Hindi films, who has made over 25,000 different records*
- Nessun Dorma *sung by Pavarotti whose album,* Essential Pavarotti, *went to number one in the UK pop charts in 1990*

- *Can you think of other examples to discuss?*

A health warning

Whatever we mean by pop (and we all mean something different), pop arouses strong feelings. We defend our taste in music more than our choice of what we watch or read. Be prepared to discuss your favourite music and that of others without feeling threatened or making fun. Remember – together you are bound to know more than your teacher on this one!

ACTIVITY 1

- In the diagram below, what labels might go in the empty circles?
- Which musicians might be examples of the overlapping areas?
- Are there more circles bordering on pop?

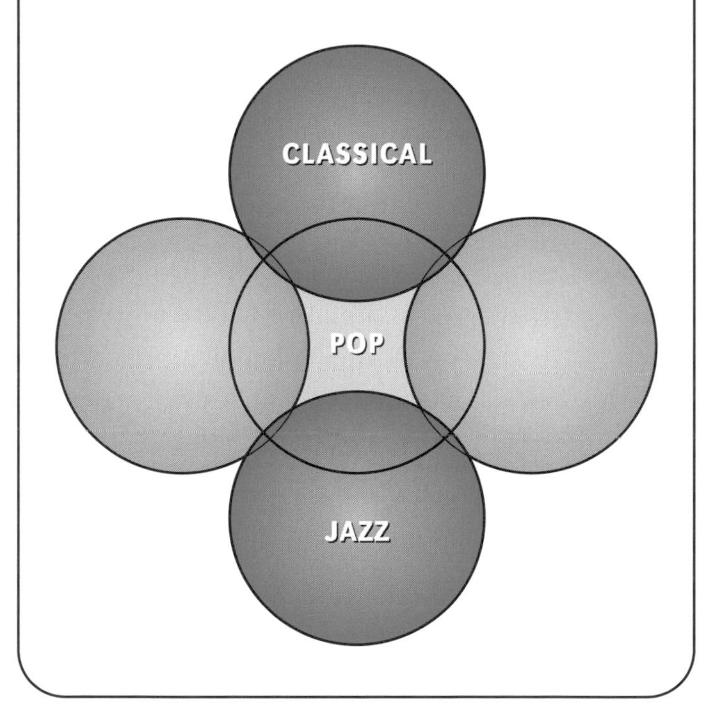

Pop and Media Studies

For the purposes of this book, pop will be used to refer to a wide range of music. Pop will not be something different from rock or rap or reggae. There is another problem before we start, however. Pop music is not really a medium like TV, radio or film although it clearly uses these other media.

- *In what ways is pop music like, and unlike, the other mass media?*

Violinist as rock star: Vanessa Mae

THE HISTORY OF POP MUSIC

THE ROOTS OF POP

All music has its beginnings in songs and dances created and enjoyed by ordinary people. During the Middle Ages, minstrels moved from town to town, playing anywhere from street corners (like modern buskers) to churches and royal courts. Some wrote their own songs, usually about being in love. These songs were called **lyrics**.

- *What does the word lyric refer to in pop music today?*

After a while, **classical music** developed away from folk music. Classical music could be written down and was for the upper class and royalty. **Folk music** was passed on without being recorded on paper although the words were sometimes written down and sold in the streets. People would sing them to tunes they already knew. (Even today many pop musicians cannot, and do not need to be able to, read music). One of the most popular types of folk song has been the **ballad**. Folk ballads tell stories and are often composed about news events and famous people.

- *What type of pop song is a ballad now? Can you think of any examples?*

About two hundred years ago, publishers started printing ballads with words and piano music for singing at dinner parties. This was the start of the music industry.

Blues and jazz

The roots of pop are found in the music of black Africans transported as slaves to the USA two hundred years ago. The slaves adapted their African singing traditions to express their bitterness about their oppression. This music became known as **the Blues**. Feeling blue is to be depressed and the Blues has been described as the music of 'a full heart and a troubled spirit'.

After slavery was ended, a more upbeat style of black music emerged. **Jazz** featured bands, even whole orchestras, of musicians, dance rhythms and more melodic tunes than the Blues. Jazz dance styles like **ragtime**, **dixieland** and the **charleston** were hugely popular in the 1920s.

Contemporary view of Anglo-Saxon gleemen or minstrels

Lady sings the Blues: Billie Holiday

The sound of the city

Pop would not exist without the opportunities and technologies of the modern city.

ACTIVITY 2

Think about how the following make the music industry possible:

- electricity and electronics
- mass production and distribution
- concentrated populations
- financial power

What other aspects of city life are important?

THE FIFTIES

Pop music, as we know it, came together in the 1950s from changes in music, society and technology.

Music

The musical development was the fusion of **R'n'B** and **Country** to create **Rock and Roll**.

Rhythm and Blues (R'n'B) is the black music of the cities - blues with drums and electric guitars for a strong beat. It had its own charts and was not allowed on white radio stations where it was called 'race music'. R'n'B is at the heart of all pop music of the past 40 years and still has its own charts.

Country is the music of white American farmers and is still massively popular. Settlers adapted their native European folk music to sing about the hardships of rural life.

Society

The **teenager** was an invention of the 1950s. The economic boom after the war meant young people had jobs and money. Entertainment and fashion industries tried to target products at this new group. White teenagers wanted a pop music which broke away from their parents' tastes.

Technology

The **single** was created in the late 1950s as a seven-inch vinyl record playing one song each side, hence the name. This proved ideal for pop music and it became the definitive format. Record players became small enough to be used in bedrooms or even carried from house to house.

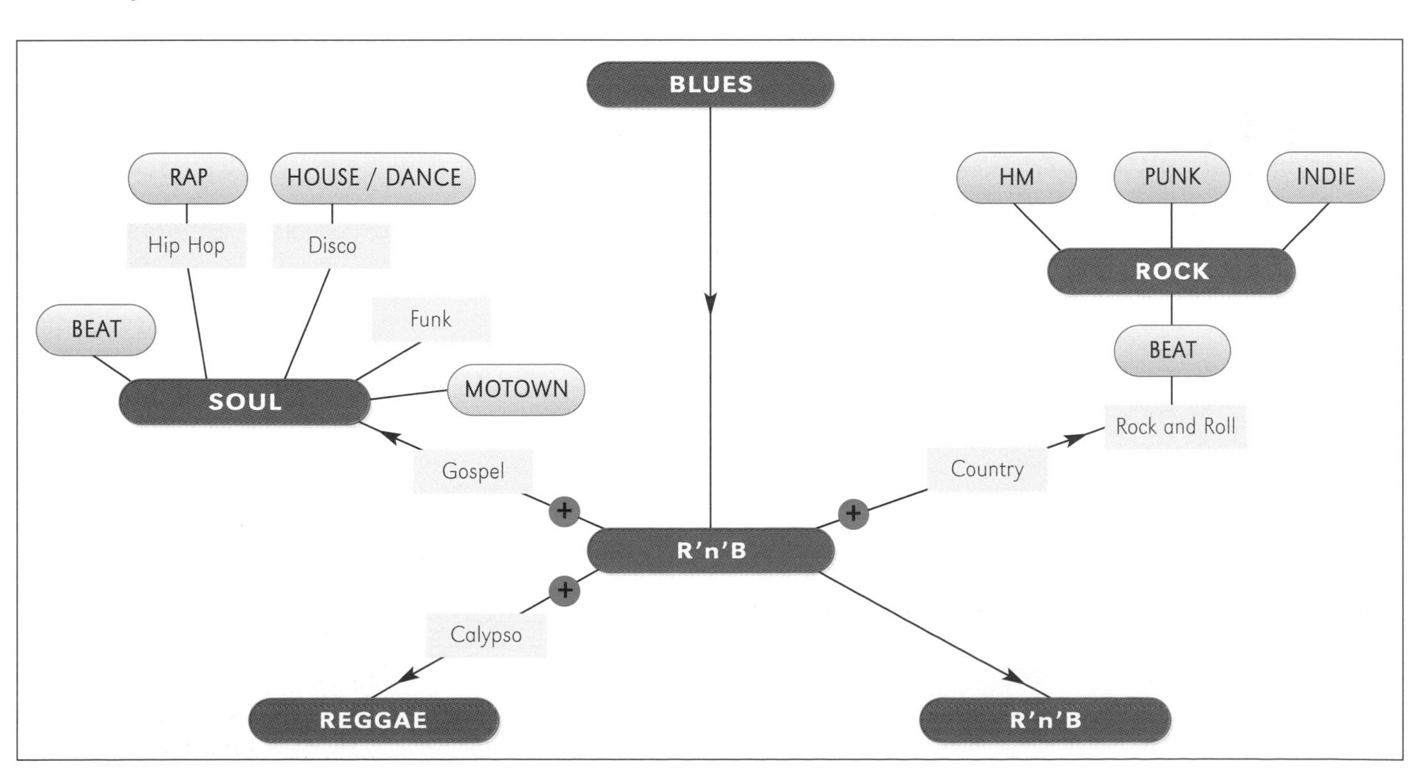

R'n'B occupies a central place in pop history

Rock and Roll

Rock and Roll mixed the energetic beat of black R'n'B and the singing style of white country music. This was not a deliberate invention. In poor neighbourhoods, whites and blacks were already blending these styles.

Then Alan Freed, an American disc jockey (DJ) on a radio station for white teenagers, started a show of R'n'B music. He disguised the fact it was black music by using the term 'rock and roll', which was not well known to whites but was actually black slang for having sex.

Under this new name, record companies promoted white performers who sounded black to white audiences. Only later did black musicians become nationally successful.

Key features: 12-bar Blues structure, sexually suggestive lyrics.

The King of Rock and Roll: Elvis Presley

ACTIVITY 3

As you read through the history of pop, here are some questions to consider:

- Which styles are still popular?
- Which performers are still going strong in their original style?
- Which performers have changed style?
- Which current performers have emerged in established styles?
- What new styles are there – particularly mixed, or cross-over, styles?

THE SIXTIES

Beat

Beat music was British Rock and Roll, blending R'n'B with the chirpy British singing style of **skiffle**. Beat was hugely popular in the 'Swinging Sixties' although Cliff Richard was promoted as the British Elvis as early as 1958.

Beat emerged in the clubs of British ports, where American records first came into the country (before transatlantic planes). The most famous 'scene' was in Liverpool and got the name **Merseybeat**. London bands went for a straight imitation of R'n'B.

Key features: groups with guitars rather than just singers, close vocal harmonies.

Tamla Motown

Soul music also developed out of R'n'B but by adding another black style – **gospel**. The first wave of soul is associated with the first successful black record company: Tamla Motown. This was set up by Berry Gordy in Detroit. (The main business of Detroit is making cars – Motown comes from motor town.) Many Motown songs were written by the Holland-Dozier-Holland backroom team.

Key features: strong melodies, poignant lyrics, vocal harmonies like choirs, tambourine beat.

The Godfather of Soul: James Brown

Soul

By the late 1960s, black music had successfully crossed over to commercial success with white audiences.

The name **soul** suggested powerful emotions and painful experience. Aretha Franklin was said to have 'quiet fire'. The visual style, however, emphasised glamour and glitz.

Soul music ranged from uptempo songs with sexually explicit lyrics to poetic ballads which showed off the vocal talents of female singers in particular. The first type developed into dance music, the second is still popular, with singers like Whitney Houston.

Key features: strong pulse, whether fast or slow; brass section, including sax.

Psychedelia

Social attitudes changed more in the 1960s than at any other time between the Second World War and the present day. Clean-cut pop groups began to seem like middle-aged entertainment to white middle-class youth.

They wanted new sounds to suit an alternative, **hippy**, lifestyle and political protests about the Vietnam War, racism and women's liberation.

The new fashion was **psychedelic** which meant the music, lyrics and artwork were inspired by hallucinatory drug experiences. **Acid rock** songs were lengthened by rambling instrumental improvisations. Concerts involved lightshows and special effects. Album covers featured clashing colours and flowery lettering.

Ironically, the '**underground**' culture created one of the biggest music businesses of all: the pop festival.

Key features: dream-like lyrics, special musical effects, keyboard instruments – organs and synthesisers.

- *Which bands or musical genres are associated today with protests or challenges to mainstream values?*

THE SEVENTIES

Prog rock and glam

In the early 1970s the social challenge of psychedelia dropped away. Musicians preferred to use the new style to show off musical talent in both songwriting and instrumental virtuosity. The challenge for so-called **progressive rock** was now seen as matching the complexity of classical music. Songs were described as **compositions**.

Meanwhile, white pop was making a social challenge of its own with **glam rock**. Although the music was straightforward, male performers pushed the glitz of soul to the point of effeminacy by wearing mascara, jewellery and furs.

Key features: Prog: 30-minute songs, solos; Glam: costumes.

Reggae

Reggae developed in the Caribbean as a mixture of R'n'B and **calypso**, building on earlier styles such as **ska** and **bluebeat**.

It was taken up by British Afro-Caribbeans but also, strangely, by white racist skinheads. This led many anti-racist whites to promote reggae as a music of political protest. Multi-ethnic British bands started in the inner cities.

Reggae has close links with Rastafarianism, a religion which foresees a home for Afro-Caribbeans in Ethiopia.

Key features: open sound, musical stress on the off beats.

Punk band The Clash

Punk

Punk erupted in Britain in 1976. In 1977, the Queen's Silver Jubilee year, The Sex Pistols went to number one with a raw, sarcastic version of the national anthem which was banned by the BBC.

Punk bands were proud they could hardly play and sang about glue-sniffing and being unemployed. Fans had fun by spitting at each other. The media claimed to be outraged but record companies snapped bands up, just in case. Nobody knew whether this was a revolution or just revolting.

Key features: angry out-of-tune singing, spiky hair and safety pins through noses.

Heavy metal

Heavy metal developed as a hard version of prog rock. Guitar-heroes were not just talented but used their **axe** (guitar) in a theatrical and sexually suggestive manner.

The audience remained largely white, male and middle-class but the prog rock fantasy style changed to an aggressive look of black leather and metal studs which was as contrived as glam.

Key features: fast guitar solos, macho lyrics, long hair, loudness.

THE EIGHTIES

Rap

Rap developed out of **hip-hop**. Hip-hop was the New York street culture which embraced breakdancing and body popping, the culture of track suits and trainers, hard drugs and spray-can artwork. Hip-hop DJs would improvise words over a music track. This was rapping. The rhyming and rhythmic pattern of the words, and their boastful style, came from street talk. DJs would also turn records back and forward to produce a distinctive **scratching** sound. Later rappers recorded their own backing tracks, often using samplers to borrow drum **breaks** from other records. Although some raps have been anti-drugs, rap has been heavily criticised for its **gangsta** glorification of violence and its attitude to women.

Key features: basic drum beat, prominent vocals with emphatic rhyme and rhythm.

Indie

Indie (from independent) refers to the sort of music promoted by small record companies. It has been particularly connected with Manchester. Indie music is simple and folky. Lyrics emphasise real, rather depressing, experience. Indie clothing is deliberately dull. Because indie is popular among students some see it as a modern prog rock. The most extreme type of indie was American **grunge** – typified by the group Nirvana whose lead singer Kurt Cobain killed himself.

Key keatures: acoustic guitar-based songs, lyrics about ordinary life.

House / Dance

Dance has been the most important musical genre of the past 10 years in Britain. The name now covers a range of styles: **Techno**, **Trip-Hop**, **Jungle**, **Drum'n'Bass**, **Garage**, etc. **House** developed as a frenetic version of **disco** which was itself a light speedy soul music popular in the late 1970s.

House came to Britain when four DJs came back from a holiday together in Ibiza (*ibeetha*, a Spanish Mediterranean island) and set up clubs to imitate the atmosphere they had experienced. It soon caught on and was closely linked with the spread of the drug Ecstasy (E). This chemical association prompted the name **'Acid' House**.

The drug connection, the psychedelic artwork, the emphasis on mindless pleasure and the underground origins of dance culture led to comparisons with the hippy culture of the 1960s.

Dance culture is not really about musicians. The dancers are the performers. The music is fairly easy to produce at home using samplers and small tape machines. In this way, house was a bit like punk.

The public reaction was similar too (see *Moral panics*, page 209).

Key features: thudding bass beat, repetitive vocal phrases, whistles, snatches of sampled sounds.

Smiley culture: Acid House

KEY DATES

1948 The 33 rpm LP album is introduced

1949 The 45 rpm single is introduced

1952 Gibson Les Paul electric guitar

1953 Elvis Presley makes first record

1955 Bill Hayley's *Rock Around the Clock* goes to No. 1

1956 Elvis sells 10 million records in first year with RCA record company, creates half the company's turnover

In the UK, coffee bars are the place for teenagers to hear records on jukeboxes

1957 First US TV pop show *American Bandstand*

1958 First pop charts – called the Hit Parade – produced

UK TV show *Oh Boy* starts – one of the first performers is Cliff Richard

Portable transistor radios produced ('trannies')

1959 US scandal of Payola – radio disc jockeys bribed to play records – Alan Freed (first Rock and Roll DJ) loses his job

Portable tape recorders produced

1960 Chubby Checker's record *The Twist* sparks the biggest dance craze since the 1920s

Cassettes produced

1961 The Mecca chain of dance halls introduces DJs playing records

1962 Decca Records turns down The Beatles

1962 Stevie Wonder releases first record at the age of 11

The Beatles release first single *Love Me Do* on the Parlophone record label

1963 First broadcast of UK TV show *Ready Steady Go!*

In December The Beatles have seven records in the top 20

1964 BBC launches *Top of the Pops* on January 1

Six pirate radio stations operate from boats and forts in the Thames Estuary

1966 The Monkees are created as a group for a TV series

John Lennon says The Beatles are 'more popular than Jesus'

1967 The high point of Rock – 'The Summer Of Love'

BBC launches Radio 1

Albums begin to outsell singles

1969 Woodstock Festival lasts three days – the high point of hippy culture

First UK pop festival on the Isle of Wight

Altamont Festival closes the hippy era with the murder of a fan by Hell's Angels security guards in front of the stage whilst The Rolling Stones are performing

1970 Jackson Five release first records fronted by 11-year-old Michael

Dr Robert Moog invents the synthesiser

1973 First major reggae album in the charts – (Bob Marley and) The Wailers' *Catch a Fire*

1973 Pink Floyd release concept album *Dark Side of the Moon* which will go on to sell 25 million copies

War in the Middle East pushes oil prices up and thus the price of plastic and records

1975 Queen release *Bohemian Rhapsody* with special video

1977 Film *Saturday Night Fever* (director John Badham) released

The Sex Pistols LP *Never Mind the Bollocks* comes straight into the UK LP charts at No. 1

1978 Five-piece 'boyband' The Village People make clear the importance of gay culture to disco (or *vice versa*)

1979 The Sugar Hill Gang release *Rappers' Delight*

Nine people in the audience of U2's first London gig

1980 John Lennon assassinated

1981 Sony Walkman on sale – the first personal stereo

MTV launched

Ghetto-blasters become popular

1982 Michael Jackson's *Thriller* goes to No. 1 in every major country of the world, spends 37 weeks at the top of the US charts and sells over 40 million copies world-wide

1983 Run DMC produce first gold-selling rap album

CDs are launched in Britain

1984 *Relax*, first single for Frankie Goes to Hollywood, has five weeks at UK No 1 despite being banned by the BBC

1984 EMI and Virgin jointly release new-style compilation CD – *Now That's What I Call Music (1)*

1985 US record companies agree to put obscenity ratings on records similar to those on films

Live Aid concert on July 13 – the world's biggest rock concert ever takes place on two continents simultaneously with a TV audience of 1.5 billion viewers

1986 Run DMC sign six-figure sponsorship deal with Adidas

1990 New Kids on the Block are first boyband of the modern period

1991 Police impound 13,000 copies of rap album by Niggaz With Attitude (NWA) – police lose the court case and the records are released

After Freddie Mercury's death *Bohemian Rhapsody* becomes the only song to reach No. 1 in the UK on two separate occasions

1992 Country singer Garth Brooks outsells U2 and Michael Jackson

George Michael sues his record company for £50 million, but loses

1993 Police crack down on Ravers and New Age Travellers

Ragga music hits the charts

1996 The Spice Girls enter pop culture

1997 Paul McCartney is knighted

2000 50 million download music from Napster Internet site before record companies get the courts to shut it down

2001 Napster re-opens under record company control

MEDIA LANGUAGES AND CATEGORIES

GENRE

The concept of **genre** links study of the history of pop with ways of identifying the distinctive elements of different styles.

Genre is a French word for type or category and is used in Media Studies as a one-word way of describing a set of recognisable, perhaps even predictable, stylistic **conventions**. These conventions may be visual, verbal, or musical, for example. The conventions are part of what Media Studies calls the **language** of that medium. In pop, the term style is more common but we shall keep using genre.

ACTIVITY 4

Create an up-to-date musical genre chart which shows for different genres names of typical bands or performers, typical song or album titles, typical image of musicians and fans, key musical features and so on. A large wall version might include photos and examples of lettering, or font, styles.

Babyboomers

There is a link between history, genre and audiences. Pop is 40 years old and its audiences have grown up with it. The teenagers of the 1950s and 60s are known as the **Babyboomers** because of the huge swell in the birthrate at the end of the Second World War (1945). This huge bulge in the population still has enormous influence on the music industry because babyboomers have carried on buying records, both new and reissues, throughout their lives. As a general rule, however, we always favour the music around when we were teenagers.

It is also worth remembering that many rock musicians have just hung around getting more and more successful: from the 1960s The Rolling Stones, Bob Dylan and Eric Clapton, from the 1970s Elton John, Bruce Springsteen and Sting.

ACTIVITY 5

Chart the musical tastes of as wide an age range of people as possible, whether teachers, parents, or grandparents even.

- Do they still prefer the pop music of their teens? A (tactful) wall chart might show photos of individuals next to their preferences arranged by age or decade.

In pop music, fashions change more than those of any of the other media and a book like this cannot keep right up to date and cover everything. You may be particularly knowledgeable about **bhangra**, **soca**, **electronica**, **goth** or **speed garage**. There are always new developments in technology as well.

ACTIVITY 6

- Create a more detailed timeline for the 1990s. Prepare a summary description of a current genre of music in the manner of the preceding pages with particular attention to the values or attitudes of the genre – does it emphasise fun or sadness, love or anger, for example?

Asian Dub Foundation – new genre or just new faces?

LANGUAGE

If we want to compare one song with another, or to explain why a particular song, or even just part of a song, is so exciting, we need to be able to say more than, 'It's just good'. We need some new, Media Studies, language to do it.

The meaning of a song has just as much to do with the effect of the rhythm or the look of the singer as the lyrics. So we need to develop ways of describing pop music genres in three basic areas: the **sounds**, the **words** and the **visual images**.

In each of these areas, as in other media languages, the description can be at the two levels of **denotation** and **connotation**. The connotative level in music is fairly clear. It covers all the suggestions, associations and effects of particular rhythms, tunes, words and images. The denotative level is harder because:

- musical notes or instruments do not mean something in themselves in the same way as words or images
- many of the specific musical terms needed to get down to the denotative level are either from classical music and are therefore in Italian or are modern technical terms, such as 'fuzz' and 'reverb'

Sounds

To analyse the music we must answer these questions:

- What instruments (including the human voice) are being used?
- How is the music structured?
- How can we describe the way the music is being performed?
- What has other technology added to the music?

Instruments

The denotative answer to the first question is easiest because most pop uses a fairly small number of instruments:

- voice
- guitars (electric, acoustic, bass)
- drums and percussion
- keyboards (synthesisers)

The term **backing** is used to describe the basic combination of instruments, usually drums, bass and guitar, underneath the vocals.

- *Can we say that particular instruments have connotations in themselves regardless of how they are played? What types of voice have connotations? Try to contrast the singers' voices in a multi-vocal group such as Boyzone.*

Structure

There are three basic structural elements:

- the **tune** (or melody)
- the **beat** (or rhythm)
- the **harmony** (combinations of notes, such as chords)

A key structural feature in pop music is the **riff**. A riff is a short sequence of notes, usually played on the bass, repeated over and over. One of the most famous riffs is from *Whole Lotta Love* (Led Zeppelin) which has been used in various versions over the years for the opening credits of *Top of the Pops* on BBC1.

- *Can you think of any riffs in current songs?*

On a denotative level we might discuss how an instrument takes over the tune from a singer and alters it or which instruments are generating the rhythm. A song's harmony is usually responsible for the suggestions that it sounds happy (in a major key) or sad (in a minor key).

- *What examples of these denotations and connotations can you find? Could we say that a physical suggestion (that is, wanting to dance) is a connotation of a particular rhythm?*

Performance

There are many musical terms, usually in Italian, to describe how music is being played. However, unless we learn a musical instrument, we simply do not develop as wide a vocabulary for describing music as we do for describing words and images.

These are some of the words we might use about performance:

- **speed** – fast, slow, speeding up, slowing down
- **volume** – loud, soft, getting louder or softer
- **feel** – tight, loose, manic, big

- *Which of these are denotative and which connotative? Can you think of any other useful or common terms?*

Technology

Other musical features might be the result of electronic technology, especially in recording studios. They fall into two broad categories: mixing and effects.

- Mixing is the blending of the different instruments at different times in the song. It is controlled through a huge mixing desk where each instrument has its own channel (see *In the studio*, pages 200–201). It is what recording is all about but it is also a crucial part of live performance, whether the mixing desk is at the back of the hall or part of stage show. The **fadeout** at the end of a song is a particular feature of recorded pop music
- Some special effects might be: use of **reverb** on the voice or drums to imitate the echoey sound of an empty space; use of **echo** (confusingly) to repeat particular notes or drum beats

- *Can you think of any distinctive examples of technical effects?*

ACTIVITY 7

Read some brief reviews of new releases.

- How detailed is the description of the music itself?
- How much do the reviews rely on connotative language?

Covers and remixes

When a song is re-recorded by other musicians, perhaps in a very different style or genre, the basic structural elements stay the same – usually the tune (and words) and harmony. Quite often the rhythm, the speed or feel and the instruments are very different. In pop, this is called a **cover version** (or in jazz and classical, an **arrangement**).

A **remix** is when the original recording is run through the mixing desk again to produce a different blending of instruments and voices.

ACTIVITY 8

- Compare different covers and remixes of the same song by using some of the terminology learned in this section. Two interesting examples might be Sid Vicious' cover of *My Way* originally recorded by Frank Sinatra, and Rolf Harris' cover of Led Zeppelin's *Stairway to Heaven*.

Sid Vicious does it his way by shooting the audience in the film *The Great Rock 'n' Roll Swindle* (Julian Temple, Virgin Films, 1980)

Words

Printed words are easier to examine but we must remember that pop lyrics are not meant to be poetry and at some stage we should examine them with their music.

- *Identify some general similarities and differences between song lyrics and poetry.*

Names, however, are clearly not meant to be sung and are a good place to start.

Names

Names of performers and groups are interesting to analyse for denotation and connotation. Where people's real names have been used we might say there is complete denotation (plain fact) and no connotation. On the other hand, group names are likely to be highly connotative (that is, to have suggestive associations), especially at first before we have heard their music. Later, they become more denotative, once we have linked the band to their music in our heads. In the end, familiar names lose all connotations.

ACTIVITY 9

What are the connotations of the following names?

- Babyou Gumbo
- Catatonia
- Megadeath
- Destiny's Child
- The Rolling Stones

Collect some examples of your own for discussion.

If a name suggests a genre of music we might say that this is actually a subtle form of denotation. On the other hand, design elements of a band's logo, such as the font, will be highly connotative.

ACTIVITY 10

Create some names and logos for imaginary groups and test them out on each other to see if they suggest particular genres.

Prince demanded the use of this symbol instead of his name. What does it suggest?

Lyrics

It is perfectly possible to like a song without knowing what the words are about. Songs in the Eurovision Song Contest are not translated, for instance. On the other hand it is almost always the lyrics that get records banned: Frankie Goes to Hollywood's *Relax*, for example. The *Media messages and values* section will discuss the attitudes expressed through lyrics. Here we will look at basic features.

Although some lyrics can be simple and mysterious, such as 'You are my wonderwall' (Oasis), most are very ordinary. The emotion comes from the way they are sung. Occasionally, people find the words as moving as the music. One example might be Elton John's song *Candle in the Wind* about Marilyn Monroe, rewritten for the funeral of Princess Diana.

ACTIVITY 11

Compare the words of the two versions of *Candle in the Wind*.

- Do they express the same feelings?
- How are they different?
- To what extent, do you think, are connotations of Marilyn Monroe carried over to Princess Diana?

This song is slightly unusual because it is a love song about someone dead. Love song lyrics often use the pronouns *I*, *me* and *you*.

- *How does this make the song more appealing to us? (see also Media messages and values, page 207).*

Ambiguity (alternative meanings) can also be effective. The chorus of Lou Reed's song *A Perfect Day* sounds like a love song:

> " It's such a perfect day /
> I'm glad I spent it with you /
> It's such a perfect day /
> You just keep me hanging on /
> You just keep me hanging on. "

This song was used by the BBC to advertise the range of music it broadcasts on radio and TV. Then the song was adopted by the 1998 Children in Need appeal. This is rather odd because the *you* in these lyrics has usually been interpreted as heroin.

The emotional power of a song comes from the way the words and the music work together. In particular, we enjoy memorable lines of words which also have a distinctive tune at that same point.

- *Can you think of any examples of lines and tunes which go together particularly well?*

This most memorable point of a song is often called the **hook** and usually occurs in or close to the **chorus**, a structural feature of a song.

The lyrics to Madonna's *Like a Prayer* can be interpreted sexually and religiously, whilst the video mixes inter-racial sex with racist flaming crosses. Pepsi withdrew their multi-million pound sponsorship as a result

Structures

Songs usually have a sequence of verses and choruses. The chorus is the set of words repeated identically several times. It has the catchiest tune and usually the most powerful part of the backing. The verse has its own tune which stays the same each time but with different words. A one-line chorus is sometimes called a **refrain**.

During the fadeout, the chorus is often repeated again and again with further layers of vocals or instruments over the top. Other sections might be a subdued instrumental **intro**(-duction), which is useful for DJs to talk over, and a **break** in the middle for a drum pattern, an instrumental solo or just a different tune.

The whole sequence might look like this:

I	V	C	V	C	B	C	V	C	C
n	e	h	e	h	r	h	e	h	h
t	r	o	r	o	e	o	r	o	o
r	s	r	s	r	a	r	s	r	r
o	e	u	e	u	k	u	e	u	u
		s		s		s		s	s

Repetition of words with a change in the underlying music is a very common structure in pop music. One example is the **12-bar blues** pattern. This forms the basis of many songs in many genres but is most easily heard in Rock and Roll. Music is counted out in bars – one chord (harmony of the backing) to a bar.

ACTIVITY 12

Noticing chord changes is very helpful when analysing pop music even if we don't know the musical details. Listen to the choruses of some current records to identify when chord changes occur.

Images

Image has a double meaning when looking at pop music. We talk about the image of a pop group, meaning a set of ideas about how they look and appear to behave. In media studies, an image is a photograph or an electronic picture on a television or computer screen.

We can see pop musicians perform live but they also use other mass media to communicate visually. We can distinguish between these two situations by referring to the two codes of presentation and representation, each of which has a personal and technical aspect.

Presentation

The personal aspects of live presentation include how performers are dressed, how they stand, move and behave on stage, even their visual expressions. We read meaning into all these things which sometimes go by the name non-verbal communication (NVC). The technical aspects of live presentation are the light show, special visual effects and even the stage set design. The presentational code covers the part of pop music which is equivalent to acting in a theatre.

Representation

Representation covers the use of other mass media to communicate visually with an audience. The two most important are photographs, in magazines for instance, and videos. Obviously, these will show the actual musicians, whether performing or not, so all the personal aspects considered above will apply. These are images in the second, more specialist, sense but they are largely responsible for the creation of the image in the first, more general, sense.

However, because photographs and videos give a carefully edited or selected view of the performers we should say that they are a representation of the performers. The visual meanings are mediated through these images. They are the equivalent of a film rather than a play, or a news story rather than the actual event.

The technical aspects of still and moving images – things like shot size, camera angle, soft focus, panning and tracking etc – can all be applied from the languages of advertising, film and television.

Another important aspect of pop representation is artwork for CD covers, posters and adverts. We could even examine the font, or lettering style, of a band's name (or record company logo, perhaps).

Pop as soundtrack

We have so far considered the basic elements of pop music itself. However, pop also functions as an element of other audio-visual media. Most commonly it features on the soundtracks of films, TV programmes and adverts. There is an Oscar category for Best Original Song and film soundtrack albums are regular best sellers.

Occasionally, pop music is the focus of the whole narrative, e.g. in *The Commitments* or *The Bodyguard*.

- *What are the attractions, and disadvantages, of this for film and TV writers and producers?*

ACTIVITY 13

Think of examples when pop has been used in films or on TV as:

- period setting – to help identify when (and possibly where) the story is taking place, like an aural prop, e.g. in *Forrest Gump*
- period feel – to suggest a mood rather than a specific date, e.g. classic soul songs in adverts
- narrative backing – to support a montage of images showing the passing of time, either in a habitual way, e.g. in *Three Men and a Baby*, or perhaps to show characters falling in love, e.g. in *Four Weddings and a Funeral*
- narrative element – when characters are listening or dancing to a song, e.g. in *The Full Monty*, or the lyrics have been altered to advertise a product
- theme tune – to combine some of the above, e.g. in Bond films
- song numbers – in musicals, characters are conventionally allowed to break into song, especially in children's films, e.g. *The Lion King*

Which genres do these images of Hong Kong popstars suggest and how?

Forms and formats

The relationship between musical **form** and technological **format** provides the link between Language and Producers and Audiences. Have technological developments changed the character of songwriting or not?

- *What might be called the software and the hardware of pop music?*

Brittle, shellac **records**, and **phonographs** to play them, first appeared in the 1920s. These records had to go round the turntable 78 times a minute (revolutions per minute or **rpm**). Although the disc was the size of a modern LP, one side of a 78 lasted only four minutes.

- *How many 78 discs would be needed for a modern album? What would the packaging look like? What would it weigh? What would record shops look like?*

The **LP** (Long Player) emerged in 1948 as a 12-inch vinyl disc playing at 33 rpm and lasting 25 minutes per side. These records were used in pop for releasing a collection of songs. In the 1950s, the definitive pop format of the seven-inch 45 rpm single was developed.

- *Why do you think pop LPs got the name 'albums'? Why do you think the pressure to develop the LP came from the classical side of record companies?*

The 12-inch format produced two interesting changes in musical form. First, progressive rock groups released **concept albums** with continuous music lasting up to an hour. Second, 12-inch (but 45 rpm) singles have been used to create extended dance remixes for use in clubs.

ACTIVITY 14

- Use an encyclopaedia of rock to research the concept behind some famous albums such as *Tommy* or *Quadrophenia* (The Who), *The Dark Side of the Moon* or *The Wall* (Pink Floyd).
- Cassettes and CDs (compact discs) use different technologies for reproducing sound but how much have they altered the basic amount or character of music released as a 'record'?
- The vast majority of CDs are reissues of old vinyl LPs. Why? Who profits?

We should also note that there have been some dead ends: eight-track cartridges, DAT (digital audio tape) and mini-discs. Vinyl has been making a comeback. These show that technological progress is not always what people want.

ACTIVITY 15

- Create a classroom archive of pop formats, dead or alive, by collecting a 78, a 45 and so on.

The Internet creates new possibilities. Already it is possible to put together a customised album by making your own selection of songs from those available on the net. It is also possible to join Internet jam sessions (group improvisations) with players from all around the world. Whether these will alter the way musicians think about music remains to be seen.

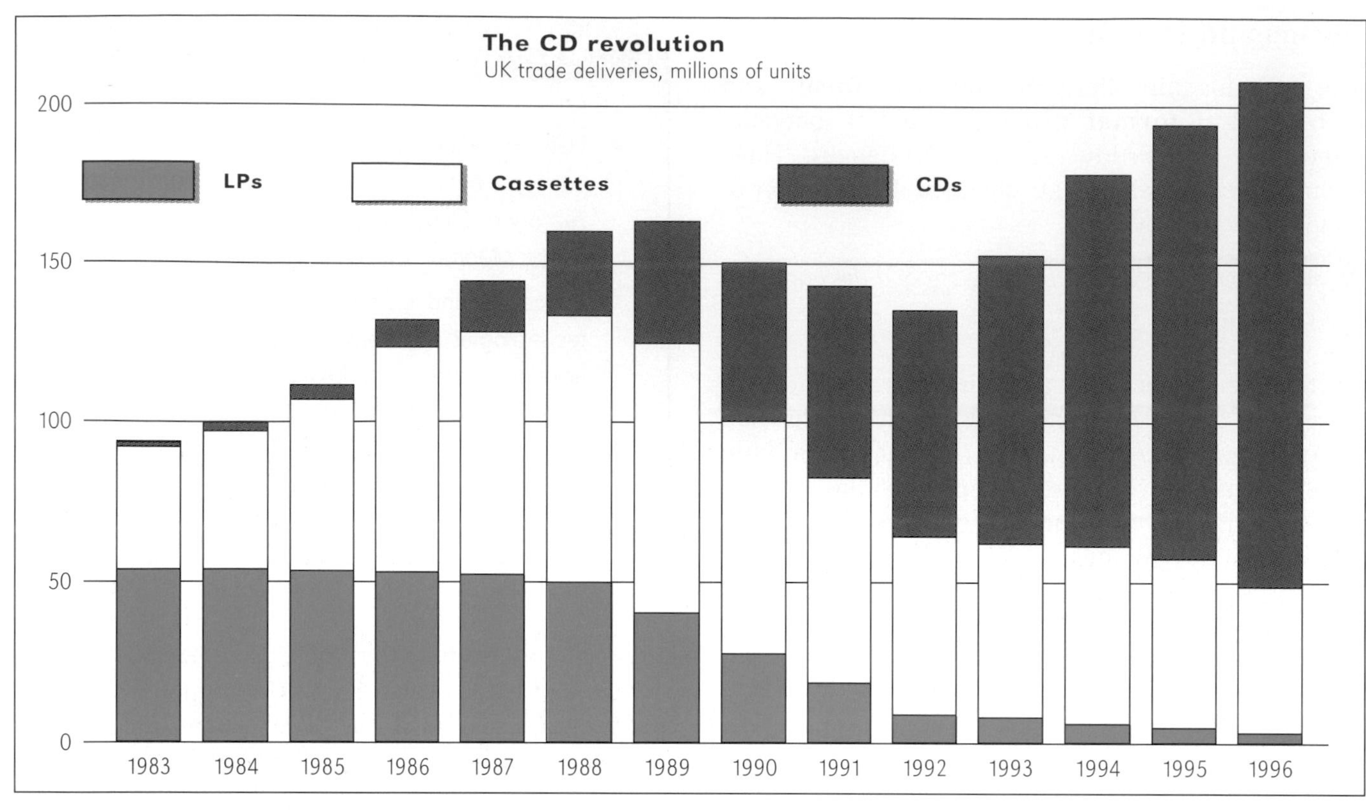

Source: *The Guardian*, 4 December 1997

MEDIA PRODUCERS AND AUDIENCES

PRODUCERS

The production of pop music involves more than just musicians. Indeed, the musicians often complain that the music has to fight through a crowd of managers, lawyers, accountants, engineers, executives, publicists, promoters and journalists to get to the fans. All these people are deciding what the audience will get to hear and trying to shape our likes and dislikes.

When looking at the industry, three key ideas must be kept in mind:

- the music business exists to make money
- producing the music and creating an audience for it is a collective effort
- the function of many people in the music business is to act as gatekeepers

Gatekeepers

At any one time in this country, there are thousands of ambitious bands. They cannot all be successful. Only some will be given the opportunity to be big and some will fail even then. However, the money from the really successful musicians keeps the whole business going. A large part of the profit goes towards finding and developing new bands.

At each stage of the production and promotion process, bands compete for the money to make the next stage possible. Not only do bands which are signed to different record companies compete, but bands within the same record company are fighting to get the best support.

The people who decide which bands should get more support (or get more space in a magazine or get more plays on the radio) are called, in Media Studies, **gatekeepers**. The analogy is with a herd of animals trying to get into a field where the grass is greener but the person on the gate lets only the best through.

Managers

The first gatekeepers that a band may encounter are managers. Managers take care of all the business interests of a band leaving them free to create music. In return, they want a cut of the profits (when the money comes in). Bands will therefore sign a management contract to fix that cut and the extent of the manager's involvement. A typical cut might be 10 per cent of all the earnings of all the members of the band.

At first, managers might have to put money into the band so managers have to be selective about their support. Money might be needed to pay for the recording of **demo tapes** or to set up a **showcase gig** in London. A demo (demonstration) tape is a small set of songs sent off to record companies to attract their attention. A showcase gig is more convenient for record companies to see the band perform.

The Spice Girls tried to do without a manager but not for long...

The contract

Signing a record contract is the most important step in a band's career. Contracts are complicated and bands are advised to get lawyers to check the contract. However, new bands have little power to force the company to make changes. Some stars later find that their contracts are so bad they take their own record company to court.

The principal elements of a record contract are:

- the length of time the contract covers
- the number and type of records (single or album) to be recorded and released
- the advance
- the royalty rate

A first contract is usually short term, say two years, although the record company will have an option to extend it written into the contract. During this period, the band agrees to record enough songs for a specified number to be selected for release as records. The company is not obliged to release them, however, if it doesn't like the songs.

- *What problems will face a band which starts making music its record company doesn't like?*

On the other hand, if all goes well, the company will be seeking to re-sign the band when the contract expires. It might offer a slightly better deal and promise to invest more money in publicity but other companies might want to 'poach' the band.

The advance

Once the contract is signed, the company will want the band to concentrate on writing and recording songs. As yet there will obviously be no money coming in from record sales but the band has to pay for time in recording studios, not to mention food, drink and somewhere to live.

This problem is overcome by the **advance**. The company lends a large sum of money to the band (and its manager) in advance of any record sales and profits. The size of the advance is a crucial sign of how important a band is to its company. The more money advanced the harder the company is prepared to work to get it back. Sometimes the size of the advance is turned into publicity but usually these figures are just hype. If a record label decides to drop a band from its list (or **roster**) the band does not have to repay the advance.

Royalties

The contract will specify a **royalty** rate. This is a percentage of the sale price – usually around 7 per cent in total – to be split amongst the musicians and, of course, the band's manager will also take his or her cut out of this straight away.

The good news for the musicians is that they get money whether the company has covered the costs of production and promotion or not. The bad news is that if they have not yet paid off the advance, all their royalties are retained until they do. Royalties are paid every six months and if success is only gradual it can take years for the band to move into profit.

- *Which looks the better deal: a large advance or a good royalty rate?*

The Sex Pistols sign to A&M outside Buckingham Palace. Ten days later they were dropped but kept the advance

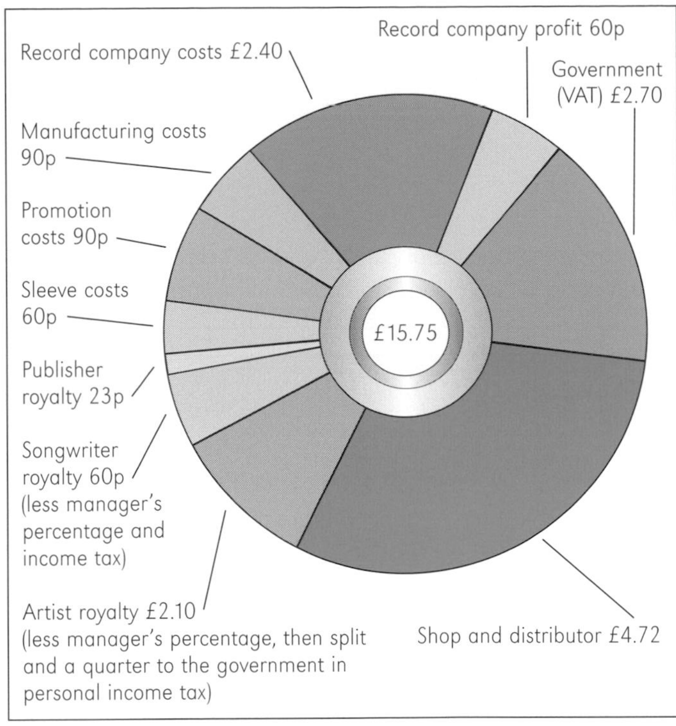

Where does the money go to when you buy a compact disc?

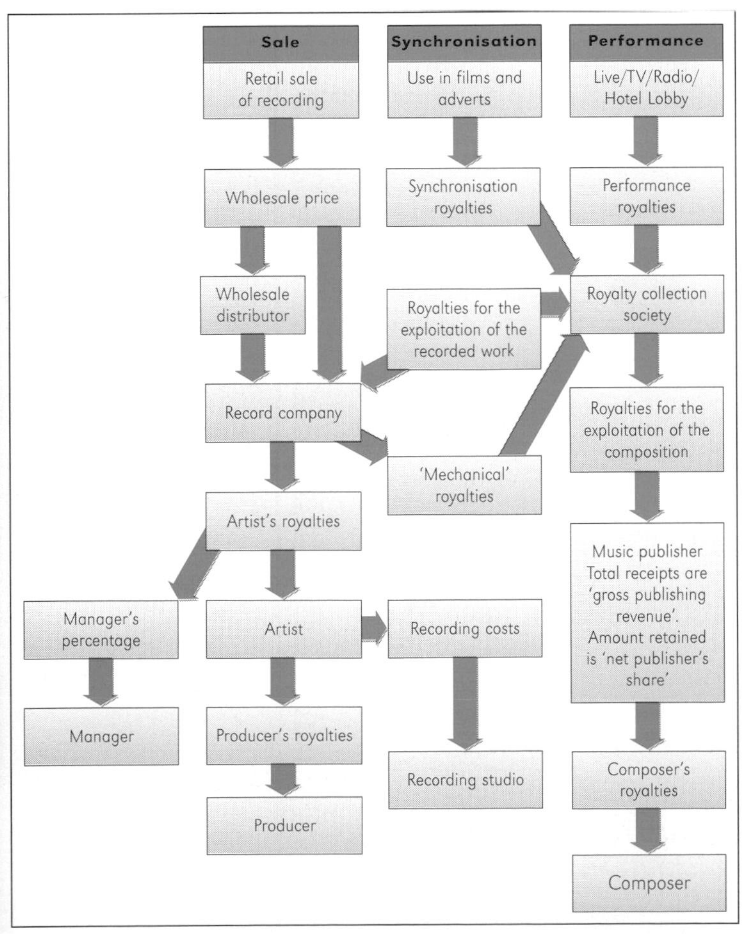

Who gets the money
(*Source*: Salomon Brothers / *The Guardian*)

Publishing

Songwriters get an additional royalty perhaps equal to the total musicians' royalty. This royalty is not kept back to pay off the advance and, because it is not split with the band, it can make songwriters much richer than 'ordinary' musicians. Freddie Mercury earned less than the other members of Queen because he wrote fewer songs.

- *If there is more than one songwriter in a band (as is common), how might this lead to tension when selecting songs to be released?*

This songwriting, or publishing, royalty is collected by a music publishing company. These publishers started by printing sheet music for people to play at home but now earn massive sums of money tracking down royalties for songwriters. Publishing royalties are payable, for example, any time anyone plays any version of a particular song in any club or on any radio station in the world.

- *Ask someone who runs a disco at school or at a club for a copy of a PRS (Performing Rights Society) return to look at in class.*

Another contract will specify the cut publishers take for this work. Sometimes the **copyright**, the right to collect the publishing royalty, is sold on.

Piracy

Piracy covers two activities: illegal sales, usually abroad, and home taping. In each case, the record company, the publishers and the band lose all their potential money. There is some evidence that home taping stimulates us into buying more records as well but record companies have been demanding as compensation a cut of the profits of blank tapes (which would then have to cost more).

ACTIVITY 16

- Conduct a survey of the amount of home taping and record buying among your class. Does it look like those who copy more also buy more or not?

In the studio

Once the ink is dry on the contract, a band will book time in a recording studio using money from the advance to pay for it. Some studios may be small, city basements; some are isolated in the country with hotel accommodation. Some rich bands choose to record in another country.

Studio recording has four aspects:

- people
- technology
- recording process
- mixing process

People 1

The most important person in the studio is the **producer**. In Media Studies, this term can be applied to anyone involved in making media texts. In pop music, as in cinema, TV and radio, the producer has a specific role to ensure that the product gets made in a particular way. It is better to have one person making decisions about the overall sound than have the band waste expensive studio time arguing. The musicians make the song but producers shape the recording. The final sound is as much their work as the band's and producers often get a royalty rate too.

ACTIVITY 17

- Make a list of the producers of your own records. Arrange with others to bring in records by the same producer to compare the style of production.

People 2

Producers have to know the possibilities of studio technology but they almost always have a **studio engineer** to help them with the details. An engineer works in the same studio all the time, whereas a producer is usually independent of both the studio and the record company. However, producers become known for their style or sound whereas most studios have the same sort of technology.

Technology 1

In the old days, a band would record a song all at once. If it didn't sound right or there were 'bum notes', they did it again. Then a very wide multi-track tape was developed which allowed all the instruments and voices to be recorded separately and at different times (sometimes in different studios on different continents).

ACTIVITY 18

- Check your local directories for recording studios and ask them to send you brochures or details.

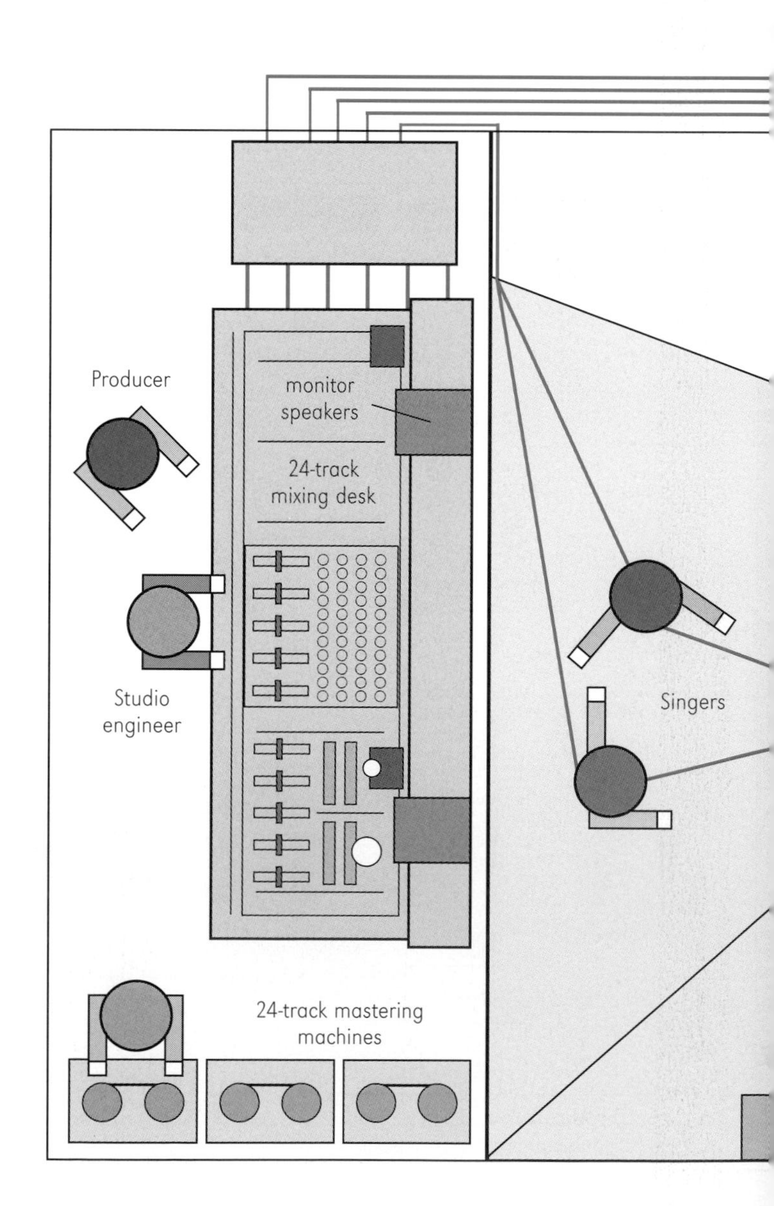

Technology 2

Nowadays, all the sounds, and even the adjustments required during the recording, are memorised by computers. Tape stores the sound electro-magnetically which means it might become distorted and copies lose quality. Computer data is stored as number codes which cannot fade or distort.

Technology 3

Before, all instruments had to be recorded using microphones. Now, synthesisers and samplers can reproduce many instrument sounds and 'play' direct into the computer. However, most guitarists still prefer to be 'miked up'.

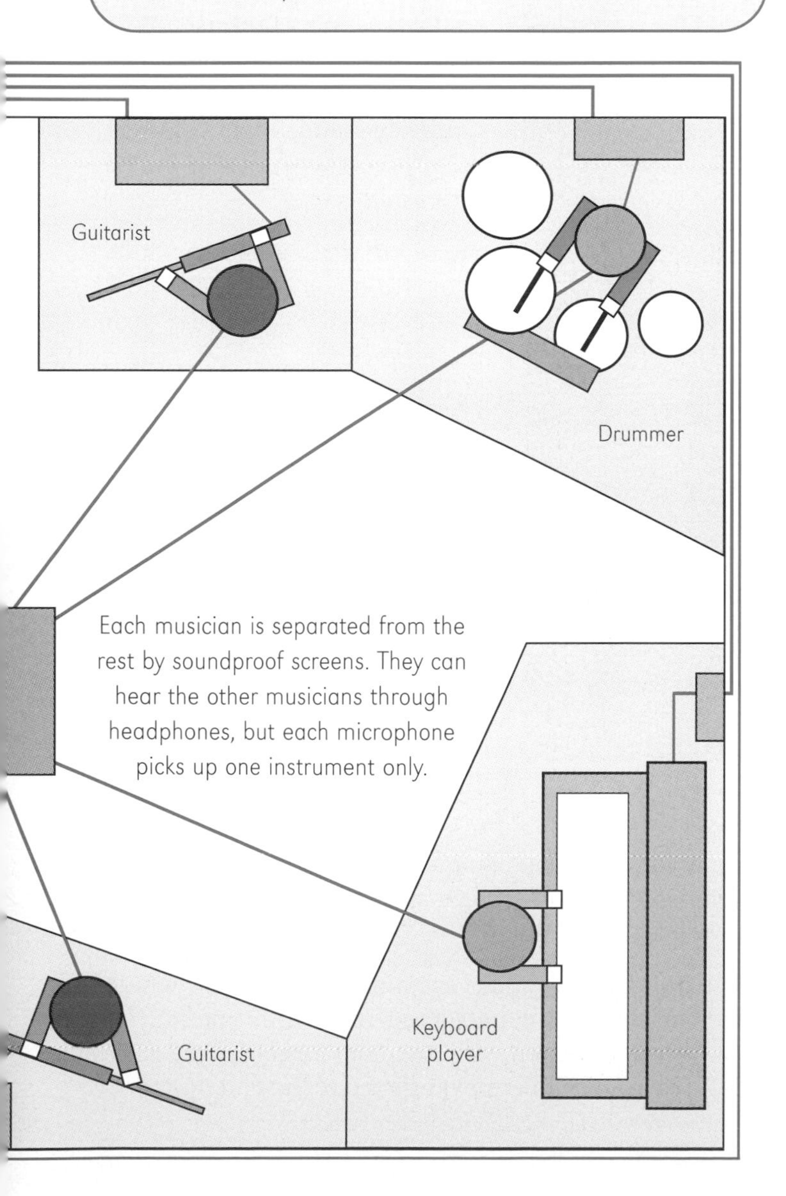

Technology 4

Sampling has been controversial because it allows producers to pinch a specific sound (say a bass drum) off another record. Some regard this as serious theft of someone else's hard work; others say it's just the way music is going.

Recording process

First to be recorded or 'laid down' is the backing: usually drums, bass and rhythm guitar playing at the same time but recorded separately. This will keep everything else in time. There might be some vocals as a rough guide. There might even be a drum machine to keep the real drummer in time! Then come the main guitar and keyboard 'overdubs' and any other instruments. Finally the main and backing vocals are added.

Mixing process

All of these are recorded as separate 'tracks' (which means here part of a recording not a song on an album). On another day, the producer will adjust the blend of these separate tracks. This is called **mixing**. When everyone's happy, the mix itself is recorded and then sent off for pressing into records. However, the original recording stays as separate tracks and can be remixed again, perhaps by a different producer.

ACTIVITY 19

- Listen to tracks where the musical instruments are mixed in and out. Compare remixes for their different blending of the same original recording.

Welcome to the Pleasure Dome

Between the company and the audience stand more gatekeepers. These gatekeepers are located in other media organisations such as radio and TV stations and magazines (*MOJO* music magazine called its review section *The Filter*). For a company to get even some of its bands through to the public, tough decisions will be made about which get more **promotional support** than others.

The aim, as in other media, is to construct a satisfied and loyal audience. In pop music, this is called creating a **fanbase**. As in other media, great effort is put into reaching the target audience and not wasting money on others not likely to be interested.

There are three areas on which promotion is concentrated. These are, in order of importance:

- **airplay**
- **press coverage**
- **live performance** or other points of reception

One rather surprising aspect of promotion should be mentioned here. For a long time, singles have not made much money for musicians or record companies. However, most people do not buy an album unless there are some recognisable singles on it. For this reason, companies regard singles as a form of advertising for the subsequent album.

The following pages examine the way in which audiences are constructed and information is managed. However, we should not forget the pleasure that we as consumers experience at the end of it all.

AUDIENCES

There has been a lot of investment in making the record but will it sell? How can the record company get people to buy this record rather than another?

- *In what ways is this challenge (of getting us to go out and buy a product) different to that faced by other media producers?*

▶ ACTIVITY 20

- Discuss ways in which you might rate the comparative pleasure you get from your consumption of different media products.
- How is the pleasure of hearing a song on the radio different from playing your own copy? How do you choose whether to watch a video or TV or listen to records?

The charts and airplay

All media industries measure sales (or viewing / listening figures) but pop uses the most visible structures to organise our listening and consumption.

- *How are the pop charts like and unlike circulation figures, TV ratings, box-office receipts, etc? What similarities might there be with, say, sports results?*

The charts are compiled by specialist independent organisations using sales information taken direct from electronic tills in record shops. However, only some shops are used each week (to make the process manageable) and this has sometimes led to the illegal activity of **hyping**.

- *If it is known which shops will be used in the week when a particular single comes out, how can their sales be distorted to affect the national chart?*

Airplay

Everyone in the music business agrees that airplay of a record on the radio is the most effective form of promotion. We, the potential buyers, can actually hear the song rather than just read a good review of it or hear about it from friends.

- *How many recent record purchases did you make*
  - without hearing the music?
  - after hearing songs on the radio?
  - after listening to friends' copies?

Radio stations do not want to play, indeed probably could not play, all the new releases each week plus all the other records already out. In fact, we would probably not want to hear so much unfamiliar music.

The stations therefore use two ways of structuring their output and our listening: the **charts** and **playlists**. Some shows are explicitly based on playing large sections of the chart (the Top 40 say) working up towards the number one.

The playlist is the weekly set of records that will be played on all the programmes on a particular station. It is devised by senior radio station producers. It will include top 10 hits, climbers (but hardly ever records slipping down the chart) and, crucially, a few **new releases**. Getting a new record on to a playlist is so important that record companies employ specialists called **pluggers** to persuade producers to include their new releases on the playlist. Plugging might involve entertaining the producers at parties or by using stunts – such as delivering the record by parachute or something.

If plugging fails, the temptation to hype a record must be very powerful because it will almost certainly then make the playlist as a fast climber.

Pluggers play games with Bruno Brookes

Radio, TV and video

Radio shows are cheap to produce so radio stations are cheaper to run than TV companies. More space on the airwaves means many more radio stations. London alone now has over 30 radio stations. This is creating a radio music culture like America's in which not just programmes but whole stations specialise in particular genres of music.

- *What is the attraction of this for advertisers?*

ACTIVITY 21

- Conduct a class survey of radio listening patterns. Compare different station schedules to see if there is competition for similar target audiences.

TV stations, or channels, are far from being so targeted. TV music shows therefore try to make the most of their magazine-type content – featuring all sorts of music, interspersed with brief interviews, videos and news. There are two major exceptions.

Top of the Pops is structured around the chart. Its format has changed little over the years. Its position at the end of the week used to be determined by the midweek release of the chart. That has changed but it seems natural that *TOTP* is scheduled at the end of the week. One of the first TV music shows, *Ready Steady Go!*, occupied an early Friday evening slot and began with the words 'The weekend starts here.'

MTV (Music TeleVision) is a specialist music channel broadcasting on satellite in Europe although originally a cable channel in the USA. MTV has been criticised for catering predominantly for white rock fans. It is, however, a commercial station, more like a specialist radio station than a broad mainstream TV channel like BBC1, which has an obligation to be varied and balanced. If its advertisers are happy then so is MTV.

ACTIVITY 22

- Conduct a viewing survey of TV music shows. What appear to be the target audiences?

MTV relies almost totally on music videos and calls its presenters VJs (video-jockeys). Music videos began as promotional material for TV shows allowing groups to 'perform' in more than one place at a time. With the growth of domestic VCRs, music videos have become sales products in their own right. In style, they have moved from performances simply recorded and edited to elaborate mini-films using Hollywood directors.

- *Compare the relative pleasures of watching a music video and listening to a record by the same artist.*

The press

The music business works through the press to reach and construct audiences. However, whereas TV and radio are used (or needed) to present the **music product** itself to the public the press is used (or needed) to build an **image** of the band. This personal and social context helps create the meanings of the music.

Record companies have publicity departments whose job it is to send out photos and **press releases** about their bands. A press release is information written up by a company to sound like interesting news. 'Band releases record!' is hardly news so the publicity department works at creating different angles on this completely normal event.

The press has a gatekeeping function because it cannot print something about every group. On the other hand, it wants good sales and will be interested in securing interviews with fashionable bands. Good sales to identifiable audiences attract profitable advertising, including adverts from the same record companies wanting feature articles about their bands.

ACTIVITY 23

- Examine some music publications to see whether articles about and adverts for the same bands occur close together.

There are four press genres in the music field:

- music magazines, e.g. *Smash Hits, Q, Megamix*
- music papers, e.g. *NME*
- general papers
- fanzines and the Web

In addition, there are specialist trade journals such as *Music Week* (UK) and *Billboard* (USA) which are very revealing about the way the business talks to itself.

> **ACTIVITY 24**
>
> Compare the content of a selection of music magazines and weekly papers.
>
> - Gauge the proportion of advertising compared with total editorial text.
> - Gauge the proportion of news compared with features (interviews, etc) and reviews.
> - Identify the target audiences for each publication.
> - How do the features and posed photographs create images for bands?

All the mainstream papers have small pop music sections – usually on a particular day of the week. Their function is again to 'collect' together readers interested in pop music for the benefit of advertisers.

Fanzines became popular during the punk period. They were home-produced, even before desk-top publishing, and were sold at gigs, in small record shops and by mail order. They have been replaced by fan-produced pages on the World Wide Web.

Reception and consumption

There are other points at which we are pop music consumers including shops, clubs and pubs and even the odd live performance.

- *Make a list of all the places in which you have heard pop music in the last week.*

Shops

Record stores play music in the shop and we can listen to certain albums on headphones. Other shops, particularly clothing shops, also play pop music, sometimes recorded with a DJ to sound like a radio station.

The media are used to build the images of bands and solo artists

Clubs and pubs

Clubs are designed for the social enjoyment of music. Listening and dancing with others increases the pleasures of the music, pleasures which are basically physical, sensual and sexual and for which certain genres of music are more suited than others.

- *How wide a range of activities does club culture now cover?*

Pop is also consumed in pubs. Every play on a juke box means money for the musicians and record company but it is also a form of promotion to those who have never heard it before. **Karaoke** (live singing over a backing track) has given pub music a new life.

Live performance

Most bands perform live at the start, doing **gigs** (concerts) in local pubs to build up a fanbase. The money from such gigs rarely amounts to a living wage for the musicians. Strangely enough, however, this remains true of almost all live performances. The cost of lighting rigs, PA (sound) systems, special effects and staging plus transport, crew and accommodation for everybody means that only world megastars like The Rolling Stones and Michael and Janet Jackson make money from touring. Everybody else loses money on the live performance but hopes to make much more from record sales boosted by the tour.

- *What are the advantages and disadvantages to bands, promoters and fans of tours as compared with festivals?*

It is now debatable whether pop music is really about live music or recorded music. This doesn't just apply to music like dance which may never be performed live. Records began as ways of preserving a performance in the sense of an historical record (as in, 'since records began'). Now, live performance is really a way of increasing record sales. All of us hear many more bands through recordings than we go to see live.

Audience and image

The last section looked at the roles of those who make and promote the music and construct and measure audiences. The next section looks at the messages and values suggested by the music and the musicians.

Why are festivals losing their popularity?

This is a good point, then, at which to consider the relationship between an audience and the overall image of a band or performer.

Both performers and business aim to create a loyal, long-lasting audience. The problem is this: new bands can be promoted more easily to younger audiences but they quickly go out of fashion and younger people tend to have less money to spend anyway. Older audiences spend more but they tend to buy new records only by artists they already know and like. The solution is to break a band or performer first of all as a pop group (in a very narrow sense of pop) but then to change their image to that of a more serious musician, partly to keep the audience which is growing up and partly to appeal to an even older audience. This is called **audience crossover**. The ultimate crossover is to appeal to the huge American market which is notoriously reluctant to like new music.

The most successful crossover in recent times has been that of George Michael who started originally as a pin-up popster in Wham! and then became a seriously moody – but seriously successful – solo singer-songwriter. Robbie Williams, formerly of Take That, is doing the same. Kylie Minogue has made a less successful attempt at being taken seriously.

- *As this book is written the future of the Spice Girls is in doubt for various reasons. Which of them, by the time you read this book, will be promoted as serious musicians with a long-term career ahead of them?*

Some big stars, of course, just stay the same (only more so!) – the Rolling Stones or Pink Floyd, for example. Others are adept at keeping in fashion: David Bowie has radically altered his image, and music, several times in his career and Michael Jackson, of course, has altered not just his image.

MEDIA MESSAGES AND VALUES

When we come to examine what pop music says about the world, we should remind ourselves that pop music messages and values are not just transmitted through song words.

As we saw in the *Language* section (page 187), there are other elements of pop music which also convey meaning: the music itself and visual aspects. In the last section, *Media producers and audiences*, we also saw that an overall image of a group is constructed and promoted in the press in particular. Each part of this section starts from a different aspect of pop language to explore a particular theme.

MESSAGES

First, however, let us consider the message of pop in general. It has been said that we value pop music, deep down, because it provides a soundtrack to our own lives so that for years afterwards we will associate particular songs with memories of particular people and places. (This might also explain the successful revivals of terribly unfashionable music.)

ACTIVITY 25

Ask a range of people about

- songs / records that always recall a particular person, moment or phase in their lives, and / or
- songs / records which bring back the memory of where they were when they first heard them

With their permission, these might be briefly published in a display or a booklet.

Love, sex and gender

Love

Have you ever noticed that whether you are falling in love or breaking up there's always a song in the charts about it? It's strange because we all think that our own happiness, and tears, are special ('You just don't understand...!') but we also like to hear someone else express it for us.

It must be true that the most common subject of pop lyrics is love. There are compilation albums of love songs and even a genre called Lovers' Rock.

In the 1950s, an American writer called Donald Horton analysed the lyrics of 235 songs printed in four magazines in the same month. He categorised the love songs (84 per cent of the total) according to the stages of being in love:

Love lyrics 84% of total	Other subjects included narrative ballads, religious and comic songs.
Wishing 4%	Waiting for the ideal lover to come along and dreaming about what they will be like when they do.
Courtship 32%	The stage of going steady. The lyrics are often written to suggest the singer is trying to overcome the reluctance of the other person, sometimes by gentle persuasion, sometimes by seeming desperate. Some lyrics are a kind of response – asking for reassurance that the pushy one is really serious.
Honeymoon 8%	The stage of complete happiness. Sometimes the singer is grateful, sometimes suspicious that it's all still a dream.
Troubles 15%	These might be unavoidable separations or hostile parents or unkindness by the other person. It might even be the worst thing of all: two-timing.
All alone 25%	The singer may be still hopeful or has given up all hope or is perhaps quite bitter when trust has been broken.

Source: *On Record*, eds. S. Frith, A. Goodwin (Routledge,1990)

ACTIVITY 26

Conduct a (smaller) survey of current songs to identify

- how many are love songs
- what other subjects there are
- which songs fall into the stages outlined above

Sex

Many contemporary lyrics are about sex – not just the activity but a person's sex. Women, in particular, are the subject of aggressive, even abusive, lyrics in two genres: heavy metal and rap.

In these lyrics, stereotypical attitudes are expressed towards women and their sexual behaviour. Women are perceived as a threat in some way and, since attack is the best form of defence perhaps, these lyrics portray women as promiscuous or even as prostitutes. This attitude of fear and hatred of women is termed **misogynistic**.

- *What is the effect of such attitudes, do you think, on pop audiences?*

Gender

Media Studies is one subject which attempts to get away from the idea that being male or female determines our behaviour. There are many different ways of being a man or behaving like a woman. Of course, there are social pressures, good and bad, to

Girlpower grown up: pop composer and producer Anne Dudley, British Oscar winner for *The Full Monty*

which we conform unconsciously. The word **gender** is used when describing these social images of masculinity or femininity rather than the term sex, which is used for the biological fact of being male or female.

Gender is important in pop when we ask questions like:

- Why is the music business predominantly male?
- Why do more boys play instruments than girls?
- Why do girls tend to be singers?
- Why are there not more girl bands?
- What does girlpower mean, in practice?

These may not be subjects that people sing about much but there are certainly powerful messages here that the business sends out whether deliberately or not.

VALUES

Moral panics and music

Moral panic is the term given to a sudden outburst of concern about a social issue, usually some form of young people's enjoyment. A good sign of a moral panic is a lack of proportion: a few drug-related deaths are given more prominence than more deaths in car crashes. The media, particularly the press, claim to be simply reporting the concerns of the public in order to prod a lazy, ignorant government to take urgent action. Many people suspect that they create the panic themselves so that they can portray themselves as protectors of public morality whilst printing lurid stories about sex and drugs and Rock and Roll.

And Rock and Roll was the first moral panic about pop music. In 1950s America, preachers smashed Rock and Roll records on television because it was 'the devil's music'. The concern was partly about violence. Cinemas showing the first Rock and Roll films were vandalised by audiences and in Britain Teddy Boys became symbols of aggressive youth.

The main concern, however, was about the openly sexual nature of the music itself. When Elvis Presley sang on television, he was framed from the waist upwards so that his suggestive hip movements were

Once upon a time, Cliff Richard was dangerous...

not shown. But this concern had a racist edge. We saw in the History section that Rock and Roll shifted black R'n'B across to white teenagers but it was only when they got interested that people wanted it stopped.

In 1956, the *Daily Mail* ran a front-page editorial headlined 'Rock 'n' Roll Babies' and correspondents wrote:

> Rock 'n' Roll, often known now as rock, roll and riot, is sexy music. It can make the blood race. It has something of the African tomtom and voodoo dance.....It is deplorable. It is tribal. And it is from America. It follows ragtime, blues, dixie, jazz, hot cha-cha and the boogie-woogie, which surely originated in the jungle. We sometimes wonder whether this is the negro's revenge.

(*Daily Mail*, 4 & 5 September 1956, quoted in *Hooligan* by G. Pearson, Macmillan, 1983)

- *Are there more recent examples of concerns about music and encouragement of sexual activity?*

The hippies of the 1960s were too peaceful to cause much of a panic. They wanted to 'drop out' of society and lie around smoking dope and indulging in 'free love'. This shifted the focus of concern about pop music from sex and violence to drugs and the challenge to '**the work ethic**' (the idea that working hard is a sign of moral purity). However, the older generation needn't have worried that society and business would just come to a stop: many hippies have become famous business people, such as Richard Branson, and, ironically, the 'underground' culture created one of the biggest music businesses of all: the pop festival.

The 1970s witnessed the punk explosion. Punks saw no point in joining society because there was no hope: this was a time of rising youth unemployment. Punk behaviour was openly offensive and sometimes distressingly self-destructive. Punks flirted with Nazi fashion, pierced their bodies with safety pins and their choice of drug abuse was glue-sniffing. Punk didn't last long, possibly because punks were mainly working class (and therefore 'did not matter' again, like American blacks and R'n'B), possibly because mainstream society, led by the music business, was becoming cleverer at turning protest into profit. Punks walking around London found themselves turned into a tourist attraction.

- *Where can the effects of punk still be seen in music, graphic design and fashion? Which current performers seek out controversy or cause offence?*

Ten years later, it was Acid House Raves. These were huge events, described as parties but for which people had to pay, held all night in empty warehouses or marquees in fields. They were publicised at the last moment usually through a network of mobile phone users. These young people were well-off (rave organisers tended to be ex-public school boys) and the scene was highly commercial from the start. Perhaps because of this, the moral panic did result in swift, but indirect, legal action by the government. A police chief was quoted in the parliamentary debate:

> “When thousands of young people just drop into a field, when you have criminals running the parties, when you have drug-taking, then you have all the elements of a major disaster. Hundreds of young people could be killed or injured...The police [are] especially worried about the infiltration of East End criminals who [see] pay-parties as an easy way of making a lot of money.”

(quoted in *Hansard*, Friday 9 March 1990)

Part of the concern about acid house was actually about the sheer 'mindlessness' of the dancing (which it was thought only drugs could be responsible for). However, the new law forced organisers to get a safety licence for each rave or face criminal charges. As a result raves were effectively killed off but, very significantly, club culture took off from warehouse parties. At this point, the moral panic switched to the drug associated with dance music: Ecstasy (or E).

ACTIVITY 27

- What is the current attitude towards pop music, drugs, young people and pleasure? Collect some newspaper stories as evidence.

Rebels without a cause

Now we will look at the values of pop music as seen through the behaviour, lifestyle and, indeed, the lives and deaths of pop musicians.

Only film stars generate as much interest in their personal lives. Because films are very controlled products we rarely see on the screen what we might have read about. On the other hand, a gig is real (and arguably not a media product) and may create not just publicity but news.

Modern pop music is now 40 years old. The teenagers of the 1950s and 60s are now settled and middle-aged but they still like pop music. Indeed, some performers are in their 50s and 60s. The longer pop goes on, the greater the contrast between pop as the music of rebellious youth and pop as easy listening for parents.

Some other signs of pop being middle-aged might be:

- the Brit Awards
- Presidents and Prime Ministers who have played in bands
- educational courses and exams in studio work and band management
- council-run recording studios
- sitcoms such as *Absolutely Fabulous* where the children are anti-pop because their parents are embarrassingly keen

On the other hand, there has always been a career path for pop stars which moved from obscurity and rebellion to prestige and conformity.

The stages of this development might be set out as below:

ACTIVITY 28

- Think of current bands or performers who fit the stages shown in the table below. Who are the delinquents, the cowboys, the new superstars and aristocrats? Are there others who do not fit this pattern at all?

The Rolling Stones were once the bad boys of British R'n'B. They achieved notoriety by being caught urinating in public in a petrol station. The wall now has a plaque commemorating the event. The police raided Mick Jagger's house and found not only marijuana but Marianne Faithful, naked on a rug. Jagger's now a grandfather and shops for antiques and paintings. At the 1968 Altamont festival, the Stones allowed Hell's Angels to provide the security but then failed to stop the concert when the Angels murdered a man in front of the stage. Nowadays, their tours are sponsored by Volkswagen.

LABEL	ARENA	ACTIVITY
Hooligan	Onstage	New pop music begins being associated with generally anti-social behaviour (and starting moral panics as we have seen). The point is to get attention.
Outlaw	Public but offstage	More famous bands, usually all-male, play up to the image of Rock and Roll outlaws riding into town, causing trouble, riding off again. Trouble in this case usually means wrecking hotel rooms, getting drunk on aeroplanes or getting off with supermodels.
Superstar	Private but over a long period	Those who get really rich turn to less violent pastimes and indulge their excesses – childish spending sprees, huge drug consumption, orgiastic parties. But still we love reading about it – if only to speculate how long before they burn out for good.
Rock aristocrat	World's media and celebrity publications	Some stay clean but indulge their inflated sense of self-importance by taking up good causes like saving the rainforest or playing concerts for royalty. This was a particular feature of the 1980s, beginning with the unique *Band Aid* record (and *Live Aid* concert) which was then copied every time there was a disaster but got tackier every time. Some end up receiving official honours. Britain now has two pop star knights: Arise Sir Cliff (Richard) and Sir Paul (McCartney)!

Rock and role model? All Saints' Melanie Blatt – blamed for encouraging teenage pregnancies

Protest and politics

Music has been used for explicitly political purposes throughout history, not least in wartime for raising the morale of soldiers and civilians. However, the relationship between pop and politics is an uneasy one.

Why and how?

The *Rebels without a cause* section sketched out the tension in pop between the desire to stand outside the mainstream of society – to be a rebel – and (later) to display wealth and importance. The former desire makes pop musicians eager to protest but reluctant to commit themselves to particular political parties. The latter desire tempts them to prove that they can not only entertain the world but also change it.

This tension can be resolved in the more general public campaigns, particularly humanitarian ones. Then pop musicians can take an outsider stance which criticises governments for not doing enough whilst appearing concerned and compassionate – rebels *with* a cause. Perhaps because of this, many of the campaigns associated with pop have an oppositional sound: anti-Vietnam, anti-racism, anti-apartheid. Others have championed human rights (civil rights, Amnesty) or humanitarian causes (famine and AIDS relief).

Musicians can bring about political change in three ways: by increasing awareness (raising consciousness) largely through the songs and explanations at concerts; by raising and donating money largely from record profits; and by lending their fame as public support largely through personal comments in interviews. It is arguable which is the most effective.

Stevie Wonder's record *Happy Birthday* turned a flagging campaign to mark Martin Luther King's birthday as a national US holiday into an unstoppable success. *Band Aid, Live Aid* and the record *We Are the World* raised huge amounts of money for famine victims in Africa. On the other hand, the largest political pop concert in history at Wembley in June 1988 climaxing with the best political pop song ever written – *Free Nelson Mandela* – had no apparent political effect at all. It did, however, put decidedly unpolitical performers like Whitney Houston (who never mentioned Mandela once) in front of a global audience of millions.

Style and authenticity

We saw in the History section that the roots of pop are in the Blues. The Blues were political songs in the sense of making an oppressed people feel stronger. Folk music, too, has a long tradition of political protest song. In both these genres the strength of the message has come as much from the perceived authenticity of the performance – the emotion, the sincerity, the importance of bonding with the audience rather than simply entertaining or getting them to buy a commercial product.

This concern with authenticity continues to this day when pop and politics get together. Indeed, it has been suggested that certain genres are better suited to political messages: rock and rap are better than pop and soul. The lifestyles, behaviour and personal comments of the musicians are scrutinised as much as, if not more than, the music. After all, it is hard to define political music as such.

What's more, the message is not under the control of the musician. Bruce Springsteen's anti-Vietnam War song *Born in the USA* became almost a second national anthem in the 1980s because the irony of the lyrics was simply ignored.

Bob Marley was the world's first Third World superstar. With his group the Wailers he made reggae commercially successful among white audiences. In Jamaica, politicians wanted his support and his funeral brought the country to a halt in the same way as Princess Diana's did in Britain. In this country, however, reggae was championed not only by British Afro-Caribbeans and white sympathisers but by skinheads more usually known for their extreme right wing and racist political views. Meanwhile, reggae is intimately associated with Rastafarianism which has mystical religious roots as well as political dimensions such as returning to Ethiopia. *Live Aid*, in support of mainly Ethiopian famine victims, was criticised for not having many black, especially reggae, performers. White pop stars seeking to show they cared lost sight of an even bigger political message.

Rocking all over the world?

Pop-rock is a largely American English-language commodity. It is infiltrating every culture and country in the world. In some cases it might be a good thing. It is said that the Communist system in Russia and eastern Europe collapsed not because of a military threat but because the population wanted their share of western culture: McDonald's, Levi's, Coke (or Pepsi).

On the other hand many people, and not just fuddy-duddy traditionalists, do not want their lives and their children's lives taken over by American values or by envy of all things American. What is perhaps harder for us to understand is that even English itself threatens other languages. The French government has passed a law requiring 40 per cent of all pop records played on French radio to be sung in French. World Music exists as a genre category in record shops and provides us with a change from mainstream pop. It is hard for us to understand, perhaps, that some people regard American pop music as a form of global pollution spoiling people's pleasure and pride in their own music and culture. The trouble is they can't really write a pop song to promote their campaign...

Bob Marley – the first Third World superstar

It'll be all white on the night: Live Aid 1985

SUMMARY

- It is hard to define what pop music is and whether it is one of the mass media.
- Pop developments are the result of converging musical, social and technological changes.
- Pop history shows repeated adaptation of black musics for white audiences.
- Analysing the elements of pop music requires new vocabulary which is largely connotative.
- The production and promotion process is dominated by non-musicians, many of whom function as gatekeepers.
- Audiences are shaped and measured in great detail.
- Pop music communicates messages and values through much more than the lyrics.

GLOSSARY

A&R – Artists and Repertoire, the record company department responsible for finding bands and developing their recording careers

advance – the money loaned to a band before it starts selling records and earning royalties

back catalogue – collection of recordings, possibly even by dead artists, which record company tries to repackage and reissue

backing – the instruments playing under the vocals

crossover – moving from success with one audience to another.

DJ – Disc jockey (**VJ**: video jockey) – the person who plays the record on radio or on stage

gatekeeper – someone whose actions decide which artists are selected for access to higher levels of support and success

gig – a performance or concert: the name comes from American anti-alcohol campaigners singing from the back of their wagons called gigs

improvisation – when performers, including singers, play a spontaneous variation on the tune

karaoke – a Japanese word meaning *music minus one* referring to songs re-recorded without vocals for amateurs to sing over

mixing – important recording process where the different instruments, vocals and sounds are blended into the final version

PA – Public Address: PA systems (or the PA) are the huge banks of speakers either side of the stage at gigs and festivals

playlist – set of records decided weekly by producers (not DJs) for airplay on a radio station

riff – a short musical sequence repeated throughout a song

solo – when a musical instrument takes over the lead from the vocals, usually for an improvisation

7 Cartoons, comics and animation

COLIN BULMAN

Coming up

In this chapter we will be looking at:

- the universal popularity of cartoons, comics and animation
- the forerunners of cartoons in prehistoric and historic times
- the importance of caricature
- when and why comics developed
- the importance of cartoon films to the film industry
- how animated cartoon films are made

INTRODUCTION

Almost everyone over the age of five has heard of Mickey Mouse and Superman. Both started life as simple drawings with words attached and over 60 years later they are as popular as ever.

Their popularity is fundamental to the subjects of this chapter. While comics, cartoons and animated films are usually thought of as just light entertainment they are, in fact, financially very important to the film, newspaper and magazine industries.

The reason for their importance is to be found in the universal language of pictures.

Although many books do not have pictures, we learn much from pictures as well as words. As infants we looked at pictures in books before we could read. People from different countries often cannot understand each other's languages but people of all countries understand the same pictures.

This chapter is concerned with particular types of pictures – cartoons, comic strips and animated films. The first two appear in magazines and newspapers, and comics may be magazines in their own right. Animated cartoons are, of course, a type of film which uses drawn and painted characters instead of live actors.

All three are based on the same things: drawings and paintings. A cartoon is usually a single drawing, comics are often series of pictures which tell a story, and animated films tell a story but the figures in the pictures appear to move.

Prehistoric cave painting at Lascaux, France, dating from *c.* 13,000 BC

THE HISTORY OF CARTOONS

PREHISTORIC TIMES

Cave paintings still exist which were done in prehistoric times before people could write or read at all. The earliest cave paintings are believed to have been drawn from about 15,000 BC and were found in a cave in Lascaux, France.

It is thought that these drawings were done not just for amusement. They may have been designed to please the gods or as a kind of prayer for the tribe to be given animals to hunt for food.

THE EGYPTIANS, GREEKS AND ROMANS

Throughout history important people and events have been portrayed in pictures as well as words, and sometimes only in pictures. Often the portrayals were on canvas; sometimes they were statues or carvings.

The ancient Egyptians, around 1000 BC, produced **papyrus** scrolls which have been preserved and which portray events in the lives of their kings, nobles and ordinary people together with comments in **hieroglyphics** or sign writing.

papyrus – an early kind of paper made by pressing reeds flat

hieroglyphics – a type of writing which used pictures instead of letters

The Greeks before the birth of Christ often depicted battles, victories and other events in a series of pictures round the bulging surface of a vase or urn.

The Romans, later, were keen on sculpted pictures on monuments and one amazing example survives from the second century AD. On the column of the Emperor Trajan a story of military victories winds round and round to an overall length of 200 metres.

The pictorial nature of hieroglyphics made them popular as a decoration for statues

Detail from Trajan's Column

A scene from the Bayeux Tapestry

THE BAYEUX TAPESTRY

The Bayeux Tapestry is the most famous portrayal of the Battle of Hastings in AD 1066. It shows the preparations for the battle, the battle itself and its aftermath – William the Conqueror's invasion of the Anglo-Saxon kingdom.

The story is told in 79 scenes embroidered in coloured wool on a cloth measuring 70 metres and includes short sentences in Latin. The most famous image is of the Anglo-Saxon King Harold with his eye pierced by an arrow.

The story in the Bayeux Tapestry is remarkably like a modern strip cartoon in that the stages are shown one following another in a time sequence.

PRINTING

The invention of the printing press in 1474 made possible the reproduction of drawings very cheaply and in large quantities. Before, only the rich could afford hand-produced drawings and paintings. Once printing was established, large numbers of copies of books, paper sheets and magazines could be produced. Printing was very much quicker and cheaper than painting, drawing, embroidery and stone carving.

ARTISTS' CARTOONS

The original meaning of the word **cartoon** was a study or plan for a painting or fresco (from the Italian word *cartone* – pasteboard). Artists in the past would do a number of sketches of the various elements to be included in a painting. They would then produce a cartoon, which was a full-size drawn outline of what would become the finished painting. They would then paint over the cartoon.

In the National Gallery in London you can see a cartoon by Renaissance artist Leonardo da Vinci. It is of two women and two children, and is known as *Virgin and Child with St Anne and the infant St John the Baptist*. Leonardo never painted over the cartoon, yet it is regarded as a remarkable work of art and is priceless.

CARICATURE

Cartoons (and most comic strips and animated films) use **caricatures** of people and animals, an exaggeration or distortion of certain features often to comical effect. The word caricature comes from another Italian word, *caricare*, meaning to emphasise certain features.

The first person to make caricatures in the modern sense was believed to be the Italian, Agostino Carracci, in the seventeenth century.

Caricatures are usually thought of as portraits of a single individual – the visual equivalent of calling them names – and they appeared in Britain from then onwards.

HOGARTH AND ROWLANDSON

Two notable British artists produced drawings and engravings which could be regarded as cartoons before they became really popular in the 1840s.

William Hogarth, who lived from 1697 to 1764, produced satirical engravings which criticised life in London in the eighteenth century. He was one of the first artists to use **speech balloons** for some of his characters.

Thomas Rowlandson lived from 1756 to 1827 and his comic caricature, Dr Syntax, a ridiculous clergyman and schoolmaster, became a popular character in journals.

PUNCH

In 1841 the magazine *Punch* was founded. It can still be found in newsagents today. In the same year, a set of paintings was commissioned for the Houses of Parliament and preparatory designs (cartoons in the original sense) were put on show. A *Punch* artist **parodied** (made fun of) these rough sketches by producing and publishing in the magazine his own versions (cartoons, in a new sense).

Presumably the *Punch* 'cartoonist' thought the originals were poor quality and a waste of public money. But out of them the modern cartoon was born.

William Hogarth's works satirised the excesses of London life – this one shows the evils of drinking

KEY DATES – CARTOONS

15000 BC The earliest known cave drawings and paintings are done in Lascaux, France

c.1000 BC Egyptians produce series of drawings on papyrus depicting the lives of their kings and people

500 BC Greeks and Romans start depicting important events and people on monuments, stone friezes and pottery

AD 500-1500 Monks write out the Bible and religious texts by hand and illuminate them with drawings

1474 Invention of printing press

1600s Agostino Carracci draws the first caricatures, stylised and exaggerated studies of well-known people

1700s William Hogarth (1697–1764) makes engravings using caricature to satirise London life

Caricatures become fairly common in publications

1812 Thomas Rowlandson (1756–1827) creates the comic character Dr Syntax who becomes popular in magazines

1840s The cartoon in the modern sense becomes popular in newspapers and magazines

1841 *Punch* magazine founded; it uses many satirical cartoons

MEDIA LANGUAGES AND CATEGORIES – CARTOONS

Nowadays when we talk of cartoons, we mean the word in the sense that came into use in the 1840s. This kind of cartoon still appears in nearly all newspapers on a daily basis and in many magazines. Like the artist's cartoon, the newspaper cartoon is usually uncoloured and seems as if it has been drawn quickly. But this is not to demean the skill of the cartoonist: speed is essential, as we shall see.

THE LANGUAGE OF CARTOONS

Words and pictures

Most cartoons are a drawing with a caption or perhaps some text in a speech bubble. The language of cartoons, in other words, is quite different from that of the other elements in a newspaper or magazine.

A newspaper article may stand alone or it may be illustrated with a photograph. A photo may illustrate an article or stand alone with a brief caption. In each instance the photo and the article remain distinct from each other. Each makes its own individual impact.

The effect of a cartoon, however, depends on words and picture together. The reader must take them in almost simultaneously. Some cartoons are purely visual, but where the cartoonist has deemed a caption or words to be necessary, they carry equal importance. The words and the drawing are **interdependent**.

Let us take an example but without seeing the cartoon. This shows how important both words and pictures are and also how a cartoon's impact may rely on an apparent contradiction between the two.

The caption on the cartoon stated simply: 'Country gentlefolk at leisure'. What do these words conjure up in your mind? Picnics by the riverside, walks in the hills, cricket on the village green?

The cartoon picture in question actually showed red-faced, angry-looking men and women mounted on straining horses, following mad-looking dogs which were in turn pursuing a terrified fox.

The message of the cartoon was clear and it depended on the irony of the innocent-seeming words contrasting with the fearsome picture. Separately they would have been construed differently; only together did they convey the complete message and the cartoonist's own point of view.

ACTIVITY 1

- Make as large a collection of newspaper cartoons as possible. Choose two or three with captions and analyse how the words complement the picture in each. Would the picture mean much without the words? Would the words mean something different without the picture?

Humour and caricature

Most cartoons have an element of humour in them and the use of **wit** (cleverness or wisdom which may also be funny) is common. Occasionally they can be grotesque or very serious – it depends on the event portrayed and the cartoonist's attitude to it. Some events may be so tragic that it would be in bad taste or inappropriate to use humour. Wars, famines and cruelty are examples.

The humour in cartoons is often born out of the cartoonist taking the implications of a news item or a speech by a public figure to their ultimate extreme. We recognise a germ of truth in the new, immoderate version of the original, perhaps rather banal, event, and it makes us laugh.

The cartoon form best suited to deal in these extremes is **caricature**. By contrast with a photograph, which captures a realistic likeness of the subject, a caricature is a drawing which deliberately exaggerates or distorts some of the subject's features. Through this exaggeration, the person is often made to look comical. The distortion sometimes makes the person look almost inhuman.

ACTIVITY 2

- Look at your cartoon collection. Try to identify examples of the use of caricature. Why has the person been caricatured? What effect does the caricature have? Examine the article the caricature accompanied to see what the link is.

A photograph of Prime Minister Tony Blair and a caricature of him by cartoonist Graham Waters

These exaggerated drawings rarely compliment their subject. In the caricature of Tony Blair, notice the way his teeth and smile have been emphasised and made unpleasant.

- *Which other features of Tony Blair are distorted? What effect does this have on our attitude to him?*

CATEGORIES OF CARTOONS

In his book *The Cartoon Connection* (Elm Tree, 1977), W. Hewison suggested that all cartoons were 'drawn humour' and divided them into eight categories:

- **Recognition humour** – the viewer recognises as funny or absurd some *common human behaviour*
- **Visual pun** – a pun is a play on words so a visual pun would be a *play on a visual feature*. The last frame in the *Dennis and Gnasher* strip from *The Beano* (right) plays visually on the word 'fireworks'
- **Sick humour** – commenting on the toleration by society or law-makers of *bad behaviour* e.g. one cartoon showed some bystanders watching a car mowing down half a dozen people on the pavement; one of the bystanders remarks: 'Oh, he's probably drunk; he'll only get 18 months'
- **Simply crazy behaviour or situations** – *bizarre behaviour* by a public figure e.g. a stubborn politician might be shown as a mule with his face in place of the mule's
- **Social comment** – commenting on a *current event* e.g. the ban on fox-hunting
- **Geometric** – lines and dots seem to take on a life of their own: they *represent* something else; there is no attempt on the artist's part to make the situation seem real e.g. a startled character might be represented in part as an exclamation mark
- ***Faux naif*** – a French phrase meaning 'pretending to be simple': some cartoonists who may be good artists deliberately use very *simple figures* to make their point
- **Strip cartoons** – cartoon stories drawn in a series, or strip (see section on Comics, pages 226–237)

ACTIVITY 3

- See if you can find a cartoon in your collection to fit each of Hewison's categories.

Dennis and Gnasher get involved in a play on words in *The Beano* © D C Thomson & Co Ltd. *The Beano*

MEDIA MESSAGES AND VALUES – CARTOONS

The people whom we are likely to see caricatured in newspapers and magazines are nearly always famous. Politicians are caricatured more than any other group, but entertainers and business leaders also feature frequently in cartoons.

The obvious reason for famous people being caricatured is that we recognise them; we would not recognise caricatures of ordinary people, even if they were in the news.

But there is another reason for caricaturing famous people, and politicians in particular. They are people who have power over us. They are able to make laws which affect our lives; they can raise taxes which we might not like; and they can force us to do things. Many of us do not like this even though we realise it is necessary.

So politicians come in for a lot of criticism and sometimes they become objects of fun, dislike or even hatred. One way of showing disapproval is to make them look comical or ridiculous. And we let the caricaturist or cartoonist do it for us through the use of **satire** – holding up to ridicule some human weakness or foolishness.

The cartoon frequently gives a **message** (of disapproval of a person and what he or she has done) and it probably reflects the **values** or beliefs of the cartoonist who may disapprove of the politician's behaviour or actions.

It may also, or alternatively, reflect the editorial bias of the newspaper in which it appears (see *Newspapers*, below); or the presumed preferences of the publication's **target audience** (see *The audience*, page 225, and Chapter 4 (Magazines), pages 128–129).

Let us take again the example of the cartoon on fox-hunting (see *The language of cartoons*, page 220). We may infer the cartoonist's values and opinion on the subject of fox-hunting from the way he drew the participants. Many pictures of fox-hunting do not convey anger on the part of the hunters or terror on the part of the fox.

We can also conclude that the newspaper in which the cartoon was published took an anti-fox-hunting stance. The newspaper's editor would be unlikely to have published the cartoon if he was an avid supporter of fox-hunting.

ACTIVITY 4

Look at your selection of cartoons and at an article or news report which refers to an incident or person a cartoonist has drawn.

- Discuss what the cartoonist has tried to do and why. What is his or her message to the reader?
- How has the use of satire put that message across?
- What values are inherent in the choice of subject for the cartoon?

MEDIA PRODUCERS AND AUDIENCES – CARTOONS

NEWSPAPERS

Newspapers in Britain (and in most other countries, too) are said to have political **affiliations**, that is, they take the side of one of the political parties, Labour, Conservative or Liberal Democrat. (There is also a Communist newspaper, the *Morning Star*, not to be confused with the *Daily Star*.)

The newspaper reflects the values of the political party it supports. Sometimes a newspaper may change its political preferences (see Chapter 3 (Newspapers), page 103).

Some newspapers, e.g. *The Guardian*, claim to be independent of any political party; some, like *The Daily Telegraph*, support the Conservatives; some, like

The Mirror, support Labour. This does not mean, of course, that they never criticise the party they are most sympathetic towards.

All national newspapers employ one or more cartoonists who draw a daily single-frame cartoon, nearly always on a political or social theme. Like most other people, cartoonists sympathise with a particular political party and each editor will employ a cartoonist who suits the political sympathies of the newspaper.

It is important to be aware of the difference between **broadsheet** and **tabloid** newspapers (see Chapter 3 (Newspapers), page 87) with regard to cartoons. All newspapers contain cartoons, but the broadsheets use only one or two a day and they will usually be of a political or social nature, that is, they will have a more 'serious' subject or message.

The tabloids, on the other hand, are likely to print a number of single-frame cartoons. One may be political, some may be simply for amusement and most tabloids also have a few strip cartoons for entertainment. Some even have a strip cartoon which is of particular appeal to young children, such as *Rupert the Bear* in the *Daily Express*.

Cartoonist Peter Brookes of *The Times* shows Tony Blair having nightmares about slaughtered sheep during the foot and mouth crisis (*The Times*, 15 March 2001)

ACTIVITY 5

- From your collection of cartoons, try to analyse the message of each cartoon. Does this message accord with the political sympathies of its newspaper? (Consult your teacher if you are not sure which party the newspaper supports.)
- Compare the cartoon content of a tabloid and a broadsheet newspaper. How many cartoons in each are political and how many appear to have no message or are purely for entertainment? Are strip cartoons mainly for entertainment or do they contain a message?

The cartoonist

The political cartoons which have been discussed above are nearly always a single **frame** or picture, although occasionally, if the subject demands it, two or three frames or drawings may be used as a single cartoon. The subject is almost always of a topical nature.

This means the work of a cartoonist is rather different from the work of people who create comic strips or animated cartoons – although all of them have to be competent artists. The most notable newspaper cartoonists include Peter Brookes, Gerald Scarfe, David Low and Posy Simmonds.

Cartoonists who work for a newspaper or magazine tend to work alone. They must have artistic skills, and the skill to caricature people, and be able to produce drawings quickly. They must be able to think quickly of ideas for their cartoons and have a good knowledge of what is going on in the world and in politics. The cartoonist will usually start drawing soon after the event happens.

Some cartoonists discuss their ideas with the editor of the newspaper the day before the cartoon will appear. Sometimes editors may say they want a cartoon on a particular subject. The editor's view may be shaped by what is known about the newspaper's target audience and the values that audience expects its newspaper to uphold or challenge.

Finally, however, it is down to the cartoonist to produce a witty drawing with or without a caption. The key thing is to make readers think about the issue.

THE AUDIENCE

We can easily find out how many people read a particular newspaper or magazine from published circulation figures (see Chapter 3 (Newspapers) page 101, and Chapter 4 (Magazines) page 123). For many years *The Sun* has been the most popular daily newspaper in Britain and the *News of the World* has been the most popular Sunday paper.

It is not as easy to find out how many people read different sections of a newspaper. Some readers may turn straight to the sports pages; some may never give them a glance.

We do not know, therefore, exactly how many people look at a newspaper cartoon; but it seems safe to conclude that most people probably do, if only because

- it stands out
- it is simply and quickly viewed / read compared with an article

The popularity of cartoons with the public is shown by the fact that no newspaper is without them. Editors clearly conclude that most readers want a cartoon. The fact that newspapers often publish annual compilations of their cartoons also demonstrates that there is a demand or a market for them.

Most readers choose a newspaper which is in tune with their own values or is at least not dead set against them. But what will a loyal readership make of a cartoon which runs counter to their beliefs?

Take once again the example of the fox-hunting cartoon. It is unlikely that the readers of the newspaper in which it was published would *all* be against fox-hunting. Those who were against it would probably be pleased and admire the cartoonist's ingenuity and artistry; a few people would perhaps be made to think; some people would be enraged.

A newspaper editor must accept that he or she cannot please all readers on every issue. Some readers will accept that the newspaper may occasionally express values they do not share; some few may decide to change their newspaper. Their reaction will probably depend on how controversial the cartoon is and how strong their loyalty is to the newspaper concerned.

ACTIVITY 6

- Do a survey of some of your adult acquaintances to find out about their responses to cartoons. Ask questions such as:
  - Do you look at cartoons in a newspaper?
  - Do you find them amusing? clever? a good comment on the news? annoying?
  - Do you read comic strips in newspapers?

SUMMARY – CARTOONS

- Cartoons may be just humorous drawings, but most cartoons in newspapers have a political content.
- The cartoonist interprets visually the news or report, commenting on it in a witty way and reflecting the editorial bias of the publication.
- A good cartoon will make readers think about the issue.

THE HISTORY OF COMICS

Most countries have a comics industry, but we will look at the history of comics in Britain, and briefly examine some features of American comics to note some national differences.

BRITISH COMICS

Penny Dreadfuls

While we often assume that comics are for children, this was not so at the beginning.

From the middle of the nineteenth century publications called **Penny Dreadfuls** appeared. They cost one penny and the stories – for adults – dealt with murders, riots and horror, often based on true crimes. They were not set in strip form. Critics deplored the *Penny Dreadfuls*, regarding them as exerting a bad influence.

Comics, with their better and more numerous drawings, became more popular than the *Penny Dreadfuls*, which had disappeared by the beginning of the twentieth century.

The first comics

What is generally regarded as the first **comic strip** or paper appeared in Britain in 1884 and was called *Ally Sloper's Half Holiday*. This strip also cost one penny and was also designed for adults. Ally was a working-class fellow who got up to various forms of mischief and often suffered for it.

The pictures of Ally were carefully drawn and quite elaborate and included captions. In the early comics speech balloons were not much used even though they had been used earlier by the artist William Hogarth (see page 219).

Ally's adventures appeared in a number of publications until 1929.

Comics for children

The first comics for both adults and children were *Comic Cuts* and *Illustrated Chips*. They were introduced in 1890 by the publisher Alfred Harmsworth. Harmsworth published magazines and newspapers and later, as Lord Northcliffe, became

The first comic, *Ally Sloper's Half Holiday, appeared in 1884*

one of the significant British press barons (see Chapter 3 (Newspapers) page 83).

Harmsworth did not like and therefore did not publish *Penny Dreadfuls*. He wanted to drive them out of business. He charged a halfpenny for his new comic papers and they became instantly popular. *Comic Cuts* gained a circulation of 300,000 in a matter of weeks. Both comics followed the style of the *Ally Sloper* publication. They consisted of strip stories and single cartoons and jokes. The stories had captions, not speech balloons.

These early comics did not use colour printing although some were printed on tinted paper.

The most famous comic characters in *Illustrated Chips* were Weary Willie and Tired Tim, two tramps. They appeared in the comic for 57 years until it closed down in 1953.

Weary Willie and Tired Tim were created by an artist called Tom Browne and although he died in 1910 other artists continued to draw his characters. Browne's tramps were so popular that he created other tramps for other publications.

- *What do you think would be the appeal of a pair of tramps? Could it have anything to do with the later popularity of anti-heroes?*

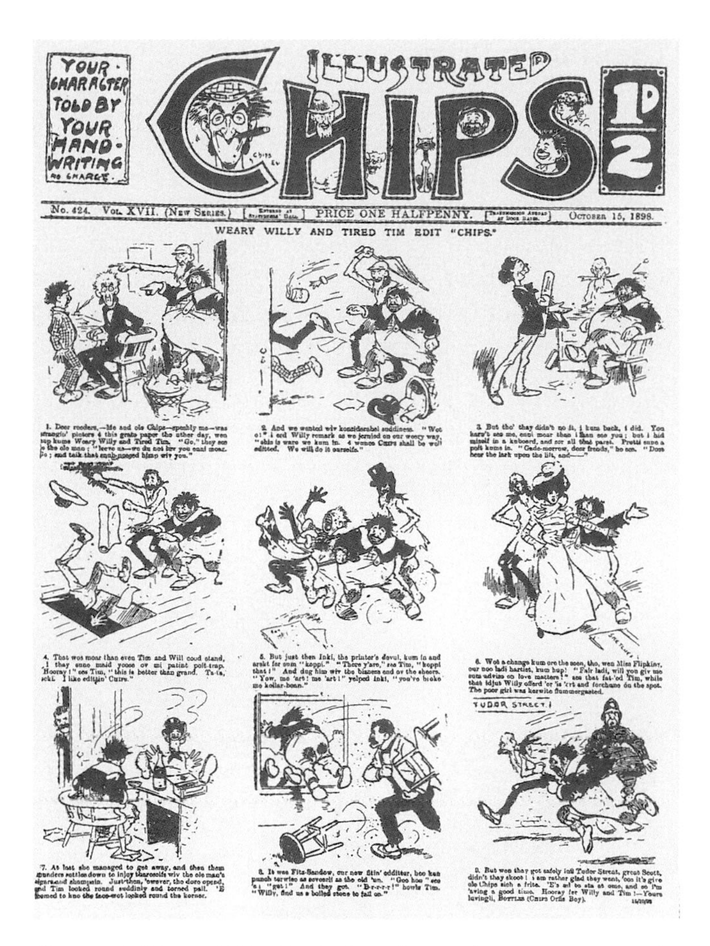

Illustrated Chips, published in the late nineteenth century, was one of the first comics for children

Expansion of comics

The success of *Illustrated Chips* and *Comic Cuts* led other publishers to create comics of a similar nature and during the twentieth century hundreds of different titles came and went.

We will examine here only a few of them, particularly those which exemplify significant developments in the comics industry.

Rainbow

Rainbow, first published in 1914, was the first comic especially for young children. Many of the characters in the stories were animals, and Tiger Tim, who appeared regularly, became probably the most popular comic strip character during the first half of the twentieth century. *Rainbow* had a colour printed cover, but used black and white printing inside.

Film Fun - 'The paper with all the stars'

Films and comics

The popularity of the growing film industry in the early part of the twentieth century led to the publication in Britain of *Film Fun* in 1920. This was a well-drawn comic which featured the fictional adventures of popular, real film comedians, such as Laurel and Hardy. An even more famous comic actor, Charlie Chaplin, featured in comic strip form in another publication.

- *Why would famous actors allow their likenesses to appear in comics?*

The D.C. Thomson Company

A Scottish firm, located in Dundee in the late 1930s, began a comic tradition which has lasted until the present day.

In 1937 D.C. Thomson introduced *The Dandy* and in the following year *The Beano*. These two comics still exist but a third, launched at around the same time and called *Magic*, was published for only a few years.

The success of *The Dandy* and *The Beano* depended on the aggressiveness, liveliness and colour of the stories and on the absurdity of the characters. Children did not seem to care that they were not realistic.

Desperate Dan, the lead character in *The Dandy*, was from a fictional Wild West. He was immensely strong, rather clumsy, and had a huge appetite for cow pies – horns and all!

Lord Snooty, who appeared in *The Beano*, was a nuisance to policemen, teachers and officials of every kind. He often triumphed over authority, but not always – occasionally he would get a 'whacking'!

Comics like *Hotspur*, *Wizard* and *Rover*, as well as containing comic strips, mainly consisted of written stories and the amount of reading in a single issue was almost that of an average-sized novel. Later, children seemed to prefer stories with pictures.

D.C. Thomson's comics were the first to use speech balloons for all the dialogue. Only brief captions were added to the frame to give a necessary piece of information like 'Later...' or 'Next day'.

Amalgamated Press

D.C. Thomson's comics were very successful and Amalgamated Press in London changed its style of comics to compete. *Radio Fun* used characters from radio comedy as *Film Fun* had used film stars. Amalgamated Press also published the successful *Knockout*, which was as lively as its name implied.

The Second World War

The Second World War (1939–45) caused a temporary decline in comics sales. A shortage of paper reduced the size and number of comics that could be published. Swapping comics became a widespread practice among children. If you were short of money you could sell your comic to a second-hand shop, which in turn would sell it on again. A single comic might go round a dozen times before it was thrown away.

Television

Just as film and radio had influenced comics, so did television, which resumed in 1946 after the War and became popular in the 1950s. *TV Fun* came out then. It did not last long but TV-based comics and magazines for children continue to this day e.g. *Barney*, *Teletubbies*. Titles change frequently according to which TV characters are popular. Another influence of television, of course, was to make comics generally less popular. Many children found television a better source of entertainment.

The Hulton Press

In the 1950s, another revolution in comics occurred. The Hulton Press, best known for an illustrated news magazine called *Picture Post*, moved into the comics business. Hulton, together with the first editor, Marcus Morris, produced *Eagle* in 1950. *Eagle* was very successful for 19 years. Its main character was Dan Dare, Pilot of the Future, and he was for a long time as famous as Desperate Dan and Lord Snooty.

Eagle was by the standards of the time much better designed, drawn and coloured; the paper was of a higher quality, glossy instead of just **newsprint**.

> **newsprint** – low-grade paper made from wood pulp, used for printing newspapers

Eagle's Dan Dare caused a revolution in the popularity of comics

All the Hulton comics managed to combine an educational and moral flavour, appealing and exciting stories and a dash of humour. The moral tone was probably the influence of the executive editor who was a priest and may have wished to depict his leading characters as suitable role models. *Eagle* carried a Bible story in almost every issue.

None of the Hulton comics exists today. They found it hard to compete with television.

COMICS IN AMERICA

The first American comic strip appeared in *The San Francisco Examiner* in 1892. It proved popular and other newspapers across the country followed suit. All US newspapers except for two serious broadsheets carry comic strips today.

It was in America also that the **comic book** began and became popular. This was an A4 size soft-bound book of around 64 pages containing usually three or four long stories in strip form. They were similar to the modern **graphic novels** (see *Media languages and categories*, page 231). Comic books used elaborate art work but were often printed on very cheap paper.

Good art work first appeared in 1929 when the *Tarzan* novels of Edgar Rice Burroughs were redone in strip form for newspaper comic supplements.

In 1938 Superman appeared in a story in the first *Action Comics*, which contained other stories as well, although Superman was featured on the cover.

When circulation figures soared to 1.4 million per issue the publishers did a survey to find out why. They discovered the most popular element was the *Superman* strip written by Jerry Siegel and drawn by Joe Shuster.

Batman followed in 1939 and many other superhuman heroes and heroines were created to cash in on the popularity of these figures: *Captain Marvel* (1940), *Captain America* (1941), *Wonder Woman* (1941), *The Incredible Hulk* (1962), *Tank Girl* (1989).

Superman on the cover of the first *Action Comics* in June 1938

ACTIVITY

- Discuss the various superheroes and try to explain why they have become so popular as fictional characters.
- Do you think there is any significance in the date of Superman's arrival on the comics scene?

The **syndication** of comic strips also began in America. Syndication means that a strip (or an article or news item) which has been created for one publication is sold to another in a different region or country.

After the Second World War in America, detective comics were in fashion, with Dick Tracy, who had first appeared in 1931, becoming the favourite hero. But they declined in popularity in the early 1950s.

KEY DATES – COMICS

- **1850s** – *Penny Dreadfuls* appear – sensational, often crime, stories with illustrations
- **1884** – *Ally Sloper's Half Holiday* appears; usually regarded as the first comic, it is designed for adults and will remain popular until 1929
- **1890** – *Comic Cuts* and *Illustrated Chips* introduced by publisher Alfred Harmsworth; they cost a halfpenny. *Comic Cuts* achieves a circulation of 300,000 within a few weeks
- **1892** – The first American comic is published as a supplement to the newspaper *The San Francisco Examiner*
- **1896** – Weary Willie and Tired Tim begin their careers as popular comic characters, lasting in various publications until 1953
- **1914** – *Rainbow* comic is launched; it makes more use of colour than previous comics
- **1920** – *Film Fun*, a comic with stories centred on real film stars, appears
- **1929** – The first *Tarzan* comic is published in America; it heralds higher artistic standards
- **1937** – Scottish publishing firm D.C. Thomson publishes *The Dandy*
- **1938** – *The Beano* appears, also published by D.C. Thomson

  Superman comic strips published in America
- **1950** – *Eagle* comic published, ushering in a higher quality of paper, colour and art work
- **1950s** – Horror comics are imported from USA and then banned in Britain
- **1954** – *TV Fun* published

  American publishers set up Comics Code
- **1980s** – Graphic novels, long cartoon stories mainly for adults, published

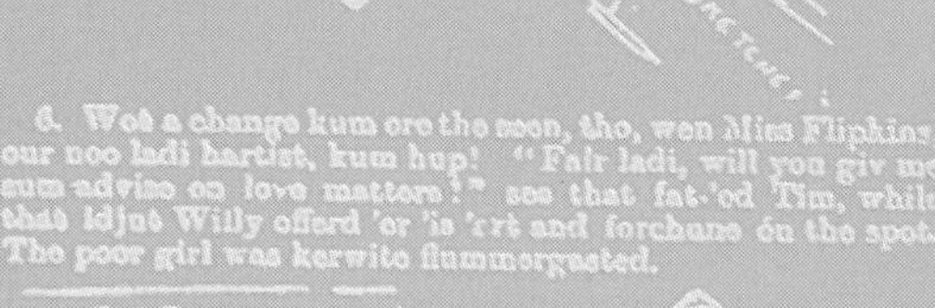

MEDIA LANGUAGES AND CATEGORIES – COMICS

Jarvis

A gag strip from the *Funday Times*, September 2001

Whereas cartoons are nearly always a single drawing which makes a point, comic strips are a series of pictures which tell a **narrative** or story. These pictures are called **frames** or **panels**. The number of frames can vary enormously in a single comic strip. In newspapers the strip is often just three or four frames long e.g. a **gag strip**, a strip ending in a single joke line.

In **comic papers** for children such as *The Beano* and *The Dandy* the number of frames may be between 10 and 30, although some stories are serials.

Comic books are almost like a novel in comic strip form and may be hundreds of frames, even hundreds of pages, long. Examples are *Where the Wind Blows* (1982) by Raymond Briggs and *The Dark Knight Returns* (1986) by Frank Miller, about Batman.

Graphic novels, mainly for adults, were published frequently in the 1980s but, although some are still being published, they have never become very popular in Britain. The art work is of a very high standard and scenes are depicted from a wide range of angles and distances, mirroring cinema film techniques.

Another comic for adults is *Viz*, which, remarkably, in the mid-1990s became the biggest-selling magazine in Britain. Its vulgarity and lack of political correctness for a time had great appeal. After 20 years on sale, it is still one of the biggest-selling comics in Britain.

GENRES OF COMICS

The stories in comic strips are as wide-ranging as those in novels. **Humour** and **fantasy** are probably the most popular **genres**, but **detective**, **romance**, **science fiction** and **adventure** all have their followers.

Examples are (dates indicate first publication):

- **Fantasy / science fiction** – the many *Superman* (1938) and *Batman* (1939) stories; *Flash Gordon* (1934); *Tank Girl* (1989)
- **Detective** – *Dick Tracy* (1931)
- **Romance** – *Young Love* (1951); *RanXerox* (1987)
- **Adventure** – *The Savage Sword of Conan the Barbarian* (1977)

Very often the genres will be mixed, so some stories may be **romantic adventures** or **sci-fi detective**. *Conan the Barbarian* is a mixture of **adventure** and **fantasy**.

LANGUAGE OF COMIC STRIPS

Any comic strip consists of three elements: the story, the pictures and the speech or dialogue.

Usually at least three people work on creating a comic strip: a **scriptwriter**, an **artist** and a **letterer**.

Occasionally an artist may also write the story and do the lettering, but this is rare.

If we examine some frames, we can see the 'language' and the related techniques used. A scriptwriter creates the story and breaks it down into tiny scenes to provide each picture or frame. He or she also provides a brief description of the scene together with the dialogue.

Here is an example of a script for a single frame:

```
FRAME 3

PICTURE 3:     Ray and Adela are
               facing each other and
               speaking.
               They look happy.
               Medium close-up.
               School in background.

CAPTION:       Later - at break-time

RAY:           I'll see you tonight
               at 7 o'clock. On the
               Piazza.

ADELA:         Okay, I'll be there.

ADELA
(thinks):      If he thinks I'll
               turn up he's got
               another think coming.
```

What the picture will look like here is fairly obvious. There would be three balloons: one for Ray's words, one for Adela's words, and one for Adela's thought. There is also a caption, to be printed at the top of the frame.

Notice that the description of the picture is very brief. The artist has considerable freedom to interpret the scene and the look of the strip. He will already have given faces and general appearance to all of the characters.

Comic artists often use techniques reminiscent of films. There are close-ups, distant shots, and sometimes the scene is shown from the point of view of one of the characters. Here the writer has specified medium close-up, which means both characters' heads and shoulders will be in the frame.

At the beginning of the script, the writer will have described the characters briefly, giving details which must be kept to if they are important to the story e.g. their ages, whether a person is blonde or brunette, if they have any special characteristics.

The following frames from a *Beryl the Peril* comic strip show some common elements and techniques:

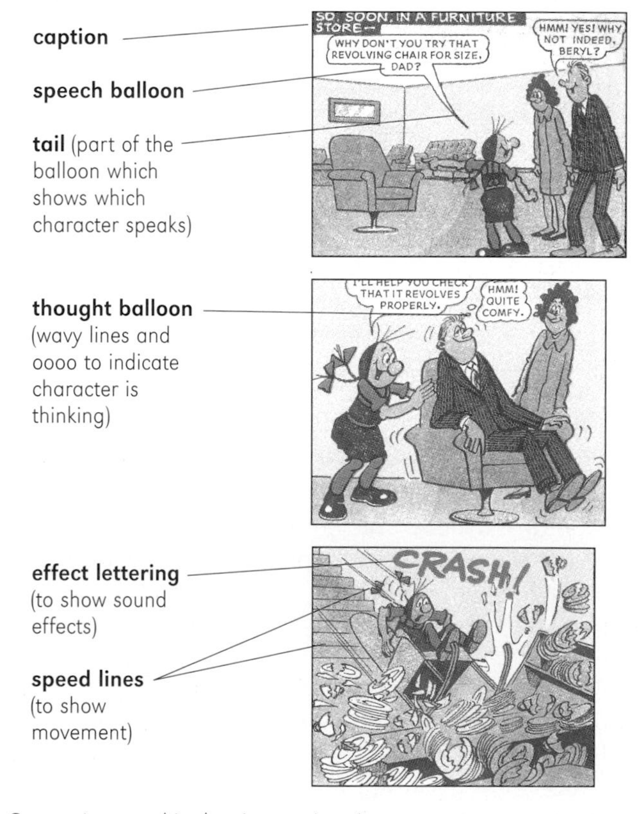

Conventions used in drawing comic strips

Some frames from a photo-story

All three contributors to a strip are important. The story must be good, the art work must be attractive and the lettering clear but not dominating the picture. **Effects** are important and there are many strange 'noises' and 'words' which comic readers will be familiar with. Those shown opposite indicate different states of action, pain, snoozing, and so on.

Large drops of perspiration dripping from someone's face indicate extreme worry. Speed lines (see Frame 3 in the *Beryl the Peril* strip opposite) are very important because comic stories often involve a lot of action and this has to be conveyed in still pictures.

Some modern comics, especially those aimed at girls, now have what are called **photo-stories** instead of drawn comic strips. The principles are just the same but instead of an artist drawing pictures, a photographer hires young actors, finds a suitable location, then photographs the actors in a real setting.

ACTIVITY 8

- Try to create a comic strip. See who in the group can think of a story and write a script in the way shown and who can draw scenes for the frames. You will also need a letterer. Or you could create a photo-story if you have access to a camera. (You should read *Production processes* on page 246 before you do this Activity.)
- Discuss why the photo-story has superseded the drawn strip in many comics.

MEDIA MESSAGES AND VALUES – COMICS

We saw earlier that newspaper cartoons usually have a moral, social or political message and attract attention to this message by being funny, witty or satirical.

Comic strips, on the other hand, are primarily for entertainment. Children and adults who read comics want exciting, funny, escapist stories. They want light relief, not heavy moralising.

This does not mean, however, that comic strips do not carry a message or uphold certain values while they entertain. As British comics are mainly for children, publishers would not risk parents' disapproval, or even a ban, by printing stories promoting immorality.

These messages and values are always secondary to the entertainment value of the story and some comic strips appear to have no message at all. Where one does exist, it is as a **sub-text**, that is, it is hidden below the surface of the story.

The *Eagle* comic, as we saw, featured Bible stories which encouraged heroism and caring for others, but were also exciting. Oddly enough, even the **horror comics**, banned in Britain for their gory graphics, were moral in the sense that the 'baddies' always came to a sticky end.

Comics have had a long tradition of anti-authority characters, like Lord Snooty, Desperate Dan, Dennis the Menace and Beryl the Peril. But comics are not really encouraging anti-authority attitudes in their readers. These characters frequently help the less fortunate and the bullied, and when their mischief gets out of hand, they get punished – justice is done!

Another comic tradition uses fictitious sports heroes and heroines as the main characters in strips. Typical of the genre are stories about footballer Roy of the Rovers and athlete Wilson, or school stories featuring children achieving their sporting ambitions. Almost always these stories endorse the importance of competition and team spirit – values much admired in contemporary society.

CULT FIGURES

One of the reasons for the vogue in superheroes is that they provide **escapism** for readers who may imagine themselves in the role of the all-powerful hero. But beneath the entertainment, these **cult figures** – like Superman, Batman, Captain America and even James Bond – are also directing two clear messages at their public:

- If you have special gifts or powers, you should use them for the good of society and to help the less fortunate.
- A powerful government or leader is necessary to create a just society.

Indeed, comic stories have often promoted values judged to be especially necessary at a particular point in history. The adventures of Jane, the attractive and sexy heroine of a comic strip in *The Daily Mirror*, were said to have increased the morale of soldiers during the Second World War and so were deemed to be performing a public service!

Jane kept the troops' spirits high during the Second World War

GENDER

While comics nearly always reflect values which are important in society at the time they appear, there is one area where rather unexpectedly they seem to have been ahead of their time.

Long before feminism campaigned for greater equality for women, comics were portraying female characters who were just as rebellious, naughty or heroic as boys.

Keyhole Kate, a very mischievous girl, was followed later by Beryl the Peril. Girls at boarding schools had adventures, solved crimes and saved the school! The fantasy figure, Wonder Woman, put the world to rights and achieved justice for all in the same way as Superman. Girls in comics certainly did not do what they were told and were more at home with catapults than needlework.

ACTIVITY 9

- Discuss why anti-authority characters in comics would be particularly popular with children.
- Examine copies of *The Beano* and *The Dandy*. Study the major characters and try to explain their appeal.
- *The Beano* dropped the character of Lord Snooty in the early 1990s. Why do you think that was? (He was soon revived in another comic!)

ORDINARY PEOPLE

We have referred to superheroes and to larger-than-life characters like Desperate Dan and Dennis the Menace but, in fact, some very ordinary characters have become the most popular subjects in comic strips.

Charles Schulz (1922–2000) created the *Peanuts* strip, which featured a group of characters aged three to five and Snoopy the dog, in 1950 and he continued drawing it until his death. The main character was Charlie Brown who was an everyman figure, an ordinary child, nervous, unassuming, sensitive, lonely sometimes, and occasionally the victim of bullying and jokes.

Schulz confessed that he based the characters on facets of his own personality and life and he clearly gained sympathy from readers. *Peanuts* has appeared in over 1,000 newspapers and magazines around the world. Its popularity seems to derive from people recognising parts of themselves in one or other of the characters. They represent our own values and problems.

Peanuts is unusual in its world-wide appeal. Many comic characters (particularly English ones) never get beyond their own shores. *Tintin*, by the Belgian artist Hergé, is another comic strip which has gained international popularity, and Tintin is also a fairly ordinary boy. He has been described as a boy scout type, but he does get up to some remarkable adventures.

Asterix, written by René Goscinny (1926–1977) and drawn by Albert Uderzo, is a French comic strip character who has gained international recognition. The setting is Gaul (France) in Roman times but some of the things that happen have a modern ring.

Asterix is a tiny man who frequently gets the better of the enemy (the Romans). He represents the ordinary or little man overcoming overwhelming odds. New *Asterix* adventures have been written by other people since Goscinny's death.

It is quite common for strips to be drawn and written by different people at different times. It is, however, unlikely that Charles Schulz can be replaced.

MEDIA PRODUCERS AND AUDIENCES – COMICS

We have already seen how even the early comics were produced in a competitive commercial environment. Publishers used an increasingly popular medium – the comic – to undercut each other's prices (Harmsworth's *Comic Cuts* was 50 per cent cheaper than the *Penny Dreadfuls* and *Ally Sloper's Half Holiday*) in a bid to win the circulation battle.

Since it appealed to children as well as adults, *Comic Cuts* had a circulation of 300,000 within a few weeks of its launch in 1890.

In the twentieth century hundreds of comics came and went, prey to changing fashions and the greater popularity of other media.

Most of the British titles mentioned in this chapter have disappeared and comics sales in the UK have declined to less than half what they were in their heyday. Television is one cause of the decline, computer games another. In general, comics cannot compete with the effects created by computers and in action films.

Even so, it is unlikely that comics will disappear completely and comic strips in tabloid newspapers are regarded as important by their editors. Broadsheet newspapers such as *The Times*, *The Daily Telegraph*, *The Sunday Times* and some others now include a comic supplement which is aimed at children, the newspaper purchasers of tomorrow.

Research shows that strips are the first things that many readers look at in the paper. This is probably because:

- they are quick and easy to read
- some of them are humorous
- most of them are in serial form and readers want to know what happens next

ACTIVITY 10

Find out what comics are available now in Britain and which age groups they are aimed at.

Americans are probably more enthusiastic about comics – the 'funnies' as they call them – than the British. In the USA it has been estimated that 100 million people read comics every day (the US population is about 260 million). Probably as many adults as children read comics and this is partly because comics in the USA started as supplements to newspapers – many were written for adults as well as children.

This is still the situation today. In general, comics continue to be popular in the USA and the decline in their sales is not so marked as it is in Britain.

American comic strips are syndicated to other countries, including Britain. *Peanuts* is one example. Syndication has advantages for the writers and artists and for the newspapers the strips first appeared in, because they will all be paid again for the reappearance.

ACTIVITY 11

Examine the comic strips in some British tabloid newspapers (or the comic supplements to the broadsheets). Which are American in origin and why do you think the British newspaper has bought them? (You may need to look carefully for clues to the origin.)

REGULATION

At various stages in their 150-year history the sometimes lurid content of comics, often masked by the innocent-looking format of the medium, has been regarded as likely to exercise a bad influence on readers.

In the 1850s *Penny Dreadfuls*, the forerunners of comics, were roundly condemned for their descriptions of grisly events.

A century later horror comics again came under scrutiny from the authorities and were actually banned in Britain. The reason for the concern was not just that they might frighten children, but that children might imitate the violence portrayed in them.

In the USA they were also frowned upon and comics publishers were eventually driven to create a **Comics Code** in 1954 which set out rules the publishers agreed to abide by to make sure their comics were decent. A regulator was appointed to see that the rules were kept.

ACTIVITY 12

- Find out what evidence there is to suggest that comics, or any aspects of the media, such as films and computer games, affect people's behaviour.
- If you had to construct a Comics Code (or a Computer Games Code) today, what rules would you put in it for the publishers and why?

SUMMARY – COMICS

- Comics are a series of pictures arranged in a strip which tell a story.
- Comics or comic papers are usually aimed at children and include strips of between 10 and 30 frames.
- Comic books or graphic novels are like novels in comic strip form – for adults or children.
- Genres of comics include fantasy, detective stories, romance, science fiction and adventure.
- Comics sales have been declining in Britain since the advent of television, but in the USA comics are still very popular.

ANIMATION

THE BASIC PRINCIPLES

The figures or characters in both ordinary and animated films seem to move like people in real life, even though we know they are made up of separate still pictures. They seem alive or to move naturally – they are **animated** – because *the human eye is not perfect.*

When we look at something, the image is retained on the eye for a fraction of a second. If another image quickly takes the place of the first image, our vision 'merges' one with the next. Thus, still pictures in sequence seem continuous and the figures in them appear to move.

This phenomenon is called **persistence of vision**. It was discovered by an Arab astronomer called Al Hazan in AD 1020. He saw someone spinning a flaming torch in a circular movement and noticed that it seemed to be a continuous circle of flame.

- *Try this in the dark with an electric torch.*

If human beings did not possess persistence of vision, movies would be impossible.

Flip books

Another experiment demonstrates persistence of vision. You may have seen a **flip book**, a little book containing cartoon characters, one per page, each picture slightly changed from the one before. When you flip though it the figure in the pictures appears to move.

ACTIVITY 13

You can easily make a flip book.

Take a large piece of thin white card (or a number of postcards) and cut out 30 pieces roughly 5 cm by 3 cm. On the right-hand side of each piece draw a matchstick figure – standing upright in the first picture for page 1 and gradually page by page going through the stages of walking a few steps or bending down by the 30th picture. Hold the 30 cards at the left in your left hand and flip through them fairly quickly. You will not see separate pictures – it is as if the stick figure is moving. Practise a little to get the speed right. When you do, you will have demonstrated persistence of vision and the basic animation of still pictures.

Try other simple drawing sequences if you find stick figures too difficult (see below).

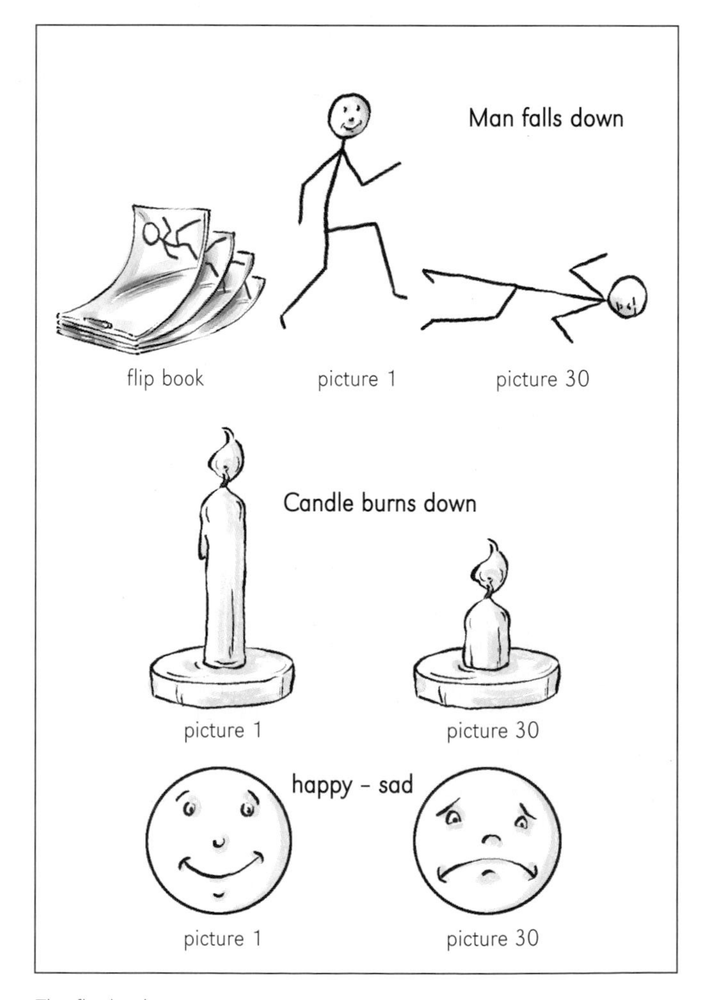

The flip book

The thaumotrope

Persistence of vision can also be demonstrated by making a **thaumotrope**. This was a simple device invented by J.A. Paris in 1826, 70 years before the invention of cinema, but it contained the main principle of film-making.

ACTIVITY 14

Cut out a disc of fairly thick white card about 10 cm in diameter. On one side draw the outline of a bird cage and on the other a bird on a perch, slightly smaller than the cage. (It could be a rectangular cage with any animal on the other side.) The two sides of the card should be like the ones shown below, one apparently upside down.

Make small holes at each side of the disc as shown and thread through a loop of string at each side. Holding the ends of the two loops of string, loosely whirl the disc round. When you pull the two strings taut, the disc will spin fast and if you look at it, the bird will appear to be in the cage. The eye cannot keep up with the quick changes.

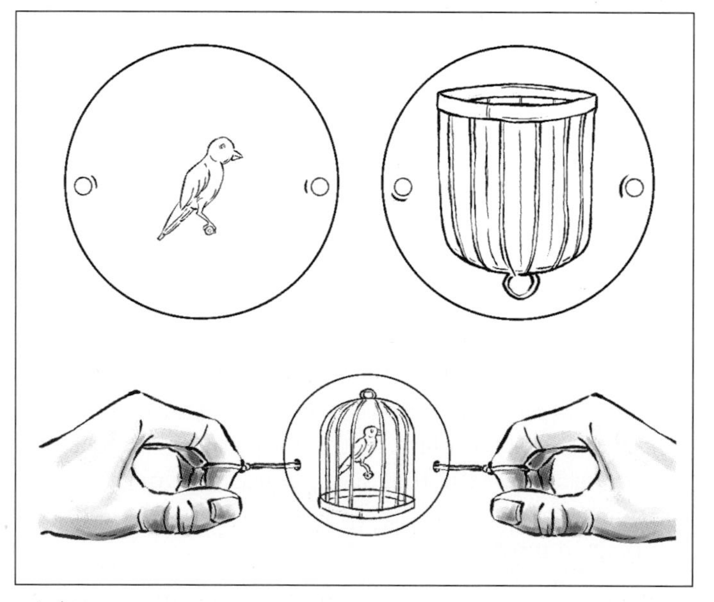

A thaumotrope

Live action and cartoons

In live action films, the actions and movements are photographed continuously for each **take** or scene at 24 frames a second. In cartoons, drawings representing stages of movement each lasting 1/24th of a second are photographed one by one. In both cases, smooth movement results.

Cartoon films are made by a process called **stop motion photography**, which simply means the movie camera shutter is opened for one painting, closed, and then opened again when the next painting in the sequence has been placed in the frame beneath the camera lens. Ordinary motion cinematography is, of course, not so laborious but is a continuous process for the length of the take or scene.

Live action film

THE HISTORY OF ANIMATION

Interestingly, the moving cartoon drawing pre-dates live action moving pictures. A Belgian, Joseph Plateau, invented the **phenakistoscope** in 1832. This consisted of a sequence of staged drawings (rather like the ones we put in our flip book) stuck on the outer rim of a circle of paper attached to a metal disc. Another metal disc was placed in front of it with a frame cut out of it about the size of one of the pictures. When the rear disc was rotated and someone looked through the cut-out frame, they saw what appeared to be a moving sequence.

An improved version of this, called a **zoetrope**, was invented by an Englishman, W.G. Horner. The principle was the same but a sequence of pictures was glued to the inside of the drum on a spindle which had slits around it just above the pictures. The eye was placed at one slit, the drum rotated, and the eye saw the progressive stages of the drawn sequence as one slit was replaced quickly by the next.

The next development came in 1877 when a Frenchman, Émile Raymond, combined a similar device he called a **praxinoscope** with a method of **projection** using light, mirrors and drawings on transparent **celluloid**. In the 1880s the device was used for public performances so it could be regarded as the forerunner of the cinema.

The invention of the cinema in 1896 clearly meant that cartoon films could be made although the essential stop-motion cinematographic method was not used until 1906, when the American J. Stuart Blankton made a cartoon film called *Humorous Phases of Funny Faces*, usually regarded as the first real cartoon film.

Between 1908 and 1918 a Frenchman, Émile Cohl, made over 100 popular cartoon films, usually just using matchstick figures doing a series of movements and tricks.

In America, cartoonist Winsor McKay made *Gertie the*

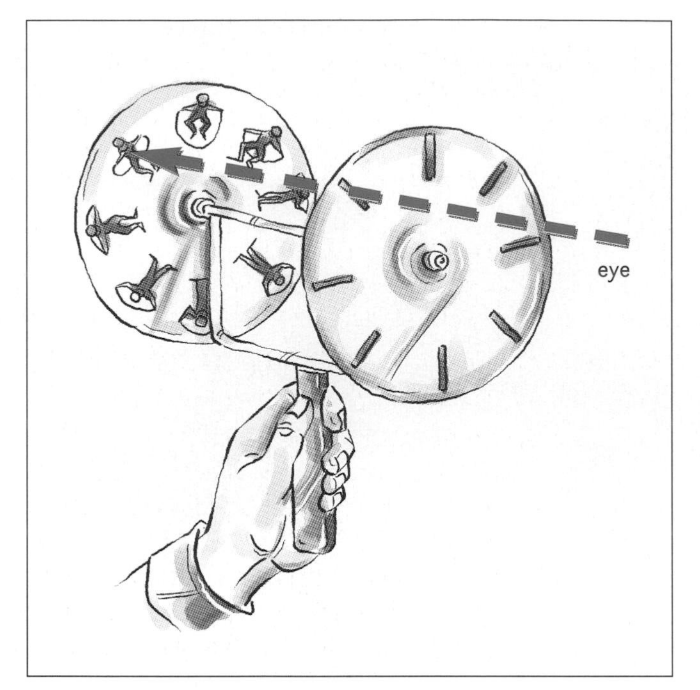

Phenakistoscope

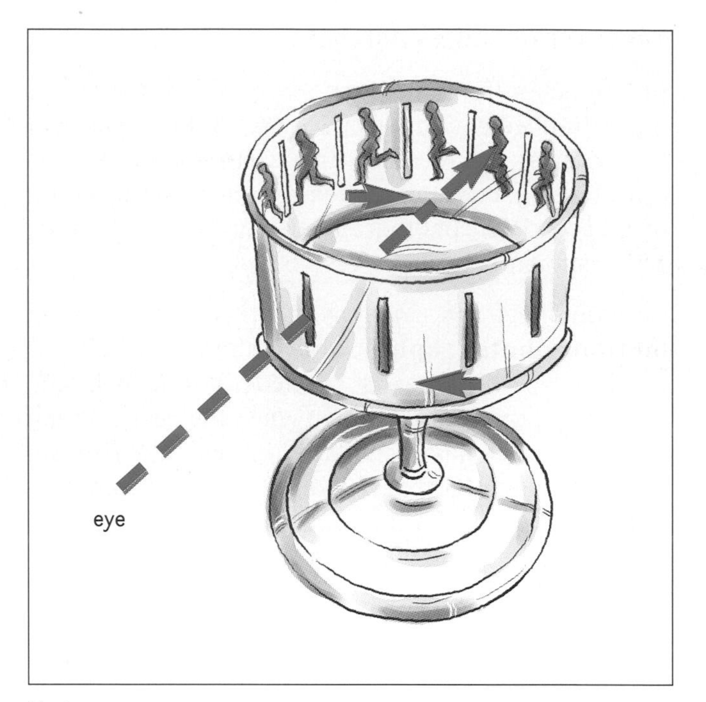

Zoetrope

Dinosaur, which proved popular in theatres in 1909, and he later made a feature-length cartoon film, *The Sinking of the Lusitania*. This was a rare cartoon on a serious theme.

DISNEY

From 1918 cartoons, although crude by today's standards, became popular and regular features in cinemas. *Krazy Kat* and *Coco the Clown* were both well known.

It was Walt Disney and his brother Roy, and Ub Iwerks (an artist friend), who began the Disney Company in 1923. They made advertising films and short cartoons but their success owed a lot to Mickey Mouse.

ACTIVITY 15

Mickey Mouse was not called Mickey in his first few cartoons. Find out what he was called and why his name was changed.

Mickey's first two screen appearances were silent, but Disney quickly used the new possibilities of sound which had come into the cinema in 1928. By the mid-1930s all his cartoons were also done in colour.

Mickey Mouse was followed by other animal characters: Donald Duck, Pluto etc.

The production of cartoons at Disney was like a factory process with hundreds of employees doing specialised tasks: background artists, animators, colourists, sound engineers, cinematographers etc.

Disney's first feature-length cartoon was *Snow White and the Seven Dwarfs* in 1937. It was immensely popular and other features soon followed: *Fantasia* (1940), *Dumbo* (1941), *Bambi* (1942). Disney continued to make cartoon and live action films until his death in 1966. The Disney Company still makes films and television programmes of many kinds and is one of the largest media companies in the world.

OTHER COMPANIES

MGM produced the popular *Tom and Jerry* features; Warner Bros made *Looney Tunes, Bugs Bunny* and others; all the major studios had cartoon departments. There were also some independent cartoon producers, and European studios sometimes made innovative cartoons.

KEY DATES – ANIMATION

- **1826** The thaumotrope is invented by J.A. Paris, using the principle of persistence of vision necessary for film animation
- **1832** Joseph Plateau invents the phenakistoscope, a forerunner of the animated film
- **1895** The film projector, which makes cinema possible, is invented independently in France, the USA and Britain
- **1896** The French Lumière brothers begin cinema as we know it
- **1906** The first proper animated cartoon film, *Humorous Phases of Funny Faces*, is made by the American, J. Stuart Blankton, and shown in cinemas
- **1909** The popular *Gertie the Dinosaur* is exhibited in cinemas and sequels follow. Its maker, Winsor McKay, later makes a serious cartoon called *The Sinking of the Lusitania*
- **1918** Cartoons become a popular and regular part of film programmes
- **1923** Walt Disney, his brother Roy and Ub Iwerks set up the Disney animated film studios
- **1928** Mickey Mouse appears in his first cartoon film called *Plane Crazy*
- **1932** Colour comes properly to cinema films; cartoon-makers exploit it
- **1937** *Snow White and the Seven Dwarfs*, Disney's first feature-length animation, appears
- **1940** Disney's *Fantasia* premieres; this film combines music and cartoon characters in a completely original way
- **1941** Disney's *Dumbo* is produced
- **1942** One of Disney's most popular films, *Bambi*, is shown
- **1964** Disney's *Mary Poppins* combines live action with cartoon animation for the first time
- **1966** Walt Disney dies
- **1988** Disney joins forces with director Steven Spielberg to produce *Who Framed Roger Rabbit?*, which combines live action and cartoon characters in a very sophisticated and believable way
- **1994** Disney's *The Lion King* is the most financially successful film of the year
- **2000** Disney shows *Fantasia 2000* in selected IMAX cinemas on the first day of the new millennium

MEDIA PRODUCERS AND AUDIENCES – ANIMATION

FILM STUDIOS

To make a 90-minute feature-length cartoon film, hundreds of **animators** (so called because their paintings appear lifelike) may work on as many as one million drawings and the complete process can take up to four years.

Is it worth it? The film studios think it is. Most children and many adults love animated films and in the history of the cinema some of them have been the most successful films.

In 1994 Disney's *Lion King* took 298.9 million dollars at the US box office. Financially, it was the most successful film of the year. In 1999 the Disney cartoon feature film *Tarzan* went straight into the film charts' top 10 in both the United States and Britain.

Snow White and the Seven Dwarfs (1937), *Fantasia* (1940), *Pinocchio* (1940) and *Bambi* (1942), all made by the Walt Disney studio, are regarded as classics and characters like Mickey Mouse, Donald Duck, Pluto and Goofy are known to most children throughout the world even though some of them were created over 60 years ago.

ACTIVITY 16

- Find out about the working methods in the Disney studios during Walt Disney's lifetime. Why did Disney's attitude to his staff lead to the opening of the UPI animation studio?
- Find out about the various activities of the Walt Disney Company now.
- One of Walt Disney's most famous sayings was: 'All the world owes me a living.' Discuss what you think he meant by this.

One of the reasons the film studios continue to invest so heavily in animated cartoons is the revenue generated by **merchandising**, sales of products linked to the film's characters or theme.

Spin-offs (toys, books, clothes etc linked to a film) are now big business for film-makers. As much money can be made from the merchandise as from the film itself in some cases.

Merchandising is not confined to animated films. You will probably have seen some of the hundreds of products related to the *Star Wars* or *Batman* films.

ACTIVITY 17

Find out what spin-offs have arisen from recent Disney and other cartoon films e.g. *Dinosaurs*.

- *Do you think these days animated feature films could be regarded as just a long advertisement for other products marketed by film-makers?*
- *What about the Disney theme parks? Are they 'selling' anything beyond a fun day out?*

TELEVISION

Live action and animated films made for the cinema have been a major part of television programming since its early days. As well as cartoons appearing occasionally on most entertainment channels (and in advertisements), they also have dedicated channels such as Cartoon Network on cable and satellite TV.

In order to satisfy the demand, cartoons have also been made especially for television. These are often of a lower quality technically than cartoons made for the cinema because they must be made more quickly and cheaply.

Nevertheless, some television cartoon films have been as popular as, if not more popular than, their cinema cousins.

AUDIENCES AND POPULARITY

As Chapter 1 (Film) pointed out, film-making is an industry; that is, the companies which make films are in it for profit. They make their profit by providing a product which entertains the public.

Animated films are expensive to make, but from the early days of cinema they have proved popular at the box office; they are therefore profitable.

If we examine the most popular films for each decade since 1930, we find that animated films feature as often as or more often than any other film genre. The table (right) shows the animated films which were in the Top 10 for each of the past seven decades (the figure in square brackets shows the position of the film in the Top 10).

These films were popular at the cinema but this, of course, was not the limit of their popularity or audience. They have been re-shown subsequently, most are available on video, and some have been shown on television. Many will be seen yet again by future generations.

You will notice that most of the films listed are suitable for quite young children. There are fewer children than adults in the whole population so one might expect children's films to feature less strongly in the Top 10 lists.

But film producers know that as well as those adults who go to animated films simply because they like them, a sizeable portion of the audience will consist of parents or relatives who regularly take children to the cinema.

1930s	*Snow White and the Seven Dwarfs* (1937) [1]
1940s	*Bambi* (1942) [1] *Pinocchio* (1940) [2] *Fantasia* (1940) [3] *Cinderella* (1949) [4]
1950s	*Lady and the Tramp* (1951) [1] *Peter Pan* (1953) [2] *Sleeping Beauty* (1959) [5]
1960s	*101 Dalmatians* (1961) [1] *The Jungle Book* (1967) [2]
1970s	No animated films made it into the Top 10. Films such as *Star Wars* (1977), *Close Encounters of the Third Kind* (1977) and *Jaws* (1975) dominated the lists
1980s	*Who Framed Roger Rabbit?* (1988) [8]
1990s	*The Lion King* (1994) [5]
2000	In just one single year, three animated films got into the Top 10: *Toy Story 2* [1], *Chicken Run* [3] and *Stuart Little* [5], which was partly live action.

MEDIA MESSAGES AND VALUES – ANIMATION

SATIRE OF SOCIETY

In the same way that newspaper cartoons and caricatures may invite readers to subject a figure in public life to closer scrutiny, to look in a different, more critical way at his or her values and what he or she stands for, so cartoon films and television series may put the values of a whole society under the microscope.

One of the first cartoons made especially for television which became immensely popular was *The Flintstones*, which ran from 1960 to 1966. It was made by the Hanna-Barbera Company and concerned a prehistoric family living in a place called Bedrock.

Although set in prehistory, the cartoons were amusing **satires** of the American passion for shopping and desire for consumer goods that reached new heights after the Second World War – the Flintstone and Rubble families had prehistoric versions of vacuum cleaners, record players, even a car to go to a drive-in movie!

The message was, of course, lost on the children who were fans simply because it was funny; but the broad humour coupled with the satire also appealed to adults, who doubtless recognised modern America in amongst the cavemen and women.

THE ANTI-HERO

More recently, another type of animated character who could be seen as an **anti-hero** has become fashionable. The anti-hero in fiction is someone who tends to challenge society and its rules; he or she is an outsider who does not belong and does not want to belong. Anti-heroes often despise the kind of values which are generally approved of.

As we have seen, rebels and outsiders have been central to the comic tradition from the very beginning. The comic strip tramps Weary Willie and Tired Tim, and later the anti-authoritarian Desperate Dan and Lord Snooty, paved the way for the modern breed of outsiders such as Daria, Bart Simpson and the children in *South Park*.

The Simpsons television cartoon series has enjoyed huge success. Created by Matt Groening and developed by Fox TV in America, it appeals to children and adults alike, providing different levels of enjoyment ranging from slapstick humour and jokes to satire of American politics and culture.

Both the father, Homer Simpson, and his son, Bart, rebel against authorities of various kinds – the government, employers and teachers. In 2001, after 11 years, *The Simpsons* was as popular as ever.

Daria – a 'cool' rebel

Another successful American cartoon series at the turn of the century was *South Park*, featuring a pack of four brats more rebellious, vulgar and even violent than any of their predecessors. The show was considered unsuitable for children and broadcast late in the evening on British television. But it quickly achieved a cult status none the less.

Daria also became popular at this time – she was an anti-hero or outsider in the sense that, unlike most teenagers, she was not particularly interested in fashion or boys, did not want to go out on Saturday night and did not mind if people did not like her. But she was, in a word much used at the time, 'cool' i.e. admired by the young.

As with the earlier comic strip characters, we have identified three main elements of animated films and cartoon series which account for their continuing popularity:

- humour
- heroic characters seeking justice and protecting the weak or innocent
- anti-heroes or characters who defy authority

ACTIVITY 18

- Discuss why the features listed above are popular.
- Can you spot any other features that hold a particular appeal?
- Take any cartoon film which you know well and identify its appeal. Are one or more of the three features mentioned above to be found?

MESSAGES FOR CHILDREN

The most successful animated films, the ones attracting the biggest audiences, are those designed for young children whose primary purpose is to be entertained, amused and excited on their visit to the cinema.

However, certain values which are important to youngsters in the process of growing up are conveyed as a **sub-text** (see page 234). Films like

Bambi or *The Lion King*, among others, introduce children to the notions of tragedy, death, love and the importance of relationships.

The fact that these films are about animals rather than people **distances** extreme emotions and makes them easier to cope with for children. Few youngsters, though, will not have cried at some scenes in *Bambi*, just as they may have laughed at others.

MEDIA LANGUAGES AND CATEGORIES – ANIMATION

ANIMATED FILM GENRES

Most animated films are made with children in mind (see *Audiences and popularity*, page 242) and this clearly conditions the subject matter or genre of animated films. Animated films are traditionally based on one or more of the following:

- **Animals** – animals in stories often have human characteristics e.g. Toad in *The Wind in the Willows*. If you compile a list of the films about animals it will probably include the *Mickey Mouse* and *Donald Duck* cartoons, and also films like *Bambi* (1942), *The Lion King* (1994), and *Chicken Run* (2000)
- **Fairy tales** – a rich source for the animated film-maker since the first full-length feature *Snow White and the Seven Dwarfs* (1937). Others include *Cinderella* (1949), *Aladdin* (1992) and *Pinocchio* (1940). Several versions of these and other stories have been filmed over the years
- **Children's literature** – examples include *101 Dalmatians* (1961), *The Jungle Book* (1967), *Tarzan* (1999) and *The Iron Giant* (1999)
- **Comic strip superheroes** – Superman appeared first as a comic strip character, then as an animated film hero (1941), and later in several live action films and a TV series
- **Music** – the most acclaimed of these is the Disney film *Fantasia* (1940)

Some films are more difficult to categorise. Examples are the very popular Wallace and Gromit films and *Toy Story* (1995). The former contains human and animal characters and the latter the same except in toy form.

ACTIVITY 19

- Compile a list of all the animated films you know and categorise them by genre.

ANIMATED FILM CONVENTIONS

Many films, especially action films, contain unbelievable events – car chases, fights, falls, stunts, escapades of many kinds. Animated films probably contain more unbelievable events than live action films: talking animals, for instance, or a flattened mouse which revives in seconds!

In animated films, we accept that certain **conventions** hold sway and do not question these incredible twists and turns. This acceptance of the unbelievable is called **suspension of disbelief** – we ignore our normal experience of reality for the duration of the film. This is because most of us have watched animated films from an early age. We know what to expect. Imagine how an adult who had never seen a cartoon film would react on seeing one for the first time.

Some of the main conventions of the animated film are:

- animals can talk
- animals can have emotions normally reserved for human beings
- an amazing degree of violence can occur without anyone being hurt
- 'superhuman' behaviour is common
- colour is much more intense than in real life

All these factors add up to **fantasy**, that is, characters and action far beyond the ordinary and realistic.

One of the most interesting things, though, is that within the fantasy world of the animated film, real and recognisable human emotional situations occur. Think, for instance, of examples in films like *Bambi* and *Chicken Run*, to name but two.

PRODUCTION PROCESSES

MAKING AN ANIMATED FILM

A 90-minute feature-length animated film is made by photographing some 130,000 separate paintings called **frames**. Some of these separate frames consist of four or five drawings or paintings on transparent plastic sheets called **cels** (short for **cellulose**), placed one on top of another to give the scene an impression of depth.

If you add in the rough drawings and the mistakes which were thrown away, well over a million separate drawings will probably have been made to complete a cartoon film.

What follows is a simplified account of the complete process – it can best be seen as a series of stages, which usually follow the same pattern.

producer – in charge of the finance and business side of the film

writer – produces the film script

director – in charge of all the filming processes

designer – creator of the film's overall look

composer – creates the music

animator – artist who draws the characters / background scenery

editor – puts separate pieces of film together to make the finished film

Stage 1

The film studio decides to make an animated feature and obtains the finance. Senior executives appoint a **producer** who, in turn, hires a **writer**. A **director** may be chosen, or this may be left until the writer has produced the first draft of the **script**.

Stage 2

The finished script is given to a **designer** who produces a **model sheet** – hundreds of drawings of the characters in different poses and showing their comparative sizes, their facial expressions and gestures. By using the model sheet and their imagination, the producer and director may envisage the finished film.

Stage 3

The designer uses the script and the model sheet to produce a **storyboard** – a comic strip version of the whole story, complete with **dialogue**. Backgrounds are rudimentary and the figures are drawn only in outline. Storyboards are usually 60 frames and 30 boards are needed for a feature-length film i.e. roughly 1,800 drawings. The storyboard also shows where distant shots, medium shots or close-ups will be used.

The director and producer audition and hire actors to say the lines. They are chosen for the suitability of their voice and sometimes, too, if they are a big name star, for their ability to 'sell' the picture, e.g. Tom Hanks as Woody in the *Toy Story* films.

Stage 4

The actors, under the director's guidance, record the **voicetrack**. Sound engineers divide it up and fit the pieces to sections of the storyboard. A **dopesheet** is put together, listing the frames of 1/24th of a second and which sounds relate to them – all before final drawings are done.

Music is composed or chosen. The **composer** is given the storyboard which shows which sections contain dialogue, when dramatic music is required, or when quieter music is needed.

Stage 5

The **animators** are given the storyboard and dopesheet, suggestions for backgrounds and details of the action. Hundreds of animators and assistants are employed and most specialise in different tasks. Some do backgrounds, some figures, some faces, some action, some weather effects, explosions etc. They are not required to be creative – they must use the models created by the designer and chief animator.

Each 1/24th second frame is not necessarily done as a new single picture each time. The drawing and painting is done on transparent cels so a large background painting can be used many times and only the characters that move have to be drawn differently for each frame. Exceptions to this would occur if, for instance, a storm was moving the background trees. In such a case, the background has to be animated as well and more separate paintings will be necessary.

The chief animator often does the two **key drawings** for the beginning and ending of a character's movement, then assistant artists paint the stages in between. At this stage, movement drawings of characters are just in outline.

All the time, the artists must refer to the storyboard and dopesheet and listen to recordings of the dialogue so that the finished result is life-like. Note how spoken words in a cartoon meticulously fit the mouth movements.

Stage 6

More artists now colour in the moving characters. The paint is put on the back of the transparent cel so that when it is reversed, the paint will look very even.

The finished 'cel'

Stage 7

Finished cels are checked against the dopesheet to make sure they are in order and are then sent to the cameraman. A **rostrum camera** is used, that is, a camera that is fixed to an arm above a flat plate on which the cels are placed in turn to be photographed one by one. The camera can move up and down and from side to side so that, for instance, a close-up could be created by the cameraman from a cel which shows a medium-distance shot. The director works with the cameraman and makes the decisions about exactly what is wanted.

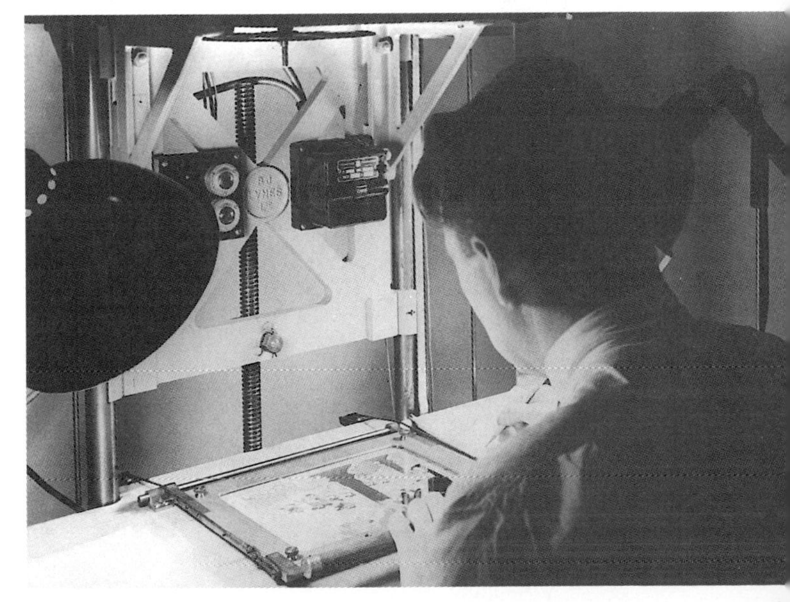

A rostrum camera

Stage 8

The reels of film are now available and an **editor**, again under the director's eye, will add the **soundtrack**, on which both dialogue and music have been **dubbed** together. Last-minute changes may also be made. Much cutting and editing will be necessary to synchronise everything. A **master film** of both vision and sound is created from which copies can be made for distribution eventually to cinemas.

The producer and director have been involved in all the processes of production. The actors may have recorded their dialogue up to three years before the movie is shown.

ACTIVITY 20

In groups:

- Devise a story suitable for a four- or five-minute cartoon film.
- Write an outline of the story.
- Create a storyboard – rough drawings will do.
- Write the dialogue using the story outline as a guide, and fit it to the storyboard.
- Find suitable 'voices' / actors for the characters and make a recording or voicetrack of the dialogue.

COMPUTER TECHNOLOGY

Films which combine live action with cartoon characters have a long tradition. Have you ever seen *Mary Poppins*, which was made by the Disney studio in 1964? The combining process was fairly crude in those days, but by 1988 it had been almost perfected in the film *Who Framed Roger Rabbit?*, a co-production between Disney and director Steven Spielberg.

To achieve a smooth integration of live action and cartoon characters, computer technology was necessary but, even so, two million drawings were made by 320 animators. Some single frames required over 20 separate drawings, the movements were so complicated.

The use of computers has now become widespread, and not just for special effects.

Computers have been used with great success in putting together the finished film e.g. the *Toy Story* series.

ANIMATED MODELS

Some animated films are made by filming puppets or models – you may be familiar with the Wallace and Gromit films made in the 1990s. Instead of an artist painting characters, Plasticine models are made and moved 24 times for every second of film time. The separate stages are photographed one at a time on the reel of film. When the film is fed through the projector at normal speed, the models seem to move quite naturally.

SUMMARY – ANIMATION

- Animated films were born out of the discovery of the phenomenon known as persistence of vision and are now a billion-dollar industry.
- The Walt Disney Company was consistently the most successful producer of animated films from 1923 to the present day.
- Hundreds of animators work on feature-length animations, producing more than a million separate drawings to achieve the effect of natural movement from still frames.

GLOSSARY

caption – line of text beneath a picture commenting on or adding to the content

caricature – a drawing of a person or animal which exaggerates or distorts characteristics to comical or even grotesque effect

cel – short for cellulose; transparent plastic film on which the final drawing is done to provide a single frame of an animated film

comic book – a paperback A4 size book of 64 pages or more containing a long comic strip story or several

dopesheet – sheet of instructions containing film soundtrack information

dubbing – process whereby sound is added to dialogue and music to make a film soundtrack

effects – decorative words used in comic strips to indicate explosions, physical blows, gunshots etc

frame – a single cartoon; a drawing for a comic strip; one picture lasting 1/24th of a second of film time

graphic novel – a novel in comic strip form, often over 200 A4 pages long, with sophisticated art work

key drawings – drawings at the beginning and end of a single movement by a character

letterer – specialist designer of comic strip lettering

model sheet – drawings done by the chief designer to show film characters' appearance, gestures and comparative sizes

photo-story – comic strip which uses photographs rather than drawings

rostrum camera – a cine-camera which is fixed in position above a plate on which the object to be photographed is placed

speech balloon – balloon-shaped space in a cartoon or comic strip frame which contains the dialogue

stop motion photography – camera shutter is opened for one frame, closed, then opened again to photograph the next

storyboard – a series of drawings with dialogue, showing where close-ups and distance shots will be used

thought balloon – a cloud-shaped space in a cartoon or comic strip showing a character's thoughts

voicetrack – soundtrack of film dialogue

Reading list

GENERAL MEDIA STUDIES

Guardian Media Guide, Peake, S. (ed.) (Guardian Books / Fourth Estate, annually)

- An invaluable book for students and teachers alike. It contains useful summaries of the main events of the year for each of the main media industries, together with industry statistics and extensive lists of media industry and regulatory institutions' addresses and contacts.

BFI Film and Television Handbook, Dyja, E. (ed.) (BFI, Annually)

- Another valuable book, specialising in film and television in the UK.

Teach Yourself Media Studies, Downes, B. and Miller, S. (Hodder & Stoughton, 1998)

FILM

The Cinema Book, Cook, P., Bernink, M. (eds.) (BFI, 1999)

Teach Yourself Film Studies, Buckland, W. (Hodder & Stoughton, 1998)

TELEVISION

The Television Handbook, Holland, P. (Routledge, 1997)

RADIO

The Radio Handbook, Wilby, P. and Conroy, A. (Routledge, 1994)

Studying Radio, Barnard, S. (Arnold, 2000)

NEWS (NEWSPAPERS AND TV)

The Newspapers Handbook, Keeble, R. (Routledge, 1998)

Television News, Yorke, I. (Focal Press, 1995)

MAGAZINES

The Magazines Handbook, McKay, J. (Routledge, 2000)

POP MUSIC

Music Week

- The industry insiders' magazine. Available at big newsagents, especially at railway stations for some reason.

Dancing in the Streets, R. Palmer (BBC, 1996)

- A book and three videos about the history of pop music.

The Music Business, A. Blake (Batsford, 1992)

- A more detailed analysis of the business.

On Record, ed. S. Frith, A. Goodwin (Routledge, 1990)

- A set of essays about all aspects of pop music (including the Horton lyrics analysis).

Hooligan, G. Robertson (Macmillan, 1983)

- A book about moral panics.

Stairways to Heaven

- A CD which has over 20 versions of the Led Zeppelin classic in different genres.

This is Spinal Tap, R. Reiner (PolyGram Video, 1998)

- A truly wicked video documentary which 'captures the sounds, sights and smells of the loudest band in the world'. Contains swearing but highly recommended.

CARTOONS

The Great Cartoon Stars: a Who's Who, Gifford, D. (Bloomsbury, 1988)

The Cartoonist's Workbook, Hall, R. (A & C Black, 1995)

Peanuts: A Golden Celebration, Schulz, Charles M. (Harper Collins, 2000)

COMICS

The Penguin Book of Comics, Aldridge, A. & Perry, G. (Allen Lane, Penguin Press, 1971)

101 Years of American Newspaper Comics, Horn, M. (Gramercy Books, 1996)

Comics, Comix & Graphic Novels, Sabin, R. (Phaidon Press, 1996)

ANIMATION

Hollywood Cartoons – American Animation in its Golden Age, Barrier, M. J. (Oxford University Press, 1999)

One Hundred Years of Cinema Animation, Bendazzi, G. (Indiana University Press, 1994)

ADVERTISING

The Advertising Handbook, Brierley, S. (Routledge, 1997)

PRACTICAL MEDIA PRODUCTION

Making Media: Practical Production in Media Education, Buckingham, D., Grahame, J. and Sefton-Green, J. (The English and Media Centre, 1995)

Radio Production, McLeish, R. (Focal Press, 1997)

USEFUL RESOURCES

- Leisure magazines on film, television and new technologies
- Critical magazines, such as *Sight & Sound*
- Press and information packs from media companies

MEDIA WEB SITES

- Every media company and regulatory body now has its own web site and most of them contain very useful information (the addresses are published in the ***Guardian Media Guide*** and ***BFI Film & TV Handbook*** listed above)
- The Guardian newspaper has an excellent website www.mediaguardian.co.uk specifically on the media
- Film Education – www.filmeducation.org
- British Film Institute – www.bfi.org.uk
- Internet Movie Database – www.imdb.com
- Screen Studies (a website for students and teachers) – www.screenstudies.com
- *The Beano* comic's official site www.beano.co.uk
- Portfolio of online cartoons and comic strips www.cartoonscape.com

AWARDING BODIES' WEBSITES

- AQA www.aqa.org.uk
- OCR www.ocr.org.uk
- WJEC www.wjec.co.uk

Index

We are grateful to the following for permission to reproduce photographs and other copyright material:

The Advertising Archives pages 118, 120, 227 left, 228, 229; Associated Press/Nick Ut page 93 bottom left; BBC Picture Archives pages 48 bottom, 57; Bridgeman Art Library pages 216, 217 top (Louvre, Paris), 217 bottom, 218 (Musée de la Tapisserie, Bayeux, France); British Film Institute pages 239, 247 top; www.CartoonStock.com page 221 inset; Channel Four Television page 62 top; Channel Five page 63 top right; © D.C Thomson & Co Ltd. The Beano page 221; © D.C Thomson & Co Ltd. The Dandy page 232; DK Picture Library page 143; Daily Mirror page 102 left, 102 right, 121 bottom, 234; Mary Evans Picture Library pages 226, 227 right; Fotomas Index page 82, 178 left; FRANCE Magazine page 115 left; supplied by John Frost Historical Newspaper Service page 234; Ronald Grant Archive page 14, 16, 17 bottom (Buena Vista), 17 top, 19 bottom, 23 (Eon Productions), 26 top left, 26 top right, 26 bottom, 34 (Lucasfilm Ltd), 188; the Graphical, Paper and Media Union page 84; © The Guardian pages 84 bottom, 102 centre left, 102 centre right, 109; Hulton Getty page 93 centre, 143 left, 219, 247 bottom; ITC page 71; ITV page 59 bottom; ITV Digital page 56 top; Illustrated London News page 117 left; The Independent/Syndication page 89 right; Johnson & Johnson page 125; © Knight Features page 231; Kobal Collection pages 19 top, 29, 30, 31, 43 right (Michael Barnett), 43 left, 62 bottom; Liverpool Daily Post & Echo page 108; Magnum Photos/Chris Steele Perkins page 202; MIZZ Magazine page 233; "MTV's 'Daria' used with permission by MTV:Music Television © 2001 MTV Networks. All Rights Reserved. MTV:Music Television, all related titles, characters and logos are trademarks owned by MTV Networks, a division of Viacom International Inc page 244; ntl page 64 top; New Internationalist, no.333, April 2001 page 115 centre left; Newsweek page 114 top; Nokia page 55; © The Observer page 110; Philips page 56 bottom; Popperfoto pages 93 centre right, 93 centre left, 93 bottom right (Reuters), 93 top (Reuters), 105 top (Reuters), 105 bottom, 142, 180, 208 (Reuters), 209; Punch page 117 right; Radio Times reproduced with permission page 112, 145; Redferns page 182; Rex Features pages 59 top, 146, 161, 190, 198 (Richard Young), 208 (Brian Rask), 212 (Brian Rask), 214, S4C page 63 bottom left, 63 top left; S.I.N pages 183 (Antony Medley), 185 (David Corio), 186 (Hayley Madden), 195 (Robert Lewis); Sky page 64 bottom; Soaplife April 2001/IPC Media page 130; Sugar Magazine pages 133, 138; The Sun pages 89 left, 90, 103, 107; © Times Newspaper Ltd 1st January 1788 page 83; © Peter Brookes/Times Newspapers Ltd 15th March 2001 page 224; Topham Picturepoint pages 48 top, 54 top (Press Association/Matthew Fearn), 54 bottom, 63 bottom right (Press Association/Fiona Hanson), 95, 177, 178 right, 213, 221; Top of the Pops Magazine page 126; UPPA page 203; photography by John Walmsley pages 47, 81, 84 bottom, 89, 90, 99, 102, 103, 107, 114, 115, 121, 205, 233, 234.

We have been unable to trace the copyright holders of some material and would be grateful for any information that would enable us to do so.